Re-enchanting Modernity

Re-enchanting Modernity

Ritual Economy and Society in Wenzhou, China

MAYFAIR MEI-HUI YANG

楊美惠

Duke University Press   Durham and London   2020

Designed by Drew Sisk
Typeset in Portrait Text by Westchester Publishing Services

Library of Congress Cataloging-in-Publication Data
Names: Yang, Mayfair Mei-hui, author.
Title: Re-enchanting modernity : ritual economy and society in
    Wenzhou, China / Mayfair Mei-hui Yang.
Description: Durham : Duke University Press, 2020. | Includes
    bibliographical references and index.
Identifiers: LCCN 2019046700 (print)
LCCN 2019046701 (ebook)
ISBN 9781478007753 (hardcover)
ISBN 9781478008279 (paperback)
ISBN 9781478009245 (ebook)
Subjects: LCSH: Ethnology—China—Wenzhou Shi. | Economic
    development—China—Wenzhou Shi. | Economic development—
    Religious aspects. | Wenzhou Shi (China)—Religion—Economic
    aspects.
Classification: LCC BL1812.E36 Y36 2020 (print) | LCC BL1812. E36
    (ebook) | DDC 306.6095124/2—dc23
LC record available at https://lccn.loc.gov/2019046700
LC ebook record available at https://lccn.loc.gov/2019046701

Cover art: Wooden ceiling of a deity temple in Rui'an City, China,
2005. Photo by Mayfair Mei-hui Yang.

*To two people who gave generous
and crucial support:*

*Philip T. Myers,
my husband, who gave continuous and tireless
moral and practical support,
with a great sense of humor*

and

Wang Qinsheng 王勤生,
*the local Wenzhou diviner and geomantic
master who initiated the revival of the Yingqiao
Wang Lineage in Yongchang Township;
may he rest in peace!*

Contents

I am indebted to so many people and agencies for the support and assistance they have extended. In research funding, I owe the National Science Foundation for its invaluable Five-Year Presidential Young Investigator Award, which early on supported innumerable fieldwork trips to Wenzhou, conference travel to present my research, and also my documentary film on Wenzhou. I would also like to thank the University of California's President's Faculty Research Fellowship, a UC Santa Barbara Interdisciplinary Humanities Center Fellowship, and UC Santa Barbara Academic Senate Fellowship for research expenses and teaching release. I also wish to thank the University of Sydney in Australia for faculty research funds when I was Director of Asian Studies there. Several institutions granted me residential fellowships. My gratitude goes to the Institute for Advanced Study, School of Social Science, in Princeton, and the Center for the Study of World Religions at Harvard University Divinity School. I am also grateful to Prasenjit Duara for inviting me to spend time at the Asia Research Institute, National University of Singapore, in 2012. Thanks to the School of Journalism and Media Studies, Fudan University in Shanghai for a research fellowship in 2012. At the crucial time of finishing my manuscript, Peter van der Veer also extended support for a stay in Göttingen, Germany, at the Max Planck Institute for the Study of Religious and Ethnic Diversity in 2017, for which I am extremely grateful.

I owe heartfelt thanks to so many people in Wenzhou for making my research possible and extending support. Regrettably, I feel it is better not to list them at this time.

This book is dedicated to Wang Qinsheng (王勤生), former lineage leader of the Yingqiao Wang lineage in Yongchang Township, Longwan District. Despite the differences in our gender, age, and cultural backgrounds, I felt a special kinship with him and greatly benefited from his extensive knowledge of local culture, kinship, and religious customs, and his generous assistance in my research. His death was a big loss for the social memory of his community.

I must also thank many academic colleagues based in the United States or Europe. My deep appreciation goes out to Peter van der Veer, Adam Chau, Prasenjit Duara, Stephane Gros, and Adeline Herrou for reading and commenting on my book manuscript, or parts thereof. I am grateful to my colleagues at

UC Santa Barbara for providing crucial information: Xiaorong Li (李小榮) and Ronald Egan were so generous with help in classical Chinese texts. Thanks also to Dominic Steavu, and Cathie Chiu, and to Huang Yunte (黃運特), a Wenzhou native and UC Santa Barbara English Department professor, for arranging a useful visit to his hometown. Wang Xiaoxuan (汪小烜), another Wenzhounese scholar, also gave important answers to my questions. Thanks are also due to Luo Xiaopeng (羅小鵬), who went with me on one Wenzhou visit. I am also grateful to Chiu Tzu-lung (Melody) (邱子倫) and Kang Xiaofei (康笑菲) for their help. Finally, I must also acknowledge the valuable work by my graduate student research assistants at UC Santa Barbara over the years: Li Weimin (李為民), Lu Meihuan (呂美環), Lu Wanshu (呂宛書), Lin Shixing (林詩杏), and Oliver Teernstra. I wish to thank Laura Holliday for her valuable editing work and suggestions in cutting down the manuscript when I could not cut any more.

Finally, and not least, I must express heartfelt appreciation for the moral support of three very dear people in my life: my husband Philip Myers, my sister Mary Yang, and my friend Cathie Nesci. Without their moral support and encouragements through all these long years, this book would not have been completed. This book is also dedicated to Phil, my husband, for his patience, generosity, practical computer help, and good humor.

Part I

INTRODUCTION

I

From "Superstition" to "People's Customs"

An Ethnographic Discovery of Key Questions in Wenzhou

使俗之漸民久矣, 雖戶說以眇論, 終不能化. 故善者因之, 其次利道之, 其次教誨之, 其次整齊之, 最下者與之爭.

(Cultural customs have gradually flowed and become sedimented among the common people. Even though one goes to every household and engages in subtle persuasion, in the end, one cannot change these customary practices. This is why the wise and noble ruler will go along with the flow of these customs. The next best thing is to try to lead and guide them. A lesser choice is to try to educate them. An even lesser policy is to try to set up rules to regulate and reorder them. The worst is to denounce and struggle against them.)

—司馬遷著 (史記. 貨殖列傳) [Si-Ma Qian, *Historical Records* (ca. 135–86 BCE)]

The history of our Party is a history of upholding science and smashing superstition. . . . In recent years, . . . ignorance and superstition have raised their heads and anti-science and pseudo-science activities have taken place. . . . [Even] some Party members and cadres . . . now believe in constellations, divination, *fengshui*, and fortune-telling by physiognomy. They worship gods and Buddhas and have become the prisoners of idealism. . . . In some places, science cannot overcome superstition, materialism cannot overcome idealism, and atheism cannot overcome theism.

—Shanghai Renmin Chubanshe, *Smashing Superstitions*

The paranoid pharaoh and the passional Hebrew? In the case of the Jewish people, a group of signs detaches from the Egyptian imperial network of which it was a part and sets off down a line of flight into the desert.

—Gilles Deleuze and Félix Guattari, *A Thousand Plateaus*

I did not set out to study religious culture but was confronted with its salience and importance in the course of fieldwork on rural "civil society" and non-governmental organizations. In 1990 I made my first visit to the Wenzhou (溫州) area in southern Zhejiang Province on the southeastern coast of China. I stayed only a few days, but returned the next year. At first I interviewed people involved with the Wenzhou Writers' Association, private kindergartens, a private technical middle school called Dawn Light Middle School, a local chapter of the Wenzhou Chamber of Commerce, and a local Individual Entrepreneurs Association. I soon realized that these organizations were either state-penetrated or market-penetrated. The organizations that showed a truly independent grassroots character and self-organizational ability in a bottom-up, spontaneous development all had a ritual or religious orientation. These were deity temples, Daoist and Buddhist temples, lineages and their ancestor halls, and Christian churches. I was impressed by the sheer energy, persistence, and ingenuity with which their organizers and congregations stubbornly established and maintained these organizations in the face of local government obstacles. Based on ethnographic material gathered in rural and small-town Wenzhou on repeated trips from 1990 to 2016, this book explores these grassroots organizations.

The title is inspired by Max Weber, who wanted to confront the "disenchantment of the world" ([1919] 1946: 153). In his 1919 speech to Munich university students, he stated that although science no longer engages in "prophecy" with the old tools of "miracle" and "revelation," he still believed that science could be a "vocation" rather than a mere occupation. For Weber, science cannot answer the question that is most important to us: "What shall we do and how shall we live?" That is why modernity calls us as scholars to reveal and teach "inconvenient facts," to have the intellectual integrity to go against "party opinions," and to help people clarify "the ultimate meaning[s] of their own [religious] conduct" ([1919] 1946: 147, 152). In this book I try to engage in this kind of science, one that does not merely describe, nor try to predict, but explores the social significance of "re-enchanting modernity" in one corner of China after a century of powerful discourses of scientism, social evolutionism, materialism, revolution, nationalism, and progress. Trained in cultural anthropology, with its scientific and empirical legacy, on the one hand, and its recent "interpretive turn" and engagement with critical theory, on the other, I offer a "hybrid science" that combines ethnographic and historical inquiry with analysis of the significance and promise of religious imaginaries with regard to economic development and nation-state power.

This book explores religious and ritual practices among ordinary people in rural and small-town Wenzhou: peasants, shopkeepers, entrepreneurs, family enterprise owner-managers, mothers and wives, and workers of Wenzhou origin, as well as ritual practitioners and Buddhist and Daoist clerics. I focus on Chinese "popular religion," including deity worship, shamanism, ancestor worship, divination, and Chinese geomancy (*fengshui*); and also popular Daoist and Buddhist practices, rather than the elite, highly literate and philosophical realms of these two complex religious traditions. Although Wenzhou is known as the "Jerusalem of China" (中國的耶路撒冷) because Christians comprise one-eighth of its population of 8 million, I will not include detailed discussions of Christianity. I was repeatedly warned by officials in Wenzhou to stay away from Christians, so although I had some furtive contacts with Catholics and Protestants, in the interest of safeguarding my fieldwork access, I did not pursue research on Christians. Given the strong links of contemporary religiosity to the past, I will frequently refer to "late imperial China," which covers the Ming (1368–1644) and Qing dynasties (1644–1911), or the past six hundred years.

MODERNITY AND ITS DISCONTENTS: "PURIFICATION," SECULARIZATION, AND A "POSTSECULAR SOCIETY"

While Michel Foucault's (1979, 1991) scrutiny of modernity focused on the shift from monarchical power to disciplinary and biopolitical power, our concern with modernity is with the processes of "disenchantment" and "re-enchantment." Here we can benefit from Bruno Latour's approach to modernity as a "purification process" whereby "two distinct ontological zones are created: that of human beings on the one hand; that of nonhumans on the other" (1993: 10–11). In chemistry, purification is accomplished through separation: it involves removing nonessential or contaminating substances. As an anthropologist in science studies, Latour focused on modernity's insistent separation of the categories of nature from culture, of the natural world from human society and politics. These radical separations enabled and sharpened the instrumental reason that produced our modern surfeit of material goods and technologies, but they also led to the false dichotomy of objective, referential knowledge versus subjective, interpretive, and religious knowledge, and the notion that nature is merely *out there*, independent of the knowledge and actions of the human world. Since Einstein's theory of relativity and Heisenberg's uncertainty principle, we have understood that nature cannot be known without taking into account both the positioning of the knowing subject and the measurement tools mediating the access to quantum objects in nature.

While Latour was not focused on religiosity, his schema can also highlight modernity's radical separation of a third opposition to both nature and culture: the *super*natural, where nonhumans include not only animals, but also gods, ancestors, spirits, demons, ghosts, and spiritually animated material objects. Indeed, European modernity's purification process was launched from within a deeply religious world. The Virgin Mary and the multitude of Catholic saints were like most Chinese gods: once human, they became divine figures of worship through their self-sacrifice, miracles, and contributions to humanity and other beings (Overmyer 1997). During the Reformation in Europe, however, they were separated and expelled from the Christian pantheon. With the earlier Catholic human-divine traffic gone, in Protestant faiths the "true God" was elevated and set apart from humans all the more; and later, in more secular contexts, God's divine handiwork evolved into the "laws of Nature." Thus, modernity, in Latour's definition as radical purification and separation of human and nonhuman categories, cannot be understood as merely the global dissemination of modern science; it must also be seen as the result of Protestant missionizing.

A related opposition that was introduced into modern China was that between religion and economy, with the conviction that they are mutually exclusive. This was perhaps born of Protestantism's struggles against the Catholic Church's elaborate ritual expenditures. In the hands of Chinese modernizers and revolutionaries, this meant that religion must be eliminated in order to push for economic development, thus erasing the historical memory of the Song dynasty's (960–1279 CE) commercialization and the rapid growth of its religio-economy a thousand years ago.

Webb Keane (2007) extended Latour's thesis to examine how Dutch Calvinist missionaries in Indonesia separated and elevated the agency of the "true God" from human agency, while casting aspersions on the nonhuman agencies of indigenous spirits and ancestors, which the Dutch called "fetishes" or false agencies. Charles Taylor also highlights this separation of agencies in modern secularism, so different from the enchanted world in which "the line between personal agency and impersonal force was not at all clearly drawn" (2007: 32). For Taylor, the replacement of the enchanted "porous self" of spirit possession and human-god interactions with the impermeable "buffered self" was the hallmark of modern secular society.

However, I must also take issue with Latour's too-quick denial that we have ever attained the state of modernity. Latour claims that we have actually always been engaged in what he calls "hybridization," "mediation," or "translation," the crossing and merging of nature and culture. As a discussant for Latour's lecture at UC Santa Barbara in May 2002, I noted that, while I found his discussion of the purification of categories extremely stimulating and useful, I also felt uncomfortable with his statement "We have never been modern." This may have been true for the modern West, but for a while, China may have "outmodernized" and "outpurified" the West! I share Andrew Pickering's sentiment that those of us who wish to interrogate the modern "would not want to ratify what we have always done without first getting clear on the specifics of history" (1994: 258), especially in non-Western contexts, where there is often an urgent ethos of "catching up" with the modern West. This book, then, addresses the effects of China's radical twentieth-century purification program, in which social, political, and economic practices were disembedded not only from nature but also from cosmology, ritual-liturgical procedures, and the divine agencies of deities and ancestors. It also explores the post-Mao-era movement toward "hybridization" as attitudes toward religiosity soften, but remain guarded in China. Contemporary re-enchanting practices, which are strong in places like Wenzhou, can be understood as an indictment of, as well as forms of redress and repair for, the excesses of Chinese modernity's purification procedures.

Modernity's purification project was at work throughout twentieth-century China, where in order to catch up with the West, the equivalent of the Reformation, the Enlightenment, the French and Russian Revolutions, and the establishment of a modern secular state all had to be collapsed into less than a century's time. We can see it in nineteenth-century Protestant missionary condemnations of Chinese "idolatry," "heathenism," and excessive ritualism (Reinders 2004). It is evident in twentieth-century May Fourth intellectuals' calls to rid China of ignorant peasant religions, such as Chen Duxiu's article in the journal New Youth (新青年), entitled "On the Smashing of Idols" (偶像破壞論):

> These idols made of clay and carved in wood are really useless things; but just because someone respects them, worships them, burns incense and kowtows to them, and says they have magical efficacy, ignorant villagers become superstitious of these manmade idols and believe that they really possess the power to reward good deeds and punish evil. . . . All religions are idols that cheat people. (Chen D. 1918: 99; my translation)[1]

We also see it in Marxist-Maoist revolutionary romanticism and realism, where human agency is elevated above false deities as the true agency of revolution. The suppression of Buddhist notions of transmigration between human and other life-forms, and its notion that human beings can attain divine Buddhahood, paved the way for the massive efforts to conquer nature.

The removal of gods and ancestors who had sacralized local communities and territories facilitated the new identification with a massive new and abstract nation-state.

Intertwined with the purification process, modernity in China also involved the rise of antitraditional discourse, secularization, the closure of local sacred spaces, and the discrediting of transcendence over worldly life. Neo-Confucian discourse had often denigrated popular religion, Daoism, and Buddhism. However, it was not until the modern era that both the Guomindang and the Chinese Communist Party mounted campaigns of state secularization to dismantle temples, ban or restrict religious rituals and festivals, change local religious customs, and return clerics to lay life (Duara 1991; Goossaert and Palmer 2011: 43–65, 139–165; Nedostup 2008, 2010; M. Yang 2008b). The English word "secularization," which originally referred to the seizure of Christian monastic lands and church buildings, such as during the French Revolution (Casanova 1994: 13), also describes Chinese modernity well. In a similar way, the movement of "converting temple property into schools" (廟產興學) that started at the end of the Qing dynasty initiated the secularizing process in modern China. However, China's secularization was much more radical than in the modern West; its extreme was the reign of terror and systematic destruction of traditional religiosities in the "Smashing of the Four Olds" campaign (破四舊, 1966–1968) during the Cultural Revolution.

Given the extremes of Chinese secularization, the aim of this book is to come up with "postsecular" argument(s) for the historical significance of the "re-enchantment of modernity" in Wenzhou. One of the earliest thinkers to invoke the term "postsecular" was, ironically, Jürgen Habermas, the German philosopher and defender of Enlightenment rationality. From a European perspective, the recent rise of religious conflicts around the world, and the need in Europe to integrate recent migrants and refugees, who tend to be religious, have "undermine[d] the secularistic belief in the foreseeable disappearance of religion" (Habermas 2008: 20). José Casanova (1994) observed that, although the religious domain has in most modern societies shrunk in terms of social function, religious practice and discourse have not simply retreated to the private sphere; they remain public. For postsecular societies to challenge the secularization thesis and high-modernist projects, their religious and nonreligious people and members of different faiths must be able to engage with and concede to each other in the public sphere. This book hopes to show that the significance of Wenzhou as a postsecular regional society in contemporary China is the reenergizing of indigenous religiosities and rituals in the reassertion of community, locality, and religious civil society, and the resurgence of a "ritual economy" whose logic and values moderate or challenge capitalist logic.

THE ELEVATION OF HUMAN AGENCY
AND THE HUBRIS OF "HIGH MODERNISM"

Modernity gave rise to what James C. Scott has called "high modernism" (1998), a modern affliction shared by both Communist and Western liberal discourses. Scott describes three elements of high modernism: "the aspiration to the administrative ordering of nature and society"; "the unrestrained use of the power of the modern state as an instrument for achieving these designs"; and "a weakened or prostrate civil society that lacks the capacity to resist these plans" (1998: 88–89). An offshoot of the European Enlightenment, "high modernism" permeates diverse thinkers and their radical projects of modernity—from Swiss architect and urban planner Le Corbusier to the shah of Iran—all propelled by a desire for totalizing social engineering projects that would speedily overturn the hated traditional ways and institute new utopian futures. In China, Maoist high modernism deemed popular religion "backward" (落後) and "feudal superstitions" (封建迷信) as useless old elements that must be swept away to clean the slate for progress toward the ideal Communist society. I frequently encountered this rhetoric among local officials and intellectuals in Wenzhou in the 1990s, but it has subsided a decade into the new millennium. The language of high modernism in China has now become less utopian, less vilifying, and more rational. Nevertheless, the radical push for "progress" and "development" continues unabated, along with state efforts at control and containment of religiosity.

Overcoming the discourse of high modernism means that secular intellectuals need to show more tolerance, understanding, and engagement with religious discourse. Thus, this book treats Wenzhou religiosity not as a stubborn "cultural remnant" (文化遺留) but as an active engagement with modernity, a willed *re-enchantment*. I also try to extend the notion of the postsecular to the epistemological and methodological realm. That is to say, the postsecular can also be understood as a new form of modern knowledge-making, where secular knowledge seeks a dialogical engagement with religiosity. Postsecular knowledge does not merely stand outside its object of study, religion, but can infuse some religio-ethical-cosmological logic into its discourse, creating a hybrid religio-scientific way of thinking.

The twentieth century may prove to be the one that has most violated the ancient Chinese theory of statecraft known as Huang-Lao Thought, which promoted the Daoist notion of *wu-wei* (無為), or "noninterventionist action," as the ideal mode of governing. As espoused by China's ancient historian, Si-Ma Qian (司馬遷, ca. 145–86 BCE), Huang-Lao Thought taught that the best form of government allowed a certain flexibility and tolerance toward popular culture and going with the flow of local customs. When we contrast Si-Ma Qian's statement with the antisuperstition campaign rhetoric in the next epigraph, we see how the modern nation-state deployed the discourse of scientism and progress in its radical state intervention in popular customs. Of course, traditional Chinese culture had severe problems that required reform, such as monarchical-despotic power; social hierarchy and the treatment of lower class-status groups and youth; patriarchy and the treatment of women; and the terrible impoverishment of a vast population. However, in the process of addressing these problems, totalizing modernist discourses have enabled the modern state penetration of grassroots society and closed off traditional mechanisms of community self-governance and social change. In contrast, late imperial grassroots communities comprised a realm where the imperial state did not often heavily insert itself. They generated cultural, ritual and religious mechanisms for community self-governance, economic redistribution, and local community welfare and problem-solving.

FLEXIBLE RELIGIOUS BOUNDARIES AND THE MODERN NATION-STATE

In global modernity, we have seen the triumph of nation-state as the overwhelming aspiration of the new age. Since nationalism emerged very early in Europe, we must examine its relationship with the Christian culture and identity that preceded it. Prasenjit Duara (2015) suggests that positing a single omnipotent God and Truth leads the Abrahamic faiths, especially Christianity and Islam, to proselytize and convert, resulting in historical conflicts with other religious persuasions, and with each other. Even before modernity, these faiths, which Duara describes as "radical transcendence," were prone to periodic "purification" drives, excluding other faiths, divinities, and alternative modes of worship, even as they also experienced periods of syncretic hybridization and encompassment of other religious practices. For Duara, the drive for conversion and exclusivistic religious ideology have been weaker among traditional Asian religions of "dialogical transcendence," which are more open to relative truths, multiple modes of devotion, and mutual dialogical encompassment. After the major purification drive of the Reformation, the European Wars of Religion raged for a century until the Treaty of Westphalia in 1648.

For Duara, the outcome of this treaty was the modern nation-state: the radical exclusivism of each Christian faith and the tight boundedness of their collective religious identities served as the unconscious model for the first modern territorial nation-states. The positing of a single God and single Truth meant that the emerging nation-state was informed by the model of one territory having a single faith, and other faiths had difficulty coexisting.

Indeed, I am writing this passage while living in Göttingen, Germany, where in 1531 the town leaders accepted the heterodox teachings of Martin Luther. They could not coexist with Catholics, however, and eventually drove them out of town. Today all of the churches in Göttingen remain Lutheran, except one small Catholic church (St. Michael's), which was only allowed to be built in 1787. While attending a conference at the University of Utrecht in the Netherlands, I saw in St. Martin's Cathedral (*Domkerk*), a Catholic church, a stone wall carving of the faces of the Virgin Mary, the Christ child, Mary's grandmother St. Ann and sister St. Elizabeth, and other relatives of the Holy Family—all of which had been chiseled out in 1580 by Protestant religious fanatics who took offense at graven images of divinities. Such smashing of "idols" predates China's twentieth-century smashing, and there may be a genealogical connection, since the nineteenth and early twentieth centuries featured heavy Protestant missionizing in China.

The Treaty of Westphalia was not the only model for modern nation-states, but most models differed from premodern empires and civilizations in their striving for an internal mass cultural integration, a common identity and language, shared religion and ethnicity, and clear territorial borders. Once this model became globalized, demands for national homogeneity sometimes triggered horrifying ethnic and religious cleansing. This new integrated nation-state became a powerful engine of labor discipline and large-scale social mobilization for the capture of natural resources in global capitalist competition.

Moving to Asian nation-state building, what Duara calls Asian "dialogical transcendence," had to be overcome in order to integrate and homogenize the nation. Meiji Japan was perhaps the earliest to take the path of modern religious nationalism. It solved the problem of having multiple religious traditions by sidelining Buddhism, centralizing its dispersed local Shinto cultures, and inventing a modern divine emperorship (Hardacre 1989). Peter van der Veer shows how in anticolonial India, traditional religiosity was not attacked like it was in China, but deployed as a new kind of national identity, and only the Indian state, but not Indian society, became secularized (2013: 157–162). However, this path to nation-state status has created problems down the line, such as the hardening of Hindu nationalism, which seeks to desecularize the state and suppress other Indian religious traditions, especially Islam (van der Veer 1994).

In the case of China, the relative tolerance of its multiple religious traditions in the imperial-civilizational mode also did not lend themselves to constructing a modern nation-state. Nor could the old monarchical power be deployed for the Chinese nation-state, since it was foreign (Manchu) and had been toppled by the Republican Revolution. China took the radical path: the modern state positioned itself outside of and in opposition to traditional religiosities, mounting campaigns to stamp them out. In their place, Chinese modernity instilled the new "radical transcendence" of secular nationalism, Leninist-Maoist ideologies, and a grand linear and teleological narrative of history. This meant that, instead of having a religious nationalism that privileges one religious tradition against others (as in India and Meiji Japan), China has been a dominant secular state that suppresses and constrains multiple religious traditions struggling to survive and grow.

While Duara (2015) uncovers the *trans*national "circulating histories" of modern nationalist discourses, I will focus instead on religious constructions of *sub*national or local identities. In other words, while Duara challenges nation-states' self-narratives of independent invention, showing that they were actually constructed out of the dense "traffic" of globalizing discourses, I show how the revival of local and regional identities through ritual and religious practice can moderate the intense emotional attachments to the centralizing nation-state. Instead of focusing, as Duara does, on Axial Age universal religions, with their elite textual and clerical traditions, I pay more attention to the religiosity of the common people, whose genealogies trace back to archaic *pre*-Axial Age religiosity, such as deity and ancestor cults and shamanism. I have often felt that, although Chinese peasants have since ancient times been repeatedly deterritorialized and inserted into the spatialities and jurisdictions of imperial state administration, they have stubbornly and repeatedly *re*territorialized, ritually and economically reconstructing their local communal identities. The post-Mao religious resurgence examined by many scholars (Chau 2006; I. Johnson 2017; M. Wang 2004) and described here in rural Wenzhou seems just the latest historical reiteration.

MAJOR QUESTIONS AND THE PLAN OF THE BOOK

In part I, chapter 1 provides a brief social history of religious culture and secularization in modern Wenzhou, from the late nineteenth century to the present, and discusses my ethnographic methodology and experience. Chapter 2 lays out the dynamic local economy of post-Mao Wenzhou, which sets the context for the resurgence of ritual and religious life. In part II, chapters 3 through 5 provide ethnographic and historical accounts of different forms of religious and ritual life in contemporary Wenzhou: popular religion, Daoism, and Buddhism. These chapters are mainly description and survey, so if one is more interested in hearing out my theoretical arguments, one could go straight to part III, or chapters 6 through 10.

I raise three key questions in the latter half of this book. *First*, if modernity has greatly expanded the reach and penetration of the modern state, how can we understand the resurgence of religiosity and ritualism in post-Mao Wenzhou? If the construction of nation-state identity depended on radical deterritorialization and new imaginaries of space, then what is the role of the ritual reterritorialization of locality in Wenzhou? Why have the native categories of the nonstate "realm of the people" (*minjian*, 民間), counterposed to "officialdom" (*guanfang*, 官方), reappeared since the 1980s? Four chapters take up the issue of "religious civil society." Chapter 6 deals with grassroots-initiated temple organizations and the management of religious associations, which, I propose, represents an "indigenous and religious civil society." Chapter 7 focuses on the activities of the Wang Lineage revival in Longwan District. Although I engaged with other Wenzhou lineages as well, the book length allows only a focus on one lineage. Chapter 9 examines the ritualization of "the local" and "community," calling for a broadening of the modern category of "civil society" to accommodate the particular conditions of non-Western, nonurban, and religious cultures.

Second, given the historical injustices to women perpetrated by traditional patriarchal social institutions and discourses, what are the gender dynamics of today's religious revival? The Chinese Communist Revolution brought state feminism's vow to liberate women from the shackles of patriarchal authorities, such as family and lineage, but what about the patriarchy of the state itself? Chapter 7 examines how men are at the forefront of lineage revival, given that its patrilineal descent favors the birth of sons. What is the gender dimension of religious revival in Wenzhou, and is there any difference or tension between kinship and religious institutions, in terms of gendered agency? Chapter 8 addresses rural women's religious agency in spearheading temple reconstruction and launching religious civil society. It explores female agency in Wenzhou, which is often conservative, modest, and self-sacrificing despite the fact that that women play a crucial role in fueling the religious drive.

My *third* issue has to do with the economic significance of Wenzhou religiosity and the religious significance of its economy. Chapter 10, on "ritual economy," links back to chapter 2, on the "Wenzhou Model" of economic development, challenging the Wenzhou Model as conventionally conceived by economists and sociologists, by asking, "What's missing in the Wenzhou Model?" I suggest that what I call Wenzhou's "ritual economy" of religious and gift expenditures is at once a stimulus for, a product of, and a countermovement to profit-oriented industrial productivism and the ascent of the capitalist market. How has religiosity been a stimulus for economic development? How did Wenzhou's old religious culture persist and reinvent itself, despite rapid economic development, unless it was a substantive partner of the new economy? Finally, how might Wenzhou's religious economy offer the possibility of redemption and provide a check on or counterbalancing mechanism to the market economy's powerful ethos of profit accumulation?

BRIEF SURVEY OF WENZHOU GEOGRAPHY AND LANGUAGES

The Wenzhou area is located on the southeastern coast of Zhejiang Province, lying south of Shanghai and northwest of the island of Taiwan. Wenzhou is crossed by two major rivers, which flow from the mountainous west to the East China Sea: the Ou River (甌江), which flows along the northern banks of Wenzhou City; and the Feiyun River (飛雲江) to the south. Much of Wenzhou's northeastern and southwestern regions are shielded by the Yandang Mountains, and Wenzhou has historically suffered from a scarcity of arable land. The Wenzhou area is composed of six counties with large rural populations: Yongjia (永嘉縣) in the north; Dongtou (洞頭縣) on islands in the East China Sea; Wencheng and Taishun (文成縣, 太順縣) in the southwest; Pingyang (平陽縣) in the south; and Cangnan (蒼南縣), the southernmost county, which borders with Fujian Province. Cangnan County was only created in 1981, when it was split off from Pingyang. The total population of registered native residents in the entire Wenzhou region in 2018 was 8.28 million (9.25 million if one includes migrant laborers and other residents).[2]

The population of Wenzhou City, the largest city and the seat of the municipal government, is 1.52 million, which leaves about 6.57 million Wenzhounese who live in rural or mountainous areas, or in small to large towns. Wenzhou City encompasses three rapidly urbanizing rural areas that are now called "urban districts" (市區): Lucheng District (鹿城區) to the city's northwest, Ouhai District (甌海區) to the south, and Longwan District (龍灣區) to the east, where the airport lies and where I first started my fieldwork in the 1990s amidst rice paddies. Besides Wenzhou City, two other areas were counties but are now designated as "municipalities" (市)—Rui'an and Yueqing

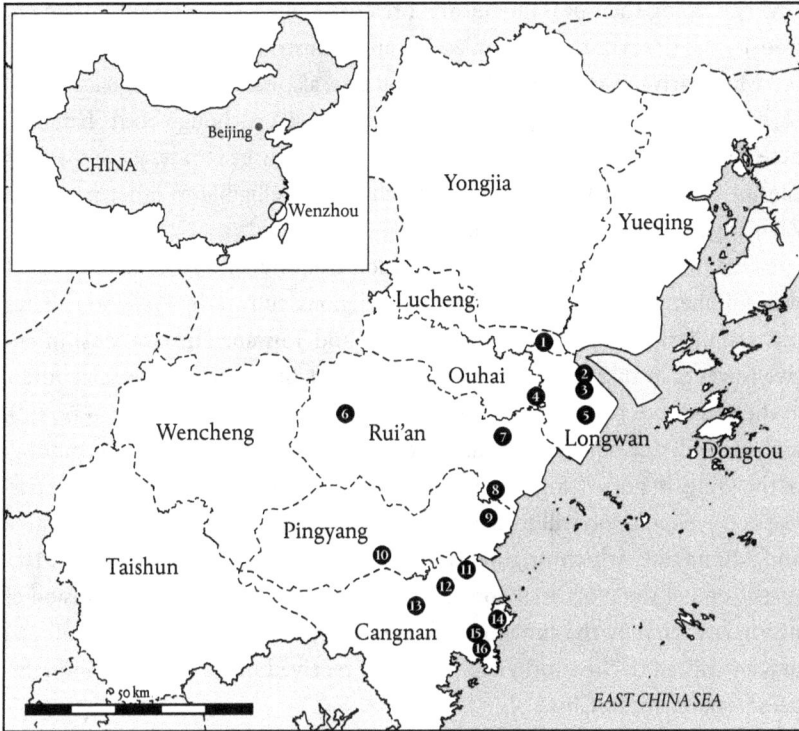

Figure 1.1. Wenzhou counties and towns visited. Map data © Open Street Map Contributors.

1. Wenzhou City
2. Yongzhong Township
3. Yongchang Township
4. Nanbaixiang Township
5. Yongxing Township
6. Guifeng Township
7. Xianyan Township
8. Rui'an City
9. Kunyang Township
10. Shuitou Township
11. Longgang Township
12. Qiangcang Township
13. Linxi Township
14. Bacao Township
15. Qianku Township
16. Jinxiang Township

(瑞安市, 樂清市), both of which have large rural populations. One important new urban area is the famous Longgang Town (龍港鎮), known as "China's First Peasant City" because it was spontaneously built up by ordinary rural folk without state investment or planning in the late 1980s.

With rapid urbanization, the labels of "peasant" and "rural household registration" have become less meaningful. As rural villages start constructing roads, electricity grids, running water pipes, and multistory buildings, and more of the population leave agriculture, "peasants" start to live like urban people, while largely keeping their peasant culture. I refer to them as "ex-peasants," living in transitional times of rapid urbanization and industrialization.

Most native residents speak Wenzhounese, also called "Ou language" (溫州話, 甌語), a branch of the Wu language family (吳語). Although both Shanghainese and Hangzhounese also belong to the Wu language family, these speakers cannot understand Wenzhounese, which is unintelligible to other people in Zhejiang Province and the rest of China.

Due to historical waves of in-migration from Fujian Province in times of war, famine, and natural disasters, the religious culture in Wenzhou shares many similarities (and deities) with Fujian and Taiwan. The two most intensive waves of in-migration from Fujian occurred, first, during the social unrest at the end of the Tang dynasty (618–907 CE) and Five dynasties (907–960 CE), and, second, during the chaos at the end of the Ming dynasty and beginning of the Qing. In both Cangnan and Pingyang Counties today, a remarkable *one-half* of the population still speaks a hybrid language, a mixture of Wenzhounese and Minnanese, which originates in southern Fujian (Lin S. 2007: 130, 133). At the end of the Northern Song dynasty (960–1127 CE), with the invasion of northern China by the Jurchens, the center of Chinese cultural and political gravity shifted to the south, and Wenzhou received many migrants and refugees from northern China.

Cangnan County also harbors two smaller languages: Jinxiang language (金鄉話) and the so-called barbarian language (蠻話) spoken near the coastal area by one-fourth of the county's population (Sheng 2004: 38–40). Jinxiang Township was first established as a fortress town at the beginning of the Ming dynasty with troops brought from across the Chinese empire for coastal defense against marauding pirates. The blending of different languages from across China produced the unique Jinxiang language. The designation "barbarian language," with its "insect" radical (蠻), is definitely pejorative; however, its speakers themselves still use this term today. Chinese linguists do not agree on the origin(s) of "barbarian language," but many believe that this language is very old and indigenous, perhaps even older than Wenzhounese, which is the product of Wu people descending into the Wenzhou area from northern Zhejiang. Thus, "barbarian language" may be the indigenous language of the original Ou people, who managed to preserve it from mixing with other invading languages whenever they fled into the mountains or out into the East China Sea in troubled times (Lin S. 2007: 135). In December 2016, I heard that Longgang Town was now being "overrun" by "barbarian language" speakers, who are the latest wave of rural people to settle into this town.

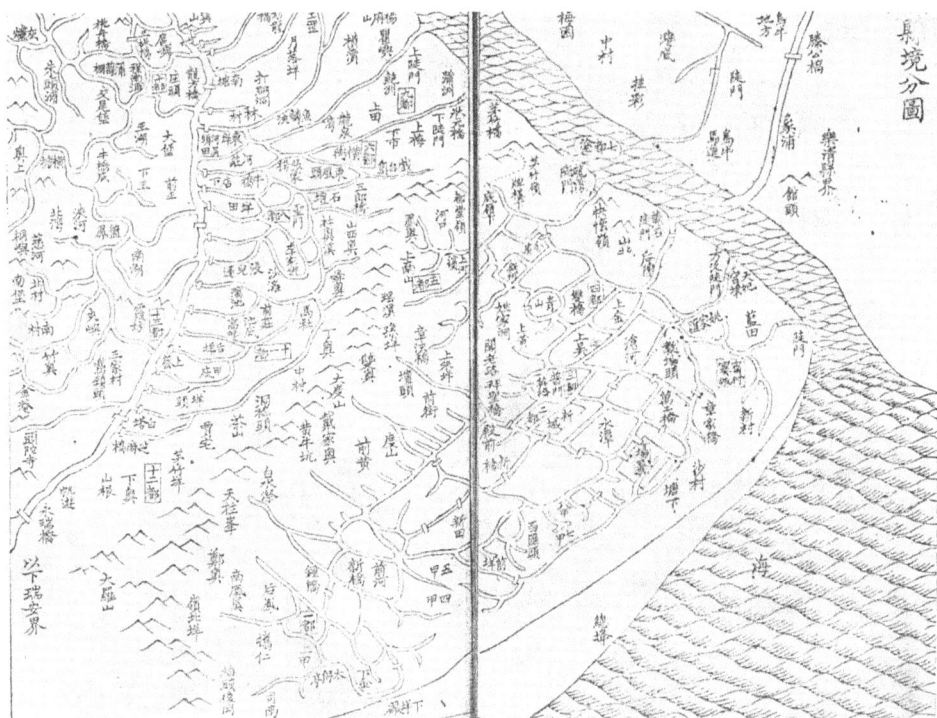

Figure 1.2. Qing dynasty map of Longwan District in Wenzhou; facsimile of original, 《永嘉縣志》 (*Yongjia Gazetteer*, Zhejiang Province, 1879).

In the modern era, Wenzhou's insular geography and its unique languages were key to the protection of its religious culture from the ravages of modernity elsewhere in twentieth-century China. The dense mountains in the northeast, west, and southwest made land travel into Wenzhou difficult. The Wenzhou Airport opened for domestic flights in 1990, but only the wealthy few could afford air travel at that time, and there was no railroad line into Wenzhou until 1998. Before train and air travel, the only ways into Wenzhou were a nauseating thirteen-hour bus ride through the mountains from Hangzhou or sailing by ship. Although Wenzhou has had a port since the commercial Song dynasty (960–1279 CE), it was not deep enough for modern ocean vessels, limiting its ability to bring in large numbers of goods and people. In addition to geographical and language barriers, a third reason for Wenzhou's stronger links with its religious past is its location on the "frontline" of possible war with Taiwan. This meant that Wenzhou received few modern state investments, requiring

Figure 1.3. Satellite image of Longwan District, Wenzhou, taken by Ikonos satellite on January 27, 2001. Satellite image © 2018 DigitalGlobe, a Maxar Company.

local people to be more self-sufficient and thus less beholden to provincial and central governments.

Wenzhou's economic and industrial development since 1978 can only be described as an "economic miracle." Wenzhounese people have since at least the Song dynasty taken to handicrafts industries, trade, and commerce. Moving into modern times, Wenzhou's strong entrepreneurial culture made it ill-suited to the Maoist collectivized agricultural life of militaristic and hierarchical discipline. In the 1970s, it was one of the poorest rural areas of China until the floodgates of economic reforms opened in 1979, lifting millions out of poverty. When I first started fieldwork in the early 1990s in what is now called Longwan District, rice paddies and water buffalo stretched to the horizon, and chickens, ducks, and pigs ran underfoot in villages and small towns. The area was crisscrossed by a dense network of water transport canals dating back to the Song-Yuan and Ming-Qing dynasties of middle and late imperial China. The favored mode of transportation around small towns was riding the cheap and efficient pedicabs. Over the next twenty-eight years, most rural families rapidly transitioned into commercialized agriculture, light industries, or commerce. They established family enterprises of cash crops or maritime resources and manufactured such products as shoes, clothing, porcelain tiles, industrial and medical instruments, small appliances, paper products, metal piping, and valve switches. They also engaged in private businesses such as retail shops, restaurants, hotels, kindergartens, pharmacies and clinics, teahouses, and even underground banks. Since then, most of the canals were filled in, paved over, and made into roads, and a private trucking industry developed to transport Wenzhou's commodities to the rest of China and the world. In 2016, almost half of urban Wenzhou families owned cars.

WENZHOU IN THE CONTEXT OF MODERN "PURIFYING" DISCOURSES OF SCIENTISM, REVOLUTION, AND NATION-STATE

Elsewhere, I have written about the cultural humiliation and collective loss of confidence in traditional Chinese culture that began in China's semicolonial era, when a Eurocentric unilinear social evolutionism was accepted by Chinese elites as "science" (M. Yang 1996, 2008b, 2011). This social evolutionist "colonization of consciousness" (Comaroff and Comaroff 1997b) subordinated the world's religious cultures into a universal system of "backward" and "advanced" religions, with the Protestant and secularizing modern West as the most developed civilization. Western social evolutionism introduced a paradigmatic shift in elite Chinese cosmological thought and senses of temporality. A linear, teleological understanding of human history developing from primitive society to "modern industrial civilization" came to supplant an ancient, spiraling sense of historical time based on dynastic units of temporality and emperor reign periods (Duara 1991, 1995).

The Protestant Reformation of the sixteenth century and its castigation of "idolatry," excessive ritualism, "magic," "superstition," exorcism, and miracles was originally leveled at the Roman Catholics (Thomas 1971). Later, Protestant diatribes against "idolatry" and "superstition" found their way from European into modern Chinese discourse, where they targeted the polytheistic deity worship of Chinese popular religion and informed elite Chinese nationalists' attitudes toward native religiosities (M. Yang 2008b). Many in the new generation of Chinese secular nationalists in Republican China were educated by Protestant Western missionaries in China. Beginning with the May Fourth Movement (1919–1929) of liberal modernism, popular religion was seen as the ignorance of the peasant masses and an obstacle to China's modernization, and groups of educated youths would go into rural temples to smash "idols" (偶像). The modern Chinese state would later take up this effort more systematically.

In late imperial China, local educated gentry wrote local gazetteers from inside a religious universe, for they did not question the existence of gods or demons, but criticized what were regarded as excessive worship, wasteful practices, or the immoral mixing of men and women in public ritual spaces. From the beginning of the twentieth century, many educated Chinese absorbed the Protestant distinction between legitimate "religions" (宗教) and backward "superstitions" (迷信) (Goossaert and Palmer 2011: 50–53; Nedostup 2010; M. Yang 2008b). "Religion" was measured against the standard of Protestant Christianity, with its own clergy, scriptural tradition, and institutional edifices. What C. K. Yang (1961) called "diffused" religiosity such as popular religion, with its scanty scriptural texts, lack of ordained clergy, elaborate pantheons of deities, "magical" and "occult" practices, and flexible organization, came to be associated with "superstition." This new label helped to justify multiple modern attempts to eradicate a whole way of life for rural communities.

Despite the overt anti-imperialist and propeasant stance of the Chinese Communist Party, these Protestant outlooks quietly made their way into Party attitudes and social policies. In the Third Plenary Session of the Eleventh Party Congress of 1979, which inaugurated a momentous policy shift away from the Soviet-style centralized command economy, we find that this distinction persists, favoring "religion" over "superstition":

By religion, we chiefly mean worldwide religions, such as Christianity, Islam, Buddhism, and the like. They have scriptures, creeds, religious ceremonies, organizations, and so on. These religions have histories of thousands of years. . . . Religious freedom, first of all, refers to these religions.

By superstition we generally mean activities conducted by shamans and sorcerers, such as magic medicine, magic water, divination, fortune telling, avoiding disasters, praying for rain, praying for pregnancy, exorcising demons, telling fortunes by physiognomy, locating house or tomb sites by geomancy, and so forth. These [activities] are all absurd and ridiculous. . . . They must be suppressed. We must criticize and educate the shamans and sorcerers, dealing sternly and striking resolutely in such cases. They are absolutely forbidden to carry out superstitious activities on the pretext of religious freedom. (MacInnis 1989: 33–34)

Although Article 36 of the Chinese Constitution protects the religious freedom of the Chinese people, "superstitions" are not considered "religion"; therefore, popular religious practices were considered illegal and dealt with by the public security organs or the police. This was the situation during my fieldwork in the 1990s. Many newly erected temples were torn down or forcibly closed by local authorities, practices that continued in the new millennium, as evidenced by the Wenzhou City government's campaign to close unregistered deity temples in 2000 (M. Yang 2004), and a similar campaign launched that year by neighboring Taizhou City (台州市) (Ye T. 2009: 286). More recently there was the "Three Reforms and One Demolition" (三改一拆) campaign of 2013–2016 across Zhejiang Province, but especially in Wenzhou (Yueqingshi 2013; Zhonggong Shamenzhen Weiyuanhui 2013). This campaign targeted for demolition unregistered deity temples and churches, or those whose construction had overstepped permissible size limits.

My fieldwork throughout the 1990s faced acute difficulties as a result of strong hostility toward popular religion from local officials and intellectuals. However, as a Chinese academic in 2014 and a Buddhist monk in 2016 both said to me, as Chinese people increasingly encounter other cultures due to China's globalization, the Chinese are asking themselves, "Who are we, and what makes us Chinese?" This question often leads them back to traditional Chinese culture, festivals, and religiosities, so recent years have brought a softening of harsh antitradition attitudes. The Chinese government itself now promotes "National Learning" (國學), traditional values such as filial piety, and lunar festivals. "National Learning" is the study of the classical texts of the Confucian, Daoist, Buddhist, and Legalist traditions. Through their publications and meetings with officials of the State Administration for Religious Affairs in the State Council, Jin Ze (2008), a scholar at the Institute of World Religions, Chinese Academy of Social Sciences, and others are credited with helping to soften state attitudes toward popular religion in the new millennium. Jin Ze argued that popular religion cannot be regarded as mere "cultural remnants" of the past, for it has "life force" and dynamism and is constantly adapting to the modern present. Nevertheless, state wariness and the resultant restrictions continue.

INTANGIBLE CULTURAL HERITAGE AS BOTH SAVIOR AND PROBLEM

In the new millennium, popular religion in Wenzhou was saved from further official persecution by the sudden interest across China in the UNESCO project of identifying "Intangible Cultural Heritage" (ICH; 非物質文化遺產) items around the globe that should be preserved for human posterity (Wu Z. 2009). "Intangible Heritage" refers to traditional customs, folksongs, arts and crafts, and so forth that are indigenous to a culture and have a long history. Professor Huang, a folklore scholar at Wenzhou University, told me the history of ICH in China. In 2005, South Korea mounted a campaign with UNESCO to get its Gangneung Dano Festival (端午祭) recognized as Korean cultural heritage. "This was the 'ignition device' [導火器] that ignited the return to tradition in China!," declared Huang. Korea's campaign prompted dismay and anger across China because people felt that this traditional lunar festival "belonged" to the Chinese. Although the Korean festival is quite different from the Chinese version, the fact that the Korean name was the same as the Chinese one and that the festival also took place at the same time of year, in mid-April to early May, was enough to raise nationalistic hackles in China. In the internet age, popular online outrage exerted great pressure on the Chinese government to pay more attention to China's own cultural heritage. China's State Council promulgated the "Communiqué on Strengthening the Protection of Cultural Heritage" (Guowuyuan 2005), calling on officials at all levels to protect Chinese cultural heritage. Officials were encouraged to nominate local ICH for inclusion in China's own ICH lists compiled every few years at the county, municipality, provincial, and national levels. UNESCO accepted Korea's festival bid in 2006, but in 2009 it also accepted China's bid. The Chinese government declared in 2007 that traditional lunar festivals would become new national holidays with paid time off from work. Thus, it was nationalism that decimated religious cultures in modern China, and nationalism is still required in order to rehabilitate and revive them.

Intangible Cultural Heritage Preservation Centers were established in Wenzhou City and in each of Wenzhou's counties and some prefectures (Wenzhoushi Feiwuzhi Wenhua Yichan Baohu Zhongxin 2009). The irony of these efforts in Wenzhou was palpable for me. Throughout the 1990s, local officials actively discouraged or prohibited local temples and lineages from launching public rituals; now they were competing with each other to nominate local rituals and festivals for inclusion as an Intangible Cultural Heritage! Whereas in the 1990s local officials were embarrassed, telling me not to pay attention to "old things" (舊東西), now they were talking about "salvage projects" (搶救工程)[3] to save Chinese indigenous traditions that they had had a hand in endangering. In nineteenth-century North America, Western colonial authorities and Christian missionaries decimated Native American cultures, and then "salvage anthropology" emerged to save the pieces and put them in museums. Similarly, after a century of officially supported cultural and religious destruction, local officials in Wenzhou finally awakened to the fact that some of this traditional culture had value and was rapidly disappearing.

Although Intangible Cultural Heritage designations are formulated from a secular point of view, they have allowed religious practices to hide under certain categories of ICH. For example, Ning Village's religious procession honoring a Ming dynasty military general–turned-god, Tang He, was classified under the category "Folk Belief Customs" (民間信俗). Legends of gods, ancestors, and Daoist immortals can also fall under the category of "folk literature." Religious rituals, operas, and deity processions can be categorized as "folk music." Back in 1993, I was not allowed to witness the Yingqiao Wang lineage's ancestor sacrifice, but now the ancestor rites of two influential lineages in Wenzhou history, the Zhang Lineage and the Yingqiao Wang Lineage of Longwan District, have been recognized as ICH. However, in the rush to get their rituals accepted as ICH, communities unwittingly enter into a new state secularization project, which continues to render religious discourse less audible.

FIELDWORK STRUGGLES: DIFFICULTIES AND INSPIRATIONS

Due to my teaching responsibilities and the difficulties of getting long-term visas, I made repeated visits during summer vacations, sabbaticals, or funded research leaves. Each visit lasted anywhere from two weeks to two months, and I made a total of thirteen trips to Wenzhou in 1990, 1991, 1992, 1993, 1998, 2001, 2004, 2005, 2008, 2010, 2012, 2014, and 2016. Added together, the total amount of time that I spent in Wenzhou was forty-two weeks, or ten and a half months of fieldwork. What I sacrificed in terms of in-depth, continuous research in one location was perhaps compensated for by my long span of time observing Wenzhou undergoing tremendous changes in social, religious, and economic development, and the many areas within the Wenzhou region that I visited.

In the early 1990s, I conducted fieldwork in an area just east of Wenzhou City, at that time a very rural part of coastal Ouhai County, but now swallowed up by the expanding city of Wenzhou and redesignated as Longwan District. This area includes the newly built Wenzhou Airport, and the townships of Yongchang, Yongzhong, Yongxing, and Shacheng (永昌鎮，永中鎮，永興鎮，沙城鎮), later relabeled "street committees." The local people, however, still often prefer the older pre-Communist administrative name, Yongqiang Prefecture (永强區).

I also interviewed people in nearby Yaoxi, Chashan, Wutian, and Nan Baixiang Townships (瑤溪鎮，茶山鎮，梧田鎮，南白象鎮).Beginning in the late 1990s, I started conducting fieldwork in Rui'an, Pingyang, and Cangnan Counties. In Rui'an, I visited Rui'an City, Xianyan Township (仙岩鎮), and Guifeng Rural Township (桂峰鄉) in the Southern Yandang Mountains. In Pingyang County, I visited Kunyang Town and Shuitou Town (昆陽鎮，水頭鎮). In Cangnan County, I visited the famous town of Longgang (龍港鎮), as well as Lingxi Town (靈溪鎮), and the townships of Jinxiang (金鄉鎮), Qianku (錢庫鎮), Dayu (大魚鎮), and Bacao (肥艚鎮) on the coast. I also visited Gutian Township (古田鎮) in the mountains of northern Fujian Province, where the most popular goddess in Wenzhou, Mother Chen the Fourteenth, died and ascended to Heaven.

Getting to the Field: Putting One's Foot in the Door

Many scholars know the difficulties of doing fieldwork in China, even for Chinese nationals. There are all sorts of political sensitivities, and one must work hard to reassure a nervous local government and to overcome the local people's guardedness toward strangers. My interest in popular religion made the situation worse, since religion was perceived as a threat to official "ideology" (意識形態) (M. Yang 2013). Instead, local officials wanted to show me the great strides in local economic development, and they were always asking whether I had business contacts in the United States who could invest in Wenzhou's economy.

Not having any relatives or academic contacts in Wenzhou, I was thinking of quitting Wenzhou research when an opportunity dropped into my lap. I was invited to help as an interpreter for a delegation of the mayor of Wenzhou, Chen Wenxian (陳文憲), who was visiting Los Angeles in 1992 (Anonymous 1992; Xu Q. 1992). Many Wenzhounese have settled in the New York City and Los Angeles areas, and there are three Wenzhou native-place associations (溫州同鄉會) in Los Angeles. I accompanied the mayor's delegation on their tour of local industries, water-processing plants, Chinese American associations, and Chinese restaurants. We also videotaped a session at the Chinese-language North America Satellite Television Corporation station, where they had a public dialogue on Wenzhou-US trade with March Fong Eu (余江月桂), a Chinese American woman who was then the secretary of state for California. On the basis of my good *guanxi* (關係), or social connection, with the Wenzhou mayor's office, they agreed to arrange two months of fieldwork for me in rural Ouhai County in 1993. That year, one staff person from the mayor's office accompanied me wherever I went. Although I made friends with my "minders," I longed for a more natural and unsupervised fieldwork experience.

Many local people advised me not to reveal my American provenance, and I found that I could easily pass as a scholar or journalist from northern China come down to "collect local customs" (採風). I decided to enter Wenzhou on my own, protected by my Chinese features and near-native fluency in Mandarin. Going incognito would ensure that no one would be responsible for me or my actions or have to face any guilt by association. On the other hand, being a foreign scholar elevated my social status, and some people sought to be seen with me to bolster their own status. One man even posted a photo of himself seated next to me as his profile image on his account with WeChat (微信), the popular and ubiquitous Chinese messaging and social media app started by Tencent in 2011.

I am forever grateful to the generosity of local people who supported my research, spent time talking with me, took me to local temples and ancestor halls, and opened their homes to me. I also stayed in two Buddhist monasteries. Fortunately, the market economy and its profit motive also made staying in small private hotels much easier, as hotel owners did not mind my US passport and wanted my business. I often wandered the streets and back lanes of rural villages and small towns by myself, approaching strangers to interview, which sometimes got me into trouble. Once, construction work on a residential street diverted me into a cul-de-sac of private homes, each with its own vicious guard dog. A hairy experience ensued: I was chased for three blocks by a pack of four snarling dogs.

Language Difficulties

A major limitation of my fieldwork was the local Wenzhounese language, which was so different from Mandarin Chinese that I was never able to pick it up, as I did with Sichuanese, Shandong, or Jiangxi, languages spoken in my father's hometown. In 1990s rural Wenzhou, most people had little formal schooling, and Mandarin was seldom heard except on television. The language problem meant that I was not able to chat with women above their thirties except through a Mandarin interpreter, which disrupted the flow of conversation. More men could speak Mandarin Chinese: some had learned it while serving in the army, and men tended to have junior high schooling, whereas rural women only went to school one to three years. The language problem also prevented me from eavesdropping on casual conversations around me, a method which had been valuable in my earlier fieldwork in Beijing. This meant that I had to work twice as hard to gather ethnographic information.

In the 1990s, a common strategy for upward social mobility among rural well-to-do families was to donate money to an elementary school in Wenzhou City and pay a teacher to house and raise their child, who was sent there to be educated in Mandarin. In turn, wealthy Wenzhou City families would donate money to a school in Hangzhou or Shanghai so that their child could gain entry to that school. Less educated Wenzhou people had a clear understanding of education's value. As local family enterprises became increasingly connected with supply sources and markets across China and even overseas, husbands and sons ventured out of Wenzhou to do business, while their wives stayed behind to manage the family factory or retail shop at home. Adult women increasingly felt the need to learn Mandarin so that they could communicate with their employees, migrant laborers from China's poorer provinces, and non-Wenzhounese customers. I visited an evening Mandarin class run by Zhennan Village in Yongzhong Township, where the thirty students were mainly women in their thirties and forties. Today the language problem in Wenzhou is less acute, due to higher educational levels in the younger generation and exposure to television. By 2016, a growing proportion of youths in Wenzhou City no longer spoke Wenzhounese.

Police Surveillance and Entanglements

China is still something of a police state; nothing can remain unknown to the local public security forces for long. One Daoist priest told me that after one of my interviews, the police paid him a visit to ask about me and warned him not to talk to me anymore. In order to protect him, I had to stop my visits. Similar police warnings were given to others who dealt with me. In 1993, shooting a documentary film with my Sony Hi8 Handycam video camera, I took the precaution of shooting interviews on the rooftops of people's private multistory homes, always with a fast-beating heart (see my film *Public and Private Realms in Wenzhou, China* [M. Yang 1994b]). In 2001, my Sony CCD-VX1 Handycam video camera broke down, so I hired a local videographer to videotape an ancestor sacrificial ritual for me. His sister later told me that "four men in black" came to their studio and asked who I was. She got rid of them by saying that I was their relative from northern China, who was just curious about local customs.

One terrifying night in 2004 at three in the morning, while staying at a cheap private hotel, I was rudely awakened by a loud pounding on my door and a male voice yelling for me to open the door immediately. Confused and frightened, I opened the door in my nightgown. Three policemen burst into the room, ordering me to show my identity card (身份証). Not wishing to reveal my US passport, I told them that I did not have the identity card. Outraged, they yelled, "Of course you have one! Pull it out right now!" Not waiting for me to find it, they started rifling through my suitcase, tossing my clothing around and pulling out my fieldnotes. They found my small business card folder, which contained the cards of local businessmen, officials, and ritual specialists. Flipping through the cards, they abruptly paused when they came to the cards of a former Wenzhou mayor and other top Wenzhou officials. Their facial expressions turned from self-righteous authority to creeping nervousness. Finally, they asked, more subdued now, "Who are you?" I showed them my US passport, explaining that I was an American scholar doing research on local customs. With a great sigh of relief, one of them asked in a gentler voice, "Why didn't you tell us that at the beginning? You would have saved yourself a lot of grief!" Then they told me that they were part of a local "Sweeping Away Yellow" campaign (掃黄運動). "Yellow" is a code name for illicit sexual culture, whether pornography or prostitution. This culture had grown dramatically in the past decade, leading the police to conduct periodic surprise raids of hotels. I suddenly remembered those young women who milled around the hotel: they were prostitutes who did their business inside the hotel! What worried these policemen when they came across my business cards of important Wenzhou officials was the thought that I might be a high-class prostitute who had done "business" with these officials! They were anxious that my powerful connections might get them into hot water for disturbing me. They reassured me that, now that they knew I was not a prostitute, they were no longer interested.

Early the following morning, I went downstairs and asked the hotel owner whether he had heard the commotion. He at first pretended not to know what I was talking about but later sheepishly acknowledged that he knew what had transpired:

> We knew the police were going to conduct a raid here. We have a connection [guanxi] inside the Public Security Bureau, who gives us early warnings of raids. We warned all the girls not to show their faces here last night. Since we thought you are "as white and pure as the snow," we did not see the need to warn you. We never imagined that the police would think you are a prostitute! Probably because you were the only single woman living here.

The next day another group of police, this time from the Border Protection Office instead of the vice squad, came to ask me to show up at the Public Security Office to answer questions. With great trepidation, I dutifully made my way there. Shaking their heads as they examined my passport, the police told me I was not permitted to conduct research on a tourist visa. After two hours of questioning, they said that they would let me off lightly with a modest fine. However, I still had to go through the unique Chinese police ritual of writing a confession and showing contrition for my mistake. Under their guidance, I composed a written acknowledgment of my wrongdoing, made a formal apology, and promised never to repeat my mistake. Ever since, I have taken care to conduct research only on an "M" business visa, with an invitation letter from a Chinese educational institution.

In September 2014, I arrived in Wenzhou to carry out more fieldwork with an official invitation letter. Just as I was sitting down with my local hosts for lunch, my host received a phone call warning him against allowing me out of Wenzhou City to do fieldwork in the countryside. Evidently, if one flies into Wenzhou City Airport, the authorities immediately know of any foreign national's arrival from the airplane passenger list. After being forced to stay five days in Wenzhou City, I was finally allowed to leave the city, accompanied by two scholars to ensure that I would not get into trouble. Later, I learned that the police I was dealing with was *not* the local Public Security Bureau, but the national Ministry of Security (Guojia Anquan Bu), the equivalent of the FBI and CIA rolled into one. That year, in the wake of the controversial state destruction of the giant Protestant cathedral at Sanjiang in April 2014, they were concerned that I had come to do an exposé of Wenzhou Christian protest and anger (I. Johnson 2014). My past fieldwork in Wenzhou should have shown them that my research interests are on Chinese popular religion, not Christianity.

RE-EMBARKING ON INDIGENOUS "LINES OF FLIGHT"

In their unique philosophical exploration of the movements of power across geological, biological, and historical time, Gilles Deleuze and Félix Guattari (1987) write about "arborescent" structures of thought and social system, which organize movements into circular repetitions, always referring back to the center, like the rings in the wood of tree trunks, and tree branches, which are always dependent on the main trunk. A prime example of these circular self-referential signifying regimes are what they call "state apparatuses of capture," which have increasingly taken hold of human life since the invention of archaic states. States have the desire not only to capture and increase territories, but also to put their own stamp and instill their own mode of organizing the captured space. Thus, states continuously *deterritorialize* the spatial organization of tribal societies, clans, and multiple other social and political formations they capture, and *reterritorialize* them into spaces for easier state administration and control. These processes have only intensified in modernity; Foucault (1979) has shown how modern social-scientific and technical knowledges have arranged new compartmentalized spaces of discipline and panoptic control, launching what James C. Scott calls modern "state projects of legibility" (1998: 2–3, 183–184) to increase state knowledge of the population and resources.

Under certain historical conditions, however, certain movements may elude or partially escape state capture. New conditions may introduce a break in the mechanisms that assured the reproduction of the system, thus enabling a significant new movement: "[The] line of flight [is what] the signifying regime cannot tolerate, in other words, an absolute deterritorialization; the regime must block a line of this kind or define it in an entirely negative fashion precisely because it exceeds the degree of deterritorialization of the signifying sign" (Deleuze and Guattari 1987: 116). No matter how flexible and deterritorializing the modern globalizing state-capitalist complex has become, it still cannot stomach certain kinds of movements. In the age of the powerful discourses of industrial productivism, progress, and nation-state, something as archaic as traditional religiosities, gods, and ancestors exceeds the permitted deterritorialization and must be negated, captured, and tamed.

In the epigraph at the beginning of this chapter, Deleuze and Guattari turn to a major discursive theme in Judeo-Christian civilization, the flight of

Jewish slaves from the arborescent formation of ancient Egypt in search of the Promised Land. In this ancient "line of flight," the Jews were able to flee and establish a separate alternative community far from the pharaoh's territory. When considering China, we will need to change the Judeo-Christian religious background when examining the resurgence of religiosity in rural and small-town Wenzhou today as a "line of flight."

In ancient China, two Daoist religious movements emerged in the waning years of the Han dynasty (second century CE): the Celestial Masters (天師道) in Sichuan and the Way of Great Peace or Yellow Turbans Rebellion (太平道，黃巾起義) in Shandong. These are the ancient religious "lines of flight" that elude or retreat from the arborescent state order in the Chinese cultural zone. With a sacred written edict from the god Lord Lao delivered to their religious leader Zhang Daoling (張道陵), the Celestial Masters in Sichuan took advantage of the weakening Han imperial state to quietly form an alternative religious community of ritual healing and repentance for sins (Kleeman 2016; Kohn 2009: 86; Wang K. 1999: 16–18). The Yellow Turbans were also propelled by a divine text, the *Scripture of the Great Peace* (太平經), which harked back to an era of "Great Peace" when rulers knew how to govern through "nonaction" (無為), they consulted the common people, and there was social and material equality (Hendrischke 2006; Wang K. 1999: 14–16). However, the Yellow Turbans were more millenarian and overtly rebellious, aiming to overthrow the "blue skies" of the Han dynasty and replace it with their "yellow skies."[4] The Celestial Masters lived on and prospered in medieval Chinese history, especially the Song dynasty, and persisted into modernity as the Daoist Orthodox Unity Sect.[5] The Yellow Turban rebels, however, were exterminated by Han imperial troops. Unlike rebellions or revolutions, most "lines of flight" seek not to overturn the "despotic signifying regime" or arborescent order but merely to open up escape routes that lead to alternative ways of life. This difference between lines of flight and revolutions, and the likelihood of success for the former, are important insights to hold on to, given modern China's own experiences with two revolutions. It would seem that revolutions or rebellions tend to reproduce or strengthen and expand the state. Thus, ironically, lines of flight, in the form of modest shifts such as the repetition of ritual actions in the *longue durée*, seem to have more promise for making a real difference than sudden totalizing transformations like revolutions, as Deleuze suggested in *Difference and Repetition* (1994).

The resurgence of religiosities in Wenzhou after a century of antireligious discourse and state-building represents a nonrevolutionary "line of flight." It avoids confronting and tackling the state head-on; it has no desire for rebellion or revolution. It is a line of flight that establishes alternative communities *in situ*, without having to leave the territory, although many Wenzhounese have indeed ventured far and wide across China and the globe. This line of flight *reterritorializes* state administrative space and *recodes* state legal and social codes to form new spaces of communities defined by deity cults, cultivation of religious transcendence, scriptural study, ritual practices, and lineage affiliations.

2 The Wenzhou Model of Rural Development in China

A basic feature of Wenzhou's economic development is its populism (民間化) and self-organizational (自組織) ability. The veins and pathways in this process reflect how deeply imbricated are the relations between economic development and traditional culture. Traditional social capital and the social networks of family and kinship culture have exerted an extremely important influence. The main reason for Wenzhou's economic success lies in the ability of its people to adapt traditional cultural resources as an impetus and tool of economic development.

—Li Renqing 李人慶 2004

When noncapitalist forms of economy are coded as primitive, backward, stagnant, traditional, incapable of independent growth and development, and *opposed* to the modern, growth-oriented, and dynamic capitalist economy, development is defined as a process that necessitates the elimination or transformation of noncapitalist forms.

—J. K. Gibson-Graham, *The End of Capitalism as We Knew It*

Feminist economic theorists J. K. Gibson-Graham boldly take on the reigning Marxist theorists of their time, critiquing David Harvey, Immanuel Wallerstein, and Ernest Mandel for their representation of modern Euro-American capitalism as a monolithic juggernaut. Gibson-Graham (1996: 254–256) suggest that these Marxist portrayals of capitalism as a unified and integrated system, rather than a shifting set of diverse practices, actually *enhances* capitalism's ability to reproduce itself and resist change. Arguing that discourses actually bring power into being, Gibson-Graham question the image of capitalism as a unified and coordinated organism that regulates itself according to universal laws, with a preordained trajectory of growth. Within any political economic system, they assert, there is a multiplicity of economic practices, and relations among those practices continually shift.

In 1996, when their book was published, the global economic powerhouse of China had yet to gain notice as a new arena for critique of political economy. Now that the world is confronting the latest potent form of capitalism, Chinese state capitalism, Gibson-Graham's exhortation to look for the hitherto invisible traces of internal difference and multiplicity is all the more compelling and important. Most Western media discussions of China's economy seem fixated on giant state-owned enterprises (e.g., Sinopec), powerful new private economic empires (Tencent, Alibaba, Huawei), or state investments like the $1 trillion for China's "One Belt, One Road" project to build infrastructure across the old landed and maritime Silk Roads. Within today's Chinese economy, however, there is great economic complexity and difference, and embedded uncomfortably within lies a mode of economy with genealogical linkages to China's commercial and urban revolution of the Song dynasty, a thousand years ago (Chen and Xi 2003: 85–199; von Glahn 2016: 242–278).

I would like to focus on one such anomalous mode within China's multifaceted economy, called the Wenzhou Model (溫州模式) of rural economic development and industrialization. It has been of great interest to Chinese economists, sociologists, and officialdom since 1985, when the term first appeared in a *People's Liberation Daily* newspaper article (Y. Liu 1992; Zhang Zhichen 1998: 1029). The anthropologist Fei Xiaotong gave further prominence to the Wenzhou Model in a series of articles celebrating its pattern of rural small-town development (Fei 1992, 1997). In a state-dominated society, the Wenzhou Model epitomized the notion of "the realm of the people" (*minjian*, 民間), because it relied on bottom-up popular initiative, the spontaneous entrepreneurial energy and financial creativity of ordinary Wenzhou residents, most of whom were peasants. This model is based on the private ownership (私有制) of factories and businesses by local families and households. In the first three decades of the post-Mao Reform period, before the rest of the country caught up, Wenzhou was known as the nation's "wellspring of private business" (民營經濟的發源地). By 2016, an astounding 99.5 percent of industrial and commercial enterprises in Wenzhou were private, numbering 556,000 household or joint-stock enterprises, with 93 percent of the employment-aged population working in this sector.[1]

In this chapter, I discuss the Wenzhou Model as conventionally understood, which reveals its difference from the dominant state capitalist and large private corporation models. Yet, even as it represents an alternative economy to the hegemonic large companies, the conventional understanding of the Wenzhou Model misses an important dimension. In chapter 10, responding to Gibson-Graham's exhortation to search for economic difference, I will lay out in detail this missing element, what I call a "ritual economy." We will then have a fuller understanding of the Wenzhou Model and how it might contribute to our critique of both state and liberal capitalisms.

The Wenzhou Model is distinguished from such other models of rapid rural development as the "Sunan Model" (蘇南模式) of Jiangsu Province, based on village- and township-owned enterprises, and the "Zhu River Triangle Area Model" (珠江三角洲模式) of industrialization in Guangdong Province based on foreign and overseas Chinese direct investment and joint ventures (Li R. 2004: 2). Due to the Wenzhou Model's impressive economic achievements, countless official delegations across the country, from the central government to provincial, prefectural, county, and township-level local governments, all descended on Wenzhou to learn from this model.

In the 1980s and 1990s, Wenzhou transformed itself from a geographically isolated and impoverished area, where electricity only arrived in many rural areas in the 1960s and bicycles in the 1970s, to an economically dynamic, prosperous, and rapidly urbanizing region. Wenzhou's gross domestic product jumped from 1.3 billion yuan in 1978 to 252.7 billion yuan in 2009, an increase of 193 times in only thirty-one years. In 2014, gross domestic product jumped further up to 430.3 billion yuan (*Wenzhoushi tongjiju* 2015: 2), with increased exports around the globe. Rural per capita annual incomes shot up from an average of 113.5 yuan ($67.55) in 1978, which was 15 percent *below* the national average, to a high of 2,000 yuan ($232) in 1994, which was 63.9 percent *higher* than the national average (Zhang Zhichen 1998: 1032). In 2014, rural per capita income increased further, to 19,394 yuan ($3,122) (*Wenzhoushi tongjiju* 2015: 16). Across China, Wenzhou people became a force to be reckoned with—at once admired, feared, and resented for their business acumen and economic success, as they invested in real estate, industries, and businesses across China and abroad.

The economic gains from 1978 to 2016 were not simply by a small group of elite entrepreneurs. A surprising proportion of ordinary Wenzhou people have acquired capital to invest and run their own businesses, and most have seen gains in household income. Most Wenzhou households I got to know were engaged in private business: family-run factories, workshops, retail outlets, or service businesses. Of course, Wenzhou also became a class-stratified society, with migrant laborers from China's poorer interior at the bottom. Migrant laborers are structurally discriminated against by the "household registration system" (户口制度) put in place by the state in the 1950s, which prevents them and their children from settling permanently in the area. If we do not count migrant laborers, the sheer number of Wenzhou households who were able to leave backbreaking agricultural labor and go into business for themselves has moderated social stratification.

According to sociologist Zhang Jianjun (2007), Wenzhou's relatively egalitarian class structure contrasts with the class-polarized "Sunan Model" of development in Jiangsu Province. The Sunan Model built its economic reforms on a historical legacy of strong local government funded by heavy state investments throughout the Maoist era. It enriched a small group of elites by awarding them control of collectively owned enterprises. Wealth in rural Jiangsu mainly fell into the hands of an exclusive club of government officials and managerial elites, and they had no interest in widening access to economic ownership. By contrast, in Wenzhou, where the starting point was a weak local government with very meager state investments (largely because of its proximity to Taiwan, a potential war zone), economic reforms mobilized a huge new private sector made up of ordinary people going into business, without benefit of ties to officialdom. With prosperity, this class of small family businesses remained relatively independent of the state and even counterbalanced it. Zhang argues that the new Wenzhou entrepreneurial class flexed its muscles by organizing local chambers of commerce (商會) and industrial and professional organizations, resulting in popular participation in local elections. However, Zhang does not mention other nongovernmental organizations that Wenzhou entrepreneurs are involved in, such as lineages, deity temple associations, Buddhist and Daoist temples, religious charities, and what Nanlai Cao (2011) called "boss" Christian churches.

Chinese and Western economists have generally focused on a narrow and conventional understanding of Wenzhou economy: capital accumulation, economic ownership, rates of industrialization, production outputs, and specialized commodity market volumes (Li and Zheng 1991; Nolan and Dong 1990; Shi et al. 2002; Wang X. et al. 1985; Zhang Zhichen 1998: 1029–1054). Wenzhou's geographic and linguistic isolation may have shielded Wenzhou's traditional commercial culture, allowing it to spring back quickly after rural collectivization in the Maoist era. Scholars have recognized Wenzhou's entrepreneurial "regional culture" (區域文化) and "maritime culture" (海洋文化), as distinguished from rural areas in northern, central, and western China, where the commercial impulse has not been as strong. As a coastal and seafaring people, some Wenzhou people have traditionally engaged in fishing, trading, and smuggling on the high seas, which involved interactions with foreign merchants, smugglers, and pirates, thus preserving the spark of commerce.

In the 1960s and 1970s, economic anthropology was embroiled in a debate between the "formalists" and the "substantivists." The formalists believed that Western neoclassical models of economic behavior, models predicated on the rational maximization of utility and efficiency in conditions of resource scarcity, could be applied universally to all human societies regardless of culture, history, or geographical place (LeClair and Schneider 1968). The substantivists believed that the formalist approach to economic behavior could not be extended to premodern, noncapitalist, and non-Western economies. According to Karl Polanyi (1957), whose work inspired the substantivists, the economy is an "instituted process"; it cannot be understood outside of the particular social and historical institutions and culture it is embedded in, which impart meaning and motivation, give shape to, and impose constraints on economic activities. For Polanyi and Marshall Sahlins (1972, 1976), neoclassical economics cannot explain or understand economic practices found in societies where the market has not separated off from or attained autonomy from the larger social and cultural institutions that encased economic processes, such as kinship, religiosity, and kingship.

This chapter shows how the Wenzhou Model is embedded in "family and kinship culture" (家族文化), as pointed out by Li Renqing in the epigraph above. Chapter 10 will show its embeddedness in ritual and religious institutions, a feature that is missing from the conventional understanding of the Wenzhou Model. The chapter ends with the suggestion that the secret of the Wenzhou Model's "success" may be that its market economy has eluded serious disembedding from traditional kinship and religious institutions. Thus, Wenzhou's market economy is able to tap into the deep economic and cultural *habitus* of a commercial culture that has been evolving for over a thousand years. Below I summarize the four conventional understandings of the Wenzhou Model of rural economic development.

PRIVATE FAMILY ENTERPRISES

The first defining feature of the Wenzhou Model is the "privatization" (*siyouhua*) of ownership and management of economic activity. Wenzhou was one of the earliest places in China to privatize collective agriculture; the rest of the country only caught up after 2000. The basic unit of production and commerce became the family or household in the 1980s. Most family enterprises started out with small-scale, low-tech production or sales. In a climate when it was still politically dangerous to openly engage in private enterprise, Wenzhou businesses were the first in the country to initiate the strategy of "hanging and leaning" (挂靠) (K. X. Zhou 1996: 121). For a fee paid to local cadres of collective- or state-owned enterprises, private enterprises disguised themselves as "collectives" by using the letterhead and seals of these more legitimate enterprises. There is often a gender and generational division of labor, where the wife stays at home to manage the factory, store, or restaurant, while the husband travels to other cities in China or even abroad, to secure raw materials and engage in sales and marketing. Meanwhile, adult children are assigned to different cities to manage branch family enterprises. In the late 1990s and 2000s, shareholding cooperatives (合資合作社) and joint-stock enterprises (股份企業) combined several families into larger enterprises, moving industrial production to a more capital-intensive and higher-tech level and scale. This "scaling up" has seen some larger factories relocating to Hangzhou or Shanghai, attracted by those cities' tax incentives and better-educated, tech-savvy workforce (Wei, Li, and Wang 2007).

Already by 1994, Wenzhou's industrial output was mainly generated by private enterprises rather than state- or collectively owned industries, a forerunner in China at the time (Wei, Li, and Wang 2007: 440). In 2014, the share of Wenzhou's total gross industrial output produced by nonstate enterprises, including family-owned, joint-stock, and joint-foreign ventures, had risen to 94.6 percent, while state- and collective-owned enterprises comprised a mere 5.4 percent of total industrial output (*Wenzhoushi tongjiju* 2015: 5). There is a common saying that in Wenzhou "everyone wants to be a 'boss' [*laoban*, 老闆], not an 'employee' [*zhigong*, 職工]." The main initiative and energy for economic development comes from the *minjian* (民間), or "the people," rather than the state. Thus, economic growth was a spontaneous popular explosion in which the local government merely followed the lead of the entrepreneurial current engulfing them.

However, "privatization" may not be the best term to describe this economic dynamism of "the realm of the people" (民間), because it carries cultural baggage from the history of capitalism in the West, which is based on the nuclear family and private individuals. Rural Wenzhou household enterprises are both families and corporations that are embedded in local communities and larger kinship structures, such as lineages. There are strong social and religious expectations for family and joint-stock enterprises to donate to temples, lineages, community projects, and local public ritual events, thus conveying a decidedly communal or public quality to "private" economic activities.

Figure 2.1. Family-owned shoe factory in Yongxing, Longwan District, 1998. Photo by the author.

INGENIOUS LOCAL CREDIT AND CAPITAL GENERATION

A second feature of the Wenzhou Model is that its economic growth is fueled by an indigenous self-generating capital. Chinese state banks, with their attractive low annual interest rates of 3–6 percent across the past four decades, rarely lend to private small and medium enterprises. State banks favor large state-owned companies or large private companies with social connections to state bureaucracy. This discrimination has forced Wenzhou private entrepreneurs to turn to informal credit schemes or "shadow banking" lying in the gray zones of legality. Since outside investments by the Chinese state or foreign overseas capital have been scarce, Wenzhounese have resorted to this gray zone, which they call, tongue in cheek, "primitive accumulation" (*yuanshi jilei,* 原始積累). Wenzhou was the first area in China to have private banks in 1986 (K. X. Zhou 1996: 98), and ingenious Wenzhou entrepreneurs ventured into underground credit associations of all stripes and sizes.

Startup capital in the early 1980s came from the savings and loans of local people, earned through their own hard work, ingenuity, and sometimes trickery. Many enterprising persons scouted out the garbage dumps of large state-owned textile factories in northeastern cities, such as Shenyang, Dalian, and Changchun. They shipped truckloads of discarded snippets of cloth back to Wenzhou, stitching them together into colorful clothing and quilts, and sold them back to the Northeast. Family enterprises developed ways of making fake shoes with cardboard that were so convincing that their buyers did not discover the deceit until it rained. In the 1980s, Wenzhou earned a dubious national reputation for making fake products, especially shoes. Other entre-preneurs combed the country for old Republican-era silver coins of the 1920s, called "big heads" (*datou*), after the head of Yuan Shikai displayed on these coins. They sold them to smugglers, who ventured on the high seas and ex-changed them for Taiwan's cheap electric appliances (televisions, cassette and video players), which found a ready market in the consumer-goods-starved Mainland. Looking back on that period, one factory owner in Jin Xiang Town-ship said to me in 2004, "What a pity that was. Such a great outflow of silver currency to Taiwan for what is now waste metal [*feitie*] today! And to think we gave away real silver for that junk—great loss for the country!" Another item smuggled out was marine eel fry (*manyu miao*) that were sold to Japanese nurseries for high prices. These marine eels, highly prized in East Asian *haute* cuisine, lived mainly around the river estuaries of the Wenzhou area, where the fresh water of rivers mingles with the salt water of the East China Sea. Due to industrial pollution in the 1990s, these marine eels disappeared from Wenzhou waters, and consumers of precious marine eels must now import them back from Japan.

In Wenzhou, loans came primarily from the private sector. Most Wenzhou small businesses turned to indigenous methods for capital accumulation: traditional "rotating credit societies" (*lunhui*, 輪會) or "people's money asso-ciations" (*qianhui*, 民間錢會). These rotating credit societies trace back to late imperial times, and Western anthropologists and Chinese scholars have exam-ined them in early twentieth-century Taiwan and Southeast Asia (Freedman 1979a; Li Y. 2002; Shi et al. 2002: 205–231; Tsai 2002). Informal credit associa-tions are called "mutual aid credit societies" (*huzhuhui*, 互助會) or "petition societies" (*chenghui*, 呈會) in the Yong Qiang area of Longwan District, while elsewhere they are simply called "associations" (*hui*, 會).

Rotating credit associations were especially important in the 1980s and 1990s, starting out among networks of kin, neighbors, and acquaintances. Women were well represented in such groups. People joined to take out loans or collect interest; those who borrowed early from the common pot of money paid higher interest, while those who waited longer to borrow collected the interest.[2] A credit association would unfold in the following way. The initiator might be the person who needed to borrow money. She would assemble ten friends and neighbors together from her *guanxi* network to form a group, sometimes hosting an initial dinner for group members. Each member contributed say, 500 yuan toward a common pot of 5,500 yuan. The host or primary borrower then took the accumulated sum first, borrowing it for a set period of time, say three or six months without interest. When the loan period was up, the second borrower would get only 4,900 yuan (5,500 yuan minus the interest he incurs). When the second loan period ended, the third borrower might get 5,000 yuan because the interest has decreased. By the time of the fifth borrower, since he is in the middle of the eleven borrowers, he would neither pay nor receive interest. The sixth borrower starts to receive the interest paid out by the earlier borrowers. The tenth or eleventh borrowers would receive the most interest, but they also waited the longest and ran a higher risk of earlier borrowers defaulting on their loans. Compared to private "shadow banks" in Wenzhou, whose interest rates were at an astounding 3 percent *per month* or 36 percent per year in the late 1990s, the interest rate of rotating credit associations was generally lower, about 1 percent per month. Although these informal credit associations were not quite legal, local officials chose to turn a blind eye.

As Li Yuanhua (2002) and Kellee Tsai (2002: 120–165) have both shown, these innocuous small-scale credit societies that helped ordinary people start up their small businesses were later overtaken by more speculative high-interest pyramid schemes such as "elevation associations" (*taihui*, 抬會), where the organizers sometimes tricked the other members into putting up their money. "Money shops" (*qian zhuang*, 錢莊) also flourished underground or in disguise as "collective-owned credit cooperatives" that extended loans at high interest rates. Instead of investing in substantive industries, these private banks sometimes invested in get-rich speculative ventures that did not always deliver, while giving out risky loans. Thus, it was inevitable that many ran into serious liquidity problems. The mass entanglement of so many creditors and debtors meant that the collapse of one pyramid scheme led to financial ruin for hundreds or thousands of people.

The global recession of 2008 and declining overseas demand for Wenzhou products exacerbated this problem of speculative investments and transformed what had been a strength of the Wenzhou Model, its ability to creatively produce investment capital and credit, into its major liability. The Chinese state's response to the global financial crisis was a major state economic stimulus package of $586 billion in easy credit to keep the Chinese economy going. State banks gave out generous loans to stimulate the economy. Those few in

Wenzhou who were fortunate enough to obtain state bank loans at low interest turned around and loaned the money to credit-starved small and medium private enterprises at stratospheric interest rates, anywhere from 2.5 percent *per month* to 60 percent or above *per year*. Due to low returns in manufacturing, private entrepreneurs soon turned to speculation, such as relending their loans at higher interest to others, or buying real estate and creating a bubble economy. Most of these high-interest loans were for brief periods of a few weeks, and the borrowers thought they could pay back quickly. As a Wenzhou economist explained to me, when the People's Bank of China suddenly tightened state credit in 2011 to beat inflation, and when the housing bubble burst and property prices crashed, borrowers could not repay their high-interest loans. This caused a chain-reaction collapse of private credit societies (Bradsher 2013; Ren 2013; Richburg 2011).

Many indebted businessmen and borrowers just simply "took to the road" (跑路), in local parlance. Some escaped abroad, leaving their lenders, investors, and employees high and dry with unpaid debts and back wages. Some defaulters were under such pressure and shame that they committed suicide, usually by jumping off tall buildings. Indeed, in 2012, a Buddhist abbot informed me that in the past year, many desperate entrepreneurs facing dire economic distress had sought him out for emotional, psychological, and spiritual counseling. The abbot personally knew several businessmen who had committed suicide. The problem became so severe that President Wen Jiabao payed a visit to Wenzhou in 2012.[3] The Wenzhou credit crisis of defaulted loans was bailed out by the central government in 2013, because the problem threatened to become contagious across the nation.

The Wenzhou Model of creative credit represents one region's strategy of dealing with a national banking system that denied loans to small private businesses, propelling them into the unregulated dangerous world of high-interest "shadow banking." The state banking system is a holdover from the Maoist command economy, whereby the state sector remains indifferent to the needs of local small and medium private entrepreneurs. Indeed, contrary to what some Western anthropologists have called China's "neoliberal economy," in Wenzhou people understand that the system still favors large state-owned enterprises. Those scholars who rush to critique China's "neoliberalism" are simply imposing a Western critique of Western neoliberal policies on a very different historical situation in China. They forget how risky and tenuous the beginnings of the Wenzhou Model were in the 1980s, when private entrepreneurs were accused of joining the "going capitalist faction" (走資派). These scholars also seem unaware of the *longue durée* history of the early Ming and

Qing dynasty "Maritime Prohibitions" (海禁), which banned small private Chinese coastal merchants from trading with foreigners (Ryuku Kingdom, Japan, Korea, and Southeast Asia), in favor of the state-organized tributary trade (M. Yang 2019a; Z. Zhao 2005). In recent years, there have been calls on the internet for the state to reduce its steep taxes, government fees, and surcharges in order to help small private enterprises to survive (Anonymous 2011). Whereas creative credit acquisition produced remarkable economic growth early in the Reform period, the 2008 global recession revealed that the Wenzhou Model could not overcome a national economic system that still discriminated against small private businesses. The credit squeeze is perhaps a major reason that most Wenzhou enterprises have been unable to upgrade beyond the low-end manufacturing that originally carried them out from agricultural poverty of the Maoist era (Liao C. 2014).

MOBILITY OF PEOPLE AND GOODS

The third characteristic of the Wenzhou Model is the high mobility and movement of goods and people into and out of Wenzhou. The light industrial products manufactured in Wenzhou are marketed across the whole country, and to Southeast Asia, the United States, Europe, Russia, and the Middle East. One noteworthy Wenzhou international export was the official metal badges for diverse organizations such as the New York City Police Department, United Nations patrols, Ghanaian customs inspectors, the Chinese army in Hong Kong, and American Lions Club members (Rosenthal 1999). These badges were manufactured in Jinxiang Township (金乡镇), which I visited in 2004. In the new millennium, I started seeing African merchants in Wenzhou placing orders for athletic shoes and long white tunics that are imported into North Africa.

Out of Wenzhou's population of 8 million, at any given time, over 1 million are traveling or residing in other parts of China, doing business, buying raw materials, searching for new sales opportunities, managing their factories, and operating small stores, tailor shops, or beauty salons. Many of them go back home to Wenzhou to celebrate the lunar New Year Festival with their relatives every year. Virtually every town or city in China has its Wenzhou quarter, such as "Zhejiang Village" in Beijing, studied by anthropologists Zhang Li (2001) and Xiang Biao (2004), where most residents are Wenzhounese. Wenzhou people have a reputation as astute business people who stick together and support each other, unified by their incomprehensible language. Many Wenzhou extended families form a business network across Chinese cities. A daughter

Figure 2.2. Old water transport canal in Yongzhong Town, Longwan District, dating back to late imperial times, 1993. Photo by the author.

and son-in-law may run a branch factory in Northeast China, while a younger son gathers raw materials in Sichuan to supply the family business. A grand-daughter may attend college in Singapore or Hong Kong, building a better-educated and more cosmopolitan generation for the future.

Wenzhou people have also embarked on journeys of labor migration or emigration to Italy, France, New York City, and Africa, some paying high sums to be smuggled abroad. These migrants generally come from the poorer re-gions of Wenzhou, such as Wencheng and Qingtian Counties, and neighbor-ing Lishui Municipality. In Italy and France, the majority of Chinese are from Wenzhou who start out as sweatshop workers; many of them graduate to local business owners (Cao 2013; Wang C. 2000). On a visit to Florence, Italy, in 2011, I came across a Wenzhou wedding, which drew the attention of international tourists assembled in the Piazzale Michelangelo. It was an impressive display, complete with white bridal gown and tuxedos, white stretch limousine, a pro-cession of bridesmaids, flower bouquets, and firecrackers. I have also visited the offices of Wenzhou native-place associations in New York City and Los Angeles; the latter has three Wenzhou native-place associations.

Figure 2.3. View of new high-speed railway line in Qiancang Township, Pingyang County, 2008. Photo by the author.

In any given year, over 1 million migrant laborers from the poorer interior of China are found in Wenzhou, working in factories, hotels, restaurants, and homes. These young people come from Sichuan, Jiangxi, Anhui, and other provinces, some of them sent in groups by their village labor organizations to help improve local finances. They work on renewable one-year contracts, generally without benefits except work injury compensation, and live in the homes of their employers or in abandoned low-end buildings. By about 2005, in some towns the migrants outnumbered native residents.

All this movement of people and goods has created transportation and communication arteries that have transformed Wenzhou from an impoverished backwater into a busy hub connected to all parts of China. A railroad line was built, connecting Wenzhou to Shanghai, Hangzhou, Xiamen, and Guangzhou, whereas before, passengers could only take a winding, nauseating thirteen-hour bus ride through the mountains to Hangzhou. An airport was established with flights to major cities, including a direct flight to Hong Kong.

Wenzhou boasts the first private airline company in the country, founded by Wang Junyao. Countless roads and highways now link up Wenzhou with the rest of China, and many privately run trucking businesses flourish.

GROWTH OF TOWNS AND RAPID URBANIZATION

A fourth feature of the Wenzhou Model is the remarkable growth of new or expanded towns. In 1978, there were only 18 towns in the Wenzhou area, but by 1994, there were 137 towns, and 40 percent of the Wenzhou population resided there (Zhang Zhichen 1998: 1048). A typical example is Yongzhong Township (永中鎮) in Longwan District. It was first established as a small settlement in the Ming dynasty, in the fifteenth century. In 1984, the town leadership developed urban plans for expanding the town and opened up a process of bidding for apartments by any family, regardless of their household registration (hukou, 戶口) status. This process of inviting investment from the people and encouraging them to buy apartment units and storefronts (about 80,000 yuan per unit in 1993) to be constructed was called "accumulation of funds from the people" (minjian jizi, 民間集資). By 1985, the township government had gathered the requisite money and construction was started. When I first went to Yongzhong in 1991, I saw how the old part of town, with narrow lanes and two-story wooden houses and water transport canals, was now engulfed by the expanding new town. Brand-new street blocks and four-story apartment buildings had just been completed, and families from the countryside had already moved in. From an area of 0.7 square kilometers, the town expanded to 3.2 square kilometers.

Thus, urbanization in Wenzhou allowed the local people to bypass the "household registration" or hukou system of strict state controls of population movement and the caste-like separation of rural from urban people, instituted by the state in 1957. Indeed, Wenzhou boasts China's "first peasant town," Longgang Town (龍港鎮) in Cangnan County. Beginning in 1984, the town of Longgang arose from a humble collection of six fishing villages of 7,000 residents to a thriving regional economic hub of 80,000 residents in 1994 (Shi et al. 2002: 298–309). In 2014, its population, including migrant workers, had reached 540,000, and there was talk during my visit in 2016 of upgrading it into a municipality (shi).

THE DARKER SIDES OF THE WENZHOU MODEL

One of the darker sides of the much-admired entrepreneurialism of the Wenzhou Model is the class tension that sometimes flared up between Wenzhou entrepreneurs and migrant laborers. Locals often blamed the rise in theft, robbery, and rape on migrant laborers. A rich local man in Longwan District, whose family spent 2 million yuan to start a new ceramic tile factory, showed me the impressive scar on his kneecap. During the New Year's celebrations of 1993, a Sichuanese thief broke into his home. The rich man chased and grabbed the thief, but the thief had a knife and slashed his kneecap before others subdued the thief and turned him in.

I spoke in 1993 to five young male migrant laborers from a village along the Yangzi River near the city of Chongqing. The villagers were resettled due to the Three Gorges Dam project, so their village sent the young people to work in Wenzhou. They bemoaned the injustice of the fact that they possessed high school degrees but had to work for Wenzhou bosses (*laoban*, 老闆) who had only an elementary school education. One of them had missed passing the national college entrance examinations by a mere two points. Outside a Buddhist temple in 1998, a middle-aged Sichuanese man declared bitterly, "Wenzhou people look down on migrant laborers. They treat us like slaves! They are like the landlords of times past. They are like how the Japanese treated the Chinese!" One night in 2010, I witnessed a knife fight where local Wenzhou people ganged up against a Sichuanese man. The locals claimed that the Sichuanese had refused to pay for his pedicab ride and they wanted to teach him a lesson. These class and ethnic tensions may subside with better working conditions, rising wages, improved state welfare, and intermarriage with Wenzhou residents. In 2016, a migrant pedicab driver told me that he could now enjoy free lunches offered by the local government. So long as the household registration system makes it difficult for migrants to educate their children, bring their families to reside with them, or establish local businesses, these ethnic and class tensions will remain.

A second dark side of the Wenzhou Model is a certain culture of defiance against the law, which may trace back to the late imperial coastal legacy of smuggling and piracy. This defiance ranges from mild transgressions such as the manufacturing of fake shoes and products with fake labels in the 1980s and early 1990s, to serious criminal acts such as drug smuggling and the manufacturing of fake baby formula in 2004. The poisoned baby formula manufactured in Cangnan County and sold to Anhui and Hubei Provinces resulted in the horrible swelling of infant heads and their deaths. One colorful example of "businesses that bring decapitation" (*shatou shengyi*) was the story I heard several times of a Cangnan County heroin drug lord operating in Yunnan Province. When he was captured and about to be executed, his last private words to his son were, "It's still better to deal in white powder." His son took this advice seriously: when he received his executed father's ashes in a box, he dumped the ashes out and substituted heroin powder, which he smuggled back to sell in Wenzhou (Shi et al. 2002: 329).

A third dark aspect of Wenzhou's economic development is the common problem of environmental degradation that has accompanied industrial development across China. From the 1990s, developers and industries seemed to violate antipollution laws with impunity. Everywhere the old waterways and transport canals became badly polluted. Whereas the canals used to provide water for drinking, bathing, and laundry, now they ran black and oily with industrial discharge, clogged with garbage. I encountered several temples whose peaceful atmosphere was ruined when a noise- and air-polluting factory set up shop next door. No amount of complaining or written petitions to local authorities seemed to make any difference; it was already too late to withdraw the official permit, which should not have been granted in the first place. Wenzhou local officials are rewarded based on industrial output in their jurisdictions and the number of new enterprises. Protection of the environment was seldom considered important from the 1980s until about 2012.

THE WENZHOU MODEL: THE GENEALOGICAL AND THE SALUTARY

One could say that, before modernity, the Wenzhou Model was not limited to the Wenzhou area, but was an economic model found across late imperial southern China, tracing back to the commercial revolution of the Song dynasty (von Glahn 2016). The Wenzhou Model accords with what anthropologist Hill Gates has called "China's petty capitalist mode of production" (1996). Gates found a long history of family-based production for profit in a commercialized society with highly developed markets stretching from the Song dynasty to modern Taiwan. She also found that the size of these units of production was always kept in check by predatory imperial state officials. State taxation and surcharge fees prevented most family businesses from getting too large, and confiscation of property could control them once they did. I would add that the Chinese cultural system of family division of equal property among all sons, in contrast with Japan's primogeniture, reinforced the small size of the vast majority of family enterprises. The insecurities brought by state predation prodded most wealthy elite families to convert economic capital into political capital through the imperial examination system and the winning of official posts.

If much of southern China (including Taiwan) followed this petty commodity model of commercialized agriculture, handicraft production, and small family businesses in late imperial China, why do we only talk about the

Wenzhou Model today? In the post-Mao economic revival, Wenzhou stands out for two reasons. In other areas of China, either the local state dominance of the economy or foreign and overseas Chinese capital investments were too strong. In Wenzhou, a poor and neglected part of China during the Maoist era, Wenzhou's unique language and regional culture and its geographical isolation partially sheltered it from the radical social engineering going on in other parts of the country. No doubt, these factors have allowed Wenzhou, more than elsewhere in China, to maintain more continuities with China's economic *longue durée*.

In 1998, a public security officer came to check up on me, and I engaged him in extended conversation. I offered congratulatory remarks about Wenzhou's economic miracle and was surprised when he replied dismissively, "Yes, we have become better off, but this should not be the model for the rest of China! Wenzhou can only produce small family enterprises. This is no progress! What we need are *large* firms, then we can compete in the world and that is *real* economic development." "But you need to start somewhere," I countered. "Small firms mean that ordinary people have more control over their own lives. They don't have to be ordered around by higher-ups in a large bureaucracy." I proceeded to tell him about the British economist E. F. Schumacher's notion of "Small Is Beautiful," and pointed out that humankind's dream of "bigger is better" has been extremely wasteful of our finite natural resources. He was not convinced, and he complained about the "smallness" and "backwardness" of local religious establishments. "You in the West have giant cathedrals," he lamented. "We just have these tiny temples making people more ignorant [愚昧] and dependent on the gods." I defended local temples by saying that they allowed ordinary people to take the initiative in doing things for the public good. It was an uphill battle trying to convince him. However, I could see that at least I had gotten him a bit confused: he was puzzled that someone from the West was not looking down on Wenzhou small businesses and temples but was actually defending their "smallness."

Part II

RELIGIOUS DIVERSITY
AND SYNCRETISM
IN WENZHOU

3   Popular Religiosity

Deities, Spirit Mediums, Ancestors, Ghosts, and Fengshui

甌越間好事鬼, 山椒水濱多淫
祀。其廟貌有雄而毅、勵而碩
者, 則曰將軍；有溫而願、晰
而少者, 則曰某郎；有嫗而尊嚴
者, 則曰姥；有婦而容艷者, 則
曰姑。

(The Yue people of the Ou River [Wenzhou area] love to worship their gods; in their mountains and along their waterways are many unorthodox deity temples. These temples cast an image of grandeur and resoluteness. Whoever displays strength and decisiveness, people will transform him into a god and call him "General." When there is a contagious disease, they will make vows to repay the gods if they bring relief. They will make a god out of those rare clairvoyant people, and call him "Lord" something. If there is a matron whom they greatly respect, they will turn her into a goddess with the title of "Grandmother." If there is a beautiful woman, they will make her a goddess and call her "Lady.")

—陸龜蒙: «野廟碑» (唐) [Lu Guimeng, "Stele Inscription for a Temple in the Wilds" (Tang dynasty, ninth century)]

As this Tang dynasty quotation attests, the Wenzhou area has long been inhabited by people who worshipped all manner of deities and spirits, built countless temples to house them, and consulted with spirit mediums. The fact that travelers and locals alike have repeatedly made this observation in texts dating back to imperial times suggests that the intensity of popular religiosity in Wenzhou may have exceeded other parts of imperial China. Today, Wenzhou's popular religious culture continues to be stronger and more tenacious than many other rural areas in China, with the possible exception of Fujian and Guangdong Provinces.

DEFINING CHINESE POPULAR RELIGION

Studies of Chinese popular religion (Fan and Chen 2016; Sangren 1987; Weller 1987) generally include practices such as deity worship, spirit possession, divination and Chinese geomancy (*fengshui*, 風水), lunar calendar festivals, ancestor worship, placating of ghosts, funerary rituals, and pilgrimage. These ritual practices are all part of the everyday lives of peasant communities, so we could also think of popular religion as a "communal religion" that is a local way of life (W. Tam 2011). Indeed, this was the idea in late imperial times, when religious practices were grouped under the indigenous label of "local customs" (風俗) that were recorded in texts called "local gazetteers" (地方志). These texts included local geography, community customs and festivals, histories of local temples and lineages, hagiographies of deities and their miracles, and biographies of local notables and virtuous women.

In Western scholarship, few have tried to define Chinese popular religion, but John Lagerwey offered a provocative definition:

> It is a machine for the production of gods who demonstrate their existence and their power by taking possession of people; in exchange for their blessings, they then require of the people, their bloody sacrifice.... [The gods] "attach themselves to the body" [*fushen*, 附身] of men and women, through whom they then speak.... This religion ... has ... its own officiants, gods, temples, faithful, and rituals—is that not enough to qualify as a religion? ... I believe [popular religion] to be the bedrock of all Chinese religion, that on which the others build and over against which they define themselves. *It is essentially autonomous*; it is also by definition local. Possession and bloody sacrifice being its two basic features, it is to them that China's "higher religions" had to react. (Lagerwey 1999: 167–168)

Lagerwey's definition stresses three components: *spirit possession, animal sacrifice*, and *localism*. When we apply Lagerwey's tripartite definition to contemporary rural Wenzhou, we find that Wenzhou's religious culture today resonates well with spirit possession and localism, but less so with animal sacrifice.

I did not witness and seldom heard about animal sacrifice for deity temples in Wenzhou. The exception is in Cangnan County, where large-scale pig sacrifices have occurred in recent years, performed by immigrants from southern Fujian (Zhang C. 2016: 196–198, 206–210, 222–225). Most Daoist and all Buddhist temples in Wenzhou offer vegetarian fare to the gods and buddhas as well as to worshippers, in keeping with their long tradition of discouraging blood sacrifice. At the Heavenly Immortal Temple (天仙宮) to the local goddess Mother Lu in Pumen Village, Yong Zhong Township, in the 1990s, worshippers offered things like a pig's head or raw hunks of fatty pork in wooden or bamboo "ritual containers" (禮盛), which are used to carry ritual gifts such as food for the gods and engagement presents (see figure 10.1). Back then, the temple was a small, dilapidated local deity temple. After it was rebuilt and registered with the Daoist Association in 1996, these meat offerings tapered off. Later, when the temple organized celebrations of the god's birthday, the gathered worshippers were only served vegetarian meals. In Wenzhou, the Communist state has domesticated and toned down the bloody and effervescent features of sacrifice and spirit possession.

Lagerwey's definition of Chinese popular religion omits a fourth dimension: class and social status group. Popular religion is distinguished from the literate philosophical and meditational religious culture of the elites. In Wenzhou, where wealthy entrepreneurs of peasant backgrounds enthusiastically donate to deity temples and ancestor halls, it seems that educational levels, more than economic class, predict participation in popular religious culture. The more education people have attained, the more they aspire to enter mainstream Chinese urban secular culture. While some local elites, such as local cadres, might subscribe to the more respectable Buddhism, other social elites may become attracted to Christianity.

Beginning around 2005 in Wenzhou, I noticed a decline in the local use of the pejorative term "superstition" (迷信), in favor of a neutral term, "popular beliefs" (*minjian xinyang*, 民間信仰), which had been adopted by Chinese academics in the 1990s. Of course, there are occasional throwbacks: in the summer of 2014, I attended a lunch graced by the presence of a local official who still used the term "superstition." His young assistant quietly corrected him, murmuring deferentially, "Nowadays, we use the term 'popular beliefs.'" In local Wenzhou parlance, the phrase "worshipping gods and chanting scriptures" (拜經懺) is often used, and refers not only to popular religion but also to popular Daoism and Buddhism. This term describes a kind of religiosity where one approaches the gods to ask for favors, and salvation is sought by chanting sutras or hiring others to chant them.

According to Philip Clart (2014), in Mainland Chinese academic debates, the Chinese translation of *minjian zongjiao* (民間宗教) to the English academic term "popular religion" poses problems. The word "religion" now connotes the "sectarian" or millenarian "secret societies" of late imperial China, which now have negative connotations as rebellious movements. Gone are the days of Marxist-Leninist-Mao-Zedong Thought and their studies of peasant rebellions as progressive "class struggles"! In China the category of "religion" has also come to be associated with political unrest, such as global Islamism and the Catholic Church in 1980s Poland. Thus, in a strange about-face, just as the term "superstition" is subsiding, its counterpart, "religion," may now inspire more concern in China as a threat to the secular order.

I have also noticed a new term creeping into common usage in Wenzhou since about 2012, which can be translated as "belief customs" or "customary beliefs" (信俗). Here the term "customs" (*su*, 俗) reconnects with the late imperial Chinese category of "local customs" (風俗), which connotes the local and the routine. A Wenzhou scholar explained to me that this new term gets around the problem of having to acknowledge that local customs are a form of "religion," which is "still a sensitive issue" (宗教還是很敏感) in China. Thus, "customary beliefs" serve to renormalize popular religion as a way of life or peasant culture, by invoking a historical category of Chinese civilization, reversing a century of modern labeling as "superstition." This new term also tones down the dangerous force that is often associated by officialdom with religion, what Émile Durkheim called "collective effervescence," the ritual suspension of everyday norms with intense outbreaks of religious passions and wild behavior (Durkheim [1912] 1995: 218–220).

However, the problem with using the phrases "popular beliefs" (民間信仰) or "customary beliefs" (信俗) to translate the notion of "popular religion" is the word "belief" (信). It introduces a Protestant slant on religion as primarily a mentalistic, doctrinal, and discursive practice, which Talal Asad (1993), in his important critique of Clifford Geertz's definition of religion, pointed out is a problem when applied to non-Protestant traditions. Chinese popular religious traditions do not share this overriding emphasis on "belief," doctrine, and textualism. Ritual actions are more important as modes of religious practice, a point that James Watson (1988) also made when he wrote that Chinese religiosities privileged "orthopraxy" over "orthodoxy." Furthermore, while Buddhist and Daoist traditions *do* focus on scriptures, the main approach to sacred texts is not hermeneutical, to discursively analyze or interpret them, but to chant, absorb, and embody them through ritualized repetition.

Therefore, I propose the Chinese phrase "popular custom religion" (*minsu zongjiao*, 民俗宗教) to translate "popular religion" into Chinese. The "religion" part of the phrase avoids the demeaning modernist association with mere "superstition," while also introducing the elements of divinity, sacrality, and transcendence that are missing in the indigenous notion of "folk customs." The inclusion of "custom" (俗) reconnects with late imperial China and suggests that popular religion is still a whole way of life for the folk, who resist the modernist move to split religiosity off from "normal" secular life. Foregrounding the word "custom" may also decrease the sense of danger and rebellion that Chinese officialdom associates with the term "religion" (宗教) at the end of the phrase. The "popular" or "folk" (民) part of the term connects up with the notion of "folk civil society" (民間社會), to be addressed in chapter 9.

DIVERSITY, HYBRIDITY, AND "DIALOGIC TRANSCENDENCE"

We must also consider the relationship between popular religion and the "Three Teachings" (三教) of Daoism, Buddhism, and Confucianism, which are China's established religious traditions, each with their highly literate cultures. Both Daoism and Buddhism had their own formal religious institutions, and Confucianism operated through the state institution, with its system of "cultural temples" (文廟) honoring Confucius, and the imperial examination system based on the study of the Confucian classics. With Song dynasty Neo-Confucianism, Confucian culture took what Peter Bol (2001, 2003) has called "a localist turn," expressing itself through local lineages and their ancestor halls across the empire (Ebrey 1986, 1991). This localist turn meant that Confucian gentry were actively involved in funding, building, and sometimes running local temples and monasteries.

The Three Teachings have each sought to tame, control, "civilize" (化), and absorb popular religion into their own religious institutions. Both Daoism (Kleeman 2016: 14, 257–258) and Buddhism (von Glahn 2004: 144–145) discouraged blood sacrifice and spirit possession in popular religion. Both tolerated but sought to absorb the cults of local gods, by placing their own Daoist gods or Buddhas above local gods in a hierarchy of divine authority and efficacy, a process I call "hierarchical encompassment." While Confucians had no problems with animal sacrifice in their ancestor rituals, in the *Analects* the Confucian attitude toward popular religion is clear:

樊遲問知, 子曰: 務民之義, 敬鬼神而遠之, 可謂知矣。(論語 。雍也)

(Fan Chi asked Confucius about Wisdom, and the Master replied, "To work for the benefit of the people; to honor ghosts and deities, while keeping one's distance from them. This can be called Wisdom." [*Confucian Analects, Yong Ye*])

Late imperial Confucian culture did not refute the existence of ghosts and deities, but sought to moderate the common people's otherworldly obsessions, dampen excessive religious devotion, and restrict ritual expenditures. Thus, long before modern times, the three established religious traditions had already worked to domesticate and integrate popular religious practices (Watson 1985), but had by no means fully succeeded. Chinese popular religion remained closely embedded into the myriad local cultures of China.

Scholarly works on Confucianism, Daoism, and Buddhism tend to present them with doctrinal and institutional boundaries, coherent identities, unique histories, and discrete organizations. This tendency may be more a reflection of our own need for classification than the realities of popular practice. In Wenzhou, I found that the boundaries between popular religion, Daoist, Buddhist, and Confucian religious cultures are often blurred, with much fluidity and interpenetration. Timothy Brook (1993) has highlighted the prominence of Chinese religious syncretism in late imperial China, showing how different religious teachings melded into a single body of religious practices. This process started in the Yuan dynasty, when it was explicitly called "the Three Teachings Combining into One" (三教合一). Under foreign Mongol rule, Confucian orthodoxy was relaxed during the Yuan, allowing for cross-fertilization between religions. Brook also noted that it was popular religion among the common people, rather than among elite gentry, where syncretism really took hold (see Hoskins 2015 on Vietnamese Caodai).

Although this book arranges these religious traditions into four chapters (popular religion, Daoism, Buddhism, and lineages as popular Confucianism), I must also stress that they are often interpenetrated and not mutually exclusive. The permeability of religious boundaries in Wenzhou can be seen in two ways. *First*, there is often a seepage of symbolic, mythological, and ritual elements from one religious tradition to another. Deities in Wenzhou are called the following terms interchangeably: "gods/goddesses" (*shen*, 神), "Daoist gods and immortals" (*shenxian*, 神仙), "Buddhas" (*fo*, 佛), and "bodhisattvas" (*pusa*, 菩薩). It is common to find statues of popular religion deities, Daoist, and Buddhist divinities together inside a single temple. Scriptures and ritual procedures from different religious traditions may also be mixed together: Buddhist scriptures may be chanted in Daoist temples, although usually not the reverse. I have participated in rural funerals where the ritualists first dress up as Daoists, then change into Buddhist robes. *Second*, membership and participation in religious associations and rituals is not exclusive, but multiple and overlapping. When a family faces an illness, it will seek out doctors of traditional Chinese medicine or Western biomedicine. When medicine fails, the family may seek help from a local shaman, communicate with an offended ancestor or god, offer incense and food to a favorite deity in a temple, exorcise a demon through a Daoist ritual, or ask Buddhist monks to chant sutras for the family. People might even try their luck with the Christian deity Jesus, for good measure.

Indeed, some people in Wenzhou seemed confused about religious boundaries. While visiting the home of a vegetable seller at the market in Wutian Town, she asked me whether Guanyin, the female-gendered Bodhisattva Avalokitésvara in China, was Daoist or Buddhist. She had reason to be confused, because this Buddhist divinity also appears in Daoist iconography and pantheon. The Daoist god Great Heavenly Stem Divinity Who Rescues People from Hardship (太乙救苦天尊) resonates with the figure of Guanyin. Although he is portrayed as an old man, like Guanyin, he shows mercy and responds to human pleas for help. His image shows him sitting on the Buddhist symbol of the lotus and the green lion. The most important goddess worshipped in Wenzhou after Guanyin is Chen Jinggu (陳靖姑), discussed below. She is claimed by both popular religion and Daoism, but the circumstances of her birth have to do with Buddhism. Mother Chen was born of a drop of Guanyin's blood that flowed into a stream where her mother did the washing: that drop of blood brought her mother an immaculate conception.

In Wenzhou's religious hybridity, there is special intimacy between popular religion and Daoism: both engage in divine technologies to exorcise demons and communicate with gods. As chapter 6 shows, the modern state has pushed for deity temples of popular religion to register as Daoist temples and transform their religious identities and rituals into Daoist ones. By the new millennium, the Daoist Association had absorbed most deity temples in all Wenzhou counties except Cangnan, where in addition to Daoist and Buddhist Associations, there is also a Popular Religious Affairs Network Center (民間信仰聯絡處). Through interviews in 2016, I learned that it oversees 1,553 registered deity temples. The Cangnan Buddhist Association lists only 280 temples, and the Cangnan Daoist Association manages 80 (Xu and Xue 2005: 19). Thus, only in Cangnan has popular religion been allowed to maintain a separate identity, and work within its own institutional framework. This intimacy between popular religion, Daoism, and Buddhism in local religious culture is seen in this common saying: "Having a deity's head and a Buddhist tail" (神頭佛尾。). This phrase refers to the nature of much religious worship, which is like a strange beast cobbled together from elements of different religious traditions.

A study carried out in twenty-one villages in Longwan District in 2008–2009 even made a note of local religious hybridity, in which popular religion is "combined with Daoism and Buddhism into one" (道佛合一) (*Zhengxie Wenzhou Shi Longwanqu Weiyuanhui* 2011: 38–39). This survey examined the distribution of different faiths in local households. Of a total of 10,009 households surveyed in Longwan District, 88 percent, or 8,809 households, followed the Buddho-Daoist-popular religious tradition; 8 percent, or 815 households, described themselves as Protestants or "followers of the teachings of Jesus" (耶穌教徒); and only 4 percent, or 441 households, described themselves as Catholics (天主教徒).[1] Thus, Christians comprised 12 percent of households in Longwan. Startlingly, only *two* households described themselves as "atheist" (無神論), and one of them was said to belong to a "mentally ill" person, as if implying that only such a person would be atheist. The whole tone of this extensive volume on local folk religions and customs is celebratory, a strikingly different tone from the derisive antisuperstition discourse of the 1990s.

In the following sections I discuss some different features of popular religion in Wenzhou: deity worship; spirit possession; ancestors, ghosts, and death rituals; and divination and *fengshui*.

Deities: Hagiographies and Geographical Spread

Deity worship forms the centerpiece of Chinese popular religion. When I first visited Wenzhou, I was bewildered by the huge pantheon of gods and goddesses, many of which I had never heard of before. While some gods represent forces of nature (mountains, constellations, thunder, etc.), most gods were once human beings and left historical records. Newly installed deity statues must undergo the ceremony of "opening the light" (開光), in which a Daoist priest dabs the eyes of statues of gods, and a Buddhist monk does the same to Buddha and Bodhisattva statues. This ritual divinely activates the statue, transforming it into a living receptacle of the god, who descends into the statue and can hear people's prayers.

The cults of gods and ancestors both exhibit the Chinese penchant for recording histories, biographies, and genealogies. Since most gods were at one time human beings, there are written hagiographies (傳) providing the god's birthplace and year of birth, and accounts of their childhood, occupation or political office, acts of self-sacrifice or self-cultivation, and miracles performed. Usually brief hagiographies are carved into temple stone steles, following a certain formulaic construction. For influential gods, there are long orally transmitted legends, many of them written down at some point by an educated gentry, and some have been transformed into operas and vernacular novels (Shahar 1996).

Many gods are represented like human officials in the imperial bureaucracy, wearing official waist rings and headdresses, sitting on official thrones flanked by attendants, and carried outside in palanquins in ritual procession, with assistants clearing the way. Gods are also thought to have different rankings; local gods are thought to be of lowly rank, just like local officials rank lower than prefectural, provincial, and national officials stationed in the capital, Beijing. Also like human officials, many gods enjoy local territorial jurisdiction. These tutelary gods are periodically brought out in ritual procession to inspect the boundaries and ensure that their human population is protected from demonic incursions into their territory. Scholars have called this bureaucratic ranking of gods in Chinese popular religion and

Daoism the "celestial bureaucracy" (Wolf 1974) or the "imperial metaphor" (Feuchtwang 2001). Other anthropologists have pointed out that not all gods fit into the celestial bureaucracy; there are many goddesses and vagabond gods who do not resemble officials (Weller and Shahar 1996). Nevertheless, this bureaucratic presentation of gods is so culturally entrenched that even many goddesses are shown in official guise, as female civil officials sitting at a desk with the accoutrements of office: writing brush, ink well, and seal of office.

A slightly lower category of celestial beings are Daoist "immortals" or "transcendants" (仙人), who are less effective than gods at working miracles and intervening in human affairs. Immortals keep their human forms and are said to never die. They are people who have led a life of self-cultivation (meditation, detachment from worldly desires, and dietary and exercise regimens) and virtuous conduct. This conduct allows them to "attain the Way" (得道) and immortality. They are ethereal beings, light of body, who ride the winds, clouds, waves, and storks, flitting about in carefree abandon.

While the dominant view of gods and immortals sees them as benign protectors, there is also an undercurrent of fear toward some gods, whose alter egos can be vindictive and punishing. There are malignant spirits, who are called by at least four terms: "demons" (臜), which means literally "vicious and dirty"; "baleful spirit" (煞神); "demonic spirits" (鬼邪); and, finally, "monsters and demons" (妖魔鬼怪). All these terms describe spirits who have sinister intentions toward human beings. In Daoist rituals, the priest sometimes adopts the role of exorcist, commanding spirit armies to defend the community from these marauders. Stephan Feuchtwang emphasized the understudied demonic quality of popular religion in Taiwan, contrasting the "more abstract and harmonized cosmos of imperial regulation" with a "military imperium . . . in which malign and aggressive forces fill the universe" (2001: 46). Richard von Glahn (2004) also wrote about the demonic in Chinese religious culture, such as the "mountain goblins" of Jiangxi and the cult of Wutong, as expressions of the fears of civilization against the "barbaric" frontiers.

In Wenzhou today, I found that most people subscribed to an image of benign and virtuous gods, which may reflect the historical context of religious revival after a long drought. As Daniel Overmyer (1997) observed, Chinese gods are very similar to Catholic saints: they were once human beings, people of rare virtue and selflessness who performed miracles, and a cult developed around them after their deaths, with religious festivals and sometimes pilgrimages. However, in China, the imperial state awarded honorific titles, or enfeoffed (封) certain gods, and promoted them to higher ranks (Hansen 1990), and selectively inducted some gods into the imperial pantheon worshipped by imperial officials. With modernity, just as the radical Christian Reformation process of "purification" in Europe drew a hard line between humans and divine figures, abolishing the in-between saints, so also modern China's exposure to Protestant discourse against "idolatry" (偶像崇拜) as "backward" resulted in the twentieth-century smashing of deity statues.

Many deity cults trace back to the vibrant commercializing era of the Song dynasty, when they often replaced Earth God cults and were spread along trade routes (Hansen 1990; Katz 1995). Deity temples who shared in the same cult of a particular deity were often linked to each other, forming a hierarchy of temples. The "ancestral temple" (祖廟) is the divine site where the god was born or ascended to Heaven, or where the first temple of the deity cult was established. Traditionally, "dividing incense" (分香) was a common way of establishing a new branch temple, by installing an urn of incense ash taken from the ancestral or older temple at a new temple site (Schipper 1990). The older the temple, the farther up in the hierarchy it belongs, and the more it tends to spawn new temples by dispersing its incense ash. Deity cults have different geographical ranges: the most prominent gods are known and worshipped across China; others are worshipped only in the southeastern coastal region of southern Zhejiang, Fujian, Jiangxi, and Guangdong Provinces; and still others are local deities who are only worshipped in the Wenzhou area.

Local Gods

The biographies of local gods are closely tied to the area: they were born and raised in Wenzhou, lived here, or they protect local places and provide a ritual focus.

Earth Gods (土地公)

Earth Gods are worshipped all over China, but because they often incarnate immortalized local persons who protect their local communities, they must be understood as local gods. The Earth God is a local tutelary spirit *par excellence*, for he presides over a limited territorial jurisdiction, protecting the human inhabitants within its boundaries. Theoretically, all Earth Gods were once a local person. However, over time most Earth Gods have lost their specific human names and identities. Statues of the Earth God generally show him as an elderly man with a white beard, sometimes accompanied by his wife, the Earth Goddess (土地娘娘). In Wenzhou, he can be found protecting agricultural fields, urban neighborhoods, temples or ancestor halls, bridges, or restaurants or shops. The Earth God ranks at the bottom of the hierarchy of divinities. In chapter 9, I examine the etymology of the ancient term for Earth God, *she* (社), which has a "spirit" radical to the left, and the character "soil" to the right (Xu S. 1963: 7).

In Wenzhou, when new houses are built, one of the first things to be ritually installed by a Daoist priest, in the exact central point of the house, is the Earth God's "central residence" (中堂府). This central point takes the form of a four-foot-long wooden post covered with Daoist talismanic writing to ward off evil spirits. The post is inserted through the house floor into the earth below, sticking up about two feet into the house. Friends told me that the top of the pole reaches up into Heaven and the bottom reaches down into Hell, anchoring the house and positioning its human inhabitants between the powerful worlds of the gods above, who protect the living, and the gods below, who administer and punish the souls of the deceased. The "central residence" protects the house and its inhabitants from wandering ghosts (鬼), demonic gods (煞), and evil spirits (邪氣).

In 1998, I discovered that the small Earth God shrines in Longwan District that had dotted the fields and village neighborhoods on my last visit in 1993 had all but disappeared, removed by the local government in a campaign to get rid of unsightly "superstitious" shrines. Wang Qinsheng, a diviner, told me that the local government especially targeted small shrines because they proliferate too easily and are difficult to control (不好管), compared with large temples. A week later, on an old street in Yongzhong Town, I rounded a corner and, to my delight, saw a brand-new Earth God shrine set into a low stone wall lining a canal. Like new bamboo shoots sprouting up quickly after a destructive storm, these Earth God shrines and small unregistered deity temples kept popping up again after campaigns to eliminate them. Despite the determined forces of state secularization, the sparks of religious effervescence stubbornly reignite.

Although Earth Gods rank higher than the Kitchen God, whose image is found in many rural Wenzhou kitchens, they do not have direct access to the court of the Jade Emperor, the highest deity in popular religion. As one ritual expert explained to me in 1993, "The Earth God doesn't have direct access above. It's just like you can give gifts to influence your village head, but he has no audience with the likes of Chairman Jiang Zemin. However, he can protect you, or you can appease him so that he won't extort [*qiaozha*, 敲詐] from you." The celestial bureaucracy parallels the human secular administration of the state, but it is more accessible: anyone can go to a temple, offer incense and food to a deity, and receive the deity's assistance.

Figure 3.1. The Earth God and Earth Goddess, in a deity temple in Qianku Town, Cangnan County, 2014. Photo by the author.

City Gods (城隍爺)

City Gods also produce local community solidarity, but on a larger scale. The City God's jurisdiction in late imperial China was a whole walled town, usually a county or prefectural seat (Ying and Jiang 2008: 6–9). The City God was thought of as the equivalent of a town or prefecture's human magistrate, an official representing the imperial state. City God temples were the points at which state deity cults and popular religious worship overlapped (Zito 1987). On arriving at their new posts, the magistrates were expected to offer sacrifices to the local City God, their celestial counterpart. The local gentry and common folk also visited City God temples to pray for their families' well-being.

City God temples in Wenzhou were revived throughout the 1990s, and their interiors, which look like late imperial local government offices called *yamen*, have been restored, some with community opera stages. I visited the

City God temples in Ning Village (寧村), Longwan District; Jinxiang Town (金鄉鎮), Cangnan County; Kunyang Town (昆陽鎮), Pingyang County; and Yu-ao Village (魚熬村), Cangnan County, all of which used to be walled towns surrounded by moats. City God temples serve as a symbolic center of the town where public rituals and processions are held, bringing much of the town population together. City Gods were at one time human beings who made a contribution to a local area, but as with Earth Gods, many City Gods have lost their specific identities. To local people, the City God is a stern, official-like god who deploys his armed guardian gods to protect the population by exorcising the local area of demons and evil spirits (驅鬼邪) and punishing human evildoers. He is also involved in governing the Underworld (陰界) and overseeing the administering of punishments in Hell. That is why most City God temples are slightly scary places, displaying the accoutrements of a juridical law enforcement office, with mock late imperial-era weapons. Many temples display large images of the Ten Judges and their courts in Purgatory, where the souls of newly deceased people are punished for their sins. Some City God temples have revived the practice of carrying out the god seated on a sedan chair in annual ritual processions, where he inspects the community boundaries to rid the area of demons. In Wenzhou, all of the City God temples have been brought under the auspices of the local Daoist Association.

Mother Lu (盧氏娘娘)

A homegrown goddess worshipped only in Wenzhou, Mother Lu or "Celestial Immortal Sacred Mother" (天仙聖母) was born during the Tang dynasty. A local elder recounted her legend: Mother Lu and her mother were collecting firewood in the mountains when a ferocious tiger leaped onto the mother. Mother Lu begged the tiger to spare her mother's life and take her instead. So the tiger let the older woman go and carried Mother Lu away up the mountain. Later, people reported seeing the tiger at the top of the mountain with Mother Lu on his back. Before descending down the other side, they turned back to look down at the village, and that was the last people saw of them. A book on gods and immortals of Eastern Ou adds another detail to the story of Mother Lu: as a baby, she would kneel down before her mother to nurse (Ying and Jiang 2008: 45). Even at that tender age, she exhibited a natural instinct for filial piety. For her many miracles in saving people in distress, emperors enfeoffed her with imperial titles. People today celebrate her every year on the fourteenth day of the second lunar month.

REGIONAL GODS

Lord Yang (楊府爺)

In this coastal area of typhoons and ocean flooding, it is not surprising that the most popular god is a native son, a maritime god (海神) who saves fishermen and sailors (Lin Y. 2011; Ying and Jiang 2008: 35–37). Lord Yang was a historical person named Yang Jingyi (楊精義) who lived in the Tang dynasty. His cult spread throughout the southeastern coastal area of southern Zhejiang, Fujian, and Taiwan.

Lord Yang lived in what is now Green Mountain Township (碧山鎮), Rui'an County in Wenzhou, when the imperial examinations were first systematized throughout the empire. Born into a long lineage of scholars, Yang scored first in the whole empire in the military imperial examinations (武狀元). At only twenty-six years old, he attained the highest imperial degree, *jinshi*, and was awarded an official post in Shanxi Province, serving for forty years. At age sixty-five, he tired of politics, quit his post, and returned home to retire in Wenzhou. He retreated as a hermit into the mountains to pursue Daoist self-cultivation, attained the Way, and became an immortal (得道成仙), living to 108 years. He ascended to Heaven in 752 CE, and people have honored his memory ever since.

A village elder in a temple to Lord Yang told me the following miracle tale. At the end of the Qing dynasty, a Wenzhou fisherman and his two sons were fishing off the coast when a sudden gale threatened to capsize their boat. As their mast broke off, all they could do was repeatedly call out "Lord Yang, save us!" Lord Yang's visage appeared to them, calming their nerves, and soon the ferocious wind died down and they were able to return to shore. As a result of this miracle, the imperial court bestowed a new title on Lord Yang: "Sacred King of Prosperity and Protection" (福佑聖王).[2] Today some temples to Lord Yang display a wooden replica of a traditional Chinese junk, a symbol of the god who saves people from the raging waters.

On Chinese New Year's Eve in 2012, two friends from Longgang Town in Cangnan County took me by taxi to the Jingtou Village Lord Yang Temple (鯨頭楊府廟), perhaps the most prominent one in all of Wenzhou. As we approached the temple at 1:30 AM, a light rain was falling and the roads were clogged with people and cars headed to the temple. My friend told me about the Wenzhou competition to be the one who lights the "first candle" (頭燈) of the New Year for Lord Yang, which brings good luck. When we finally got inside the temple an hour later, I was amazed at the huge crowd.

At the entrance, people were engaged in brisk sales of incense and candles, including huge candles taller than a person. Through the haze of incense,

Figure 3.2. Lord Yang in his Jingtou Village Temple, outside Longgang Town, 2012. Photo by the author.

I could make out a central alcove and giant altar in the distance where the red-faced Lord Yang sat on his throne, framed by flashing red and green neon lights. People huddled around large metal incense burners, into which they inserted incense sticks after bowing three times to the gods. Near the main altar was a giant metal trough into which people threw piles of folded paper spirit money (冥幣) offerings, causing the fire inside to flare up suddenly and singe their hair. We sat amid twenty fortune-tellers who told the fortunes of a long line of people. I estimated there were three thousand people inside the temple at any given time that night. If each group of three thousand spent two hours there, about thirty-six thousand people visited the temple over the twenty-four-hour period of New Year's Day.

Mother Chen the Fourteenth (陳十四娘娘)

Mother Chen, whose human name was Chen Jinggu (陳靖姑), is the second-most-prominent god worshipped in the Wenzhou area, and her temples are

Figure 3.3. Crowds at 2 AM at Jingtou Village Lord Yang Temple, 2012. Photo by the author.

called Palaces of the Great Yin (太陰宮). She is also worshipped across southern Zhejiang, Fujian, Guangdong, Jiangxi Provinces, and Taiwan. The number fourteen refers to the date of her birth, the fourteenth day of the first lunar month in 766 CE (Ying and Jiang 2008: 39). She was born in the Tang dynasty in the village of Xiadu (下渡), outside Fuzhou City in Fujian Province, not far south of Cangnan County in Wenzhou. The prominence of her cult in Wenzhou reveals the historical settlement of Wenzhou by waves of migrants from Fujian. Her ancestral temple is located in the town of Gutian, in the mountains of northern Fujian, where she died and ascended to Heaven. Mother Chen is both a popular deity and a Daoist deity in the shamanistic and exorcistic Daoist Lu Mountain sect (閭山派). Brigitte Baptandier (2008) carried out a thorough examination of the Fujian text of her legend, *Tales of Subduing Demons in Linshui* (臨水平妖傳), in the Min (閩) culture of Fujian (Yu B. 2007). The Wenzhou legends of this goddess follow the main outline of the Fujian text but are localized to the Wenzhou area, with Wenzhou place-names, and the ritual traditions also differ from those in Fujian (Lin Y. 2009: 184–221; Xu Hongtu 2005).

Mother Chen is especially popular among rural women, who beg her for help in fertility, childbirth, and family happiness (Ye and Ye 1992). Men also pray to Mother Chen for help in business success, eliminating disease, providing safety on the high seas, relieving droughts, and granting community peace and harmony. Mother Chen is said to have two sworn sisters, goddesses Lin Jiuniang (林九娘) and Li Sanniang (李三娘). She commands a divine army of two male generals, thirty-six female spirit soldiers (女陪神), and seventy-two "granny assistants" (婆神).

Innumerable Wenzhou legends and spinoff stories about Mother Chen have been handed down orally and recorded in popular novels, operas, verse, songs, and historical texts. I first learned of Mother Chen in June 1992 from Wang Qinsheng, a diviner and head of the Yingqiao Wang Lineage. Here is the story I recorded from him in 1993:

> Mother Chen the Fourteenth is from Gutian, Fujian Province. She is a Song dynasty historical person. Her father Chen Chang was a Daoist exorcist-priest (法師) who was trained in the Maoshan branch (茅山派) [sic] of Daoist magical techniques, and he taught martial arts skills to her and her two brothers, Xiao Tong and Xiao Qing. One day, the local people begged her father to go to the mountains to kill the White Snake Demon. Since he was suffering from a back ailment, he had his two sons go instead. Unfortunately, Xiao Tong, the older son, was eaten by the snake, but the younger son managed to escape and get back home. Chen Jinggu was only seventeen years old, but that did not stop her from vowing to avenge her brother's death. She went off to Lu Mountain (閭山) to improve her martial arts fighting skills under the instruction of the immortal Old Mother of Lu Mountain (閭山老母). On her way back home, she passed through Wenzhou, including Ping Yang County, all the way dispatching demons and monsters that were harming the people. Later she learned that the White Snake Demon was harassing people in Fujian, so she went to his mountain cave. She cut the White Snake into three sections, but the snake did not perish, and changed into a woman and escaped. One year, there was a great drought which caused the crops to wilt. At that time, Chen Jinggu was three months pregnant, but she decided to abort the baby (脫胎), utilize her Daoist magical powers (施法力) to bring rain for the people, and come back to finish her pregnancy. She was successful in bringing rain to the people. However, the sly White Snake Demon

Figures 3.4a and 3.4b.
Goddess Mother
Chen as Civil God
(*wen* 文) and as
Martial God (*wu* 武)
with sword. Photos
by the author.

disguised itself as Chen Jinggu and sneaked into her home, stole the baby, and devoured it. In a great rage, Chen Jinggu chased the snake demon to its cave in Gutian and sat astride the snake so that it could not leave the cave. In this way, she died saving the people, at only twenty-four years old. Before she died, she said, "When I become a goddess, I want to protect the life and health of all babies and destroy demons!" That is why women today beg her to help them conceive and give birth. Today her corpse still lies in Gutian, Fujian province.

In this story, the listener is transported back to ancient times when certain humans exhibited great heroism and could change into gods. This was the world of interchangeable human and divine agency, before the "purification" process of modernity insisted they be clearly separated. Mother Chen at first refused to marry the man that her parents chose for her (Pan E. 2001: 114), fleeing to Lu Mountain and apprenticing herself to the Daoist immortal Xu the Perfected Lord (許府真君) to learn Daoist magic and martial arts. In chapter 8, we will see how, although she is still worshipped within a patriarchal context where women pray to her to conceive a boy instead of a girl, Mother Chen's bold exploits are ripe for future feminist reinterpretations and redeployments.

A theme not addressed in Wang Qingsheng's story above is Mother Chen's genealogical descent from the blood of the Buddhist goddess Guanyin. Two sources—Ye Dabing (葉大兵), a folklorist and former chief of the Bureau of Culture in Wenzhou City, in 1998; and two elders at the Cultural Relics Protection Office in Jinxiang Township, Cangnan County in July 2004—told very similar versions of one story. The Queen Mother of the West (西王母), who is also the mother of the Jade Emperor, holds a big birthday celebration, at which she invites all the gods, goddesses, and immortals to compete to move a giant column holding Heaven up above the Earth. Only the Bodhisattva Guanyin can move it with a flick of her fingers—but, in doing so, she cuts a finger and two drops of blood fall to earth, down into a well in Gutian County (in Fujian). Chen Jinggu's mother drinks water from this well, and Guanyin's blood impregnates her.

Here we have a matrilineal descent of goddesses, crossing the divide between Buddhism, Daoism, and popular religion.

In October 2001, I collected another Chen Jinggu oral legend from Gong Hongxin, a well-respected elderly doctor. We sat in bamboo chairs in his family-owned pharmacy in Ning Village in Longwan District, and I strained to understand his Wenzhou-accented Mandarin. As a child, he sat in rapt attention in a temple as a blind storyteller spun tales of the goddess's exploits:

In Quanzhou, Fujian Province, Luoyang Bridge was being built. Magistrate Cai, the official in charge of the project, fell ill and ran out of funds to complete the bridge. The local wealthy families, like today's children of high officials, would not donate money to finish the bridge. Wanting to help, the Bodhisattva Guanyin disguised herself as a beautiful woman and sat on a boat next to the bridge. Many handsome young men came over to gaze on her beauty. She told them she would marry whoever could throw gold into her apron. They each tried their luck, and lots of gold fell into the river. Lü Dongbin (呂洞賓), one of the eight Daoist immortals, was jealous of Guanyin's fun and wanted to play a trick on her. Just then a young peddler, aged fifteen and poor, passed by. Said Lü Dongbin, "Would you like to have her as your wife?" The peddler had only three cents, but Lü told him to throw them all the same. Lü made them all stick to Guan Yin's apron. In her anger at having to keep her promise to marry the man who could throw gold into her apron, Guanyin squeezed out blood from her fingernails, which landed in Gutian. Chen Jinggu's mother drank this blood and gave birth to her. Thus, Chen Jinggu is born of the blood of Guanyin.

In this tale, the gods are strangely human, with their petty rivalries and flights into rage. As with humans, it is important to trace the gods' genealogical descent lines, even if some gods are the products of divine virgin birth. Here we have a direct matrilineal line of descent from Guanyin, a powerful Buddhist mother goddess worshipped across China, to Mother Chen, a younger generation goddess. As direct descendant, Mother Chen inherits the considerable powers of Guanyin, as well as some of her characteristics: both are active female agents who resisted patriarchal marriage, and both are also known for their feminine compassion and capacity to relieve human distress.

In late imperial China, popular fiction and drama played important roles in spreading Chinese deity cults (DeBernardi 2006: 150; Shahar 1996). As a child, Wang Qinsheng heard many stories of this goddess and also read about her supernatural feats in a new text: (陳十四奇傳) (*Marvelous Tales of Chen the Fourteenth*), published by amateur folklorist Ye Zhongming (1985). I am grateful for the browned and dog-eared copy that he presented to me as a gift. Based on fieldwork among old "drum chant" (鼓詞) storytellers and village elders across Wenzhou, Ye Zhongming compiled this folk narrative of Mother Chen's exploits in the Wenzhou area.[3] Mother Chen passes through actual places in the Wenzhou area, such as Qian Cang (Money Storage, 錢倉) and Ping Yang (平陽). After three decades of modern antireligious campaigns, the late imperial tradition of a local educated person gathering and publishing vernacular tales of a deity has resumed.

From 1998 to 2002, Tang Zhendong, a Wenzhou native, also traveled through the Wenzhou countryside and recorded newer versions, which he published under the title *Wenzhou Drum Chant: Travels through the South* (溫州鼓詞南遊傳) (Lin Q. 2014; Tang 2008; Xu Y. 2001). In 2014, I was thrilled to chat for a whole day in a teahouse with Professor Lin Yixiu of Wenzhou University about the cult of Mother Chen and religious development in Wenzhou. He has published two excellent books on Mother Chen: a transcription of a complete fourteen-chapter drum chant that he recorded from a Wenzhou storyteller (Lin and Chen 2011), and a study of the Mother Chen cult in Cangnan County, with a list of her Great Yin Temples (Lin and Guo 2016).

Many older people in Wenzhou remember that as children they sat through public performances of "Wenzhou drum chants" (溫州鼓詞) in temples or public squares. Also called "chanting the Mother's song" (唱娘娘詞), this chanting ritual is found only in the Wenzhou area. The verse is composed of seven characters per line and was sung ritually in the Wenzhou language before Liberation. "In the old days," said Wang Qinsheng, "whenever a local community was beset by problems of disharmony and crisis, it would hire professional singers to stage the chanting of this text," a cross between ritualized scripture recitation and storytelling. Two musical instruments provide rhythmic accompaniment to the chanting: a stringed instrument made of wood with ox tendons stretched over it, and bamboo hand clappers (快板). The chanting usually lasted seven days and seven nights and was believed to be effective in exorcising the demons (妖怪) who were causing the problems. In the Yong Qiang area of Wenzhou, this drum chant was sung three times in 1949, but subsequently was banned.

In January 2012, after waiting for twenty years, I had the good fortune to attend a drum chant performance in Xiayi Village, Longgang Township, Cangnan County. The opera stage in the temple was set up as the side of a mountain, with multiple levels of little papier-maché gods and demons that the goddess encounters in her adventures. The whole incredible scene was bathed in golden light. Paper paths connected different levels, and clusters of gods were grouped around paper temples. Mother Chen held pride of place at the mountaintop, and plates of fresh fruit were offered to her at the front of the stage. Over the seven days, the story of Mother Chen would move from one cluster of gods to another on the stage. On each side of the stage, two giant paper snakes, one white and one green (白蛇青蛇), wrapped themselves around tall poles. The audience in the packed hall was expected to participate

Figure 3.5. Wenzhou Drum Chant performance, Xiayi Village, Longgang Town, with paper White Snake Demon, 2012. Photo by the author.

in the ritual storytelling: at one point, they were each given incense sticks to take outside and invited to offer thanks to the goddess for saving human life. At the end of seven days, the ceremonial master approached the two giant paper snakes with a big knife, cut them down, and burned them. The ashes were thrown into a giant paper boat that was later pushed out to sea to exorcise the community.

EMPIREWIDE GODS

Empirewide gods refer to deities that are worshipped not only in Wenzhou or the southeastern coast, but across what was the Chinese empire or is the nation today. These areas include the interior, provinces such as Sichuan, Hubei, Hunan, and Jiangxi; the southwestern provinces, like Yunnan and Guizhou; and even northeastern Shaanxi, Shanxi, Hebei, and Shandong.

The Jade Emperor (玉皇大帝)

The Jade Emperor is the supreme deity of Chinese popular religion, ruling over all the other gods. His statues show him with an emperor's headdress, a rectangular mortar board from which thirteen strings of beads dangle in front of his face and behind his head. He sits on a throne, usually flanked by the Goddess Moon and the Sun God, and other deities who are his court assistants. His temples often feature images or carvings of dragons, symbols of sovereign power. He is said to have a wife (or mother), believed to be the Queen Mother of the West, and a nephew, who some believe to be the god Erlang (二郎神). He is thought of as the divine counterpart of the earthly emperor, with a court of divine ministers and assistants and a "celestial bureaucracy" (Wolf 1974) of hierarchically ranked official-like gods who all answer to him. In Wenzhou, people have told me that he is the celestial counterpart of the general secretary of the Chinese Communist Party, or the secretary-general of the United Nations, the leader of the world's government.

The hagiography of the Jade Emperor has been heavily infiltrated by the Daoist tradition, in which he also ranks in the upper echelon of the pantheon of gods, positioned just below the three highest Daoist deities, the Three Pure Ones (三清). He commands the "Three Worlds" (三界), understood as the cosmos and heavens above, the human world in the middle, and the Underworld (or "Yin World") below. Thus, the Jade Emperor rules over the vast cosmos and the forces of nature; the pantheon of all the other gods; human life and death, good and ill fortune, and longevity; and the souls in Purgatory and the gods and buddhas there who administer them.

As a divine sovereign, the Jade Emperor bestows and promotes life: he controls the rains, winds, and weather to ensure good crops and harvests; determines the number of newborns and descendants for each family; controls people's prosperity, good fortune, wealth, education, and longevity; rewards virtuous behavior; and shows his concern for "the illnesses and sufferings" of the human population by sending down assistants to report on humanity's well-being and to save people from storms, floods, and misfortune.

The Monkey Sage-King (齊天大聖)

The Monkey King or "Great Sage, Equal to Heaven" is one of the few Chinese gods who does *not* have a human genealogy. He is a divine monkey who has not only supernatural powers but also many humanlike weaknesses. His hagiography can be found in the classical vernacular novel *Journey to the West* (西遊記), written by Wu Cheng-en (吳承恩) in the Ming dynasty (Wu C. 2010).

Figure 3.6. Jade Emperor, Fengmen Daoist Temple, Yongzhong Township, 2012. Photo by the author.

In the novel, Monkey is called Sun Wukong (孫悟空), and his character presents a rare defiance of authority. Monkey's propensity for mischief provides comic relief and satirizes the portentous gods of popular religion; at the same time, Monkey is prone to arrogance and boastfulness. In Wenzhou there are many temples devoted to Monkey, including a prominent one in Lingxi Town, Cangnan County.

Although Monkey is basically good-hearted, his mischievous nature creates great headaches for the gods who try to control him. He snuck into Purgatory and destroyed the Register of Births and Deaths, much to the anger of King Yan Lo (閻羅王), the head god of Purgatory. Monkey also dived under the sea to the Pavilion of the Dragon King and stole his magical needle that quells the seas. Hoping to distract Monkey by making him feel important, the Jade Emperor called Monkey to Heaven to assign him to a celestial office—but when Monkey discovered that "Horse Warden" was a lowly rank, he left

Heaven in a rage and returned to Flower Fruit Mountain (花果山), where he awarded himself the title "Great Sage, Equal to Heaven" (Pan E. 2001: 87–88).

The Jade Emperor sent down his celestial army to capture Monkey, but they were beaten badly. Monkey soon offended all the other gods by pulling rank and ignoring their titles. Fearing the loss of order in Heaven, the Jade Emperor dispatched Monkey to guard the celestial Peach Orchard and get him out of the way. However, Monkey ate all the precious peaches that ripen only once every three thousand years, rudely disrupted the Queen Mother of the West's divine peach party, drank the royal wine, and stole the God Laozi's golden medicinal pill. Apoplectic, the Jade Emperor dispatched ten thousand celestial troops to seize Monkey, but Monkey beat them back, wielding his magical golden staff (金箍棒). Only when Bodhisattva Guanyin sent the God Erlang to join forces with Lord Laozi were they able to subdue Monkey. They threw Monkey into the Oven of the Eight Trigrams, but the fire only made Monkey stronger, and he escaped. Desperate, the Jade Emperor appealed for help from the Buddha Rulai of the Western Heaven. Rulai entrapped Monkey in the palm of his hand. When the Buddhist monk Tang Seng (唐僧) journeyed to the Western frontier to bring back Buddhist scriptures, Guanyin directed Monkey to protect him from dangers along the way, and they had many adventures. The story of the Monkey King is tied up with a narrative of how Buddhism encompasses the gods of popular religion and Daoism. These gods are helpless against Monkey, so it takes the power of the Buddhas, Guanyin, and Buddhist monk Tang Seng to finally control the strong-willed Monkey.

MODES OF DEITY WORSHIP

We now turn to a brief examination of the modes of deity worship and communication with deities. These can be summed up in the following categories: prayers and offerings, chanting of sutras or scriptures, doing penance, transmitting legends and miracles, and religious rituals and temple festivals: communal banquets and local operas.

Communication with the Gods: Prayers, Offerings, and Divine Response

A primary mode of deity worship is to engage in individual prayer with a chosen god, presenting a request or asking for the god's advice or permission. When a person needs help, she will enter a temple and light incense and a candle for a chosen god. A villager once told me that the incense is like a mobile phone (shouji), and lighting it alerts the god that someone would like to talk to him. One must kneel down and ketou three times, knocking one's forehead on the floor or kneeling cushion. Offerings of fruit or other food to the god, periodic monetary donations to the temple, and the lighting of candles are sufficient.

If the request is more specific and hard to obtain, prayer assumes the form of "making an oath" (許願) for reciprocal exchange with the god. For example, if a woman wants help so that her husband will stop seeing another woman, she might make an oath specifying a monetary donation to the god's temple; if an entrepreneur needs help gaining more customers for his business, he might promise to volunteer his labor toward temple construction. Volunteered labor is known as "beneficial work" (益工), and many temples rely on this help.

If the god grants the request, then one must "return the favor" (還願) or incur the god's wrath and divine retributions. Many people purchase red felt pendants to hang in the temple, with gold Chinese characters singing the god's praises and expressing gratitude. The number of red pendants hanging in a temple and the wealth of the temple from donations is a gauge of the god's "divine efficacy" (靈驗). The god's reputation for granting wishes quickly spreads by word of mouth. Thus, a god's rise and fall in popularity depends on divine efficacy, an extrahuman force.

Chanting and Singing of Sutras

Those who are devout take time to chant sutras (經) to their favorite gods. For the most part, this activity is the domain of women. One frequently sees elderly women in the temples clutching their prayer beads (佛珠) and chanting for their own merit-making as well as for their family members. Since most old women are illiterate, they mainly chant simple texts, or just invoke the name of the Buddha Amitabha of the Western Paradise repeatedly: "O-mi-to-fo."

Some devout women join "worship and penance groups" (拜懺團) attached to a temple or perform sutra-chanting services at Daoist or Buddhist temples. The word "penance" (*chan*, 懺) suggests that, through the labor of chanting scriptures, the chanter is repaying for her family's sins and building up merit for the afterlife. I was told that the difference between a sutra (經) and a penance-song (懺) is that the former is chanted, while the latter is sung, and only in temples. These sutra-chanting troupes, made up of about ten to twelve middle-aged women, practice together in their spare time; those who are semiliterate memorize between twenty and forty sutras. Twice a month, on the first and fifteenth day, when their deity or Daoist temple holds a festival, they wear vestment robes and chant scriptures, interspersing the Daoist priest's incantations and ritual dance steps with the graceful solemnity of their uplifting voices, singing the deity's praises.

The troupes may also be hired by any family to assist a Daoist priest in performing a private ritual honoring a god, in hopes that the god will respond to a special request by the family. The sutra chanted depends on the nature of the request. People wishing to send their child to college will sing the sutra Precious Chant of Repentance for the Lord of Literature on High (太上文昌消劫行化寶懺). People who wish to dissolve sins chant the Precious Chant of Repentance to Dissolve Sins for the Jade Emperor on High (高上玉皇宥罪寶懺). People wishing to recover from illness chant the Precious Chant of Repentance for the God on High Who Prolongs Life and Prevents Disasters (太上歲德延生祛災度一靈華寶懺). For rituals performed to bring good luck for a woman's childbirth or new infant, the group may go to a temple to Mother Chen and sing the Precious Chant of the Celestial Immortal and Great Yin Who Prolongs Life and Promotes Progeny (天仙顯烈太陰廣生衍嗣寶懺).

Although these women receive a nominal payment for their services, the main reason women join these groups seems to be not financial need but the emotional satisfaction they derive from rendering a service to the gods. For example, Liu Lanfeng, a woman in her midfifties, told me that in addition to getting her out of the house, going to temples to chant in a troupe five or six times a month brings her close to the gods and makes it easier to gain their protection for her family. She views it as a good deed to help others win the gods' protection.

Liu Lanfeng also performs this chanting service in her home for others who lack the time or cannot read. She records her chanting on paper envelopes bearing images of different gods as well as tiny circles, which she dots with a red ink brush each time she chants a sutra for ten to fifteen minutes. When all the circles have been filled in, she seals the envelope. Each is worth six to ten hours' worth of chanting, and several hundred yuan. These envelopes are taken by the family and burned in the temple to move the gods to protect them.

Doing Penance and Mitigating Sins

Previous ethnographic studies have not stressed the importance of "sin" (罪) and "doing penance" (懺悔) in the modern practice of Chinese popular religion. I had associated notions of sin with Christianity but was struck by their importance in contemporary Wenzhou. These notions of sin and immorality are tied in with bodily illness; mathematical calculations of merit, demerit, and life span; notions of divine punishment in the afterlife; and ritual measures to mitigate the effects of sinning. These measures can be found in both Daoist and Buddhist traditions. The ancient Celestial Masters Daoist movement in Sichuan made a connection between ethical behavior and bodily health and longevity. Rituals of confession were also medical approaches to healing in the Five Pecks of Rice movement (Kleeman 2016; Wang K. 1999: 17). Similarly, in the Buddhist tradition, the notion of sin is tied in with *karma* (the cause and effect of actions) and transmigration of the soul from one life to another: committing sins accumulates negative karma, which has consequences in one's afterlife or rebirth.

In rural Wenzhou, most people believe that after a person's death, the soul must travel down through Purgatory (地獄) and appear before the Ten Judges in the Yin World (陰界十大殿王) (Teiser 1994), gods who preside over the souls of the deceased. Headed by King Yan Lo (閻羅王), they consult records of the sins and good deeds of each soul brought before them. After balancing out the accumulated merits and demerits, each judge pronounces a sentence for crimes committed during the person's lifetime. Only after the punishment is administered is the soul released and sent on to the next judge. After serving sentences in all ten courts, the soul may be released into their next life, sent up to the Western Paradise and eternal happiness, or detained eternally to suffer the tortures of Hell. Sets of ten scroll paintings of the Ten Judges in their courts, administering grisly punishments, can be found in deity temples, in Daoist and Buddhist temples, and especially in City God Temples.

In the local religious imagination, sins and good deeds are quantifiable. If one commits a sin, doing penance prevents the accumulation of demerits and decreases punishments in the afterlife. At the Jinxiang City God Temple in 2004, a giant abacus hung above the main entrance; I was told that it stood for how the City God could calculate and balance out people's merits and demerits. One way of doing penance is to meditate and chant sutras, or to pay others to chant on one's behalf; another way is to donate money to a temple. One can also do another, more public penance by participating in a ritual procession. For example, in the Jinxiang Township City God ritual procession, people with an illness may donate money to do public penance for their sins. In late imperial fashion, they dress up as prisoners wearing cangues or sit in wooden cages pulled along by horses to show remorse, and thereby be cured of illness. All these penitential actions can "dissolve sins" (化罪).

Some people still practice the ancient Daoist penance ritual of marking the Geng Shen Day (庚申日) by collectively staying up through the night. The Geng Shen Day, which occurs six times per year, is calculated according to the ancient Chinese calendrical system of Heavenly Stems and Earthly Branches (天干地支). Generally people only attend such meetings once a year. On Geng Shen Day in 2010, which fell on September 7 (lunar calendar: twenty-ninth day, seventh month), I was taken at one in the morning to a Buddhist temple called Town Center Hall (鎮中堂) in Yongzhong Township (see figure 8.1). I was amazed to find about one thousand people crammed into the small temple, preparing to spend the whole night together sitting on wooden benches. The assembled crowd was composed mainly of middle-aged and elderly folk, in their forties to seventies, with about 80 percent women. The locals call this absolution ritual "narrating one's sins and sitting through the night" (敘罪座夜), and it is an act of penance to atone for their sin of sexual intercourse, which led to "giving birth to boys and raising girls" (生男育女).

In a medieval text called "Observing the Geng Shen Day" (守庚申), we learn that in ancient Daoism, there was the religio-medical idea that the "Three Corpse Worms" (三尸蟲) reside in the upper, middle, and lower parts of the human body and record each sin of their host. On Geng Shen Day, when the host is asleep, they ascend to Heaven to report his transgressions to the "Heavenly Emperor" (天帝) (Kohn 1995a). Since they can only do this when their host is asleep, staying awake on this dangerous night prevents the worms from reporting one's sins and shortening one's life span. Today in Japan, this ritual is rapidly declining, mainly performed in rural areas and outlying islands (Kohn 1993, 1995a, 1995b). To find it resurfacing in Wenzhou, after the excesses of Chinese state secularization throughout the twentieth century, is a reminder that the deep cultural unconscious dies hard.

Transmitting Legends and Miracles of the Gods

Another way to honor the gods is to tell stories about them, especially to the younger generation. Their hagiographies include legends about their birth, parents, and childhood; their great deeds and self-sacrifices; their miracles; their attainment of immortality, the Way, or Enlightenment through self-cultivation; their interactions with other gods or Buddhas; and their ascent to Heaven. Accounts of dreams and sightings of gods keep the gods alive for people. In the early 1990s, I heard no accounts of recent miracles or god sightings, only about miracles in late imperial China. Increasingly in the new millennium, people feel more relaxed about recounting present-day encounters with gods or ghosts and being the beneficiary of a god's healing powers.

In the 1980s, Wenzhou people mainly learned about the gods through orally transmitted tales. Later, old hagiographies of the gods were republished. More recently, there is greater interest in reading the biographies of local and regional gods and ancestors. This has led to an increasing number of publications by local Wenzhou writers. One example is the volume titled *Hagiographies of Gods and Immortals of Eastern Ou* (Ying and Jiang 2008), which was collected by two Wenzhou Daoist writers and self-published through a Hong

Kong press. For many people, the writing of hagiographies creates merit, just like erecting or funding a statue or temple to honor the gods.

Religious Rituals and Temple Festivals: Communal Banquets and Local Operas

Deity and Daoist temples hold several rituals each month, usually with at least one Daoist priest presiding. Regular communal feasts and rituals occur twice a month, on the first and fifteenth lunar days, when the local villagers or a town neighborhood gather to honor the tutelary god(s) of the area. Local villagers gather to make offerings to the gods and chat animatedly with each other over the communal lunch banquet. They sit ten to a round table, drink potent yellow grain alcohol in cups, and sample the large dishes of food brought out from the kitchen. Private families may also have a Daoist priest conduct a ritual, either in their homes or at the temple, to request help from a god. These private family rituals include exorcism rituals for an illness in the family, Daoist funerals, and rituals seeking blessings for an elderly parent. Depending on the nature of the request to the gods, different gods will be called down by the priest to receive offerings and enjoy the ritual performance. Most rituals are day long affairs, but large-scale communal rituals might last two or more days. Chinese law allows religious temples to conduct public rituals only inside temple walls; rituals or processions beyond the temple confines require a lengthy permit application process.

Large-scale rituals or temple festivals may occur on the birthday of the primary deity of the temple, an important lunar festival, or Daoist *jiao* (醮) ceremony that will bring blessings to the whole community. These festivals can last several days, with local peddlers and merchants setting up temporary stalls and sell their wares and food. These fairs can be noisy and boisterous, with jostling crowds and loud firecrackers.[4] Local families will often take advantage of the festive atmosphere to throw banquets at their homes. Occasionally, larger temples may get official permission to do a ritual procession in which the resident god is carried out of the temple on a palanquin and makes the rounds of his territorial jurisdiction to dispatch demons.

Some temples have an opera stage in a courtyard where benches can be set up for a performance. Opera troupes generally perform "Ou Opera" (甌劇) in Wenzhounese; the subjects are standard opera stories dating from late imperial times. Opera is especially beloved by the elderly and children, who bring little bamboo chairs and wooden benches to watch for hours. The operas are not just for a human audience; they are presented as an offering of entertainment for the gods. At the beginning of each performance, there is a ritual to welcome the gods from neighboring deity temples. Represented by their wooden name tablets or a miniature statue, and by an incense urn carrying ashes from their temple, they are seated along with the resident temple gods to enjoy the show. Afterward these divine guests are sent back to their own temples in a ritual called "completing reunion" (團圓). By 2008, in Longwan District alone, there were temple operas performed in every month of the year; most months saw an average of 17 operas, totaling 158 operas in one year (Longwan 2009: 185–187).

SHAMANISM AND SPIRIT POSSESSION

I define shamanism (*wushu*, 巫術) as a religious culture that revolves around gifted and respected holy women or men who have rare abilities to communicate with spirits or ancestors, go into trance or ecstatic states, travel to other divine realms, heal the sick, and divine the future (Eliade 1989; Lewis [1971] 2003; Teiser 1994). I use the term as the larger category that also includes spirit possession and ritual healing. Spirit mediums are people whose bodies get possessed by spirits who speak through them to communicate with the human world. Through mediums, people can ask questions of deities or ancestors, and find out why they have gotten ill or experienced misfortune, and what measures they may take for recovery. Ritual healers may or may not communicate with spirits, but they are able to heal the sick through ritual, writing Daoist talismans, and chanting spells.

Male shamans are called "sacred-men" or "deity-men" (*shenhan*, 神漢), while female ones are called "deity-women" (神婆), "woman of the Dao" (道姑), or "spiritually efficacious women" (*linggu*, 靈姑). I was advised to avoid the pejorative term "old shamaness" (*wupo*, 巫婆). There are also the terms "deity-child" or "deity-servant" (*shentong*, 神僮) and "servant-body" (僮身), which do not seem to be gender-specific. There is also a kind of vegetarian female shaman, called a "teacher-mother" (師娘). Most shamans have less formal education and speak mainly the local Wenzhou language. In spirit possession, when a medium's body is shaking with the presence of the spirit inside, in local parlance it is called "coming on to the body" (上身) or "dancing like the body of a shaman" (跳僮身). Elsewhere in China, especially northern China, the phrase "dancing to the great deity" (跳大神) is used, but it is not favored in Wenzhou.

My friend Wang Qinsheng, an old diviner in Longwan District, told me that in the Yong Qiang (永強) area, he knows of only three male shamans, but there are over forty women shamans. There are many more in Pingyang and

Cangnan Counties in southern Wenzhou, and also in Yongjia County in the north, the less developed areas of Wenzhou. Elsewhere I have suggested that the reason for the female predominance is that men get sucked more easily into the secularized world of competitive capitalism, because they have more opportunities, so that more women's bodies remain sensitive and receptive to divine messages (M. Yang 2015).

Jin Xiulan, a middle-aged woman who belongs to a temple sutra-chanting group, told me that many shamans can be found in the villages. Many are sick or weak, but doctors or psychologists can find nothing wrong. These shamans get possessed by spirits and people ask them to help in communicating with their dead. In the villages, about 80 percent of the people believe in shamanic powers to connect with spirits and to heal sickness. According to Jin, there are both "real" and "fake" spirit mediums. Some are very effective and can really cure illness; others just pretend to be possessed in order to make money.

In January 2012 in Wenzhou, I interviewed Cao Jinling, whom I call the "reluctant spirit medium." "To be honest," said Cao, "I would rather have my health than have the gods come to me, but they chose me, and so I must comply." She lived with her husband and his parents in a modern apartment building in Kunyang Town, Pingyang County. Because of her continuous ill health, Cao did not work, and her two children were raised by her mother. At the age of forty-six, Cao had had only one year of schooling. She first became ill at age fifteen: her leg hurt, her whole body felt sore and weak, and she could not work. Over the years, she went to see one doctor after another, trying out both traditional Chinese medicine and Western biomedicine, but they all told her there was nothing wrong with her.

When she was thirty-five, Cao and her husband moved to Taiyuan in Shanxi Province in northern China to do business. There, far from home, she again fell seriously ill and started to become possessed. Cao's husband discovered that in Taiyuan there were local people who got possessed—but by their local gods, not Wenzhou gods. "I found out this thing is fairly common, so that made me feel relieved," he said. The couple even visited a few mediums in Taiyuan to find out their experiences and share stories.

Cao described the sensation of possession as "going crazy" (*fengle yiyang*, 瘋了一樣), or "like getting drunk." When she awoke from her possessed state, people described her as looking "crazy and unsteady" (*fengfeng diandian*, 瘋瘋癲癲). During her possession, her eyes were closed, as if sleeping, but her body was not shaking convulsively, nor did she have saliva or foam flowing out of her mouth. However, following each possession, she "hurt in her stomach and intestines," and since she started getting possessed, she has lost a lot of weight. In her possessed state, people would talk with her and she would reply, in a strange, eerily low voice, that she was the goddess Mother Chen the Fourteenth. Sometimes a voice would also tell Cao that she was the goddess Li the Thirteenth, the "shamanic sister" (*tongmei*, 僮妹) of Mother Chen. Cao was also possessed by Mother Chen's two brothers, Fatong and Faqing; and by the Earth God (*Tudigong*, 土地公), who often led the way (*yinglu*, 迎路) for the other gods who possessed her. Each time she woke up from being possessed, she felt exhausted and could not remember what she did or said while possessed. "I never wanted to be a shaman," said Cao, "but for some reason, this is my fate."

ANCESTOR WORSHIP, GHOSTS, AND DEATH RITUALS

Death does not stop communication between family members and kin, for it is the beginning of an ancestor's new life and the traffic between the living and the dead. Ancestor worship is archaic, extending back at least to the Bronze Age and the invention of writing. During the Shang and Zhou dynasties, ancestors of the nobility were consulted with written questions scratched onto divination bones and tortoise shells, and precious bronze ritual vessels were cast to hold the meat and alcoholic beverage sacrifices to them. In Confucian culture, the sons and daughters of the deceased must spare little in honoring their parents with a lavish funeral. Indeed, in rural and small-town Wenzhou, funerals are sometimes more elaborate and expensive than weddings.

Elders and Ancestors

In the early 1990s, I discovered that although most families were no longer engaged in agriculture, this was still a peasant culture of respect for the elderly. I noted the interesting lack of a generation gap in the 1990s, compared with the urban China I knew (and what later developed in Wenzhou). Nor did I feel the oppressive weight of the old over the young, as portrayed in modernist literary or filmic representations of ossified patriarchal domination, as in the May Fourth–era novel *Family* (家) by Ba Jin ([1933] 1982). In the 1990s, different generations seemed to get along. Although the elderly in Wenzhou hold no formal positions in government office or local enterprises, their opinions and social influence had impact in local society. However, in the new millennium I have noticed more intergenerational conflict, especially between the youth of the "planned birth" generation and their parents.

Old people have been at the forefront of the revival of traditional culture and religious observances in the post-Mao era. They manage and staff such

Figure 3.7. Old People's Pavilion in Yongchang Township, Longwan District, 1993. Photo by the author.

rural organizations as Old People's Associations, lineages, temple management committees, church organizations, the Daoist and Buddhist Associations, and so on. Old People's Associations (*laoren xiehui*, 老人協會), made up of retired village elders, are found in almost every village and have no precursor before Liberation. Most villages have built Old People's Pavilions (老人亭), with traditional upward-curving tiled roofs, located next to a waterway, where retired men get together to play *mahjiang* or watch Wenzhou opera on television. These associations often mount donation drives to build or restore temples and ancestor halls and local infrastructure. Their elderly members also help write local histories, recompile lineage genealogies, collect old legends and oral tales of the gods and ancestors, and negotiate contentious issues with local government officials. It is as if closeness to death and ancestorhood awards seniors leadership roles. Thus, the advancement of age in Wenzhou does not necessarily herald a retreat from society, but often, instead, a new kind of social engagement in an emerging grassroots civil society.

Funerals

Funerals are elaborate affairs that last at least one full day, and often several days. Families of the deceased may choose to put on a Buddhist or Daoist funeral, or something that combines both liturgies. It is not uncommon for funerary ritual experts to change from Buddhist to Daoist robes for different sections of the ceremony. The work of funerary rituals is encapsulated by the Chinese term "to seek release from" (超度) Purgatory or punishments in the afterlife. Purgatory, literally "underground prison" (地獄), is a detention center through which the souls of the deceased must travel and serve out their sentences of punishment for sins committed in their lifetimes before they can enter into their next life. The ritual experts lead the family members down into Purgatory in an effort to help the soul quickly gain release from its tortures and speed the deceased on her way to either the Western Paradise or to the next life in the transmigration of the soul. Basketloads of paper spirit money are burned so the deceased will have money to spend on her long journey. Paper clothing and a large replica house made of paper and bamboo sticks are burned for the deceased's comfortable afterlife. Funerals involve elaborate banquets attended by dozens or hundreds of relatives, neighbors, friends, and local officials; often the guests are so numerous they must eat in shifts.

After the funeral, the coffin is carried in a public funeral procession, complete with a marching band, that winds through the streets to the burial ground, where the coffin is lowered into the tomb and sealed. In Wenzhou, tombs are shaped like giant sofas, their back and ridge looking like sofa armrests—indeed, people call them "sofa tombs" (*shafafen*). Of course, many participants at funerals do not really believe in the afterlife, Purgatory, and so forth, but their presence at the funeral is socially obligatory. As Roy Rappaport (1999: 107-131) wrote, participants do not have to *believe* in the words or intentions of rituals; as long as their bodies and voices perform the ritual steps, the ancient cultural codes and messages of the ritual are inculcated into their bodily habituses and conscious and unconscious structures.

During the lunar Qing Ming Festival honoring the dead, which usually falls around early April, the family makes a trip up to the burial site to sweep the tomb and clear it of the year's accumulation of dirt, weeds, and debris. They bring incense, rice wine, and cooked food to offer the dead, bowing and kowtowing, and then have an outdoor picnic.

The Struggle over Earth Burials and Cremations

In the 1990s, I often came across empty wooden coffins stored under the eaves of rural people's homes. As the elderly advance in age, they take great comfort in knowing that their coffin is prepared and that a burial plot has already been selected and purchased for them. Back then, on certain streets in rural towns, every three or four shops was owned by coffin-makers or by those who created giant paper flower wreaths and miniature multistory paper-and-bamboo houses for funerals. The houses for the dead to enjoy in the afterlife could be very intricate, with miniature garages and paper cars, microwave ovens, and stereo systems, not to mention refrigerators, washing machines, and televisions. Death and its ritual business had clearly carved out an important niche market here.

Elaborate death rituals smack of overindulgence in the afterlife, and the Wenzhou Communist Party promoted cremation and criticized traditional funerals as "wasteful." Reforming death rituals did not assume a high priority, however, until the Great Leap Forward (1958–1960) and the Smash the Four Olds campaign in the first three years of the Cultural Revolution (1966–1976), which saw the greatest push for mandatory cremation (Whyte 1988). In the 1970s, the Wenzhou City government banned earth burials for all urban residents, but not rural ones. However, the law for urban Wenzhou residents was not properly enforced until 1987, when a new Office of Changing Habits and Simplifying Customs (移風易俗辦公室) was established (Zhang Zhichen 1998: 2278), charged with implementing the cremation policy for urban residents, simplifying funerary customs, and reducing "waste and extravagance" in funerary expenditures.

In the 1990s, I often came across a puzzling sight on rural roads: tricycle carts ferrying a human figure wrapped tightly inside thick bedding. Since they were completely covered, including their faces, I wondered if they were dead bodies. I was told that they were still alive, but barely. They were urban residents who were close to death in Wenzhou City hospitals, smuggled out of the hospital by family members to die in a relative's home in the countryside. That way they could enjoy a proper funeral and earth burial at a secret plot in the rural areas. Had they died in an urban hospital, their bodies would have been whisked away by hospital staff for cremation, without enough time for a proper funeral.

In 2001, the ban on earth burials was extended further to include all peasants residing in rural areas. Thus, the lucrative coffin industry was demolished by administrative fiat. Since then, the Wenzhou government has continued to mount periodic campaigns to demolish or remove the family tombs dotting the hillsides. Tomb-makers, stonemasons, and *fengshui* (Chinese geomancy, 風水) masters have been adversely affected. The government ban on earth burials not only offended old people facing impending death; it also threatened the

Figure 3.8.
Yongzhong Township government sign: "Smash Feudal Superstitious Thought; Promote the New Wind of Civilized Funerals," 1998. Photo by the author.

well-being of family units. It is only by providing the dead with a good funeral send-off and resting place, sited propitiously according to *fengshui* principles, that they will become benevolent ancestors who look after their descendants.

I heard stories of old people organizing collective suicides on the eve of the 2001 ban on earth burials—as both an act of protest against the ban and a last-minute effort to enjoy a proper funeral. I was unable to verify them until 2008, when I met a young official, Mr. Luo, who had worked in an office in a Wenzhou county overseeing the cremation policy. When I confronted Luo with the stories of suicide, he tried to dodge the topic. His reaction, however, spoke volumes: he immediately stiffened uncomfortably and asked me where I had heard these stories and who had told them to me. I gave a vague answer, and he responded: "I'm sorry, I cannot talk about this topic with you; you're a foreign national, after all. This is rather sensitive."

Those who die violently or without descendants do not become benevolent ancestors, but restless "orphan souls and wild ghosts" (孤魂野鬼) who resentfully prey on the living. Ghosts (鬼) are also thought of as strangers who did not receive a proper funeral and burial, so they bear grudges against society. There is a mixture of fear and sympathy for ghosts, who have no one to remember them. Making offerings to these hungry ghosts is a way of expressing sympathy and care for them, as well as appeasing them in order to stem their wrath and ensure self-protection. The Festival of Ghosts (鬼節) takes place in the period around the fifteenth day of the seventh lunar month. Families in Wenzhou present food offerings and incense on the streets outside their homes to wandering ghosts. Many pierce pomelos (Chinese grapefruit) with incense sticks and offer these lighted "incense balls" (香球) to ghosts, and some neighborhoods will set up long tables with food offerings.

Both Daoist and Buddhists celebrate this festival to the dead, but they call the festival by different names. For Daoists, it is called the Mid-Primordial Universal Salvation Festival (中元普渡), while Buddhists have their Ullambana Festival (盂蘭盆節). For Daoists, the year is divided into three sections, each with its festival day honoring one of the Daoist trio of gods, the "Three Officials and Great Emperors" (三官大帝). The Upper Primordial (上元) is the Heaven Official's birthday; the Mid-Primordial (中元) is when the Earth Official descends to Earth; and the Lower Primordial (下元) commemorates the Water Official at the beginning of winter. During the Festival of Universal Salvation, Daoist priests perform rituals begging the Earth Official to absolve the sins of ghosts so that they can win release from their punishments in the afterlife.

The Buddhist Ullambana Festival's (盂蘭盆法會) name comes from the Ullambana Sutra of Mahayana Buddhism, in which a disciple of Buddha Sakyamuni named Maudgalyāyana, or Mulian (目連) in Chinese, travels down to Purgatory and sees his mother suffering as a "hungry ghost" for her sins (Teiser 1988: 20–21, 43–56). He is agonized that she is condemned to see the food offered to her but be unable to eat anything. The Buddha advises him that on the fifteenth day of the seventh month, he and all filial persons must make food offerings in Ullambana basins to the *sangha*, or Buddhist monastic community, to win their ancestors' release from their sins. Thus, this festival promotes filial devotion to ancestors and provides a time when hungry ghosts can enjoy some satiation of their hunger. I witnessed the Ullambana Festival in the summer of 2008 in Jinxiang Town (金鄉鎮), Cangnang County. Parts of the town's old Ming dynasty wall and moat still remain, and local residents floated myriad candlelit paper lanterns on the moat to light the way for the orphan souls who visit Earth.

DIVINATION AND FENGSHUI

Divination (占卜)

Wenzhou people are avid pursuers of insight into their individual or family fortunes. Before they undertake an important life-changing decision or activity, they often seek divine guidance for their actions. Diviners also set the most auspicious date and time for starting important activities such as weddings, opening new stores, embarking on big trips, or lowering coffins into the ground for burial.

People call on professional diviners to peer into the future to guide action, to take precautions to avoid disaster, to prepare psychologically and accept what lies ahead, and to gain peace of mind. Secular people often mistake this eagerness to consult diviners as a passive acceptance of fate, or lack of agency in allowing higher divine forces to decide one's life. As I understand it, the reliance on divination bespeaks a reverence for the larger hidden and unknown forces that move the cosmos, and acceptance of the relative insignificance of human beings in these larger equations. It bespeaks a desire to align one's actions and life according to powerful patterns of divine nature and cosmos, and a wish to avoid violating whatever cosmic patterns the diviner is able to glean. Thus, to consult diviners is to take an active rather than passive stance—to peer into the unknown, anticipate future events, and plan appropriate actions. Professional diviners engage in "calculating with trigrams" (算卦). "Trigrams" (*gua*) refers to the eight trigrams (八卦), eight different combinations of six broken and unbroken lines found in *Yi Jing* divination, which dates back to the Zhou dynasty. Instead of the ancient milfoil stalks, today most diviners shake three coins in a turtle shell, then spill them out and read them.

Fengshui (Chinese Geomancy, 風水)

Another important ancient religious technology to ensure good fortune is Chinese geomancy or *fengshui*, literally "wind and water." *Fengshui* masters are

Figure 3.9. Wang Qinsheng, compass in hand, surveying a public cemetery for a woman buying a tomb for her mother, Yaoxi Township, 2010. Photo by the author.

primarily hired to help people position tombs and residential homes in the surrounding landscape. Other constructions, such as temples, ancestor halls, and even factories, stores, and whole villages, may also require *fengshui* siting. A house positioned correctly and facing in the right direction will bring good fortune to the family residing within, and a correctly sited tomb will bring prosperity for generations to come. Manmade structures must be properly aligned with the geographical formations and bodies of water in the natural landscape, so as to ensure the smooth flow of qi (氣), or "primordial breath," that runs through the veins of the earth.

Wang Qinsheng often took me out on his *fengshui* siting trips into the mountains, where tombs are still being quietly built. In the new millennium, we also visited new public cemeteries (公墓), where a company has carved out a whole hillside with endless rows of tightly packed tombs. The buyers still consult *fengshui* masters to choose the most auspiciously positioned tomb.

Figure 3.10. Wang Qinsheng's old geomantic compass, 1998. Photo by the author.

The Chinese compass (羅盤), with its magnetic needle facing south, was originally employed for *fengshui* siting of tombs, not geographical navigation, until centuries after its invention. *Fengshui* work also requires familiarity with the theory of yin and yang (陰陽) and the Five Material Elements (五行) of gold/metal, wood, water, fire, and earth, and how these cosmic forces wax and wane and interact with each other.

4 Daoism

Ancient Gods, Boisterous Rituals, and Hearthside Priests

It used to be that the strength of Daoism was in the north. Laozi lectured at Lou Guan Tai in Shaanxi. Shamanistic tradition [巫] came from the north. Ancestral teachers Wang and Qiu [王祖師, 邱祖師] [founders of the Quanzhen Sect] were both based in the north. There was even a saying, "Buddhist monks in the south; Daoist priests in the north" [南僧北道]. However, a third generation priest of Zhang Daoling's Celestial Masters lineage moved south from Sichuan to Dragon Tiger Mountain in Jiangxi, and this started the southward movement. In the Tang dynasty, Sima Chen Zhen [司馬承禎] came to settle in the Tiantai Mountains in Zhejiang. He and Zhang Boduan [張伯端] played important roles in establishing Daoism in the south. The famous Tang poet Li Bai was his student, and Li Bai's poetry shows the Daoist influence. From the Song dynasty onward, there was Emperor Huizong and his Daoist adviser Lin Lingsu [徽宗, 林靈素], and popular Daoism and Buddhism were both strong in the south. Then came the rapid economic development of the 1980s, and it was in Wenzhou that Daoism revived especially fast.

—Master Liu (pseudonym), a Daoist priest in Wenzhou

The *Dao De Jing* 《道德經》, *The Classic of the Way and Power*, is an ancient text said to have been written by Laozi (老子). It has much appeal as "Eastern philosophy" for a modern Western secular world. Similarly, the figure of the Daoist hermit who retreats to the mountains to engage in meditation and self-cultivation also appeals to a post-Reformation modernity that avoids ornate religious rituals and engages in forms of self-knowledge where the individual is central in the practice. In contrast, few people outside China and the Sinophone world know about Daoism as a religion of local communities or about its rich liturgical tradition. These ritual and community dimensions are prominent in Wenzhou's Daoist revival today, continuing what Terry Kleeman (2016) calls the "alternative community" of ancient Celestial Masters (天師道) that emerged during the collapse of the Han dynasty.

Kristofer Schipper (1993) suggested that, contrary to approaches that separate Daoism's philosophical and religious strands, they are one and the same tradition. The Celestial Masters religious movement in Sichuan emerged in the second century CE, several hundred years after the *Dao De Jing*. For Daoist practitioners, the *Dao De Jing* is not philosophy, but a sacred salvational scripture sent down from Heaven. Laozi is a personification of the Dao, the god Taishang Laojun (太上老君), who repeatedly descended to Earth to save humanity.

A good example of religious understanding of the *Dao De Jing* text is the Efficacious and Charitable Daoist Temple (靈善道觀) in Jinxiang Township, Cangnan County, which I visited on July 19, 2004 (Zhou and Ruan 1999: 332–333). In 1989, Master Li Chengsong (李誠松) gathered funds and built a new temple on the site. Master Li, then in his seventies, did not speak Mandarin, so we communicated through his young assistant. Inside Master Li's temple, two walls were covered from floor to ceiling with the five thousand characters of the *Dao De Jing*, written in beautiful *kaiti* script, a very readable form. The text of Immortal Lü Dongbin's *Hundred-Word Stele* (百字碑) covered another wall; Master Li explained that it could teach people to "have a good moral character." When I asked him why he put up the *Dao De Jing*, he said that he wanted everyone who visited his temple to absorb some of the words. Even if they do not understand them at first, he explained, once they start to memorize passages here and there and to repeat them, they will come to understand them. When he saw that I had a book about Daoism written by a Chinese scholar, he shook his head and said that the scholarly understanding was not complete. "Scholars are very good at giving the history of the texts they study," he said, "but scholars do not fully understand the rich meaning of the classics. They remain outside the teachings." One must "feel" or "intuit" (*wu*, 悟) the full meaning, he said, employing a term that also means "to attain enlightenment" in both Daoist and Buddhist traditions. Here, in a nutshell, is the Daoist suspicion of language and intellectualism. Although Daoists also treasure texts, their religious approach emphasizes intuition and bodily cultivation, quite different from the academic emphasis on intellectual and rational thought. Daoists also deploy writing ritualistically, where talismanic writing (符) does not transparently represent the real world but, rather, functions as an opaque, self-referential instrument for ritual healing or transformation of the world.

WHAT IS DAOISM?

The question of what Daoism is has vexed many scholars because, more than other religious traditions, Daoist teachings and practices seem to lack cohesion and standardization, perhaps owing to its strong localistic ethos. Despite the difficulties, let me attempt this simple working definition: it is a religious teaching, community liturgical tradition, and program of self-cultivation that seek to harmonize and align human life with the patterned movements of the cosmos, called the Dao (the Way). It embraces life, health, longevity, and immortality through healing rituals, meditation, breathing exercises, and dietary and yogic practices. Through ethical conduct, repentance for sins, food and incense offerings, and elaborate rituals, Daoists also communicate and gain the protection of the gods and exorcise harmful demons. Daoism is concerned with the well-being of communities and seeks to bring them under the protection of larger divine cosmic forces.

One difficulty in defining Daoism may be due to what I call "hierarchical encompassment," in which other religious cultural elements are absorbed (albeit positioned at a lower level) instead of remaining clearly separated. For example, Daoism and popular religion are mutually imbricated, and it is hard to figure out where one ends and the other begins. Wherever Daoism has spread, it absorbed popular local gods into its pantheon, while keeping its own gods at the top. Hierarchical encompassment was stronger in Daoism than in Buddhism, since Daoism built upon the shamanic, healing, and exorcistic traditions and deity cults of popular religion, whereas Buddhism downplayed the gods, redirecting attention to a new order of divine beings, the Buddhas, and taught about the ephemerality of this life in the endless cycle of reincarnation. Like Buddhism, early Daoism tried to change popular religion's culture of bloody animal sacrifices and promoted vegetarianism. Another difficulty stems from the fact that, in rural Wenzhou since 1994, the state has been marshaling deity temples to join the Daoist Association, and these new Daoist members have not completely shed their identities as local deity associations. As the new state-sponsored Daoist Academies, with their standardized classroom curricula that override traditional master-disciple lineage transmission of localized traditions, produce more Daoist priests, this problem of defining Daoism may recede. For now, Daoist priests who are the products of urban Daoist Academies are still uncommon in rural and small-town Wenzhou.

Over the years, I asked various Daoists how they would explain Daoism to people who know nothing about it. Master Cui, a monastic Daoist priest in Wu Yan Township, replied with this description of the Dao (the Way):

The Dao is very mysterious; it is the law of the universe. This law is like the laws of physics. We cannot see it, but it works to control the movements of all things in the universe, both living and nonliving things. If you try to go against the laws of physics, you will not only fail, but you will bring harm to yourself, right? It's the same with the Dao. So we Daoists do not like to force things, because then it is not spontaneous [unnatural, 不自然].

Master Cui then explained what he called a "core principle" of Daoism, "purity and stillness" (清靜) or quiescence:

Daoism teaches the importance of tranquility. One's thoughts must be calm because it is only though stillness that we can obtain wisdom. The source of much suffering in the world is noise. Today, machine noise is very irritating and disturbing (煩躁); so is a lot of the ghastly popular music blaring on the streets. All the noise prevents people from understanding what is important in life. Daoist teachings emphasize something quite different: we emphasize the spontaneous/natural way (自然), not things that are manmade.

He went on to anticipate a common misunderstanding that people have of Daoism:

Many people believe that Daoism stands for passivity or fatalism. Daoists are not passive at all. They are actively engaged with life and with the world. There is a Daoist saying: "My fate is in my own hands, not in those of Heaven" [我命在我, 不在天]. We have another saying, "[Seek] purity, quiescence, and nonaction" [清靜無為]. This does not mean escaping reality, but that the way of dealing with aggression and anger from others is to keep calm. One should not resist or confront head-on, but just rechannel the aggressive force [轉換力量].

Despite what Master Cui said about how Daoists respect the natural order, environmentalist consciousness among Daoists did not seem particularly high during my fieldwork. Perhaps this is because, in the economic hyperdrive mode of Wenzhou, environmental consciousness only developed very recently.

Master Cui also talked about three emphases in Daoist teachings: First, there are techniques (重術) or "Daoist technologies" (*daoshu*, 道術) to attain longevity and immortality, such as "inner and outer elixirs" (內丹, 外丹). Inner elixirs include self-cultivation techniques like meditation, breathing, and yogic exercises. Outer elixirs include substances that one ingests, such as herbs and chemical compounds mixed and heated on stoves. The second emphasis is life (重生). "Daoists value life," said Master Cui. "We are different from the Buddhists, who focus on the illusory and transitory nature of life, and focus on past and future lives." Many Daoists practice special diets and inner and outer elixirs to live longer and become immortal, he said. Finally, there is peace and harmony (重和). Daoists try to live "in harmony" with nature, the Dao, society, and the body. Examples of the harmony between thought and the body are such mind-body techniques as *taiji quan* (太極拳), a system of exercise with smooth, flowing motions in tune with the breath. When I asked Master Cui how many Daoists actively pursue these practices, he acknowledged that nowadays very few people do, except for *taiji quan*, which is a common sight in public parks in the early mornings.

In August 2005, I was chatting with Mr. Luo, a retired military man and self-taught scholar of Wenzhou Daoist rituals and music. When asked what came to mind when he thought about Daoism, he answered, "Daoists are into freedom [spontaneity, 自由] and nonaction [無為]. They ask the state not to control and manage things too much, to let the people alone and govern themselves." He went on to talk about the Daoist immortals, or transcendants (仙), people who through self-cultivation and bodily exercises have attained the Way (修身得道). With a hint of wistfulness, Mr. Luo said, "Immortals are free-spirited, blissful, and carefree [逍遥自在]. They easily ride on clouds or storks and fly around between Heaven and earth."

Master Liu provided another typology in 2004, about three levels of Daoism. The upper level is "official Daoism" (官方道教), the kind of cleaned-up Daoism imposed by organizations like the Daoist Association, a quasi–civil society, quasi-state organization found in every township, and the Bureau of Religion, a state office with branches in local governments. According to Master Liu, official Daoism is interested in getting rid of the "superstitions" of Daoism and focusing on the question of what Daoism can contribute to society. The middle level is composed of the Daoist clergy, who are excited about the different teachings, techniques, and schools of Daoism and eager to build up the religion. However, Daoist clergy are often frustrated by official restrictions and obstacles. The lower level is the popular Daoism of the "old hundred surnames" (*laobaixing*), or the common people, focusing on the worship of gods. "Their Daoism is to beg the gods for protection of their families, and the healing of the sick. They worship sacred persons who have done great things for humankind," said Master Liu. As he saw it, in order for Daoism to recover from its long historical decline, it must first develop at this lower level:

This is a necessary step because you must get the emperor to recognize and grant a title to your god. Once you get this recognition and approval, then you can survive and expand. Everything in society works this way. For anything you do, you must get acknowledgment and permission from the state. Otherwise, you are treated like a rebel or traitor [*pantu*]. You must always get the [imperial] court's recognition and approval [朝廷的認可].

If Daoism were merely the province of the clergy, it would be much easier for the state to deny its importance and eradicate it. Master Liu's logic is that when so many ordinary people are engaged in Daoist practice, it is hard for the state to deny it as a religious force. Without state approval, it would be very risky for any group to develop Daoism; they would be hounded by the state. What is noteworthy about Master Liu's wording is that there is a smooth conflation of the modern state with the old imperial court, suggesting the structural continuity of the binary tension of "official" versus "the people" (官 vs. 民). Since the ascendancy of Xi Jinping in 2012 as Communist Party General Secretary, traditional Chinese culture and indigenous religions are now upheld, and Daoists worry less about religious survival. However, they must still contend with state restrictions, commercialization, and the penetration of "official Daoism" and its nationalist discourse that undercuts Daoist transcendent aims.

DAOIST HISTORY AND PRACTICE IN WENZHOU

Wenzhou is one of the strongholds of Daoism in the country, along with Sichuan and Fujian Provinces, Jiangxi's Dragon Tiger Mountain area, and Shaanxi's Lou Guan Tai area, where Laozi is said to have engaged in an ancient debate with Confucius. Of the Ten Daoist Caverns, Thirty-Six Grottoes, and Seventy-Two Blessed Lands scattered throughout the Daoist sacred geography of China, five of these sacred sites are located in the mountains of Wenzhou (Ying and Qian 2008).[1] Said to provide passageways to Heaven and the playing grounds of Daoist immortals, Daoist caverns and grottoes attract hermits engaged in self-cultivation because it is easier to be transformed into an immortal in these sacred terrains. The Daoist movement established a foothold very early in Wenzhou. The city of Wenzhou was geomantically sited by the famous *fengshui* master and diviner Guo Pu (郭璞, 276–324 CE), an early disciple of the Celestial Masters (Lin S. 2013: 83). During the Southern and Northern dynasties, Tao Hongjing (陶弘景, 456–536 CE), a famous Daoist pharmacologist and doctor, became a recluse in the Da Ruo Yan Mountains of Yongjia County. He practiced "inner elixir or alchemy" (內丹), the cultivation and circulation of the body's "primordial breath," or *qi* (氣), through techniques such as meditation, breathing, and gymnastic exercises to maintain good health, achieve longevity, and attain transcendence and become an immortal (仙).

The epigraph at the beginning of this chapter traces a historical movement for Daoism from northern China to southern China. Zhang Boduan (aka 張紫陽, 984–1082 CE), an inner alchemist, promoted the growth of Daoism's Southern Lineage (南宗) (Kong 2008). During the Northern Song dynasty, Emperor Huizong (徽宗) was a strong patron of Daoism who built up Daoist culture across the empire. He was especially influenced by Lin Lingsu (林靈素, 1075–1119 CE), his Daoist adviser, a Wenzhou native who helped establish the Divine Empyrean Sect (神霄派), combining inner alchemy with talismanic and divination arts (Kohn 2009: 164). Wenzhou has been a stronghold of this sect. In 1127, when the Jurchen army of the Jin dynasty invaded the Northern Song capital and took Emperor Huizong and his son prisoners, Huizong's other son, Gaozong (高宗), fled to Wenzhou, where he hid out in the Buddhist Temple on Jiangxin Island in the Ou River. Later, Gaozong established the Southern Song dynasty, launching a massive population migration and shifting the Chinese empire's center of gravity from the North to the South. The Wenzhou area was a beneficiary of this southward movement of Daoist culture.

In 1999, there were 426 registered Daoist temples listed for all districts and counties of Wenzhou (Zhou and Ruan 1999). This was a large number at that time compared with almost any other area of China. Certainly the numbers have greatly increased since then. In 2016, just one Daoist Association in Longwan District oversaw 218 registered Daoist temples, including 88 Daoist and 130 deity temples.[2] The number of temples in this small area of Wenzhou in 2016 is around one-half of the total number of temples across Wenzhou in 1999. Here we also see that, even though the authorities have ordered all deity temples across Wenzhou (except Cangnan County) to become Daoist, the local people still maintain a distinction between them.

Today in Wenzhou there are two major Daoist sects. The Orthodox Unity sect (*Zhengyi pai*, 正一派) is descended from the ancient Celestial Masters order; its male priests reside in local communities, and they can marry and have families. This is by far the largest sect in Wenzhou, with the most priests. Many come from a long line of father-to-son priesthoods tracing back many generations (Ai L. 2013). Then there is the Complete Perfection sect (*Quanzhen-pai*, 全真派), founded by Wang Chongyang (王重陽, 1112–1170 CE), which developed throughout northern China during the Yuan dynasty. Its priesthood includes men and women who have "left the family" (出家): in other words, they live in separate monasteries, follow a vegetarian diet, and take a vow of sexual abstinence.

Wenzhou Daoist culture has played an inordinate role in the national revival of Daoism. For example, the music of Wenzhou's Eastern Peak Daoist Temple (東岳觀) was incorporated into the teaching curriculum of the White Cloud Temple, the Beijing temple that houses the National Daoist Association and trains new generations of Daoist monastics. In September 2010, a local historian took me to visit the Eastern Peak temple in Kunyang Township, Pingyang County. This is a venerable Daoist temple established in 1066 CE, during the Northern Song dynasty, that has been in almost continuous Daoist usage for a thousand years. The Shenzong Emperor built an eighty-meter-long road to the temple and gave it a plaque with "Sacred Longevity" (聖壽) written in calligraphy. In the early twentieth century, it became an important center of the Longmen Sect of Daoism, and one of its priests went on to become the abbot of Tongbai Palace (桐柏宮), a major Daoist center in the Tiantai Mountains of Zhejiang. Eastern Peak Temple was damaged and lost much of its temple grounds during the Mao years. The temple priests were harassed and forced to return to lay life.

However, in the 1980s, Eastern Peak Temple bounced back to life and made a major contribution to the national revival of Quanzhen Daoism. The temple's elderly priest, Master Ma Chengqi (馬誠起), was invited go to Beijing's White Cloud Temple and train the young Daoist acolytes from across the country (Xu and Xue 2005: 19; Zhou and Ruan 1999: 274–275). Beijing's White Cloud Temple had lost much of its own music and scripture-chanting traditions during the Cultural Revolution. Since Wenzhou's Daoist ritual, chanting, scriptural, and musical traditions were "relatively intact," an effort was made to import Daoist music from the South to the North. Thus, the music and rituals of Wenzhou Daoism were brought to Beijing's national Daoist revival effort. From there it was disseminated across the country as the new standardized form shared by a new generation of monastic Daoists. Furthermore, the vice chair of the National Daoist Association in Beijing is a Daoist priest from Cangnan County: Master Huang Xinyang (黃信陽), a student of Master Li Chengsong, mentioned above.

DAOIST GODS AND POPULAR DEITIES: THEIR PLACE IN THE CELESTIAL BUREAUCRACY

As discussed in chapter 3, the lines between Daoism, shamanism, and popular religion are difficult to draw, as they share much iconography and many gods, rituals, festivals, and temples (Liu Z. 2000: 41). Daoism is the closest tradition to shamanism, as its priests also communicate with the gods to bring down blessings and conduct exorcism rituals. In 2010, a Daoist priest in Longwan District told me that "Buddhist monks do not exorcise demons" (和尚不驅鬼) but that "Daoist priests have a strong ability to exorcise demons," on account of their self-cultivation practice (修身). I attended a Daoist exorcism ritual in Wenzhou, in which the priest used his body to vigorously draw out the demons that had taken over a woman patient. According to Piet van der Loon (1977), there is a deep "shamanic substrate" to Daoism, and this phrase has struck a chord with other Western scholars (Dean 1993: 17; von Glahn 2004: 260). However, in contrast with spirit mediums, the Daoist priest holds back: he does not *become* a god, nor do gods speak *through* him; he remains merely a bearer of messages and a supplicant to the gods on behalf of his clients.

When I asked Masters Liu and Cui in separate interviews what the difference was between Daoism and popular religion, they gave similar answers. They said that in Daoism there is a distinction between two realms of divine beings: the Originary Heavenly Deities (先天之神) and the Later Heavenly Deities (后天之神). The former category is stressed by Daoism and refers to deities who are powerful forces of nature tracing far back to the origins of the cosmos, such as the Three Pure Ones, the Jade Emperor, the Queen Mother of the West (西王母), and nature gods of stars and constellations, Thunder, Grain, and so forth. The second category are generally the gods of popular religion, cultural heroes who were once human beings, who performed good deeds or sacrificed themselves for others. Over the centuries, as certain gods from the second category became prominent and worshipped across regions, they have been absorbed into the Daoist pantheon. These include Lord Guan, Goddess Mazu, and Goddess Chen Jinggu.

Daoism has often been described as "inclusive" (Lee, Chan, and Tsu 1994: 140), and several Daoist priests in Wenzhou have described their religion as having an "encompassing heart" (包容心). According to Master Cui, "The Dao teaches us that we should 'empty our bosom so that we become like a valley' [虛懷若谷]." By this, he meant that Daoists must embrace and absorb different elements, be flexible and open, allowing different streams to flow into its valley. Over the centuries, wherever Daoism spread, it absorbed and integrated the local shamanistic cultures, deities, and demons across China into its own religious imaginary. According to the scholar of Daoism Liu Zhongyu, whom I interviewed in Shanghai: "Many Daoist gods and immortals were originally local popular gods, whose positions were made more prominent by Daoism, and some of them were even promoted in rank in the Daoist pantheon"

Figure 4.1. Hierarchical seating of Daoist and local gods in Great Sage Who Equals Heaven Temple, Lingxi Town, Cangnan County, 2010. Photo by the author.

(Liu 2000: 41). Although Daoism absorbs popular and local gods, it imposes its order and hierarchical system on them, so that local gods are positioned below Daoist deities. The principle of "hierarchical encompassment" enables the Daoist tradition to absorb and build on local popular religion, wherever Daoism spreads.

Both popular religion and Daoism position their gods into a "celestial bureaucracy" resembling the hierarchy of the imperial state, with different ranks of the gods. The Daoist pantheon arranges the gods into three levels, called "the Three Worlds" (三界): Upper, Middle, and Lower. At the beginning of many Daoist rituals, the presiding priest will invite the gods to come down and enjoy the ceremony and food and incense offerings. These gods are seated in empty chairs placed in three rows at three different elevations. The upper row of chairs seats the highest Daoist gods, like the Three Purities, the Four Emperors, the Three Officials, and the Queen Mother of the West, all discussed below. The middle level includes major gods like Wenchang, Lord Guan, the God of Thunder, and Xuanwu. The lower level includes local Wenzhou deities, who may not be known in other parts of China, and the local Earth God, who welcomes higher-level gods when they descend to localities.

This hierarchical ranking often extends to the relationship between Daoist priests, who are usually men, and shamans, ritual healers, and spirit mediums, who in Wenzhou today tend to be women. In May 2005, I met with a Daoist priest of the Quanzhen sect at his temple in White Elephant Township. He was dismissive of the women shamans who frequent his temple, but felt it necessary to be polite and paternalistic:

> Most shamans [巫人] are women. They usually have some emotional problems and they are usually not married, or their man has died early or left them, so shamanic activity is an outlet for them. Their "will" [yizhi] is not very strong, so they are easily open to outside influences, like hearing voices. Their bodies are usually not very healthy. Their social position is low in society. They can heal the sick and foretell the future [預測]. They can hear voices and see visions and images: the Jade Emperor, the Western Queen Mother, Guanyin, and local deities, and so on. Actually, gods don't really enter into them or speak through them, gods do not possess them. That's just how these women describe it. It's actually a yin force [陰形的力量], a negative force [fumiande liliang] that affects them. These shamanesses will come to our temple to pay respects to us [Daoists]. They are very respectful to priests, and our priests warmly welcome them. The relationship is like that between teachers and students. One must have both teachers and students; neither would be complete without the other. So we priests are not arrogant toward them, because this relationship is necessary.

On the topic of the teacher-student relationship between Daoist priest and shamaness, he quoted an ancient saying: "Those who are virtuous must be teacher to those who are not virtuous; those who are not virtuous are the resources of those who are" (善者為不善者之師，不善者為善者之資). Here shamanism is regarded as an inferior form of religiosity compared to the literate and institutional religiosity of Daoists. Despite the priest's denial of arrogance on the part of Daoists, one can detect the condescension in his words when he speaks about women shamans as "students" or "resources" or describes their powers as a "negative yin or female force."

There is a sense in which local gods and Daoist gods are so intertwined that they seem to belong to a single religious system serving local communities, in contrast with Buddhism. In February 2001, I was exploring a newly completed Daoist temple in Shipu Village, Yongzhong Township, called Loyal and Upright Temple (忠烈道觀). I engaged a local elder in conversation, and he told me:

> Nowadays, Buddhist temples don't have much money. People do not go beg Buddha for help much. They feel he is too high and remote from them. Most people prefer to beg the gods [求神]. The gods feel closer and people find it easier to understand them. They don't understand Buddhist teachings. So deity temples and Daoist temples get lots of donations.

I knew that this observation was not completely true, because I have seen many ordinary people, especially old women, fingering their prayer beads at Buddhist temples, and since 2000 a new, educated Buddhist culture has been growing, in both wealth and membership. At the same time, the old man's statement also expressed an important insight into local religious life, as borne out by this common saying:

皇天緊, 大悲咒慢。

With the sovereign celestial deity, one gets results faster; with the Buddhist Great Compassion Dharani 《大悲咒》 chant, it is slower.

Here we see that for many, the gods of popular religion feel closer and more responsive to their prayers, while the Buddhas seem higher, more aloof, and less responsive. At the same time, local people are also aware that in the mind-sets of officials and urban people, Buddhism is regarded as more sophisticated. They know that Daoism and folk religion are looked down on. In the next section I describe some important Daoist deities.

THE THREE PURE ONES (三清)

Daoism set up its own Originary Heavenly Deities as higher gods above those of popular religion that it absorbed. In chapter 3, I discussed how the Jade Emperor is the highest god in popular religion. In the Daoist pantheon however, the Jade Emperor is below the Three Purities (三清), the three highest Daoist deities, all of whom trace back to the origin of the cosmos and reside in the highest of Heaven's thirty-six levels. Their residence in three Palaces is located in an area of Heaven called the Purities, hence these deities' names: Lord of the Primal Origin and Jade Purity (玉清原始天尊); Lord of the Numinous Treasure and High Purity (上清靈寶天尊); and Lord Laozi of Great Purity (太清道德天尊). The Lord of Primal Origins emerged from the original breath or energy of the primal chaos, before any divisions, boundaries, or limits. He oversees all of the natural forces of the universe, the multiple deities and immortals, and the ten thousand things. The Lord of Numinous Treasure is the second-highest deity to emerge from this original breath of the primal chaos. Lord Laozi emerged as a third personification of primal breath, a god with the image of Laozi riding a water buffalo, used in many Daoist rituals. There is a Daoist saying, "Out of one breath are produced the Three Purities" (一氣化三清). These deities represent the three original pure energies from the origin of the cosmos, the primal breath that each new human infant also harbors, until it is dissipated through aging. In Daoist paintings, the Three Purities are always arrayed at the top, above a gradation of lower-level gods.

THE FOUR EMPERORS (四御)

Below the Three Purities are the Four Emperors (四御), important astrological deities that are commonly invited down to earth by Daoist priests performing rituals. They are the Jade Emperor (玉皇大帝); the Purple Profound Emperor of the North Pole Star (紫微北極大帝); Emperor Gou Chen of the South Pole Star (勾陳南極大帝); and the Emperor of the Land (后土皇地祇). The Jade Emperor is in charge of the Three Worlds of Heaven, Earth and the human world, the Ten Directions, the lower gods and immortals, and all of the fortunes and misfortunes of human life. The Purple Profound Emperor resides in the constellation around the North Pole Star, which is centrally located in the cosmos. He assists the Jade Emperor in holding together Heaven and Earth; maintaining the Sun, Moon, and stars; and ensuring the four seasons and the climate. In Daoist exorcism and healing rituals, he is a major god whom the priest summons down. Emperor Gou Chen assists the Jade Emperor in controlling the North and South Poles and the stars, and in maintaining links between Heaven, Earth, and Humanity. The Emperor of the Land is the only goddess among the Four Emperors, and she assists the Jade Emperor in monitoring the interaction of yin and yang forces, ensuring the reproduction of life-forms, and protecting the ten thousand things and the gods of the earth, mountains, and rivers (Zhang Jintao 2000: 55–57).

THE THREE OFFICIALS AND GREAT EMPERORS (三官大帝)

This trio of empirewide nature gods straddles the boundaries between popular religion and Daoism. The three statues of the Heaven Official, Earth Official,

Figure 4.2. The Three Officials—gods of water, Heaven, and earth, 1993. Photo by the author.

and Water Official are found in both deity and Daoist temples in Wenzhou, no matter which god occupies the central altar. In Daoist mythology, these Three Officials came to life from the Lord of the Primal Origin (原始天尊), one of the Three Purities. They are very ancient gods, as shown by historical records that date their cult back to at least the end of the Han dynasty, when religious Daoism first began on the Chengdu Plains in Sichuan Province. In the *History of the Three Kingdoms*, there is a passage saying that the Five Pecks of Rice followers would pray to divine officials (鬼吏) when they became ill, by writing down their names, with a confession of the sins they had committed, on three pieces of paper. Then they left one piece of paper on top of a mountain for the Heaven Official; buried a second piece of paper in the earth for the Earth Official; and threw a third piece of paper into a river for the Water Official (Lu 2001: 39; Wang K. 1999: 267). Although this form of ritual healing is no longer practiced, people pray to the Three Officials because they control our natural surroundings and the cosmos and shape human lives, fates, and fortunes.

THE GOD OF LITERATURE (文昌爺)

The God of Literature is also called "Emperor Wenchang" (文昌帝君). In imperial times, he was the patron saint of scholars facing the difficult imperial examinations that made them eligible for scholar-official posts in the imperial state. In ancient times, this god was the six-star constellation known as the Northern Dipper (北斗) or Wenchang Pavilion (文昌宮) (Kleeman 1994; Lu 2001: 66–84; Pan E. 2001: 95; Ying and Jiang 2008: 17–18), which is Ursa Major, or the Big Dipper, in Western culture.

Today in Wenzhou, Wenchang is the chief god that students and their parents turn to for help in negotiating the arduous series of examinations that will gain them entry into a good high school and later into college. Indeed, in Wenzhou, where the average educational level is lower, most people want their children to have much higher educational attainments than themselves. Thus, after the anti-intellectualism of Maoism, the God of Literature has enjoyed a renewed ascendancy. On Wenchang's birthday, the third day of the second lunar month, his temples are mobbed with people seeking his assistance in academic pursuits.

Two examples are instructive here. First, inside a small Wenchang Temple in Yong Chang Township, countless red paper slips were pasted onto the walls, each bearing the name of a student about to take an exam, along with the exam location, date, and time, and even the student's seat number. Students place these slips on the wall after praying to Lord Wenchang so that he will know exactly when and where to help them. Second, the central deity ostensibly worshipped at the Palace of the Heavenly Immortal (天仙宮) in Yongzhong Township, Longwan District, is the local goddess Mother Lu, described in chapter 3; Lord Wenchang is only a secondary presence. However, the God of Literature is the main reason the temple has thrived and become a major attraction to worshippers from other areas of Wenzhou. The popularity of Wenchang, with his promise of upward mobility, has eclipsed that of Mother Lu, whose traditional filial and feminine virtues no longer have great appeal. In the newfound economic prosperity, the local people beg the gods to help their children gain the symbolic capital of higher education.

THE PERFECTED LORD XU (許府真君)

The Daoist immortal Lord Xu was an early Daoist healer named Xu Sun (許遜), born in 239 CE in Jiangxi Province (Brokaw 1991: 43–50; Fan, Zhang, and Liu 1996: 83–84). As a young hunter, Lord Xu shot an arrow into a pregnant female deer. He watched with horror as the wounded deer gave birth to her baby and then, without regard for her own safety, licked her baby clean before she expired. Heartbroken, Lord Xu threw away his bow and arrow, resolving never to kill animals again. He threw himself into studying the classics, history, astrology, *fengshui*, law codes, the five elements, and divination arts, and attained enlightenment. Under the Jin dynasty, he served as an official in Sichuan, developing a reputation for honesty and helping the common people deal with rapacious government clerks and officials. Legend has it that he slew a few dragon and snake demons that were terrorizing local communities. In 374 CE, he ascended to Heaven and became an immortal. Of course, this would make him 135 years old when he died, but perhaps these are the longevity effects of Daoist self-cultivation!

A cult developed around Lord Xu that gained a significant following in the late Tang and Song dynasties. Emperors Zhenzong and Huizong of the Song dynasty bestowed two imperial titles on him. He is the founder of the Daoist sect "Clean and Bright" (淨明派), which historically intersected with the Lü Mountain Daoist order of Fujian and Zhejiang but was based in Jiangxi Province (Brokaw 1991: 45–50). I visited his ancestral main temple, Wanshou Palace (萬壽宮), located in the city of Nanchang, Jiangxi, which draws many pilgrims to its festivals. It was first built in the Eastern Jin dynasty in 376 CE, but the impressive buildings that still survive date back to the Ming and Qing eras.

In Wenzhou, Lord Xu is honored in a unique temple, the Sacred Well Temple (聖井道觀), on top of a mountain near the town of Da-nan in Rui'an County. Lord Xu is often associated with dreams, and many of his temples offer dream interpretation. In May 1993, I made the long trek up to the Sacred Well Temple on the mountain of the same name with my friend Wang Qinsheng, the diviner, and a woman local government representative. First we had to cross over a steep valley to get up to the base of Sacred Well Mountain. A primitive pulley system ferried us in a basket carrier suspended from cables high above the valley. Creaking precariously along and gazing down at the valley hundreds of feet below, I wondered if I would soon meet the gods after we crashed to the ground below. I was soon distracted by the sheer beauty of the landscape. No wonder the Yuan dynasty Daoist painter Huang Gongwang (黃公望, 1269–1354 CE) depicted these mountains and river valley when he stayed at the Sacred Well Temple.[3] On the mountainsides, hundreds of steep terraces of rice paddies and sweet potato and vegetable patches were carved into the slopes, and any space not terraced was covered by thick green bamboo forests stretching toward the blue sky and swaying gently in the breeze. I saw no signs of machinery; it seemed that machines did not make sense anyway on the narrow footpaths and steep terraces. After landing on the other side of the valley, we still had to climb a steep stone stairway up the mountain to the temple, which took over an hour of strenuous exercise.

First built in 1262 during the Southern Song dynasty (Zhou and Ruan 1999: 260–261), the temple was a marvelous archaic-looking place, completely constructed of large stone blocks, whose rear backed into a naturally formed mountain cavern. Inside, even the main altar and seats of the gods were made of stone. Under the temple altar, a natural mountain spring fed a stone well dug into the mountaintop. It is said that drinking this pure water would heal many illnesses. However, the temple was in a dilapidated and sorry state when I was there. Over the years, the black soot from countless candles had covered the ceilings, walls, and statues of the gods. Fragments of stone stele and statues lay around the temple grounds in disarray, and sheets of newspaper flew about in the wind. Sixteen old peasant men made up the temple management. They were supposed to care for the temple, but seemed more concerned with their income from fortune-telling and interpreting the dreams of temple visitors. Mr. Wang was visibly upset by the mess and scolded several old men that this was no way to run a famous temple and honor a powerful immortal.

There is a Wenzhou legend about the famous Ming dynasty official, Zhang Cong (張璁, 1475–1539 CE), a native of Yong Zhong Township, where his tomb still lies. In his forties, Zhang still had not passed the highest level of the imperial examination, the *jinshi*, nor been appointed to an official post. He traveled to the Sacred Well Temple to "request a dream" (*qiu meng*) and look into his future. That night, he dreamed that someone gouged out one of his eyeballs and nailed it onto a wooden pole. He took this dream as an inauspicious sign indicating that his prospects for officialdom were not good. Indignant, he left the temple in a huff. Years later, Zhang Cong attained not only the *jinshi* but also a high office, as prime minister in the imperial state's Inner Court. Having become a big official, he became angry about the false prophecy he received in his dream at this temple, so he ordered that the Sacred Well Temple be dismantled. At the temple, he and his troops were stopped by the resident Earth God of the temple, who asked what they intended to do. When the Earth God heard about the bad dream, he laughed and explained the dream's real meaning. "The character for 'eye' is written with the radical *mu* (目). Then the wooden pole onto which the eye was nailed is 'wood' (*mu*, 木). If you put the two *mu* characters together side by side, then you get the character *xiang* (相), which is the title of prime minister (*zaixiang*, 宰相). So your dream here *did* predict your future," said the Earth God. Thus humbled, Zhang Cong called off the troops and spent his own money to restore and expand the temple. From this story, one can see that the Chinese tradition of dream interpretation is quite different from the psychoanalytic approach pioneered by Freud. The aim of many Chinese dream interpretations is to glimpse the future rather than understand current unconscious turmoil or desires of the individual psyche. The Chinese approach often focuses on the written script for images that emerge in the dreamscape, unearthing hidden meanings in key Chinese characters.

THE DAOIST PRIESTHOOD

The priests of the Orthodox Unity sect (Zhengyi, 正一派) are all men, and many come from a long lineage of father-to-son inheritance of their occupation. Since Zhengyi priests can marry, have families, and reside in local communities, they are often called "hearthside Daoist priests" (*huoju daoshi*, 火居道士). Most Zhengyi priests have their own family business or other line of work besides their Daoist activities, which mainly involve performing Daoist rituals for their clients. A Wenzhou Daoist Association publication wrote that in 1999, there were 2,452 Zhengyi Daoist priests in all of the eleven counties, municipalities, and urban districts of Wenzhou (Zhou and Ruan 1999: 14). This number seems very low to me; most likely it represents only priests who have registered with the authorities. The Quanzhen Sect (全真派) is comprised of monks and nuns, who, like Buddhist clergy, are celibate and live in monasteries. The Daoist stronghold in Wenzhou is Cangnan County, in southern Wenzhou, where the Daoist priests have the reputation for providing the best liturgical services. In 2005, there were over seven hundred Orthodox Unity Daoist priests and about two hundred Quanzhen priests in Cangnan County (Ai L. 2013; Xu and Xue 2005: 19), well over one-fourth of Daoist priests in Wenzhou.

Zhengyi Daoists must have at least three years of training with a master before they can undergo ordination as priest. Some hearthside priests get ordained at home or in a temple with a two- to three-day ordination ritual. Many now choose to travel to Dragon Tiger Mountain, the Orthodox Unity religious center in Jiangxi Province, to get ordained. There are priests who are not ordained, but they cannot serve as the head priest (主持) in any ritual. Theoretically, all hearthside priests are supposed to have an altar devoted to their "ancestral Master" (祖師), Zhang Daoling, at home, and to offer prayers and incense daily at morning, noon, and evening (早課, 午課, 晚課). However, they have become quite "secularized" (世俗化) and often neglect this duty. For many, a Daoist priesthood is more akin to engaging in a business to support a family than a religious calling. Once when I asked some priests why they chose to become priests, they said frankly, "It's because we have no talent for doing business, so we can only perform Daoist rituals" (不會經商, 沒本事。). Quanzhen priests living more regimented lives in monasteries are perhaps more serious and disciplined about the priesthood, but one man told me that even Quanzhen priests sometimes just play a recording of chants and prayers instead of taking the time to perform the daily ritual themselves. Thus, although Daoist resurgence is impressive in Wenzhou, the religious spark is often dimmed by secular and commercial forces. Below are a few portraits of some of the Daoist priests I interviewed.

The Vegetarian Who Was Forced to Marry

Master Li was ordained into the Quanzhen monastic order before the Communist Revolution. He was seventy-five, with his long hair tied into a topknot, when I interviewed him in July 2004. He grew up living in a Daoist temple with his mother because they were poor and had nowhere else to go. Although he only received a few years of formal schooling, he read all the old Daoist books of liturgy, healing, and scriptures that he could get his hands on. At Liberation in 1949, only twenty-one years old, he was already abbot of a Daoist temple. At first, he kept to his temple affairs and things were going all right. However, 1958, the first year of the Great Leap Forward, was disastrous: local Communist Party branches were smashing and closing temples. Master Li was forbidden to perform any more Daoist rituals. One day people forced their way into his temple and dragged him through the temple grounds. Then someone pounced on him and cut off his hair. They forced him to renounce his religious vows and return to lay life. He had no choice but to do their bidding and get married, and he bore a son and daughter. Today his son is also a Daoist priest, and his wife lives with him in his temple. He turned to the practice of traditional Chinese medicine and developed a good reputation for helping the sick. When the Cultural Revolution came, he was dragged out again and made to march in political processions with a dunce cap on his head and a giant wooden cangue around his neck. People on the streets yelled epithets at him and accused him of fomenting "superstitions." Most Daoists of his generation went through all this, he said, and unlike many others, he was not beaten. He was thrown into prison, but released because he was well liked in the local community, having cured so many people. Despite all the twists and turns of history, Master Li has remained a vegetarian all his life.

The "Academy Priest"

Master Guo is a young educated Quanzhen monastic priest whose parents brought him up as a Daoist. He speaks quietly and has a scholarly air about him. At age eighteen, he went to live in a Daoist temple in Fujian, and later he spent time meditating in the Cavern of Female Immortals (仙姑洞) in the Yandang Mountains of Yueqing County. At age twenty-two he matriculated at the prestigious White Cloud Temple Daoist Academy in Beijing. Four years later he graduated and was ordained a priest. He was assigned to a Daoist monastery in Wenzhou, where he receives a regular salary from the Daoist Association. He feels sad that the number of new academic priests is so low. There are only five Daoist Academies in all of China: in Beijing (Quanzhen Sect), Shanghai (Zhengyi Sect), Wudang Mountain in Hubei, Qingchen Mountain in Sichuan, and the Southern Mountain Convent in the Heng Mountains in Hunan for Daoist nuns.[4] These Daoist Academies do not even recruit students every year, and each graduating class is quite small; Master Guo's graduating class, for example, was only sixty people. Only one to three students from each province in the country are selected to attend this academy in a recruitment year. According to Yang Der-Ruey (2012), a Taiwan scholar of Daoism, these Daoist Academies have totally transformed the traditional master-to-apprentice model of religious transmission, introducing secular elements into the curriculum, so they resemble secular college instruction. Until 2013, the number of Daoist Academies in China, and the number of graduates, remained relatively steady (Yang, personal communication). In 2013, the academies in Beijing and Qingcheng Mountain closed down for unspecified reasons, the Shanghai Academy only had forty-seven students, and the Wudang Academy had less than forty.

Master Guo told me that there is a major difference between "academy priests" (學院道士), like himself, and "priests of the people" (民間道士), or "hearthside priests." Academy priests have the equivalent of a college education and know much more about the world outside Wenzhou. They want to build up and strengthen Daoism and spread its teachings, even to the world outside China. The main motive of "priests of the people" is an economic one; they perform rituals and earn money to take care of their families. He said that in the Ming and Qing dynasties, there were very few Daoist priests who made a living out of performing rituals for payment. Today's priests who treat Daoism as a way of making a living mainly started to appear in Republican China in the early twentieth century. Although Zhengyi priests could always marry and have children, they used to be closely attached to temples, and less dispersed among the laypeople. After Liberation, with many temples closed down or destroyed, these priests had nowhere to go, so they began trying to make money by wandering around offering ritual services. Master Guo sighed and said that academy priests like himself would like to spread Daoist teachings to "hearthside priests," but the latter are not very interested, nor are the common people who hire them: "It is hard to educate the lower levels of society. They want miracles from rituals and the chanting of scriptures, not doctrines [道理]."

The Party Member

Master Cao is a married Zhengyi "hearthside Daoist priest" who modestly refers to himself as "Little Multitudes of Zhengyi" (正一小兆). He was born not long after Liberation and spent the first decades of his life working as a peasant, his family having lost its land at Land Reform. When I first got to know him in 1993, he possessed an innocent quality that I found among many Wenzhou peasants. He had a way of expressing himself very emphatically and loudly when he chose to speak. Although he never finished elementary school, he learned to read classical Chinese from his grandfather, who was educated in a traditional school before Liberation. He loved to read old books about history and the ancient exploits of gods and heroes, so he apprenticed himself to an old Daoist priest for three years to learn how to perform rituals and chant the Daoist scriptures (經書).

"A hearthside Daoist priest needs to be good at three things," said Master Cao. "First, you must have good vocal chords [for ritual singing and chanting]. Second, you must have good writing and calligraphy skills. Third, you must have good musician skills."[5] He admitted he was deficient in musical talents and lacked knowledge about traditional Chinese medicine, unlike some priests. However, he did have a booming voice, which was good for chanting scriptures. He observes the Five Prohibitions (五戒) for Daoist priests: no killing of humans or animals; no stealing; no illicit sexual behavior; no sowing of social discord by talking behind people's backs; and no consuming of meat, garlic, onions, or alcohol.[6] Indulging in any of these prohibited acts would weaken his will and concentration (意志不強) when he conducts rituals. "If one is not pure in heart, then the gods will not listen to you. One has to cleanse oneself before facing the gods," said Master Cao. Sometimes he bathes before conducting a ritual, but he does not engage in meditation, breathing, or yogic exercises. "These are for really professional priests, or for people who are engaged in 'the nurturing of life' [yangsheng, 養生]," he said, referring to the Daoist arts of self-cultivation and longevity. I asked him if he practiced sexual abstinence before conducting rituals. Master Cao replied that he was old now, having just turned sixty, which I took to imply that he seldom had sex with his wife anyway. Master Cao said that younger men generally avoid sex one or two days before they conduct a ritual, so they can concentrate their energies (qi) and be clean before the gods.

I took a risk and asked, "Do you really believe in the gods?" "Of course I believe! Why would I call down the gods and do these rituals if I did not believe in them? That would be a waste of time!" he reassured me. I pressed on: "When you are communicating with the gods, are you afraid?" "I'm a bit nervous sometimes, but never afraid," Master Cao replied. "The gods are good and beneficial [善良] to humankind. The demons [魔鬼] are scary, but you have to be very resolute with them and show them your power." In most rituals, Daoist priests communicate with the gods, but in others, such as exorcism rituals, they must also fight demons and command spirit armies to fight them.

Before he became a Daoist priest, Master Cao was already inducted into the local branch of the Communist Party. Local cadres thought he would make a good Party member given his literacy, but his interests were in training for the Daoist priesthood, not becoming a Party official. For many years, he quietly conducted Daoist rituals (although he was not ordained until much later). This was against Communist Party rules—no Party member can follow any religion; each Party member is sworn to atheism—and created a difficult situation not only for Master Cao but also for his local Party branch. The Party repeatedly asked him to stop, telling him that his Daoist activities were incompatible with Party membership. "I just kept going," said Master Cao. "I told them that I was trying to help the local community, looking after their well-being, asking the gods to protect the people." Finally he decided to quit the Party. Each time he made his request, however, the Party asked him to stay. Master Cao told them that he did not wish to besmirch the Party's reputation with his "superstitious" activities. "It's true that there is a deep contradiction here: the Party is about 'materialism,' and what I'm doing is 'idealism.' The Party stands for 'science,' and what I'm doing is 'religion.' These cannot go together," said Master Cao. In the end, Master Cao prevailed and was allowed to leave the Party. Knowing from my years in Beijing that quitting the Party is an affront and can get a person into political trouble, I asked Master Cao whether he had any trouble afterward. "No, there was no trouble," he replied. "It's not like I was expelled from the Party for wrongdoing, like having sexual relations with women, or for official corruption. It was I myself who asked to quit."

In 2007, Master Cao was ordained as a Zhengyi Daoist priest in a weeklong ordination ceremony held at Dragon Tiger Mountain (龍虎山), the Daoist religious center in Jiangxi Province. Over three hundred other Daoists from across the country were also ordained at that ceremony. Master Cao spent about 10,000 yuan of his own money for this ordination, paying for his expensive embroidered silk dragon robe (龍袍) and "court tablet" (*chao hu*, 朝笏), the long, narrow curved tablet that Daoist priests use to call down the gods and hold in front of their chest when addressing the gods during rituals, as if in the imperial court having an audience with the emperor. It also paid for travel and lodging, for tuition fees to prepare him for the ordination ritual, and for the big ritual and banquet that he had to provide on returning to Wenzhou. He put up a portrait of his "ancestral master" (祖師), the first Celestial Master, Zhang Daoling, in his home, and burned incense to him on the first and fifteenth day of each lunar month. At the end of each lunar year, on the thirtieth day of the twelfth month, he must send off Lord Zhang with a little ritual to Dragon Tiger Mountain, where Lord Zhang engages in meditation. Then, on the third day of the New Year, he must invite Lord Zhang back down into his home.

In 2010, I heard that Master Cao had become the head of his region's Daoist Association, a position of some influence that also made talking with foreigners more controversial. From then on, whenever I tried to meet with him, he would either not return my calls or not show up to the appointment.

The Artistically Talented but Economically Shrewd

I first met Master Tang in 2001 at a Daoist funeral for which he was the presiding priest. After attending two more of his ritual performances, I was smitten with the rituals' alluring music, impressive dramaturgy, and his beautiful, heartfelt singing voice. I arranged to go to his hometown in Pingyang County for an interview. Like most hearthside priests, Master Tang was married and had children; his older son owns and runs a store and factory, and his younger son graduated from the Shanghai Daoist Academy. Master Tang also pursued another line of work besides his ritual performances, a retail business selling traditional Chinese dried and canned foods (南貨) (lychees, peanuts, black funguses, spices, etc.). He proudly informed me that that very day, he had completed 10,000 yuan of business, and that his monthly income as a Daoist priest was over 8,000 yuan. He came from five generations of Daoist priests, and as a child he learned some rudimentary Daoist ritual forms from his father. After his father died, he was asked by Daoists in his town to follow in his father's footsteps, so he journeyed to Shanghai to apprentice for an important Daoist abbot there. This abbot was very selective about his apprentices, testing the two hundred contestants in scripture-chanting, singing, and playing Daoist music. That year the abbot chose to take on only three new apprentices, Master Tang and two Malaysians. After the training, Master Tang was ordained at Dragon Tiger Mountain in Jiangxi.

I was so entranced with Master Tang's beautiful rituals that I offered to look for funding to invite his ritual troupe to perform at the University of

California at Santa Barbara. This was 2004, when a trip to the United States was still rare and coveted by Chinese. However, instead of seizing this opportunity, Master Tang was reluctant. "How many Chinese people live in your city?" he asked. I replied that Santa Barbara did not have many Chinese, only about three hundred, not including university students. At that, he lost interest, because there would be few Chinese who would hire him to perform Daoist rituals. He said that he would rather visit Malaysia, where he could start a lucrative Daoist business catering to the ethnic Chinese community. Another Daoist priest who sometimes performs rituals with Master Tang said, "Actually, Master Tang is someone who is not very religious. He is good at accumulating money and at self-promotion. However, despite these weaknesses, his Daoist art and music are indeed superb."

The Timid "Transmitter of Intangible Cultural Heritage"

In September 2010, I visited Master Xiao, a twelfth-generation Zhengyi priest. His ancestor first settled in the Wenzhou area from Southern Fujian in the Ming dynasty to spread Daoist teachings, and their lineage genealogy is still intact to prove their heritage. Master Xiao's son is continuing the family tradition for the thirteenth generation. In the Qing dynasty, their ancestors thought that traveling to Dragon Tiger Mountain in Jiangxi for the ordination ceremony was too long and arduous, so they copied the ceremony and held their own ordinations in Wenzhou. In recent years, when Dragon Tiger Mountain revived their ordination ritual for Daoist initiates, the monastery managers discovered they had lost a crucial segment of their liturgy (失傳). Master Xiao's family still had these liturgical records in their possession, so they were able to provide it. Since his Daoist ancestors had historical stature, in 1986 the national United Front Office (統戰部), a Party organization that handles relations with non-Party people such as intellectuals, overseas Chinese, and religious leaders, even sent down a reporter to interview him.

Master Xiao is a rather timid man and repeatedly asked that his real name not be used. His family experience may have given rise to his nervousness. His grandfather and father were both ardent Daoists who devoted their lives to hand-copying Daoist texts for posterity, including liturgies for ritual performances, scriptures extolling different gods, morality books (善書) enjoining people to be kind, and texts on self-cultivation, Daoist medicine, and so on. I was shown some of the texts, which had beautiful calligraphy, and some were illustrated in color. Master Xiao's father was so dedicated to copying texts that in 1945, when the Japanese entered Wenzhou and people were fleeing, his father refused to follow, because he was in the middle of copying an important text. Their neighbor asked, "Aren't you coming with us? Don't you hear the gunfire?" His father replied confidently, "I will not die while I am copying the *Dao De Jing.*"

Somehow his family was able to keep their five thousand precious Daoist texts hidden through the Great Leap Forward. They even performed occasional secret rituals for relatives and friends at home after nine in the evening, without the music. However, disaster struck during the Cultural Revolution's campaign to "Struggle against the Private and Criticize Revisionism" (斗私批修). Sensing trouble brewing, his grandfather and father wrapped some of the texts in oilcloth and hid them in a container in the river. When they checked on the stash, they found that there had been water seepage, so they moved the texts into the walls of their house, between the wooden frame structure and the plaster. One day a piece of plaster fell, revealing the hidden trove to a passerby, who reported them to the local authorities. When they were first hauled in, they denied everything. Of course, a search of their home soon exposed them. Over half of their precious volumes were burned before their eyes, and they were even made to burn them themselves, to show their contrition. His father and grandfather were both paraded through the streets wearing dunce hats and locked up. Since their family had relatives who had fled to Taiwan, they had the added political stain of "overseas connections" on top of their crime of "pursuing superstition." After his father was finally released, the family sat together at home and cried about their lost sacred books.

This traumatic family experience is the reason Master Xiao did not wish to become a Daoist priest, nor for his son to follow. However, everyone pleaded with him not to allow his Daoist family line to "break" (斷絕). Despite his deep fears, he thought about his ancestors passing down this tradition for so many generations, and his father and grandfather suffering to keep it alive, and he reluctantly took up the priesthood. Over the years, he carefully selected ten apprentices to train and pass down the tradition.

Master Xiao still possesses five hundred remaining hand-copied Daoist texts, and he showed me a few. One precious volume that survived was a little book that his father presented to him when he was a boy, an illustrated account of what priests must do as preparations to conduct a ritual. It showed how a priest must envision certain gods, absorbing some of their energy to add to his own insufficient energy. Another image showed a stove and a pot boiling herbs for the priest to drink. Master Xiao explained the drawing of a phoenix giving birth to an egg that cracks, from which a baby pops out. The baby represents himself, and the birth of a new Daoist priest. Regarding the birth of Daoist priests, Master Xiao's daughter cannot inherit the line because she is female. When I asked her whether she would like to become a priest, she replied that, since tradition prohibited it, she had not given it much thought. Master Xiao's son interjected, "Even our clothes cannot be washed together with hers." Despite the passages in the *Dao De Jing* in praise of the feminine, and "returning to the womb," in Wenzhou Daoist practice there is a prejudice against women as polluting elements.

In 2010, Master Xiao was honored as a "Transmitter of Intangible Cultural Heritage" (非物質文化遺產傳承人). The petition to select him was filed by his county's Bureau of Culture and the Party Propaganda Department (宣傳部). The painful historical irony of this award was not lost on Master Xiao. His father and grandfather had been hounded and imprisoned for their religious dedication, but now he was receiving a prestigious award for doing the same thing!

DAOIST LITURGICAL TRADITION

I found Daoist rituals to be powerful and moving, stimulating all of my five senses. At the same time, the rich and complex system of symbols, images, sounds, and writings also made for a bewildering experience. The ritual sites were invariably festooned with a welter of colorful banners and hanging scrolls featuring images of gods and calligraphic writing in praise of the gods. Wooden tables were stacked on top of each other, sometimes three tables high. Empty chairs covered with red cloth served as the seats of the gods invited down to enjoy the ritual and the offerings. The priests' long, embroidered silk robes, with their brightly colored dragon and eight-trigram designs, glistened with reflected light. The bodies of the Daoist priests were in constant motion, whether going through the ritual pacing across the floor, ringing bells, making finger mudras, waving swords, or dancing and leaping across the ritual site. The ritual sponsors, who paid for these performances, wore dark brown robes and faithfully attended the priests. The air was filled with the acrid smoke of candles and incense, and the burning of written "petitions" or spirit money sent up to the gods. A musical troupe played traditional Chinese musical instruments in between the scriptural chanting of the priests, and the periodic loud clangs of drums and cymbals sometimes reached a crescendo.

Daoist rituals have many different appellations. Ordinary laypeople in Wenzhou simply call their performance "doing a Daoist ritual" (作道場) or "engaging in dharma activities" (作法事), revealing the conflation of Daoism and Buddhism in people's minds. Educated people might use the formal term "fasting and sacrifice ritual series" (*zhaijiao keyi*, 齋醮科儀). The "fasting" (齋)

refers to the fact that the priest is supposed to fast to cleanse himself before he appears in front of the gods. Daoist fasting includes abstaining from alcohol, meat, and foods like garlic and onions, as well as from sex for one or more days before the ritual. "Sacrifice" (*jiao*, 醮) refers to the food and incense offerings made to the gods. "Series" (科) refers to the orderly sequence of steps in a ritual performance (儀).

According to Master Kang in Lingxi Town, there are basically seven kinds of Daoist rituals commonly performed in Wenzhou:

> Rituals to help deceased souls in the afterlife, including funerals, called "transcending and crossing over rituals" (超度), and rituals for long deceased ancestors, called "rituals for accumulating merit" (功德). The objective of funerals is to quickly liberate the soul from Purgatory and send her on to the next life. In the ritual, the priest leads the relatives as they accompany the soul down to Purgatory and negotiate their way through the dangerous Underworld, appearing before the Ten Judges of Purgatory.
>
> Middle Yuan Ritual of Universal Salvation (*zhongyuan pudu*, 中元普度), which helps wandering "orphan souls" (*guhun*, 孤魂) attain liberation from their sins. These ghosts are people who died without leaving any descendants to make offerings to them, or people who died a sudden, violent, or unjust death. They bear a grudge and will take out their resentment against the living unless they are appeased with offerings and rituals.
>
> Ritual of Response for Wishes Granted (*huan yuan*, 還願). This ritual is offered in thanks when a person's prayers to the gods for help have been granted, or when a family wishes to fulfill an oath made to the gods. Two common occasions to give thanks are family prosperity or a child's success in major exams.
>
> Rituals to protect peace and security (保平安). There are at least four different types of rituals seeking blessings for a community, ranked according to who can sponsor or order them:
>
>> Great Ritual of the Encompassing Heaven (羅天大醮), to ask for blessings and protection for the whole country. In 1996, the White Cloud Daoist Temple in Beijing performed this great ritual lasting over ten days. Participating priests numbered in the hundreds and came from across China, Hong Kong, and Taiwan.
>>
>> Golden Registry Ritual Altar (金籙斋壇), to ask for the protection of a space as large as a province. Master Liu was preparing to perform

this ritual in March 2001, asking for the protection of Zhejiang and Fujian, when I interviewed him. Ninety Daoist priests from these two provinces were going to participate in this seven-day performance.

Jade Registry Ritual Altar (玉籙斎壇), a medium-scale ritual conducted in a major Daoist temple in Wenzhou over five days, to protect a county or town, and often funded by wealthy entrepreneurs.

Yellow Registry Ritual Altar (黃籙斎壇), a ritual to bless a local community or village. Generally, only a handful of priests are involved and it lasts only three days.

Rituals for Dispelling Disasters (遣災), held when there is social strife, a disease, or natural disaster. According to Master Kang, it has proven effective in averting typhoons, or in dealing with the aftermath of floods.

Ritual to Overcome the Yin and Protect the Yang (超陰護陽), an exorcistic ritual performed to heal sickness and expel demons. It promotes and extends life, allied with yang forces, while also helping to avoid death and to delay travel into the afterlife, associated with yin.

Ordination Ritual for new priests (授籙道場). After at least three years of study, a novice undergoes this two- to three-day ritual to become ordained as a Daoist priest and take a Daoist name (道號).

I showed this list of Daoist rituals to Master Ding, who added three more rituals commonly conducted in Wenzhou.

Opening the Light Ritual (開光典禮) or Thanking the Earth God (謝土). When a new Daoist temple is opened or new deity statues installed, the statue(s) must be activated, imbued with divine life, by inviting the gods to enter them. The priest dabs a brush infused with sacred water onto the eyes of each statue. This ceremony also thanks the site's local Earth God and asks him to protect the new temple.

Ritual to Celebrate Completion of a Lineage Genealogy (完譜). When a lineage updates their lineage genealogy, it will often celebrate with a Daoist ritual. Lineage genealogies trace their members' collective kinship inheritance, list the names of ancestors in each family line, and enter the names of new wives and offspring in each family. The ritual usually takes place in the ancestor hall, followed by collective feasting.

Rituals to Celebrate Birthdays (祝壽). Each Daoist temple features a different collection of gods and celebrates their birthdays according to the lunar calendar. The Jade Emperor's birthday falls on the ninth day of the first lunar month. Celebrations of the Three Officials fall on the fifteenth day of the first, seventh, and tenth months for Heaven, Water, and Earth Officials, respectively. Birthday celebrations for Goddess Guanyin fall on the nineteenth day of the third, sixth, and ninth lunar months. All Quanzhen Daoist temples celebrate the birthday of the founder of their sect, Ancestral Master Qiu (邱祖師). Recently Daoists have adapted to the needs of secular society, so families celebrating the fiftieth, sixtieth, seventieth, and eightieth birthdays of family elders may also hire Daoist priests.

A PHENOMENOLOGICAL ACCOUNT OF DAOIST RITUALS

As described above, Daoist rituals are complex and engrossing experiences, rich in sensory stimulation. They provide a stylized forum for communication between the human and divine world of gods and sometimes demons, with the priests serving as mediators. The presiding priest (高功), who leads the ceremony, assembles a team of Daoist priests, sometimes including Zhengyi and Quanzhen sects.

Daoist Ritual Spatialization

Daoist rituals pay special attention to the spatial design of the ritual site and the setting up of different altars (設壇). They create their own microcosmic ritual space inside a temple, which does not necessarily correspond to the physical directions marked by the geomagnetic compass but displays the four cardinal directions plus the center, in relation to each other. These five directions are marked by altars, tables stacked two or three high, and are said to correspond to the five elements: gold/metal (West); wood (East); water (North); fire (South); and earth (Center). There is also the distinction between the Inner, Center, and Outer Altars (內壇, 中壇, 外壇). The highest gods, such as the Three Pure Ones or a special god invoked for the ritual, are seated at the Inner Altar, which "sits to the North, facing the South" (坐北朝南), befitting all powerful rulers. The Outer Altar is formed by tables to the ritual south and facing the Inner Altar. This is often where the priests store their robes, the musicians play their instruments, and priests occasionally rest between sections

Figure 4.3. Daoist ritual layout in Great Sage Who Equals Heaven Temple in Lingxi Town, Cangnan County, 2008. Photo by the author.

of the ritual. Often there is tiered seating, arranged according to rank, for the gods who descend. The local low-ranking gods, like the Earth God, must be on hand to welcome the divine guests. "It's like when high-ranking officials from the central government in Beijing come down to visit. The local township official must be present to greet them," said an assistant to a Daoist priest. At the beginning of the ritual, there is usually a morning ritual to cleanse the site. The head priest takes a sprig from an evergreen tree and dips it into water fetched from a mountain spring, then scatters water around the site.

Recitation of Scriptures and Mantras

Depending on the occasion and which gods are invited down to the ritual site, a variety of Daoist scriptures are chanted or sung to music performed by a musical troupe. The scriptures are sung to please the gods and move them to respond to human requests or to help dissolve human sins. A scripture can be chanted by the head priest and his acolytes, or by a "penance troupe" (拜懺團), usually made up of ten or more women volunteers. By volunteering one's time to singing scriptures, one produces merit to make up for one's sins. The singing can be interspersed throughout the ritual, and sometimes the head priest leads the women troupe members on a ritual pacing expedition, weaving their steps around the ritual site. In their spare time, the women often practice their scriptural singing together. Popular scriptures include the Exquisite Scripture of the Jade Emperor for Imprinting on the Heart, the Great and Efficacious Scripture of Lord Thunder, the True Scripture of the Mysterious and Efficacious Northern Dipper on High That Prolongs Life, the Scripture of the Efficacious and Beautiful, and Precious Scripture of Wenchang on High for Dissolving and Transforming Misfortunes.[7] Throughout the ritual, the head priest occasionally pronounces mantras (咒) accompanied by hand gestures, or *mudras* (訣).

Breathing and Meditation of the Head Priest

The presiding Daoist priest(s) leading a ritual has an inordinate influence on the ritual's effectiveness: he must be a virtuous and sincere person who engages in self-cultivation (自我修養). Many Daoist rituals feature moments when the head priest pauses in silence to meditate, engage in a breathing exercise, or visualize images, called "preserving thoughts" (存想). The priest closes his eyes and may visualize the images of different gods; features of nature such as the sun, moon, and stars; his internal organs; or the "sacred fetus" inside himself. These silent moments are said to have just as much practical effects on the gods as the chanting and offerings made to them. Since the body is a microcosm of the cosmos, by moving his internal breath around the priest is also moving parts of the cosmos, and the gods to respond to his requests. Hence the saying "If the heart is sincere, then [the ritual] will be effective" (心誠則靈).

Master Xiao said that he only "exercises his *qi*" (練功) before important large rituals, for about fifteen minutes. During the ritual, he pauses and concentrates on his five organs and the millions of gods that inhabit his whole body, including the thirty thousand gods in the pores of his skin. His internal *qi* (氣) and the five elements in his body must "circulate smoothly" (*yao yunzhuan*). His "consciousness must attain a high level."[8] Thus, when he is performing a ritual, he feels he has transcended this world and has entered into Heaven (天堂). Sometimes he even feels as if he has been transported to the highest realm of Heaven, that of the Three Pure Ones.

Ritual Pacing and Dancing

Besides meditating in silence, Daoist priests also actively move around the ritual site in choreographed ritual steps or dance. The Steps of Yü (禹步) are said to have been first adopted by China's ancient sage-king, Yü, who saved the world from the Great Floods by damming the rivers. When Yü traveled to the South, he noticed a large bird perform a dance that made giant stones overturn. He copied these bird steps and developed them into an effective magical technology. The Steps of Yü belong to a corpus of Daoist pacing or ritual dance called "Stepping and Leaping through the Big Dipper" (*bugang tadou*, 步罡踏斗) (Zhang Zehong 2003). In many Daoist rituals, a large rug with a *taiji* (太極) symbol is placed on the floor, an image of the black-and-white yin-yang S-curve inside a circle, surrounded by a circle of eight trigrams, eight different combinations of broken and solid lines. As the priest meditates on the nine layers of Heaven, he paces across the cosmos, symbolized by the *taiji* rug on the floor. This stepping movement models him soaring through the heavens, flying through the Northern Dipper, and communing with the gods (與神溝通). The eight trigrams on the rug accord with the eight directions, and the yin-yang symbol shows the dark and bright forces that interact in the universe. Lagerwey suggests that each step by the priest on a trigram "activates the principles of the trigram and so summons their gods" (1987: 31). Here the Daoist priest is like a shaman who travels through the divine realms.

There are many forms of ritual pacing, sometimes performed by the head priest alone, sometimes together with his assistants and the women's "penance troupe." Besides the Steps of Yü, there are two kinds of pacing: a figure-eight form (八字型) and a four-corner square form (四方型). Both forms of pacing involve walking the S-curve found in a *taiji* symbol, which runs down the center of the square or figure-eight form.

Ritual Writing

Anyone who witnesses a Daoist ritual will be struck by the importance of writing. Paper or textile banners written with calligraphy brushes festoon the ritual site. Written petitions (章表) are an important feature of most Daoist rituals. These petitions are first read aloud to the gods, then sent up to them by burning in an urn, called "sending up the petition" (上表). These paper messages to the gods are collectively called "memorials" (*zouwen*, 奏文), a term used in imperial China to refer to written communications submitted to the emperor, or "letters and reports" (*shuwen*, 疏文). Daoist ritual petitions often list the names of the sponsors and donors for the ritual, the purpose of the ritual, names of family members who are making a request of the gods, and the place, year, date, and time of the ritual.[9]

In Daoist rituals, mysterious talismanic characters (*fu*, 符) are also very important. Talismanic writing differs from ordinary writing in that the characters have much more flourish and the meaning is hard to decipher. Rather

Figure 4.4. Daoist ritual pacing in Xuanling Daoist Temple, Longwan District, 1998. Photo by the author.

than a system of representation or communication in which the signifier refers to a signified or referent, talismans are like spells and incantations, producing results such as protecting a family from misfortune, bringing good luck, or exorcising a demon from a human body (Raz 2012). In Daoist rituals, besides ink and calligraphy brushes, talismans are also "written" with dry rice grains or incense ash onto the table altars. A hand grabs a fistful of rice or ash and allows a small amount to leak through the fingers onto the table, while the movement of the hand creates the character with a calligraphic flourish. These are temporary works of art: once this ritual segment is completed, the talisman is swept away.

Buddhist Religiosity

The Wheel of Life, Death, and Rebirth

如彼大雲、雨於一切卉木叢林、
及諸藥草如其種性, 具足蒙潤, 各
得生長。如來説法,...
究竟至於一切種智。其有眾生、
聞如來法, 若持讀誦, 如説修行,
所得功德... 眾生住於種種之
地, 唯有如來、如實見之, 明了無
礙... 如來知是一相一味之法, 所
謂解脱相、离相、滅相, 究竟涅
槃、常寂滅相, 終歸於空。佛知
是已, 觀眾生心欲、而将護之, 是
故不即為説一切種智...能知如來
随宜説法。

(The great cloud rains down on all grasses and trees, shrubs and forests, and medicinal herbs; and each, in accord with its nature and species, derives benefit from the moisture to grow. In the same way, the dharma preached by the Buddha . . . is absorbed by all different forms of intelligence. Whenever sentient beings hear the dharma, if they grasp it, read it, recite it, and act according to the teachings, then they will gain merit. . . . The living beings dwell on a variety of different terrains, but only the Buddha sees them for what they are and understands them clearly and without obstruction. . . . The Buddha knows the appropriate image and flavor of the dharma [to offer for each], such as the message of deliverance, the message of disenchantment, the message of extinction, the message of ultimate nirvana, of eternally quiescent nirvana, all finally reducing itself to emptiness. The Buddha, knowing this, observes the heart's desire of each being, and guides them protectively. For this reason, he does not preach a single knowledge for all beings. . . . The Buddha preaches the dharma in accord with what is most appropriate [for each being].)

—(妙法蓮華經) [Lotus Sutra]

The Lotus Sutra compares the Buddha's teachings to the monsoon rains, which fall down equally on a multitude of different life-forms and nourish them.[1] The Buddha, in his infinite wisdom, is able to diversify and calibrate his teachings according to the different levels and situations of understanding and thereby stimulate their spiritual growth and liberation. In this chapter, we will see differences in Buddhist practice and understanding in Wenzhou, between the common people, the clergy, educated laypeople, and officialdom, where Buddhism is making surprising inroads today.

The Lotus Sutra was a major scripture in Mahayana Buddhism, composed as early as the first or second century CE in India, and inspired the Tiantai Sect (天台宗) in China (Buswell and Lopez 2014: 729). The Tiantai Mountains are located only three hundred kilometers northwest of Wenzhou in Zhejiang Province, so the Tiantai Sect has exerted a strong influence in Wenzhou. The Lotus Sutra inspired devotional practices, such as memorizing, reciting, copying, and explicating it, that earn merit and enable miracles for the devout. Today in Wenzhou, public chanting or singing of Buddhist sutras and dharanis, short mnemonic passages, continues in homes and temples. In past Chinese Buddhist Studies, the emphasis has been on the study of Buddhist scriptural texts and history. This chapter on Buddhism in Wenzhou joins a recent wave of writings on the living practices of Buddhism in contemporary Chinese societies (Fisher 2014; J. C. Huang 2009; Ji, Campos, and Wang 2016).

THE *LONGUE DURÉE*:
THE HISTORY AND SECTS OF BUDDHISM IN WENZHOU

Buddhism made its way into China during the Han dynasty, in the second century CE, and arrived in Wenzhou during the Western and Eastern Jin dynasties (265–420 CE) (Anonymous 2009; Zhang Zhichen 1998: 459–465). During the Song dynasty, the monastic complex Yong Quan Chan Buddhist Temple on Mei Peak (梅峰湧泉禪寺) in Jinshan Township, Cangnan County, was one of two hundred recorded Buddhist temples in China, boasting over a thousand monks and eight hundred nuns. On my 2004 visit, I found that local residents had mounted an impressive drive to rebuild its past greatness. The scale of public Buddhist gatherings in Song dynasty Wenzhou could be quite impressive: Pure Land rituals and lectures by famed monks of the Chan and Regulations sects frequently gathered up to ten thousand people (Lin S. 2003: 59).

Historically, four sects of Buddhism were most active in Wenzhou: the Tiantai, Regulations, Chan, and Pure Land Sects. The Tiantai Sect (天台宗) was founded in the sixth century CE by the monk Zhi Yi (智顗, 538–597) (Ch'en 1964: 303–313; Yang Cengwen 1999: 79–84). During the Tang dynasty, the sect spread to Japan, and today it is known as the Tendai School of Japanese Buddhism. After the imperial court destruction of Buddhism in China in 845 CE, the Tiantai sect never fully recovered, leaving the Chan Sect (禪宗) and Pure Land Sect (淨土宗) as the main active ones in Wenzhou from the Song dynasty to the present. The smaller Sect of Regulations (律宗) emphasized regulations for living an ascetic monastic life. The famous monk and calligrapher Master

Hong Yi (弘一法師, aka 李叔同, 1880–1942 CE), who spent several summer retreats in Wenzhou, rekindled interest in this austere sect, but its influence was not strong.

The word *chan* (禪) in Chan Buddhism is the Chinese translation of the Sanskrit term *dhyana,* meaning "methods or states of meditation," in which the practitioner achieves inner stillness, emptying the mind of thought by concentrating on the breath or an object (Ch'en 1964: 350–364). Chan teaches that ultimate reality cannot be expressed through language or conscious thought and is only attainable through meditation, intuition, or spontaneous enlightenment. Chan Buddhism is thought to have been founded by a Persian monk named Bodhidharma who arrived in China in the fifth or sixth century CE. Chan was a reaction against the scholastic, metaphysical speculations of other Buddhist schools. Its iconoclastic dismissal of buddhas and bodhisattvas, book learning, and ritual life was radical for its time. Chan Buddhism also spread to Japan, becoming what the world knows as "Zen." Although most Wenzhou Buddhist temples today belong to the Chan sect, few espouse the original Chan teachings. Over the centuries, in accommodating the multitude of ordinary lay followers, Chan temples have adopted features of the Pure Land Sect, especially in the twentieth century.

Chinese Pure Land Buddhism emerged in the fourth century CE. Its two main inspirational scriptures, the Pure Land Sutra (阿彌陀經) and Seeing the Buddha of Infinite Light Sutra (觀無量壽經), are chanted repeatedly by its followers. The emphasis is on reaching the "Pure Land" (淨土) or "Western Paradise" (西方極樂世界), a peaceful and happy land of fragrant flowers, precious jewels, running streams, and pleasant music, inhabited by gods and humans, with none of the lower forms of existence (animals, ghosts, creatures of hell). It is presided over by the Buddha Amitabha (阿彌陀佛), or "Buddha of Infinite Light," whose love for all sentient beings propels him to help the weak and needy reach this paradise. If one possesses an unyielding faith in the Buddha Amitabha, performs meritorious deeds, and utters his name repeatedly ("O-mi-to-fo"), then one gains salvation and entry into the Pure Land.

Pure Land followers also place faith in the Bodhisattva Avalokitesvara or Guanyin (觀世音菩薩), a central figure who possesses infinite compassion and mercy (慈悲) toward the suffering of others and is always ready to give assistance. In China, Guanyin's image underwent a gender transformation around the tenth or eleventh century, when depictions changed from the male figure of Indian Buddhism to a female figure, full of maternal kindness (Sangren 1983; Yü 2001). The Pure Land Sect has exerted a vast popular appeal that has allowed it to flourish into the modern age—to the extent that actual practice in

Wenzhou's Chan temples today more closely resembles Pure Land, with Buddha images and sutra-chanting.

During the Republican era (1911–1948), Wenzhou experienced a minor revitalization of Buddhism as the winds of reform blew through the area. There was a brief proliferation of grassroots lay Buddhist societies, called "forests of reside-at-home lay Buddhists" (*jushilin*, 居士林), whose members got together to chant sutras, discuss Buddhist teachings, or perform charitable deeds (Lin S. 2003). However, this was cut short by the difficulties of life during wartime. The 1950s saw Buddhist temples and monasteries converted to other uses and a large segment of the clergy forced to return to lay life. This sudden contraction of Buddhist life was only a prelude to the terrible experiences of the Cultural Revolution (1966–1976), when countless Buddhist properties were destroyed and monks and nuns terrorized, beaten, forcibly laicized, and imprisoned. I heard stories of Buddhist monks and nuns forced to eat meat or have their teeth knocked out, or forced to marry and have children. Buddhist scriptures and statuary were burned as firewood, and Buddhist rituals and festivals were prohibited. The 1,542 registered Buddhist monks and nuns in Wenzhou in 1990 had still not surpassed the number recorded in 1949, which was 2,283. Similarly, while in 1949 there were 987 registered Buddhist temples in Wenzhou, in 1990 there were still only 978 (Zhang Zhichen 1998: 461). However, after two decades of unprecedented economic prosperity from 1990 to 2010, the number of registered Buddhist temples in Wenzhou in 2010 had increased to 1,700 temples, a 74 percent jump over 1990.

RECENT BUDDHIST DEVELOPMENT IN WENZHOU

Abbot Hong Guang (虹光方丈, Rainbow Light) has been in charge of the Xianyan Temple (仙岩禪寺) since 2001.[2] He belongs to a new generation of well-educated Buddhist monks who are changing the face of Buddhism across China. A native of Wenzhou, he graduated from Minnan Buddhist Academy (閩南佛學院) in Xiamen, Fujian, and received an MA in philosophy from Xiamen University in 1998. He also attended the prestigious Beijing University to study for an MA in Buddhist philosophy, but left because he could not pass the required English examination. Another problem was that Beijing University asked the monks to take off their saffron robes when attending classes. All six of the Buddhist monks enrolled there at that time refused.

Abbot Hong Guang's education at the Minnan Buddhist Academy means that he is greatly influenced by the modern reformer monk Taixu (太虛, 1890–1947). The academy was established in 1925, and Taixu became its director in

1927. During the Republican era, Taixu's reformed Buddhism, along with his student Yin Shun's (印順, 1906–2005) notion of "humanistic this-worldly Buddhism" (人間佛教), sought to counterbalance Buddhism's otherworldly orientation with a new engagement with social problems in *this* life. Instead of the Buddhist clergy's traditional preoccupation with self-cultivation in monastic cells, Taixu sought their active participation in addressing contemporary social needs and alleviating human suffering. He also promoted participation by lay Buddhists and sought to rid Buddhism of its many "superstitious" elements (Pittman 2001; Welch 1968). Various factors, including the ravages of war, the conservatism of Buddhist clergy, and the Communist Revolution, delayed the implementation of Taixu's ideas in Mainland China until recently. Master Hong Guang has been at the forefront of putting Taixu's ideas into social action in Wenzhou. As chapter 6 shows, he founded his own Nalanda Buddhist Academy in 2007, and the Nalanda Charitable Foundation in 2009, as well as a host of other initiatives that have made Xianyan Temple a leader in Buddhist religious innovation in Wenzhou.

In a lecture that Abbot Hong Guang gave when I invited him to visit the University of California at Santa Barbara in November 2011, he divided the post-Mao Buddhist revival in Wenzhou into three periods. Later, when I talked with him in 2016, he added a fourth period. The dates on the periods overlap and are not meant to be precise:

1. Period of initial restoration (1983–1995)
2. Period of rapid temple construction (1996–2005)
3. Beginning of the "future era of Buddhism" (佛教的未來, 2006–present)
4. Period of reconstructing Buddhist philosophy (2014–present)

The first period began with Document 19 (Zhonggong Zhongyang Wenxian Yanjiushi 1995b), promulgated in 1982 by the Central Committee of the Chinese Communist Party, which admitted that the Party had made "Leftist errors" in the Cultural Revolution and called for returning sites of worship to their congregations. Although Document 19 was an important Party directive, local governments were initially not eager to implement it, so Buddhist clergy and lay followers had to repeatedly petition local authorities to move people and work units out from the temples they were occupying. This was a period of struggle to win back religious rights and properties, but people remained nervous about a reversion to antireligious terror. The main form of Buddhist practice in this period was the ritual-oriented peasant popular Buddhism, called "worshipping gods and chanting scriptures" (拜經懺), that emphasizes the ritualistic effects of chanting on health, prosperity, and good fortune rather than understanding of the religious doctrines (道理) of the scriptures. In fact, the line between Buddhism and popular religion was fuzzy, with worshippers generally treating the Buddhas and Bodhisattvas like popular deities who granted requests in exchange for offerings.

At that time, most of the Buddhist "monks" or "nuns" I encountered were not properly ordained; they were laypeople who donned Buddhist robes and resided in a local temple as caretakers. Few Buddhist temples dared disseminate Buddhist teachings or educate society. Nor were they equipped to do so, given their lack of Buddhist scriptural education and a social vision for their historical time. Buddhist monks and nuns served their local communities by conducting rituals and chanting sutras for funerals and healing of the sick.

The second period saw economic prosperity and the rapid construction or restoration of Buddhist temples and monasteries in Wenzhou (and of sites related to Daoism, Catholicism, and other religions). Although the central government had decreed in 1980 that religious properties and sites seized during the Maoist era must be returned to their religious constituencies (Zhonggong Zhongyang Wenxian Yanjiushi 1995a), implementation of this policy took time, and local governments did not immediately give out religious building permits regularly. Nearly all villages, led by their Old People's Associations, gathered donations to construct temples and ancestor halls. Newly rich entrepreneurs led the way with the most generous donations. Also during this period, many temples began to revive rudimentary "sutra explanation festivals" (講經法會) and "Buddhist study classes" (佛教培訓班) to educate the local people in vernacular language about the teachings of different sutras (Pan Yirong 2000: 65–79). I can personally testify that this period indeed saw a frenzy of temple-building: every time I returned to Wenzhou, I saw new temples being constructed.

The third period, according to Abbot Hong Guang, reveals the sprouts of what Buddhism will look like in Wenzhou's future. A new kind of Buddhism emerged at this time, with the key features of "culture," "education," and "self-cultivation Buddhism" (修持佛教). This new, educated Buddhism emphasizes self-cultivation and meditation and the teaching and dissemination of Buddhist scriptures and doctrines. Some of the larger and more innovative Buddhist temples in Wenzhou started to move away from the typical activities of grassroots Buddhist temples, that is, providing ritual services such as funerals and festivals to their lay communities.

These larger temples, headed by abbots with degrees from Buddhist academies, began engaging in public charity and fund-raising activities, Buddhist

Figure 5.1. Monks and lay women chanting sutras during the water and land festival in Xiangyun Buddhist Temple, Lingxi Town, Cangnan County, 2005. Photo by the author.

educational and sutra-studying programs, animal protection and environmentalist activities, and group meditation sessions. Economic prosperity and generous donations relieved the pressure on larger temples' monks and nuns to perform so many rituals for the lay public. Instead, these temples have quietly taken on the mission of educating the public about Buddhist ethics and self-cultivation methods. They organize lectures by monks to explain and analyze Buddhist scriptures, translating them into concepts that people can use for self-improvement and charity. Some educated monks even started to provide Buddhist therapy or counseling for people struggling with modern life's cruel and painful challenges, such as business failures, domestic dysfunctions, juvenile delinquency, drug abuse, suicidal despair, and so forth.

The fourth period presages increasing sophistication in Buddhist philosophy and interpretation of the vast collection of Chinese Buddhist scriptures. Lectures by Buddhist Studies scholars and academic monks were organized by temples for semipublic audiences of clergy and laypeople. This period is also when Buddhism fully embraces the internet and social media like WeChat (微信), since television remains a restricted terrain for Buddhist proselytizing. Whereas in earlier decades Buddhist sermons were disseminated via cassette tapes or printed materials, then CDs and DVDs, now video sermons of famous Buddhist monks based in China, Taiwan, Malaysia, and Australia are readily available on the Chinese internet, and their scriptural interpretations can be read on social media. This is the period when maverick monks pushing their own interpretations of Buddhist philosophy vie with each other. They find an audience in the increasingly educated lay public emerging in Wenzhou. This is also the period when Buddhist philosophical sects thought to be "extinct," such as the Tiantai, Regulations, and Huayan, have sprung back to life. The abbot of Miaoguo Buddhist Temple (妙果寺), Master Dazhao (達照法師), who studied at the Beijing Buddhist Academy, bills himself as a forty-seventh-generation transmitter of the Tiantai Sect. He gives sermons, publishes on Buddhist philosophy, and teaches Yongjia Chan self-cultivation techniques. During my 2016 visit, Abbot Hong Guang announced that he was deep in studying the entire Buddhist canon and seemed to be preparing to engage with Buddhist philosophy himself.

MERIT, DEBT, AND THE WHEEL: POPULAR BUDDHISM

In the first period of Buddhist revival in Wenzhou (1983–1995), popular Buddhism was virtually the only kind of Buddhism. It was blended with popular religion and Daoist culture and shared with them an emphasis on community and life-cycle rituals. Religious persecutions of the Mao years left few properly ordained monks, nuns, or educated Buddhist clergy. A new occupational group of lay Buddhist ritualists emerged to meet the ritual needs of local communities. Some of them came from Buddhist families; others were poor or disabled, or lacked the skills or desire to go into business.

In February 2001, in the countryside of Shuitou Town in Pingyang County, I observed a Buddho-Daoist funeral, during which the ritualists wore Daoist robes in the first half and Buddhist robes in the second. During a break in the funeral, Tang Longxi, one of the Buddhist ritual performers, said that while some monks are devout, many are like himself—they only "half-believe" in the Buddhas and mainly want to make a living performing rituals for the community. In some smaller Buddhist temples, things are "not very proper" (*bu tai zhenggui*), meaning that the monks do not observe the Regulations (戒律) of monastic life. Some secretly eat meat; others get married and continue living in the temple, while quietly visiting their families. He thought this practice started outside Wenzhou: he believed that the monks at historic Buddhist temples could not speak English or connect with foreign tourists, so the government hired college students to play the part. These "monks" could have wives, earned salaries, and were given houses.

A lay Buddhist volunteer told me that he thinks about 40–50 percent of the monks in his county were secretly married and that they are called "wild monks" (野和尚). I do not know how much to believe this astonishing figure, but he also said that nuns tended to stay celibate. He told me that, after visiting Buddhist temples in Japan, the abbot of a Buddhist temple in Wenzhou was shocked to learn that Japanese monks today no longer have to observe celibacy. After he returned to Wenzhou, the abbot did not dare report it to his own monks, because he feared they might all demand an end to celibacy too.

In September 2008, I met with Master Clear Water (清水法師, Qing Shui), a middle-aged nun who resided with six other nuns in a small nunnery (庵) perched precariously on the side of a mountain in Pingyang County. The temple featured a spectacular vista of the valley below, and in the distance, one could follow the meandering line of the new elevated railway that connected the cities of Wenzhou and Fuzhou in Fujian. Inside the temple, it was dark and grungy, and the furnishings were spartan. I chatted with Master Qing Shui over two days in the small kitchen and dining room, sitting on crude wooden benches, with several cats meowing underfoot.

As a child, Master Qing Shui did not receive much education. She followed her parents around the Wenzhou countryside as they visited Buddhist temples to do tailoring work for monks and nuns. She observed how quiet and tranquil life was in Buddhist temples, in contrast with the "chaos" (*luan*) and daily suffering outside. She turned eighteen during the Cultural Revolution, but she started offering incense and praying at temples regularly. In 1980, at age twenty-four, she had her head shaved at an ordination ceremony in Wutaishan (五台山), a famous Buddhist site in Shanxi Province. She traveled there by bus, together with a group of Wenzhou women with a similar resolve to become nuns. After returning to Wenzhou, she constantly hid from officials, who often checked temples to make sure that no one secretly harbored excess clerics.

There are five Buddhist Prohibitions (五戒), Master Qing Shui lectured me: "The Buddha forbids us to kill [殺], to rob [盜], to be sexually licentious [淫], to be arrogant and greedy with ambition [妄], and to indulge in alcohol [酒]." There are hundreds of prohibitions for monks and nuns; they must memorize all the Buddhist regulations, which are "just like the laws of the Chinese Communist Party." She gave one example of how assiduously they adhere to rules of monastic life. The money from donors must be used exactly according to the donors' intentions: if the money was intended for buying incense and candles to light up the Buddhas, the nuns cannot dip into it for daily subsistence. If nuns from other temples visit, the nuns must feed the guests out of money saved from their own subsistence allowance.

Karma, Merit, and Debt

The axis of Buddhist teachings, Master Qing Shui lectured, is the endless wheel of "transmigration" or "reincarnation" (samsara, 輪迴)—of birth, suffering, death, and rebirth:

> In the world today, we have smart people and dumb people; we have people who are very fortunate and get rich, and those who are poor, with bad fortunes. Why is this? This is all due to a person's past lives: did they act honorably in past lives, or did they behave badly? They will earn their just rewards in their next life. If you commit the worst crimes, you will end up suffering the tortures of hell.

A person's reincarnation after death depends on one's accumulation of karma, which in Chinese is literally "cause-and-effect repayment and response" (因果報應 or 因緣). The term "karma" refers to one's actions that will have consequences in the future lives. In turn, one's current situation results from actions in a previous life. All sentient beings are caught in the endless wheel, until one is able through selfless acts and intensive self-cultivation (修行) to gain enlightenment (覺悟, 悟道, 開悟), and transcend or escape (解脫) from this vicious cycle.

Related to the idea of karma is the popular Buddhist notion of "merit" (功德), which is quantifiable through a point system of accumulating merit and offsetting demerits (Brokaw 1991). By helping others, giving alms, chanting scriptures, donating money or labor for Buddhist temple construction, and other activities, one can shore up merit for a better rebirth. Merit accumulation can also take the form of repeatedly uttering Buddha Amitabha's name (阿彌陀佛, "O-mi-to-fo!"), or chanting scriptures. Merit and demerit points are supernaturally recorded and will be accounted for on one's death, when the soul travels down to the Buddhist Purgatory (地獄) and appears before the Ten Judges. The balance sheet of one's merits and demerits will determine what awaits in the next life. Here the notions of "sin" (罪), "merit" (功德), "debt" (債), and "repayment of debt" (還債) are interrelated in popular belief. The more one sins, the more one becomes indebted; the more merit one accumulates before death, the easier it is to repay one's sins, and thus, the better one's rebirth in the next life. This notion of indebtedness in the wheel of life and death is encapsulated in a common saying in Wenzhou:

冤要解脱, 不能接

One must unburden ourselves from our [past] offenses and debts;

They should not be allowed to be inherited [into the next life].

As a lay Buddhist woman explained to me, "Whether it's monetary or social debts, one accumulates these in a lifetime, and they can also be carried over from one lifetime to the next. So we should try to dissolve these debts by doing good deeds, so as to prevent these debts from haunting our future lives." These interrelated Buddhist notions are also embedded in the folk logic and ethics of popular religion and popular Daoism. This religious logic also interpenetrates with Wenzhou's famous entrepreneurial business logic. If entrepreneurs rely on unethical practices to get ahead in money-making, they will feel guilty and repentant and will fear that their pool of merit has been reduced. Thus, they must repent, do good deeds, or make donations to temples in order to accumulate merit again.

Wenzhou entrepreneurs know that material wealth must often be converted into spiritual merit, as an investment in one's own or family member's afterlife. Besides doing good deeds and donating voluntary labor, one can also purchase merit, and it can be transferred to another person: one can make donations to temples or charities, or hire monks and nuns to chant sutras in order to transfer merit to a sick or deceased family member. As one Buddhist monk told me, when Buddhist temples reach out to businesspeople for donations, they avoid the word "sponsor" (贊助), for that is the secular language of officialdom (官話), and entrepreneurs may feel unpleasantly pressured, as if the state were demanding some sort of tax. Instead, the Buddhist community employs phrases like "erecting merit" or "leaving merit" (立功德; 留下功德) to appeal to entrepreneurs' desire to accumulate merit for their next life by giving away a portion of their material wealth. Since "merit" here has the double entendre of "legacy," they are also suggesting that such donations will leave a legacy for posterity. "Even if the entrepreneur is not Buddhist, the notion of merit will appeal to him, because he is used to thinking in terms of investing [投資] in something and getting something in return, or incurring debts and repaying loans [還債]," said the monk. "It's the same logic in business as well as in Buddhism." We will further explore this parallelism or blurring of religious and economic logic in what I call Wenzhou's "ritual economy" in chapter 10.

In January 2012, I spoke with Mr. Bai, a volunteer worker (義工) who was donating his time and labor to construct a new Buddhist temple, the Forever Prosperous Temple (永福寺) in the Huagai Mountains (華盖山). During the week, he is an entrepreneur, with a busy life in the porcelain tile business. That Sunday afternoon there were six volunteers, all engaged in the heavy labor of digging in the hard earth to lay the foundation of the temple's main hall. Mr. Bai told me that if he had stayed at home, he would be carousing with friends, and later he would regret eating and drinking too much. So he was happy to come here into the fresh mountain air and help construct the temple. He used to be someone who only "worshipped the Buddha and burned incense" (拜佛燒香), meaning that he only beseeched the Buddha for favors, in exchange for offerings. Most people in Wenzhou do not understand Buddhist teachings, said Mr. Bai, but only go before the Buddhas to "beg for good fortune and wealth" (求福, 求財). Only two years ago, he did not know the difference between a deity temple and a Buddhist temple. Then he started listening to sermons given by Buddhist monks. In recent years many entrepreneurs like himself have started studying Buddhist teachings (學佛). According to his observations, one difference that conversion to Buddhism makes in entrepreneurs is that they no longer pursue profit with such a vengeance. They will still make money, but they will avoid business practices of questionable ethics. In their personal expenditures too, he noted, they reflect more deeply on how best to spend their money. Before they came to Buddhism, they would go gambling and banqueting, or to a KTV outfit and sing karaoke, or imbibe alcohol in a bar, or go take a sauna (implying sexual services).[3] After studying Buddhism, said Mr. Bai, men avoid these sinful places, live more frugally, and donate money to temples.

Death, Funerals, and Purgatory

As a Buddhist nun, Master Qing Shui has personally presided over hundreds of last rites. Buddhists are often called to preside over that crucial period before sick patients breathe their last breath, called "approaching the end" (*linzhong*, 臨終). Says Master Qing Shui:

> Those approaching death are sick and weak, their breath is feeble. No one should cry out loudly or shake them. It is best to keep them undisturbed, so they can leave peacefully. . . . When we get to the bedside, our chanting helps keep them focused. Their last days are when their creditors [冤情 債主] will appear, demanding payment and retribution for past wrongs. People can carry their debts over several past lives. These creditors greatly disturb those who should be preparing to leave this world at peace with themselves. If thoughts of debts and past conflicts keep bothering them, it will give them pain and anger, which will derail them. . . . We need to persuade the dying not to cling on to life [*buyao you qiangua*], but to accept their fate and allotted time, and depart this world peacefully. . . . Otherwise, their creditors might seize the opportunity to drag the deceased down into one of the lowest paths of the six reincarnations.
>
> Before death, you can already feel their breath is cold, like refrigerator air! After the person breathes their last breath, you should keep chanting quietly. Do not move or touch the body, because the soul has not completely left the body. Dead people have different parts of the body still warm and soft after death—this shows that the soul is still residing there. Buddhists believe that you should keep the body still for at least twenty-four hours after death, and keep on chanting until the body is cold and hard.

Master Qing Shui was happy that she could personally preside over the last breaths of both her parents. "This is the greatest act of filiality [大孝] a person can perform," she declared proudly, "to chant sutras for your dying parent, to keep their minds focused from distractions and pain." Despite being a Buddhist nun who has "left the home" (出家) and entered a monastery, she still subscribes to the Confucian ethics of gratitude and care for one's parents.

Before Buddhism's entry into China, the Chinese did not have a developed notion of the afterlife (the Yin World, 陰界). Stephen Teiser (1994) has shown how Buddhism brought in elaborate imageries of Purgatory and Hell, "underground prisons" in Chinese (地獄). Purgatory is the transitional place that the soul must traverse after death, before it is reborn into a new life-form, while Hell is a permanent space of torture for those who committed heinous sins. After death, the soul appears before the judges of the Ten Courts of Purgatory (十殿閻王), who have records of their merits and demerits. The sentences meted out to sinners are gruesome and violent: there are bodies stretched on the rack, dipped into boiling vats of oil, put to the torch, flayed of their skin, stabbed repeatedly, or disemboweled. The prisoners in Purgatory are guarded by grotesque-looking wardens, some with animal heads. Chief among them is the dreaded blue-faced Wu Chang, an Asura or malicious god who drags the souls before the Ten Judges. However, even those wretches who are consigned to the lowest level of Hell can pray for mercy to Bodhisattva Kitsigarbha (*dizang pusa*, 地藏菩薩), who pledged to help those trapped in the dark Underworld. In 2004, a Buddhist ritual performer assured me that most of the ordinary peasants and townspeople in attendance did indeed believe in the Ten Courts of Purgatory. When I asked whether the ritual performers and musicians also believed in Purgatory, he sighed: "This question is very complex; it is really hard to say."

The Yulanpen Festival (盂蘭盆節; Sanskrit, *Ullambana*), on the fifteenth day of the seventh lunar month, in the summer, reminds people to have compassion for the suffering of souls in Purgatory and Hell. In popular religion, it is called the Ghost Festival (鬼節), when hungry ghosts descend to earth and prowl around, and the living offer them food, either out of compassion or to placate them. In the Buddhist *Yulanpen Sutra*, Mulian, a disciple of Sakyamuni, saw that his deceased mother had transmigrated into a hungry ghost, the fifth form of reincarnation (Teiser 1988; Yang Cengwen 1999: 215–217). Unable to swallow any food, she was always hungry and thirsty. Anguished to see his mother suffer, Mulian journeyed down to Hell to liberate her. The Buddha told Mulian that if people placed food donations in Yulan basins for the monks and nuns, then their ancestors would be released from their suffering as hungry ghosts. I encountered a vivid Yulanpen Festival event in the walled fortress town of Jinshan in Cangnan County one evening in 2004. Myriad candle lights were set on lotus-shaped paper and floated on the town moat, lighting the way for the hungry ghosts.

A common way for family members to help their deceased on her journey through Purgatory is to burn paper spirit money. The deceased can use the money to ingratiate herself with the Ten Judges, who may commute her sentences. Serious Buddhists reject the efficacy of spirit money. According to Master Qing Shui,

> Burning spirit money for the dead is not Buddhist, it's a folk custom [民間風俗]. For Buddhists, the only way one can really release oneself from

past debts is through invoking the Buddha, chanting sutras, and doing a funeral ritual to release the soul from purgatory [念佛, 念經, 超度]. . . . Spirit money should only be offered to the gods, that's where it is effective [靈]. It's no use burning it for dead people.

Despite misgivings about spirit money, many Buddhist temples accommodate this popular practice.

The Six Paths of Reincarnation (六道輪回)

"Most people cannot escape the endless wheel of birth, suffering, and rebirth," Master Qing Shui continued. After each death, one is reborn into one of the Six Paths of Reincarnations, which are ranked from the highest to the lowest forms of sentient beings:

1. Way of Heaven (天道)—the gods inhabit Heaven, but even they have desires, so they have not escaped the endless wheel; they are still subject to reincarnation and can be reborn into a lower path
2. Way of Asuras (阿修羅道)—the world inhabited by giant malicious gods (*asuras*) who "enjoy heavenly powers, yet are devoid of the virtues and grace of heavenly beings" (有天之福，無天之德); they have been driven out of Heaven on account of their fighting and aggression
3. Way of Human Beings (人道)—the human world, which is full of suffering but offers the chance to redeem oneself and attain a better next life through good deeds and self-cultivation
4. Way of Beasts (畜牲道)—the more lowly world of animals and insects that often suffer at the hands of humans, as their beasts of burden, food, or captives
5. Way of Hungry Ghosts (餓鬼道)—the netherworld of desperate souls who wander around in search of anything to satiate their thirst and hunger, because they have no living descendants who offer sacrifices to them
6. Way of Hell (地獄道)—this is the lowest form of existence, as a tortured soul trapped in Hell, subject to horrific punishments

According to Master Qing Shui, if one lived an extraordinary life and repeatedly did good deeds, after death, one could be reborn into a higher level of the Six Paths of Reincarnation. After many lifetimes of effort, one might escape this endless wheel and enter the Western Paradise (西方極樂世界) forever.

In 2004, I interviewed Mr. Dong, who traveled the countryside with a ritual performance troupe of musicians and Daoist and Buddhist ritualists.

A soft-spoken man in his late forties, his demeanor was humble and intro-spective. His father was a Buddhist monk who was imprisoned by the People's Liberation Army and forced to get married. Dong was born inside a Buddhist temple, where he grew up. He was different from other children: he liked to chant sutras with old women in secret. In 1985, he was ordained a Buddhist monk in a local ritual that may not be recognized today. In 1989, he spent one year living as a hermit in a mountain cave, growing his own food. Later he gave up monastic life, got married, and had children. To support his family, he learned his ritual trade from a talented Daoist ritual performer.

For Mr. Dong, Buddhism teaches two main principles that are very valu-able for humanity: the "capacity for responding to tragedy and suffering" (慈悲), and that all people are equal (平等), regardless of birth, occupation, and social status. He observed: "Actually, Buddhism already implemented the ideals of Communism long ago. Monks in a Buddhist monastic community are equal: they eat together, and eat the same things; they are all sworn to give up individual desires. They put all their money into a common pot and share it together." Mr. Dong thought there was no reason for the Communist Party to turn against Buddhism, when Buddhism already shared the same collective and egalitarian ideals.

THE RESTORATION OF THE TAIPING BUDDHIST TEMPLE (太平寺)

Taiping Buddhist Temple, built in 942 CE, was undergoing restoration when I visited it in July 2004. We were guided through the temple grounds by Ab-bess Wan Ru (萬如方丈), who looked to be in her late forties. Historically, this temple was one of Wenzhou City's four major Buddhist temples of the Ming and Qing dynasties—the others being Miaoguo Temple (妙果寺), Huguo Temple (護國寺), and Jiangxin Temple (江心寺). Taiping Temple is one of Wenzhou's large innovative temples, and the plan was to restore it as both a temple open to the public and as a monastic residence for nuns.

The restoration of Taiping Temple actually received state support, by Wenzhou City's mayor, Qian Xingzhong (錢興中), a keen supporter of Bud-dhism who is said to have wanted to leave a Buddhist legacy. In 1949, the Wen-zhou District Military Garrison had taken over the Taiping Temple site and damaged the historical structures, tearing down some temple halls, building barracks for troops, and converting parts of the temple into an automotive and weapons repair shop. Persuading the powerful army to vacate the temple was definitely not an easy task. Without the personal support of Mayor Qian, according to several people, the army would never have moved out. The mayor put the powerful City Urban Planning Bureau in charge of the project and exhorted them to continue their efforts even after he was reassigned to another post. Somehow the mayor found 35 million yuan to build a new site to entice the People's Liberation Army to give up the temple grounds. I asked Mr. Ma, a city official, how they managed to persuade the People's Liberation Army to move, and he replied,

> It certainly was not easy. They kept refusing, but we persisted. Basically, we had to appeal to the PLA's self-interest. We knew it was no use trying to appeal to their sympathy for Buddhism or to moral obligations for doing public good [公益]. The PLA has no sympathy for religion. So we argued that this site was too exposed to public view. It does not give the military proper secrecy from prying eyes. We also said that we could build a much bigger space in the suburbs for them, with brand-new buildings, strong walls, and security gates so that no intruders could get in.

First, they had to persuade the Wenzhou Garrison (溫州軍營), then the Zhejiang Provincial Garrison, then the Military District for the whole of southeastern China based in Hangzhou, and finally, the People's Liberation Army Headquarters in Beijing, almost insurmountable mountains. They were elated when the Zhejiang Garrison head agreed to help them plead their case with Beijing, because he was such a big shot in southeastern China. "However, in Beijing, he is nothing but a 'Rank Seven Sesame Seed Official' [七品芝麻官], lost in the 'sea of bureaucracy' [官僚大海]," said Mr. Ma, employing a common phrase for a low-level official of insignificant stature. Luckily, the Zhejiang military official *did* manage to find out that at the Beijing PLA office, the Wenzhou City petition papers were at the bottom of a heavy stack of requests from around the country. By "pulling *guanxi* strings," or using social connections, they were able to get their petition moved to the top of the pile, saving them two to three years of waiting time.

In 2004, Taiping Temple had collected 15 million yuan in donations by the people (民間集資) for the new temple halls and dormitories for the nuns, and they needed to raise another 15 million. On the temple grounds, Abbess Wan Ru pointed out to me the engineer who was donating not only his own labor and expertise for the temple construction, but also 3.5 million yuan in cash. On that summer day, he was laboring in the hot sun along with the construction workers. City officials and Taiping Temple managers worked together to select a good construction company that specialized in reconstructing ancient buildings. The Xiangshan Ancient Buildings Company Ltd. was a joint-stock company based in the city of Suzhou; they brought over their own engineer, architect, and skilled workers and hired Wenzhou manual laborers (*cugong*). Master Wan Ru did not want to construct the temple out of cement. Although it is inexpensive, cement only lasts about a hundred years, and it does not have the "feel of history" (沒有歷史感), she thought. Mayor Qian visited the temple and supported her preference for high-grade wood, saying that they must be "responsible to history" (對歷史要負責). The temple managers made nine visits to the Shanghai lumberyard where much of the nation's imported lumber supply was offloaded from freight ships bringing redwoods from Indonesian and Malaysian rain forests. Each of the one hundred large wooden posts that would support the temple halls was nineteen meters long and sixty centimeters (two feet) in diameter, and cost 50,000 yuan ($6,097).

I asked Abbess Wan Ru how she managed to raise the money. She modestly said that she did not wish to make a big public plea for money, because she is aware that Buddhism sometimes had a bad image of asking money. She was confident that people would find out on their own about the temple's needs, and they would donate on their own initiative. However, they did host a big public event, a foundation-laying ceremony. Almost four thousand people attended the banquet, and tens of thousands just came to watch. The event was covered on Wenzhou Television Station, so word got out that Taiping Temple was going to be rebuilt. Soon the money came flowing in like a flood. Thus, the reconstruction of this major Buddhist temple was made possible by different groups across society: the Buddhist clergy, ordinary lay Buddhists, entrepreneurs who donated larger sums, professionals who offered free expertise, and supportive city officials. In this rare case, the effort was led at the top by an active Communist Party mayor who managed to turn an indifferent and sometimes hostile state machinery into a supporter of local Buddhist development.

The reconstruction of Taiping Temple belongs to both the second and third periods of Wenzhou's recent Buddhist history. The third period can be seen in how Abbess Wan Ru was selected to be temple head (住持). At her interview for the position, when asked what she would do as abbess, she replied:

> What Wenzhou needs most right now is better education. So many of our young people do not know what to do with their time: they just gamble, do drugs, and go dancing. Married couples spend their time arguing with each other. People need to learn how to conduct themselves as decent human beings [作個像樣的人]. Buddhism has much wisdom to help them improve their lives.

The abbess explained that she would build a great sermon hall (大講堂) in the temple and invite famous monks to deliver sermons, which she envisioned thousands of people attending. She also wanted to build a library of Buddhist texts and teachings. Her interviewers were impressed with her answers, telling her that it was rare for a Buddhist to have such bold and farsighted ideas. At the time, many Buddhist clergy were still timid and cautious because of their memories of persecution.

I asked Abbess Wan Ru whether she planned to deliver these religious sermons on television to reach a larger audience. Everyone present smiled at my ignorance. "Religion cannot be advocated on television," one person explained. "This is not permitted in our country. Television can only briefly report local Buddhist events; it cannot broadcast Buddhist teachings." Actually, I knew only too well about this policy, but wanted to hear how they responded. In 2004, Buddhist sermons could be delivered to live public audiences, but television broadcasts were forbidden. In 2013, I noticed that the website of Taiping Buddhist Temple featured small embedded videos of lectures delivered in the temple's great hall by a rising Buddhist star, Master Jie Quan (界詮法師), on "Pure Land Notions of Being and Non-being."[4] Since then, Buddhist sermons by famous monks like Master Jing Kong (淨空法師), based in Australia, and Taiwan's Master Hao Tao (海濤法師) have become readily available on the Chinese internet and disseminated via WeChat. Thus, in the third and fourth periods of Wenzhou's Buddhist development, there are lively Buddhist discussions in the new media, but Buddhist teaching remained excluded from television in 2017.

It is also in the third period that Buddhism has made inroads into the ranks of officialdom. In 2014, I was invited to a lunch banquet in Cangnan County, at which an official was present. I ventured a remark that Wenzhou was special in China because so many people had religious inclinations. The official responded with surprising enthusiasm, in contrast to my past dealings with officials. He extolled the deep wisdom and theological sophistication of Buddhism, and affirmed Buddhist contributions to humanity. When I asked him if he were a Buddhist himself, he hesitated, but then declared proudly that he was indeed a Buddhist. That evening, the banquet host called me discreetly to say that the official had asked him to tell me that he merely "admired" Buddhist teachings, but did not practice Buddhist religion. He hoped that I would not spread reports that he was a Buddhist. I assured him that I would never mention his name. Communist Party members are supposed to be atheists; they are not allowed to subscribe to any religion. I also heard that lay Buddhists were starting to get positions inside various branches of the municipal government. It would seem that, more than other religious traditions, Buddhism has entered the government and is gradually exerting subtle influence from within the state.

THE *SANGHA* (沙門): XIANYAN TEMPLE AND BUDDHIST MONASTIC LIFE

"Sangha" (*shamen*, 沙門) is the ancient Pali and Sanskrit term for the "monastic community" of Buddhist clerics. The first step to becoming a monk or nun is to "leave the home" (出家), enter a monastery, and become a "little *shami*" (小沙彌), an initiate between the ages of seven and nineteen years. Master Longxin told me that he was sent to live in a temple as a *shami* at age nine because he did not like eating meat. I came across several cases in which a child's reluctance to eat meat was taken as a sign that he was destined to become a monk. These days, the government forbids child shamis in temples. At the age of twenty, and after serving at least five years, a shami can "seek ordination" (求戒) to become a full-fledged Buddhist monk or nun (比丘, 比丘尼). The ordination ceremony features the shaving of the head and the burning of incense sticks into the forehead, making three burn marks. Before Buddhism became standardized and controlled by the state in modern times, standards for entry into the sangha were lax and varied from place to place. For example, Master Longxin was secretly "ordained" at age twenty, in a local ordination ceremony that today is not recognized, so at age fifty-three he underwent a proper ordination in Hangzhou. Today, only large prominent temples get approval from the State Administration of Religious Affairs in the State Council of the central government for the authority to ordain monks and nuns.

Across China, leaving home goes against the Confucian teaching of filial piety. Many parents resist allowing their children, especially their sons, to become a monk or nun. The filial obligation to support parents in old age, and to produce descendants to continue the family line, have been obstacles to monastic life in China for two millennia. Nor are state controls over the number of monks and nuns ordained by monasteries anything new, for there were state restrictions on expanding the *sangha* in imperial times (C. K. Yang 1961). What is new today is the birth control program (1979–2016) that has made it even more difficult for families to allow their child to join a monastery, especially if he is their only son.

I first visited Xianyan Chan Temple (仙岩禪寺) in the Da Luo Mountains of Rui'an City in 2010, and stayed in the nuns' dormitory in 2012 and 2016. The temple was built in the Tang dynasty. In 1009, the imperial court named it Sacred Longevity Chan Buddhist Temple (聖壽禪寺) (Pan Yiheng

2000: 150–151). Historically, this is an important temple written up in major imperial-era compendiums like *The Complete Works of the Four Repositories* (四庫全書), *Complete Record of Buddhist Ancestors* (佛祖統紀), and *Biographies of Eminent Monks* (高僧傳). In the Republican era, the Southern Zhejiang Buddhist Academy (浙南佛學院) was established here by Master Wooden Fish (木魚法師), a native of Wenzhou. During the Cultural Revolution, the temple's landmark Northern Song Huiguang Pagoda was toppled by a mob of Red Guards. In 1979–1980, two brave lay Buddhists, Pan Yiheng and Chen Chunsheng (潘貽衡, 陳春生) raised donations from the local community to start restoring the temple.

Abbot Hong Guang arrived at Xianyan Temple in 2001 and continued restoring the temple. In 2012, Xianyan Temple had roughly thirty monks and seventy nuns living in separate dormitories; however, state agencies and local public opinion disapproved of monks and nuns living at the same monastery, so in 2016 the temple moved the nuns to another site. Abbot Hong Guang estimated that the temple catered to 120,000 worshippers, and major Buddhist festivals attracted over ten thousand faithful to the temple. After staying here, it was clear to me that this temple belonged to the third period of Wenzhou's Buddhist development, the emergence of innovative temples and the teaching of Buddhist doctrines.

On a cold January day in 2012, my taxi arrived at the front gate of Xianyan Temple. I gazed up the mountain, and it was a site to behold: the temple complex and its many saffron-painted halls with black-tiled curved roofs dating to the Ming and Qing dynasties extended up the slope. The abbot told me that the old temple buildings were not destroyed during the Cultural Revolution because a local elementary and middle school had moved into the temple grounds, a commune government spent 500,000 yuan to build themselves a new building inside the grounds, and three town government offices occupied the temple. This prevented the mobs from destroying the temple complex, because they did not dare go against the local government directly. However, through peasant encroachments, the temple lost a lot of land. Once the local peasants saw the reconstruction of the temple start in 2002, one by one they came to the temple on their own. They said, "Master, go ahead and take this piece of land, we don't really need it anymore." Observed the abbot, "This way they will accumulate merit."

Abbot Hong Guang received all his important guests in an impressive guest reception hall. The interior décor was extremely tasteful, with wood paneling and traditional Chinese-style furniture, framed Chinese calligraphy, a centrally placed multiheaded Thousand-Handed Buddha, and an antique

Figure 5.2. Abbot Hong Guang interviewed by author in his elegant reception room at Xianyan Buddhist Temple, 2016. Photo by Pan Qinyong 潘勤勇攝.

wooden statue of Buddha Sakyamuni with a red satin sash draped around it. From a large wooden table, he served his guests tea from his traditional Chinese tea set, complete with water heater, large tray for washing cups, little clay teapots, porcelain tea cups, and bamboo tea whisks. In this way, he was reviving an earlier period of tea sophistication at this temple. It is said that the Japanese Zen monk Eisai (榮西大師) studied at Xianyan Chan Monastery in the Song dynasty and brought its trademark tea back to Kyoto with him. In Kyoto, Eisai established the Kennin Zenji Temple and helped to start the Japanese Zen tea ceremony.

I observed that the abbot received some well-heeled guests in this reception room: successful businesspeople and professionals, sometimes with their families, officials high and low, and academics from across China. I guessed that their donations to the temple were quite generous, for the honor of a private audience with the abbot. One day, the abbot told me that these visits were not merely an exchange of pleasantries; he provides psychological counseling to some of these guests. Due to recent economic difficulties, many entrepreneurs are under great pressure, with bad loans they have given out, or debts they are unable to repay. Just two nights before speaking with me in 2012, an entrepreneur he knew had hanged himself. Another man who visited the abbot had unwisely loaned out the huge sum of 1.3 billion yuan (US$21,451,309!), but his debtor could not pay him back. This man told Master Hong Guang that he regretted his greed for the high interest, and now he may never see his money again. People also have marital failures or delinquent children abusing drugs, and officials are disciplined, expelled from the Party, or imprisoned for a number of offenses. The abbot tried his best to combine Buddhist wisdom with modern psychological and therapeutic approaches to comfort and give practical advice to people in emotional distress.

Returning to Wenzhou from his travels in India through the ancient Buddhist holy lands of Bodhgaya, Nalanda, Sarnath, and Lumbini in Nepal, Abbot Hong Guang was inspired to build several round stone stupas (佛塔), about fifteen feet high and eight feet in diameter, in the Indian Buddhist style. These stupas house the sacred relics (*sheli*, 舍利) of important monks and abbots who resided at the temple. *Sheli* are translucent beads or residues left after the cremation of a corpse; it is said that only highly virtuous and self-cultivated monks will leave them. Abbot Hong Guang also established the Nalanda Buddhist Academy (那蘭陀佛學院), which he named after the ancient Nalanda Buddhist University in Bihar, India, where the famous Tang dynasty monk Xuan Zang (玄奘) studied for several years.

Inside a monastery, monks and nuns rise before daybreak. At 4:30 AM, the temple bell and drum call people out of bed. On awakening, the nuns and monks meditate and conduct their "morning lessons" (早課) by chanting a sutra. At 6:00 AM, they take their breakfast. Afterward, they wash their face, brush their teeth, and do laundry. At 7:30 AM, their ritual work for the local community begins. People from the community come into the temple with requests to chant a particular sutra for them. The hoped-for effects of chanting include dissolving misfortune and reducing disasters (消災); gaining prosperity and good fortune (祈福); obtaining protection, peace, and security (*bao pingan*); helping a recently deceased soul gain release from Purgatory and move smoothly into their next life (超度); and helping a child in a crucial examination. At 10:30 AM, the monks and nuns present (上供) flowers, food offerings and incense to all the Buddhas and Bodhisattvas in the temple, while chanting the "offering chant" (供養文). At 11:00 AM, they take their lunch in the monastic dining hall, after which they rest or nap. At 1:30 PM, they chant sutras together, some on behalf of community members who have made requests. At 3:30 PM, they conduct their "evening lesson" (晚課). They may chant the Amitabha Sutra (阿彌陀佛經) or the Ritual Text of Repentance (禮懺悔文).

At 5:00 PM, they have their dinner, and then read or watch some television news, before going to bed at 8:00 PM.

I discovered that most of the nuns and monks spoke Mandarin because they were not Wenzhounese but from Shandong, Anhui, Sichuan, Henan, Shaanxi, Fujian, and even Heilongjiang. Two nuns explained that the reason why the monastery was full of non-Wenzhounese was that Wenzhou people were so wealthy: with such comfortable lives, they cannot tolerate the harsh discipline and boring routines of monastic life. People from the poorer interior provinces (内地) are more willing to submit to Buddhist monastic life. Since China is a patrilineal culture with a state birth control policy (until 2016), few families are willing to allow their precious single son to enter the monastery. Thus, at Xianyan Temple, more women are entering the monastery than men, and more nuns than monks are ordained. This has led to talk in some quarters about a "crisis" in Chinese Buddhism: if so many women populate Buddhist monasteries, say some men, Buddhism will have no future. A male lay Buddhist once said to me,

> Men have more pressure to produce descendants and continue the lineage line [傳宗接代]. But peasant families want to get rid of their girls so they can have another chance in the family planning program to give birth to a boy, so Buddhist temples become like garbage cans where lots of girls are dumped. This will have bad effects on the future development of Chinese Buddhism! No matter how excellent some women may be as nuns, they cannot compete with men in achieving great things [zuo da shi, 做大事]. So Buddhism is going to become weaker than Christianity. The Christians don't have this gap in the numbers of men and women.

Putting on a polite face, I thought to myself: the feminization of Chinese Buddhism might actually prove to be Buddhism's salvation. In a rapidly changing Chinese society dominated by secular and profit-seeking forces that are largely run by men, women in Buddhism may produce a clear alternative voice for a different religiosity. Indeed, the feminization of Buddhism has already occurred in Taiwan (Yü 2013), and Taiwan's major Buddhist institutions are conducting Buddhist work across the globe.

Abbot Hong Guang at Xianyan Temple discovered that the temple's venerable tradition of Chan meditation had been lost. He had spent some time at the Living-in-the-Clouds Mountain Temple (雲居山寺), a small Chan temple in Jiangxi Province, where he learned Chan meditation techniques from an eighty-year-old monk, so he brought this precious knowledge to Xianyan Temple. His assistant, a Wenzhou Buddhist monk, observed:

In historical periods of destruction, like the Maoist era, deeply religious people retreat to the mountains as hermits, wanting to have nothing to do with the "world of red dust" ([紅塵世界, the sinful mortal world]. So, although people thought that religion had been exterminated in China, eventually these hidden self-cultivating saints start to re-emerge. They are "beautiful gems" who have preserved the old ways.

Master Hong Guang established the International Chan Meditation Center, which now offers workshops and meetings on Chan meditation. In 2004, he also invited Chan Master Guangchao (廣超法師) from Singapore to come and teach meditation classes. Four hundred people came to the temple to take these classes for two weeks. He also planned to import meditation regimens from a Theravada Buddhist temple in Thailand.

BUDDHIST LAY LIFE: SUTRA-CHANTING, MEDITATION, AND STUDY GROUPS

Temples rely on a large network of lay volunteers, most of them older women, who perform myriad tasks to help maintain the temple's daily functions. These volunteers help prepare for festival days and clean up after the events. Their voluntary labor wins them merit, which will help them be reborn into a better life. Some lay Buddhists undergo a ritual called "Three Refuges" (三皈依), in which they seek refuge in the Three Treasures (三寶): the Buddha, the Dharma (teachings), and the Sangha (the clergy). This ritual transforms them into "lay Buddhist disciples," or "those who seek refuge" (guiyi, 皈依), and they receive a Buddhist name (法名) and a certificate declaring them a Buddhist disciple. Henceforth, they can wear dark brown robes when they enter the temple to help the monks officiate at Buddhist rituals. These lay devotees are also called "devotees who stay at home" (在家居士).

There are several forms of Buddhist voluntary worship and study associations in the Wenzhou area (Lin S. 2003). First, there are "groups to chant the Pure Land" (念淨土), made up of middle-aged women and men who get together to chant the Pure Land Sutra (阿彌陀經) and repeatedly utter "O-mi-to-fo" and the names of eighty-eight Buddhas. Repeated chanting has a soothing and meditative effect. Second, "sutra-chanting assistance groups" (助念團) are usually older women, who go to other people's homes to chant sutras and pray for the spiritual salvation of their sick and dying family member. These chanters are paid a modest fee for their efforts, but money is not their main motivation. Rather, they are moved by compassion and also seek the opportunity to accumulate merit. A third type of lay Buddhist group are the "sutra and repentance groups" (經懺團 or 拜懺團), which are attached to each Buddhist temple and are also composed mainly of middle-aged women. These groups assist Buddhist monks when they conduct temple rituals, serving like a choir chiming in at different points in the ritual.

Fourth, there are lay groups for the study and promotion of Buddhist teachings, called "the forest of reside-at-home lay Buddhists" (*jushilin*, 居士林). Whereas precursors of the first three lay groups can be found in late imperial times, the term "jushilin" describes groups forming in the early twentieth century who studied Buddhist teachings and provided social services. The first jushilin was formed in Shanghai in 1918 by educated elites and business people who believed that Buddhist scriptural studies did not have to be restricted to the clergy. Their activities also included charity work and disseminating Buddhist literature. In Wenzhou, the Hongqiao Jushilin was established in Yueqing County in 1923, and it built an orphanage and poverty relief station (Lin S. 2003: 60). The Hengjiang Fohua Jushilin was opened in Pingyang County in 1934, and three other jushilin were established in Wenzhou City.

Jushilin reemerged across Wenzhou in the 1990s, including the Cangnan County Fangshan Jushilin in 1988, the Rui'an Jueyan Jushilin in 1998, and the Pingyang Aojiang Jushilin in 2001 (Lin S. 2003: 60). According to the former head of one jushilin whom I interviewed in 2010, the reason why there are so few jushilin, with vast memberships for each, is that the government strictly limits the number. Some counties in Wenzhou have no jushilin at all. A jushilin must register with the local Bureau of Religion (宗教局), and permission is not easily granted. These voluntary associations are primarily comprised of educated people. Like the other lay groups, they chant sutras; however, they spend more time studying Buddhist doctrines and scriptures. They offer frequent lectures by acclaimed visiting monks, nuns, and scholars, and some also print Buddhist scriptures and literature.

The Pingan Jushilin (平安居士林) was formed through a grassroots initiative in 1983. In 2005, it became the only jushilin to be officially approved for the whole city of Wenzhou. In 2010, this organization had about ten thousand members and offered lectures, study meetings, and religious activities and outings. In 2006, the Pingan Jushilin established an affiliated Wenzhou Buddhist Youth Association (溫州佛教青年協會) for the growing number of younger, better-educated lay Buddhists. I interviewed Yu Songqing, a twenty-nine-year-old woman, who was active with this Buddhist youth organization. She is a graduate of a three-year vocational college and has worked a few accounting jobs. It was a pleasant surprise for me to be driven to the interview by Yu in her own car to an air-conditioned tea house. After the interview, she wrote about it in her online blog, where she periodically posts her latest reflections on Buddhist teachings. According to Yu, there were well over one thousand Buddhist youth members in Rui'an City alone, with about twenty people showing up at each meeting. She explained,

> Young Buddhists pay more attention to spiritual matters of the heart [*xinling*] and we are very responsive to scriptural teachings. We are less superstitious [*mixin*] than our elders, and we like to listen to Buddhist lectures in Mandarin; sometimes we even talk among ourselves in Mandarin. We all share a sense of being fed up [*yanjuan*] with life's anxieties and hardships [*shenghuo fannao*] and the ruthless "dog-eat-dog" ethos of contemporary society [*gouxin doujiao shehui*]. Some among us have a very deep level of understanding of Buddhist principles, and a few have even gone on to become monks and nuns [*chujia*]. . . . The dharma teaches us that we must smash all conceptualization [打破一切觀念] and we must not have any clinging to attachments [执着] or illusions of a self [我执]. We must practice cultivation [修行] to see through these attachments. . . . Buddhism has taught me to reflect on things a lot. I observe my changing moods. Buddhism enables us to gain a freedom of the spirit [*xinling ziyou*].

Yu's Buddhist Youth Association organizes scripture study classes, lectures by knowledgeable monks and nuns, meditation sessions, and trips to famous Buddhist temples in Wenzhou and across China. They have had discussions of the Diamond Sutra (金剛經), the Heart Sutra (心經), the Forty-Two Chapter Sutra (四十二章經), the Weimojie Sutra (維摩詰經), and the Journey of Jushi (居士行儀).

In 2014, the Xianyan Buddhist Temple set up a network of lay Buddhist meditation enthusiasts, the International Urban Chan Meditation Group, whose members are connected via WeChat, the social media cell phone app. Yu Songqing volunteered to single-handedly manage all thirty meditation classes, each with one hundred students. The three thousand members are mainly based in Wenzhou but also include people from across China, and Chinese residing in Japan, Australia, Korea, and the United States. Each member meditates at least fifteen minutes each day on their own and records their daily meditation time with the "class leader" (*banzhang*) and shares any thoughts about their meditation experience. From time to time, Abbot Hong Guang of Xianyan Temple assigns the different classes a Buddhist topic to meditate on and discuss with their class members. Yu organizes periodic offline face-to-face class meetings at Xianyan Temple, often attended by educated professionals such as officials, civil servants, academics, and doctors.

BUDDHIST VEGETARIANISM AND "RELEASING LIFE"

When I first started fieldwork in Wenzhou in the early 1990s, the vast majority of people there were avid meat- and seafood-eaters, and most of them did not understand the concept of vegetarianism. People above a certain age still had vivid memories of famine during the Three Years of Hardship (1959–1961), when some rural people starved to death or had to eat tree bark and roots. This experience with hunger is perhaps the reason for the lavish banqueting since the 1980s and the cultural amnesia about Buddhist vegetarianism in the 1980s and 90s. Indeed, I have dined with local officials and businessmen who could no longer consume meat or alcohol because, having overindulged on rich banquet fare, they were now stricken with painful gout.

In the new millennium, suddenly vegetarianism came back. Even though lay Buddhists could always justify eating meat because they did not personally kill the animal, many now switched to a vegetarian diet. Of course, Buddhist festivals and temple events always featured vegetarian meals. Surprisingly, some deity temples and Daoist temple festivals also turned vegetarian. The quality and variety of vegetarian dishes in temples was greatly improving, along with enhanced spending power. At first, the few vegetarian restaurants that popped up in the larger cities of Wenzhou were elegant and high-class; later, though, family-style vegetarian buffet restaurants multiplied in all the towns, serving people of lower incomes.

In 2008, I picked up a free pamphlet at a Buddhist temple in Wenzhou which contained a lecture given by Taiwan Buddhist abbot Master Guanghua (廣化法師, 1924–1996) on the virtues of vegetarianism (Guanghua Fashi, n.d.). The pamphlet was printed by Guanghua Temple in Putian, Fujian Province, which had a state license to publish Buddhist literature. After listing the evidence by Western scientists for the superiority of vegetables over meat for human health, longevity, and intelligence, Master Guanghua asked why it was that so many countries are manufacturing weapons of war and machineries of death:

> This is the *karma* or repayment [果報] of humanity's history of killing sentient beings and eating meat. All sentient beings have a form of consciousness and spiritual awareness [靈性], with a blood and flesh body. No matter what form it assumes, the body will always die, but the spirit will never

perish. It keeps on circulating through the six reincarnations in the cycle of life and death without end. . . . All sentient beings value life most of all: humans as well as beasts. So when this most precious life is ended by someone for meat, the killer incurs deep hatred and enmity, so a knife is repaid with a knife, a life for a life. . . . This kind of mutual killing and eating becomes a cycle of karmic retribution and transmigration of life. When one person is a professional killer, then he will suffer retribution. When one country engages in the industry of killing, then it will also experience the pain of being slaughtered. (Guang, n.d.: 49)

Here we see that in Buddhist thought, killing for meat is linked to the killing of war in a huge cycle of karmic retribution, and all sentient life-forms are equalized so that it is not just humans who should enjoy the right to live.

In 2008, I also began hearing about the revival of a late imperial Buddhist practice called "releasing life" (*fangsheng*, 放生), where people purchase a live fish or fowl at the market and participate in a Buddhist ritual to release it back into the wild. Joanna Handlin Smith (1999) has shown how this Chinese Buddhist practice of liberating captured animals traces back to the *Book of Brahma's Net* (梵網經) of the fifth century CE. During the Song dynasty, this ritual was accompanied by "rites of confession and penitence on behalf of the released creatures that would enable them to attain a better rebirth" and was a way for Pure Land Buddhism to displace the animal sacrifices to "blood-eating deities" (von Glahn 2004: 145). By the seventeenth and eighteenth centuries, accounts of *fangsheng* activities became common in gentry writings (Smith 1999). Whereas earlier Buddhist accounts placed equal emphasis on reincarnation and the liberation of animals, late Ming discussions focused on the latter, expressing the emotional and physical suffering of the animals. This suggests that what we today would call an "environmental ethics" was already well-developed in late imperial China, through a melding of Buddhist and Confucian ethics to address human-animal relations.

Today people go out in groups, sometimes hundreds of people, to the countryside on the birthday of the Buddha or other special days, and release captured wildlife into a pond, river, or reservoir. Ms. Chen, a former township government official, said that people release wildlife, not domesticated fowl or farm-raised fish. In 2016, Ms. Chen participated in a "releasing life" ritual every two months. Each time, the participants collected large bins of fish, eels, and freshwater turtles from markets and went out on a boat together. A Buddhist monk led the group in chanting Buddhist scriptures. They generally began by singing the short "Ode to Incense Urns" (爐香讚). Next, they recited the

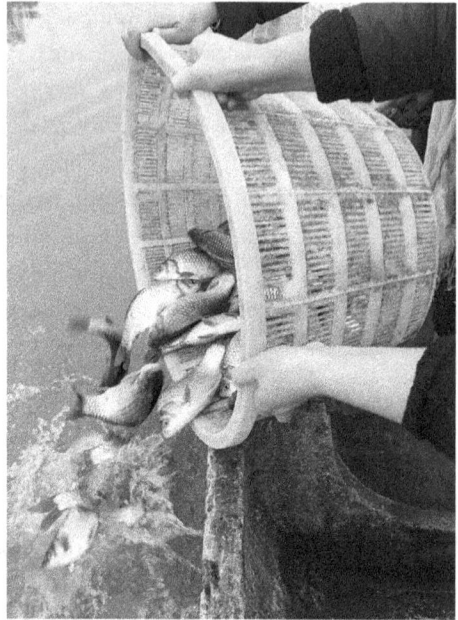

Figures 5.3 and 5.4. "Releasing life" ritual to release captured wildlife, Longwan District, 2016. Photo courtesy of Zhou Xiaoying 周小英.

Great Compassion Dharani (大悲咒) three times, followed by the Heart Sutra (心經) once. Then they recite the Prayer for the Dead (往生咒), another dharani, three times, followed by a reflection on their own sins (懺悔). Finally, they empty the buckets of fish one by one into the water and silently reflect on the meaning of this release of life and compassion for other sentient beings.

BOUNDARIES: WENZHOU BUDDHISM'S RELATIONS WITH OTHER FAITHS

Earlier, we discussed how in the first period of Buddhist revival, Buddhism and popular religion were hard to distinguish. Despite their hybridization, there are also frequent efforts to reassert the boundaries between Buddhism and other religious traditions. In this section I discuss some attempts to conceptually disentangle Buddhism from popular religion and to work out a proper relationship between them.

Mr. Dong told me that Buddhists have an older notion of *mixin* (迷信) that is different from that of the Communist Party's notion of "superstition." He explained,

Mixin for Buddhism means *mihuo* [迷惑], to get excessively bedazzled by the gods. Some people blindly believe the gods control everything. They beg the gods to help them in worldly ambitions. They assume a passive position and just obey the gods. When they place all their hopes on the gods to answer their prayers, they are still stuck with desires; they have not managed to "leap out" [*hai meiyou tiao chulai*] from this desiring world. In contrast, Buddhism promotes "wisdom" [*zhixin*, 智心], which transcends worldly desires and this illusory world. Wisdom means that one believes in the gods, but also reserves an active position to reflect on one's actions.

For Mr. Dong, even the gods have desires and are capable of wrongdoing, which will cause them to descend down the hierarchy of the six forms of reincarnation. For all their power to help or punish human beings, gods may also be transformed back into mere humans. The Buddhas and Bodhisattvas, however, have completely escaped and transcended the endless wheel of the six reincarnations. Buddhas and Bodhisattvas are *above* the gods; they transcend the gods and are much more powerful.

Although Mr. Dong regularly performs popular Buddho-Daoist rituals and funerals for rural communities, he nevertheless believes that certain ritual segments are "not authentically Buddhist" (不是正規的佛教). For example, toward the end of the Buddho-Daoist funeral he performs, there is a section called "delivering money to the bank: replenishing and repaying" (交庫添還), which involves burning several basketloads of folded spirit money, amounting to tens of thousands of yuan, that the deceased owes to the Bank of Hell in the Netherworld. In the Yin World (陰界), there are sixty officials or guardians of the Bank of Hell (庫官). So, besides burning money for the deceased to use when he arrives in Purgatory, money is also burned for the guardians of the Bank of Hell, so that they will guard the money sent down. Although he disapproves of the practice, Mr. Dong generally allows this ritual segment in his performances.

Master Hongfa, a young ordained Buddhist nun, helped establish a small Buddhist Recital Hall (念佛堂) in a coastal town in Cangnan County in 2000. This hall straddles the second (1996–2005) and third periods (2006–present) of Buddhist development in Wenzhou, because of its move toward Buddhist teachings and ethics rather than ritual efficacy. The hall encountered some difficulties with the local community, who kept asking them what sort of religion they represented. The locals had three issues with this new kind of Buddhism. First, the locals asked the hall managers why they did not allow the burning of spirit money. Master Hongfa patiently explained that if the deceased was reborn into one of the six paths of reincarnation, burning money for them to use in the next life was useless. Second, they asked why the hall charged no money for people to chant "O-mi-to-fo" or listen to Buddhist sermons. The Buddhist Hall's offering free rituals and sermons was seen as cutting into the business of traditional lay chanters. Third, the locals were confused by the hall's focus on self-cultivation (自修) and its teaching that one cannot attain wisdom and enlightenment with external aids like hiring others to chant for one's liberation. Master Hongfa tried to explain that one must pursue one's own liberation by "starting from within one's heart" (以内心開始). Here we see that even small Buddhist temples have started to differentiate themselves from popular religion, stressing individual interiority over ritual efficacy.

It seemed that, the more educated the Buddhist, the more they wished to draw a line of distinction between Buddhism and popular religion. Abbot Miao Feng (妙峰方丈) is a Buddhist intellectual who writes and publishes Buddhist philosophy. In January 2012, the abbot explained:

> The basic activity of popular religion is "begging the gods for favors and divining the future" [求神問卦]. Adherents of popular religion make requests [許愿] of the gods. When they get their wish, they must return the favor [還愿]. So the distinctive feature of popular religion is that its worshippers want to gain or acquire something. Once they get what they prayed for, then they stop their worship. Real religions like Buddhism are not like this. A true Buddhist is someone who consistently studies the teachings of the Buddha, regardless of whether the gods favor him. A Buddhist also believes in the existence of the gods, but these gods are only one of the Six Paths of the Cycle of Reincarnations [六道輪回]. The gods can indeed help people, but even the gods are still caught up in the cycle of birth and rebirth. They cannot compare with the power of the Buddhas, who have all attained Enlightenment. That is why we Buddhists do not encourage the common people to worship gods or ghosts.

In the above statement, we can see that, instead of banning other religious practices, Buddhism, like Daoism, adopts the strategy of inclusiveness and "hierarchical encompassment" toward the gods of popular religion, who are positioned lower.

While there is some disdain for popular Buddhism, I also discovered that educated Buddhists did not wish to exclude popular religion or popular Buddhism, out of pragmatic considerations. In the increasing contestation between Buddhists and Christians for religious loyalty and membership, a lay Buddhist man put the matter in these stark terms:

Buddhism must not reject those who pursue popular religion [拜經懺的人], because they are an important resource that we can use. It does not matter that these people cannot tell the difference [分不清] between Buddhas, deities, and Daoist gods. It's all right that they have "superstitions" and lack education, because they are still educable and open to our Buddhist teachings. We need them to expand our troops. If we give them up, they will go to Christianity, and then "our fishing hooks will catch no fish!" [魚鉤掉不上魚].

Some Wenzhou Buddhists feel embattled by the rapid advance of Protestantism in Wenzhou. Protestantism has greatly increased its membership through proselytizing strategies that are much more forceful and systematic than those of Buddhism. Such undercurrents of competition between Buddhism and Christianity seem to have grown stronger in recent years.

In 2012, Abbot Qingchun at a Buddhist temple in Cangnan County told me about an unpleasant experience. One day, while he was strolling on the street in his saffron Buddhist robes, a five-year-old boy called out, "Sha-dan is here!" (沙丹來了!). "Sha-dan" is the Chinese term for Satan, and the abbot knew its Christian provenance. He asked the boy who had told him to say such a thing. The boy replied that his mother told him that anyone dressed like the abbot was a "Sha-dan." This outburst bothered Master Qingchun for several days, and he finally decided to report the incident to the local Bureau of Religion. The abbot remarked, "Each religion should work on tolerance for other religions. It seems that Christianity has changed its nature [*bianyang*]." His previous image of Christianity had been positive; he had thought that it was an advanced religion because it came from the West. Now he thought that somehow in China, it had become more aggressive and intolerant. He worried that in some mountainous areas, almost 80 percent of the villages have recently converted to Christianity. Buddhism does not have the same dynamic expansion, he thought, because it is too tolerant (太包容心).

Wenzhou Buddhists have also become increasingly aware of the nature and strength of Taiwanese Buddhism. Master Ling Kong toured Taiwan in 2009 with other monks from China, visiting all the important Buddhist organizations there: Buddha Light Mountain (佛光山), Tzu Chi Merit Foundation (慈濟公德會), and Dharma Drum Mountain (法鼓山), as well as smaller Buddhist establishments. He sighed and said that it would take another thirty years before Wenzhou could catch up with Taiwan Buddhism. In terms of finances, he thought the Four Sacred Buddhist Mountains in China—Emei Mountain (峨眉山) in Sichuan, Putuo Mountain (普陀山) in Zhejiang Province, Wutai

Mountain (五臺山) in Shanxi, and Jiuhua Mountain (九華山) in Anhui—and other large and famous Buddhist establishments like Lingyin Temple (靈隱寺) in Hangzhou and Shaolin Temple (少林寺) in Henan had all surpassed the wealth of any Buddhist organization in Taiwan. The problem, however, lies not in the wealth itself but in what one can do with the money: in Mainland China, there are all kinds of government restrictions on religious activities, so Buddhist establishments can only sit on their money, with their hands tied.

In China, Buddhist organizations cannot run schools or kindergartens, nor can most temples print their own religious literature, disseminate their teachings, or advertise their activities on television or radio, and public schools are not permitted to teach Buddhism. Thus, Buddhism has trouble attracting educated people into its ranks, and the vast majority of people still know very little about Buddhist teachings. Another difference Master Ling Kong pointed out was that in Taiwan, there are democratic elections: "When a political ruling group [*zhengzhi jituan*] needs to get elected, they will always support Buddhist organizations, because that is what makes them look good in the eyes of the people." For him, these two differences—that Buddhism is shut out of the educational and media systems in China, and that political rulers do not have to be elected—are the major obstacles to Buddhism in Mainland China catching up with Taiwan Buddhism. Pointing to how Christians in Taiwan only make up 3.5 percent of the population, but in Wenzhou, Christians are about 10-12 percent, he laid this at the doorstep of government restrictions on Buddhist development. "Under our current political system, we cannot hope to produce global Buddhism like in Taiwan, or maverick monks like Master Xingyun [星雲法師]. There is only one reason for this: the government simply does not wish to have such a person emerge."

Part III

RELIGIOUS CIVIL SOCIETY RITUAL ECONOMY:

Grassroots Initiative,
Gendered Agency,
and Alternative Economic Logic

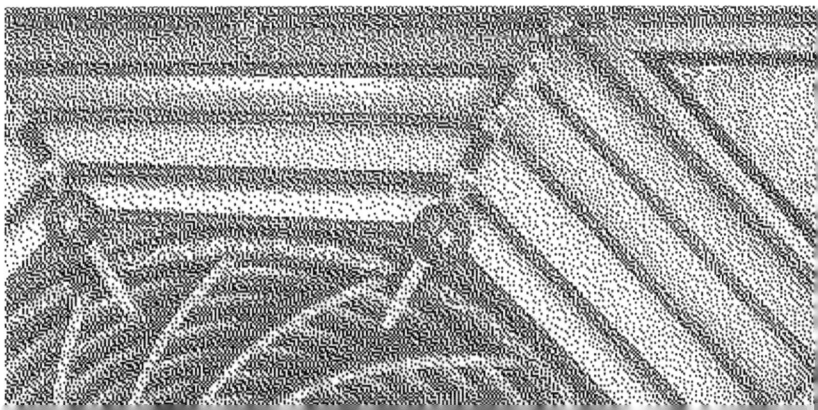

6 Sprouts of Religious Civil Society

Temples, Localities, and Communities

We can say that nearly all the great social institutions were born in religion. For the principal features of collective life to have begun as none other than various features of religious life, it is evident that religious life must necessarily have been the eminent form and, as it were, the epitome of collective life. If religion gave birth to all that is essential in society, that is so because the idea of society is the soul of religion.

—Émile Durkheim, *The Elementary Forms of Religious Life*

In July 1998, I was chatting with Mr. Zhang, a retired entrepreneur in Longwan District, and he told me:

The local people are much more willing to give money to people's organizations [民間組織] like temples and lineages than to the government. We seldom see the direct benefits of government projects. The government spends a lot of effort on propaganda about their latest projects, which they want the people to support, but the people do not really know just where their donations will end up.

Mr. Zhang contrasted the local people's eagerness to donate to a local deity temple with their reluctance to contribute money to the government's effort to clean up polluted waterways. In 1997, the local Celestial Immortal Temple burned down due to a faulty electrical switch. Two million yuan (US$242,000) had just been spent in 1994 replacing the decrepit old temple. Before the temple management committee had even made a public call for help, people from surrounding villages spontaneously came forth to donate money for a brand-new temple. Within two months, the temple construction fund had accumulated well over 2 million yuan, surpassing the amount collected in 1994. By contrast, the local government required every family in the township to contribute money to clean up the canals, which were clogged with foul-smelling garbage and toxic black factory discharges. However, nothing came of this effort, and the project seemed to have been dropped in 1998. Mr. Zhang commented that too often government leaders and the media spout off good intentions and slogans, but they do not always follow through with substantive action. He thought it was better to allow the "realm of the folk" (*minjian*, 民間) to step in to solve problems themselves, since people can organize themselves and get things accomplished more effectively.

Implicit in this indigenous notion of the "realm of the people" is the contrast with the "realm of officialdom" (*guanfang*, 官方). We can see from this interchange that local residents possess a strong community spirit that makes them eager to donate money for the "public benefit" (公益), as well as the initiative and organizational skills to convert these donations into new temples, road and bridge repair, and lineage ancestor halls. For community infrastructure improvements, they prefer their own local *minjian* organizations to top-down state efforts.

I have been repeatedly struck by the local initiative, voluntarism, dynamism, and organizational abilities of rural and small-town Wenzhou people. In this chapter I will show how these abilities have been deployed in erecting, restoring, or expanding religious organizations. Ironically, Wenzhou's highly "privatized" economy produces a local culture with a public, communitarian, and religious ethos of donations and service for public benefit. Since the 1980s, a renewed social realm has opened up, composed of countless nongovernmental religious groups and associations. Can these religious associations serve as the building blocks for a modern rural and small-town "civil society" of self-organizing associations?

By "civil society," I mean a society or social group with the ability to initiate an activity or organize and govern itself for the public good. The notion of civil society is a category of modernity, evolving out of the experiences of the modern West. Since the modern state's prerogatives and functions overflowed the boundaries of traditional monarchical states, a new discourse of civil society arose in modernity as formerly nonstate space rapidly vanished. This was the historical background of civil society discourse in the eighteenth-century European Enlightenment as a countermovement to the expansion of the absolutist state (Habermas 1989; J. Keane 1988a, 1988b; Taylor 1995). Thus, the concept of civil society is always a relational one, predicated on a number of stark comparisons. First, it is contrasted with and mutually defined by its relationship with the modern state. Second, standing for notions of the public good, it is contrasted with private interests, such as those of the market or capitalist economy or the individual and the private family. Civil society stands for the society realm that is not directed by the state, whose membership is not composed of state officials, whose goals transcend the private interests of individuals, families, or for-profit economic enterprises, and whose organizations have relative social and financial autonomy from the state. Key concepts associated with civil society are grassroots initiative and voluntarism; self-governance; nonprofit group identities that counterbalance state or nationalist identity; group selection of association leaders; and group formulation of goals and activities.

This chapter presents a diverse array of self-starting grassroots religious organizations I encountered in rural Wenzhou. In chapter 9, I reflect on the relevance and applicability of the modern Western category of "civil society" to a non-Western cultural tradition such as China and call for new ways to rethink civil society theory.

LOCAL INITIATIVE AND GRASSROOTS ORGANIZATION IN WENZHOU TEMPLES

In the three decades of the Maoist era (1949–1979), the only organizations that could organize society for the public good were branches and hierarchical levels of a Party-state apparatus that threaded through all aspects of Chinese society. This vast bureaucratic administration was designed with a centralized and hierarchical chain of command that discouraged local initiative and the integrity of local communities. Beginning with the radical campaign to completely collectivize agriculture and set up rural communes in the Great Leap Forward (1958–1961), old historical temples were seized by local authorities and converted into government offices, schools, factories, and storage facilities. After the religious destruction and terror of the Cultural Revolution, the Chinese Communist Party's landmark Document #19 permitted religious communities to reclaim their lost religious properties. Along with the return of a market economy and increasing prosperity since the 1980s, rural and town residents in Wenzhou found that they had surplus money to donate for reestablishing community temples.

The process of acquiring funds, petitioning multiple bureaucracies to reclaim a religious site from its current occupants, acquiring land to build or expand, legally registering a temple, and doing construction work, was arduous and could stretch over many years. It required a strong *guanxi* network of social connections and good relations with local government, and endless patience and ingenuity. Many initiators of temple building or rebuilding were fired up with the desire to do something on behalf of their native place (家鄉). Many voiced religious motivations: they were propelled by a dream in which a god spoke to them; they wished to build up their divine merit for their afterlife; or they wished to do penance for their past sins. Many were also motivated by a desire for "face" and local prestige. Of course, there might be a mixture of these motivations, along with economic gain for the local area in expanding tourism and pilgrimage. The desire to properly house powerful gods is also propelled by the expectation that they will protect the local community.

Today, most villages in Wenzhou have at least one deity temple or Daoist temple devoted to a god worshipped as a sort of patron saint or tutelary spirit protecting the village, and the temple serves as a community center for important ritual and social gatherings. There are also multivillage temples that draw worshippers from several neighboring villages. Some villages have two or more temples, while towns have even more. In some villages, a major lineage ancestor hall, Buddhist temple, or Old People's Association headquarters may also serve as the village center. Where temples serve as community center, most village families will contribute money or voluntary labor for major ritual events, and participate in temple-sponsored religious festivals. The exceptions are Christian families, for whom these activities are "idolatrous worship" (偶像崇拜). Thus, the major deity or Buddha residing within the community center temple is often treated as an icon of community and local protector.

Many temples hold a temple ritual and communal banquet twice each lunar month, thus bringing members of the local community together. Additional feast days for social gatherings and collective rituals fall on the god's birthday and on lunar calendar festivals. Most temples are equipped with a kitchen and round banquet tables and benches for these festival celebrations; some also have stages that are used for opera performances at temple festivals. These temple gatherings provide opportunities for people to inform each other about public issues, discuss recent events, and exchange family stories and community gossip. Sometimes the chatter at these gatherings can turn to exposing and criticizing certain local officials for alleged corruption or controversial decisions. This suggests a rudimentary face-to-face local public sphere, what Adam Yuet Chau has called an "agrarian public sphere" (2006: 10–12).

Before Land Reform in the early 1950s, many temples owned land, from which the rent collected from peasant tenants was used to fund temple maintenance, operas, and festivals. Land Reform confiscated and redistributed the communal lands owned by temples, churches, and lineage organizations. In the post-Mao era, religious entities have been able to recover their religious site of worship, but not their attached land. Technically the Chinese state owns all of the nation's land and offers usufruct rights, for a limited but renewable time period, to individuals, groups, or businesses. Land is controlled very tightly, and since local governments prefer that the land be used for agriculture, industry, shopping centers, or apartment buildings—which generate profits—they are reluctant to award land to religious organizations. Without land to rent out, Wenzhou temples now rely almost solely on candle and incense sales and community donations. The names, work units, and companies of major donors to the temple reconstruction are etched into stone temple steles. In an effort at transparency, each year, temples will also hang on the wall a large poster showing the total amounts of donations and temple expenditures. If there is any public suspicion about the honesty of temple finance managers, temple attendance and donations will drop.

Temples depend a great deal on the public reputation of their resident god(s): the more a god shows his or her "divine efficacy" (靈驗) in helping people or performing miracles, the more word will spread and attendance will increase. Some modest village temples have developed wide reputations for "efficacy," so they no longer just serve their own village; rather, they draw people from across townships or counties.

Below are some compelling examples of grassroots energies and local organizational initiative in the running of temples in Wenzhou. Each entry is designed to reveal a different dimension of temple life as the "sprouts of religious civil society."

The Shamanic Ignition Spark of Divine Presence

The initial establishment of a temple and its community often relies on what I call a "shamanic ignition spark" provided by a shamaness, spirit medium, or ritual healer who can suffuse a temple with divine presence and help build religious civil society. In 2008, I traveled with two friends to the Golden Rooster Mountains (金鷄山) in the western region of Rui'an City (瑞安市). We went to interview a remarkable village head, Mr. Wu, who was spearheading a drive to convert the agricultural economy of his picturesque mountain village into the "green economy" (綠色經濟) of ecotourism and religious pilgrimage. The village lay next to a clear, rushing mountain stream surrounded by mountains, green and lush with swaying bamboo and pine trees.

The rebuilding of an old run-down Lord Yang Family Temple (楊府廟) was the centerpiece of Mr. Wu's effort to kick-start a green economy. He needed a sacred site housing the awesome powers of the gods to attract religious pilgrims and urban tourists. He brought in a Daoist shamanic ritual healer and housed her and her husband in the newly restored temple. Elsewhere, I have

Figure 6.1. Ritual healer and shaman who provided the spark to activate a Lord Yang Temple in Western Rui'an County mountains. Photo by the author.

called her Luo Jinhong, and she described herself as a "deity-child" (*shentong,* 神僮) (M. Yang 2015). She told me that she came from three generations of Zhengyi Daoist priests, but she was mainly a ritual healer and diviner. She had a three-year contract with the village to manage the temple and share a certain proportion of her earnings with them. Mr. Wu said her presence was important because it allowed people to feel that the gods had come down into the new temple.

In a study by a Chinese ethnographer in neighboring southern Jiangsu Province, we find a further example of the importance of shamans in jump-starting a temple. A woman referred to as ZBM was possessed in 1993 by the god Lord Zong Guan, who asked her to spearhead the rebuilding of his decrepit old village temple (Luo 2008). Soon ZBM's ability to cure people of illnesses began attracting villagers to the new temple, inspiring them to join together to get the temple rebuilt. In rediscovering the deity Lord Zong Guan, the villagers were able to reconstruct their lost "collective memory" (*jiti jiyi,*

集體記憶) and community identity (Luo 2008: 290, 294–295). Alas, only two months after its erection, the new deity temple was rudely torn down by state authorities, who regarded the temple and its shamanic authority as "feudal superstition." The higher state authorities refused to accept the new temple until it was converted to Buddhist uses—and ZBM, the shamaness who had originally inspired the ritual solidarity of the village around the old deity temple, was driven out of the new Buddhist temple. Shamans—most of whom, in Wenzhou, are women—are a common presence in small temples, especially start-ups. The reason may be that, when spirit mediums are possessed by a deity, their shaking bodies and unintelligible speech make the presence of a god palpable and highly visible. With ritual healers, any improvement in a patient's health is a testament to the presence of a spirit who favors that particular temple space. Thus, we can posit that shamanic presence in a temple provides the spark of divine presence, reactivating the spiritual authority of a derelict or new temple space and transforming it from a secular space into a sacred space capable of drawing crowds. To the extent that shamans play important roles in jump-starting the ritual solidarity and collective identity of grassroots communities, when officials harass shamans or tear down their small temples, they are throwing a wrench into the delicate process of rebuilding indigenous civil society.

The Temple as a Communal Institution and Icon of Locality

Mountain Stream Daoist Temple (pseudonym) was constructed in 1558 during the Ming dynasty. Before becoming a Daoist temple in 1994, it was a modest deity temple called Dual Residence of Gods Yang and Chen (楊陳二府), honoring two gods worshipped only in the Zhejiang area. One, Yang Chongye (楊崇業), from Shanxi Province, served as a military official in Zhejiang Province during the Wanli reign of the Ming dynasty; the other, Chen Tao (陳陶), was born in Jiangxi Province in the Tang dynasty. In Zhejiang, both men fought Japanese pirates valiantly, but they were sacrificed on the battlefield near Wenzhou in 1553. After their heroic deaths, they were honored as gods by the local people. Today, Mountain Stream is a good example of a small community temple.

During the Maoist era, the three-room temple was turned into a shed for raising silkworms. It burned down in 1958, but somehow was rebuilt. When the Economic Reforms started in 1978, "virtuous men and devout women" (善男信女) from surrounding villages gathered donations, and the decrepit wooden temple was rebuilt. The temple serves four neighboring villages, who take turns sponsoring temple festivals. These festivals, held on the second and twentieth day of each lunar month, gather people from the four villages together to participate in rituals and a banquet. The temple also holds birthday festivals for the gods Yang and Chen, the Three Officials, and the Jade Emperor, for a total of over thirty festivals per year. There is a regular Daoist priest, who is assisted in festival rituals by a local scripture-chanting group (拜懺團). This group, mainly composed of women, chants Daoist and Buddhist scriptures, including the Amitabha Scripture (阿彌陀佛經), the Scripture of the Three Officials (三官寶懺), and the Lotus Sutra (蓮華經).

In 1992, the flame from a large candle spread to the rafters, engulfing the entire wooden structure in flames. A funding drive followed, which netted 50,000 yuan for rebuilding the temple. This time, they built a cement structure with five rooms totaling four hundred square meters. Their quiet expansion of the temple did not go unnoticed by local authorities, and they were fined 10,000 yuan for expanding the temple without official permission. At a boisterous festival in the new temple on May 8, 1993, I shot video footage that is included in my documentary (M. Yang 1994b). The large wooden outer doors of the temple were painted with brightly colored door gods. Inside, behind the central altar, sat the god Yang himself, behind a glass panel; to his right sat the Earth God, guardian of the temple and the local area; and to his left were the Daoist gods, the Three Officials (三官大帝) of Heaven, Earth, and Water. The temple had dropped the other god, Chen. Over five hundred people attended this gathering, sitting around banquet tables, sipping potent Shaoxing rice wine, eating vegetarian dishes, and chattering in good spirits. The kitchen was a busy scene, with men cooking in giant woks; outside, women were washing the dishes.

In 2015, Mountain Stream Temple got permission to organize a large-scale five-day ritual procession, which cost the temple about 400,000 yuan. They brought out the god Yang on a palanquin, carried on bamboo shoulder poles by eight men, and, amid huge crowds, made their way to each of the four villages the temple served. At stops in each village, the local residents presented the god with incense and food offerings laid out on "incense offering tables" (香案). The purpose of this outing was to ask the god "to preserve peace and protect the people of the locality" (保平安，保护地方人民). The big event took three months to organize, with two hundred participants, including musicians, drummers, and people dressed in traditional costumes, walking on stilts; and an estimated forty thousand people thronged to see the procession. The organizers assembled thirteen Daoist priests to conduct Daoist rituals, and teams of women chanted the Scripture of the Jade Emperor. The temple arranged for the local police to direct traffic and keep order.

Divine Efficacy, Temple Finances, and Social Redistribution

The Palace of the Celestial Immortal (天仙宮) is dedicated to Sacred Mother Lu (discussed in chapter 3), a local goddess born in 742 CE and worshipped only in the Wenzhou area. Locals described this temple as a place where "the incense fire is very strong" (香火很盛), meaning that it was a successful temple to which multitudes flocked to burn incense, including visitors from other townships and counties.

I first visited this temple in 1992, when it was a small, rundown wooden temple with faded walls, its pillars leaning unsteadily with age. The painting of Mother Lu on the wall outside was barely discernible, and the courtyard stones were cracked and uneven, with weeds growing in the crevices. There was no temple management committee, so the temple was overseen by an old man who had no other place to live. Since then it has been rebuilt twice, and by the new millennium, the temple was about eight times larger than before. In the first rebuilding in 1993–1994, the old temple was torn down, and a more impressive temple was erected at a cost of 1.8 million yuan ($216,000). Unfortunately, an electrical fire destroyed the new temple, so the second rebuilding, which cost another 1.2 million yuan, took place in 1997. In 2000, the temple's total income was 740,000 yuan ($88,800). By 2004, the temple was receiving an annual total income of 1 million yuan ($120,000).

Although the temple name refers to Mother Lu, and she is still positioned at the central altar, the main attraction today is the deity Lord Wen Chang (文昌爺), God of Literature, whom people hope will assist their child to pass examinations. In these days of fast-paced economic development, urbanization, and jobs that require educational success, the filiality and feminine virtue embodied by Mother Lu seem to have diminished in importance. The birth control program has also meant that, with only one or two children, parents can now afford to send their daughters to school alongside their sons.

So many people were granted their prayers that they brought in an overabundance of red velvet banners (錦旗) declaring thanks to the gods. The banners lined the temple walls and reached almost to the ceiling. Finally, temple managers had to save space by taking photos of each banner and posting the photos on the walls instead of the banners. They also asked the public to refrain from bringing in more banners and, instead, to donate money to build, outside the temple, an Educational Advancement Pavilion (升學亭), where students can study and rest.

The temple holds religious services and a community banquet twice a month, on the second and sixteenth days of the lunar month. Like most deity temples here, it was converted into a Daoist temple after 1994. They invite a local Zhengyi Daoist priest to preside, and a scripture-chanting group chant and accompanies the priest in Daoist pacing in the temple courtyard, including "walking in the five directions" (走五方). About every three years, the temple organizes a large-scale Daoist ritual (作道場) to beg for peace, health, and prosperity for the community. Twice a year, the temple organizes opera performances, each of which lasts eight to ten days.

In 1999, the temple started to engage in "public benefit work" (公益事業), making charitable donations to fund public needs. With their impressive income, they donated 257,300 yuan to build a nearby road. At New Year's, they gave 300 yuan to each elderly resident of a local old-age home and invited all villagers above the age of sixty to an annual feast in the temple; at this event they fed nearly six hundred elderly people. They also gave 200 yuan to any villager who got sick. Assistance to the poor amounted to 50,000 yuan. By 2004, financial aid to the needy had increased: they gave out 500–6,000 yuan to "hardship families" (困難戶)—those with illness, death of a working adult, and so on. For those whose house or business burned down, the temple offered assistance of up to 15,000 yuan ($1,800). They were also planning to give out scholarships for children of poor families attending high school, technical school, or college.

In 2001, a novel way of increasing temple revenue was introduced, called "peace and prosperity lamps" (平安發財燈). These are large cone-shaped racks, nine feet high, that are filled with rows of little candles in glass cups for people to pay to light them. Originally invented in Taiwan, a Daoist temple in Taiwan gave two of them as gifts to the White Cloud Daoist Temple in Beijing, the national headquarters of the Quanzhen sect of Daoism. A Wenzhou man from Rui'an County happened to visit that temple and was very impressed with them. He scrutinized their composition and structure carefully, came back to Wenzhou, and started to reproduce them by hand. Now he manufactures large numbers of them in a Wenzhou factory. The Celestial Immortal Temple purchased one peace lamp from him for 26,000 yuan ($3,120) and charged worshippers 50 yuan to keep a small candle lit for the gods year-round. The temple committee was swamped with eager people wishing to purchase a lamp. In just three days, the temple sold 50,000 yuan ($6,000) worth of lights and had already ordered a second cone rack. Wiping his brow, the temple director said his "head was full of sweat" (滿頭大汗)! Each cone tower could hold twelve hundred candles—and the temple sold every one, earning 60,000 yuan ($7,200), which at that time was a very impressive sum.

Figure 6.2. Peace and Prosperity Lamp at the Palace of the Celestial Immortal, in Yongzhong, Longwan District, 1998. Photo by the author.

Grassroots Resistance: Protecting a Religious Heritage Site from the Profit-Seekers

The original Jinxiang Township City God Temple (金鄉城隍廟), a small temple, was built in 1387 at the beginning of the Ming dynasty (Jinxiang Chenghuang-miao Bianji Weiyuanhui 2007). The City God to whom the temple is dedicated is Tang He (湯和, 1326–1395 CE), a general sent by Emperor Zhu Yuanzhang, the founder of the Ming dynasty, to China's eastern coast to fight pirates. Tang He and his men established the town of Jinxiang when he built a military fortress, one of fifty-nine that he erected on China's eastern coast to defend against the pirates. During the Cultural Revolution, the temple was attacked, and the gods inside were smashed to pieces. On July 20, 2004, I interviewed Mr. Tao and Mr. Cai, two elders who had participated in reviving the temple.

The County Grain Bureau occupied the site for many years, and they refused to move out when the Economic Reform period started. In 2001, the Grain Bureau decided that it wanted to tear down the dilapidated temple buildings, build new residential apartments with storefronts downstairs, and sell them for profit. When they approached the town's mayor, he told them that this temple was a symbol of the town and beloved by the local people; he dared not approve this action and incur the wrath of the people. He suggested that the Grain Bureau gather one representative from each of the nine Old People's Associations—representing four sections of the town and five surrounding villages—and see if it could win their approval. The nine elders refused to accept the bureau's plan. The Grain Bureau then demanded that they pay 300,000 yuan to purchase the site. The mayor told the nine elders that the government did not have any money for this and that they would not be getting any government help. So these nine elders decided to "strike out on their own" (*zili gengsheng*), employing a Maoist-era slogan. They were not wealthy, but each of them donated about 1,000 to 1,600 yuan. They got together 15,000 yuan, but it was insufficient. Some of the old people wanted to give up, but others were more resolute: "We've come this far, we cannot give up! We've got to persevere and press on." So they filed legal suits (*da guansi*) with different agencies of the local government, spoke out at town meetings, and sent petitions up to higher levels, above the township. Their activity got the attention of generous entrepreneurs who wanted to contribute to their hometown. Soon they assembled the 300,000 yuan and successfully bought the site from the Grain Bureau.

The organizers immediately got to work to restore the temple to its former glory. Between 2001 and 2004, they collected another 2.6 million yuan in donations and formed a preparatory committee to oversee temple reconstruction. The temple was completed in 2004. Neither the township nor the county government gave them money for the temple construction or helped with organizational work. "This was entirely a spontaneous organization [自發的組織], and the donations came from the local people themselves. The only thing the government did was to sign the approval," they told me. Furthermore, it was only through the repeated petitioning by the nine elders that the temple finally gained official approval to take out the City God twice a year in ritual procession around the town.

However, the wording of the temple's stone commemorative stele suggests that the township government took the credit. The stele says that the temple was restored "under the leadership of the township government" (在金鄉鎮政府的領導下), and the stele announcement is signed by the township government. Certainly this goes against local accounts that it was a collective effort by the local citizens themselves. The temple organizers may have awarded credit to the township government for two possible reasons. First, the temple elders may have wanted to "give face" (*gei mianzi*) to the local government and thereby gain official support for the temple. This kind of flattery is akin to taking out an insurance policy against possible temple destruction in the future. Second, if the temple organizers could demonstrate official leadership and support, the temple would gain a certain legitimacy and command more respect. However, future historians and archaeologists who read only the stone stele may come to some faulty conclusions about the absence of grassroots initiative in Chinese culture: they may simply assume that most social initiatives come from the state.

From Local to National Buddhist Institution: Xianyan Buddhist Temple's Nalanda Charitable Foundation and Buddhist Academy

In chapter 5, I introduced Xianyan Chan Buddhist Temple in Rui'an Municipality. Here I wish to show how local initiatives may take off and create a strong institution that breaks through onto the national stage. In 1979–1980, following the Cultural Revolution, a few devout Buddhist laypeople—Pan Yiheng, Chen Chunsheng, and others—stepped forward to lead in collecting donations and rebuilding this temple. In his published recollections, Pan Yiheng wrote of the tremendous risks to their own political safety:

> Since I was a Buddhist disciple, I could not push away this responsibility [of rebuilding the temple] onto others. So I discussed the matter with some local elders who were enthusiastic about the public benefit [公益]. They were all opposed to my initiating this work. They were anxious about the still dominant Leftist tide, and concerned that I risked getting struggled against and thrown into jail. In addition, they thought this task was too monumental; we lacked the funding, and the occupying work unit had many people on its side and was very powerful. . . . At that time, the new state religious policy had not yet been implemented, and Leftist thought exerted a lot of pressure . . . , so I was fighting a lonely battle. (Pan Yiheng 2000: 248)

However, after several more lay Buddhists and monks came forward to support him, he boldly threw himself into the effort.

> Although a few leaders of the occupying work unit went to the provincial authorities to report us, and used both hard and soft tactics to scare and threaten us, however, we Buddhist disciples also used some aggressive tactics and kept on fighting. We are capable of great patience, and we have great tenacity and fearlessness. After one year of construction, the high beamed and green-tiled roof of the central hall emerged against the green mountainside, startling the whole country. (Pan Yiheng 2000: 248)

Since those difficult years, this historically prominent Buddhist temple has attracted visits and donations by many prominent Wenzhou citizens, officials, and wealthy entrepreneurs. Under the capable leadership of Abbot Hong Guang (formerly Nengxian), the temple has added many new buildings and a new Huiguang Pagoda, making it one of the largest in Southern Zhejiang. This temple's prominence and wealth has meant that it is more penetrated by the state than smaller temples. For one thing, the local government, seeing the temple as a sort of cash cow, requires it to charge an entrance fee of thirty-five yuan (in 2010), which may deter many ordinary worshippers from entering. None of the entrance fees have made their way to the coffers of the temple, who did not wish to charge any fees. Instead, all of the money has gone to the Bureau of Religion.

In 2012, I attended an impressive lunch at an elegant vegetarian restaurant, along with a few temple monks, local writers, officials, and entrepreneurs. I could see that prominent professionals and officials in Wenzhou increasingly support Buddhist development. Given that the abbot hobnobbed in these influential circles, it was not surprising that he was able to win official approval to set up two ambitious temple projects, described in the next sections.

Nalanda Charitable Foundation (那藍陀慈善基金會)

Abbot Hong Guang registered the Nalanda Charitable Foundation with the Wenzhou City government's Charity Office in 2009, making it the first formal religious charity in Zhejiang Province. In the past it was very difficult across China to establish foundations or charities, but after the Chinese government saw the tremendous contributions of charities to victims of the 2008 Wenchuan earthquake in Sichuan, it relented and allowed many to be established. Technically, a "charitable foundation" differs in nature from a "merit foundation" (功德會). Foundations are more powerful and subjected to fewer restrictions, while the latter are set up by religious organizations and are considered "folk organizations" (民間團體), which have less legitimacy and influence. Since the Nalanda Charitable Foundation organizes many fund-raising activities in cooperation with government officials, who also attend its social functions, it can be understood as partially secularized and partially integrated with the state. The advantage of the foundation working closely with the city is that its donors can enjoy tax breaks for the money they give, which encourages more donations. That year the foundation accumulated 270,000 yuan in donations for the 2008 Wenchuan earthquake victims in Sichuan.

In its very first year of operations, 2009, the Nalanda Charitable Foundation engaged in an impressive list of projects and activities:

1. Poverty Relief and Aid to Hardships Group. This group held a public fund-raising event on Wenzhou Television Station, raising 50,000 yuan to help leukemia patients. They also brought gifts to a local orphanage and collected 45,000 yuan to buy food for thirty families.

2. Saving Migrant Workers' Children event (救助民工子弟). The foundation organized artists and calligraphers to donate fifty artworks and held this fund-raising event, raising 60,000 yuan to support one year's school tuition and living expenses for sixty migrant workers' children. This event was co-organized with state or quasi-state agencies: Wenzhou's Communist Youth League, the Wenzhou government's Main Charity Office, the Wenzhou Hope Project Office, and the Wenzhou-Chongqing Chamber of Commerce, an organization of Wenzhou entrepreneurs who do business in Chongqing City.

3. Environmental Protection Group. The foundation brought together the Asian Animal Foundation, the Wenzhou Wandering Dogs Foundation, and the Green Eyes Wildlife Protection Society to discuss joint projects and activities to protect the environment and animals. They held a Buddhist wildlife-releasing ritual activity outdoors.

4. Environmental Protection of the Mind program (心靈環保). This program teaches Chan meditation, sutra-chanting, and physical exercise to help people cleanse their minds. They invited a professor of psychiatry and a psychological counselor to provide free lectures on forging loving social relationships with other human beings.

5. On October 1, the sixtieth anniversary of the Communist Liberation of China, the foundation held a large public event to promote compassion and charity (慈善). The event featured a mistress of ceremonies wearing an elegant *qipao*; a choir composed of Buddhist clergy and laypeople; and performances by monks and laypeople. This event demonstrates the interweaving of religious and secular nationalist activities, where religious civil society can merge with state projects.

6. The foundation organized a lecture by a professor of philosophy from People's University in Beijing on how to develop Buddhism.

Nalanda Buddhist Academy (那藍陀佛學院)

The Nalanda Buddhist Academy was established at Xianyan Temple in 2007 in accordance with the guiding principle for all Buddhist Academies across the country: "Love one's country, love one's religion; learning and self-cultivation are equally stressed" (愛國愛教, 學修并重). In the first four characters of this phrase, one can see the state expectation that patriotism must have precedence over religious doctrines. The academy's teaching philosophy is encapsulated in the phrase "The eight sects are equally important; the five fields must all be absorbed" (八宗並重, 五明兼顧). The eight sects of Chinese Buddhism are Huayan, Tiantai, Three Doctrines, Faxiang, True Speech, Regulations, Chan, and Pure Land. The "five fields of learning" refer to the ancient Buddhist curriculum: phonology and language; handicrafts; medicine; karmic knowledge and ethics; and Buddhist religious principles.

The academy recruited students between the ages of eighteen and thirty-five years. In 2014, there were about twenty students taking four years of undergraduate classes, and about ten graduate students studying three years for the Buddhist equivalent of a master of arts degree. Instructors came from the Minnan Buddhist Academy (in the city of Xiamen), Wenzhou University, and other universities. Classes included Buddhist Studies, Confucian Studies, Foundational Principles of Religious Studies, and Textual Methodology for the Study of Buddhist Texts. The academy is active in proselytizing Buddhist doctrines and organizes public lectures by monks and scholars. It also offers classes on China's literary classics, foreign language (usually English), cultural history, comparative broadcasting (a media production class), and Buddhist sutras. The students, monks, and nuns attend psychology classes twice per week. The academy also publishes a Buddhist magazine, *The Light of Wisdom* (慧光).

Besides educating a new generation of monks and nuns, the academy also makes classes such as Chan meditation, youth education, Buddhist scriptures for adults, and calligraphy available to laypeople for a nominal fee.

Xianyan Temple also established several other initiatives. The Nalanda Calligraphy and Painting Institute has a membership of calligraphers, painters, and art lovers in the Wenzhou region. The Nalanda Dharma Dissemination Group, founded in 2010, organizes Buddhist sermons to win new converts. The Buddhist Cultural Exchange Association between the Mainland and Taiwan promotes religious and academic exchange between Wenzhou and Taiwan Buddhists across the Taiwan Strait. Finally, the Institute of Xianyan Buddhist Culture was established in the Philosophy Department at East China Normal University in Shanghai, a top university in the country. Here monks, nuns, and lay intellectuals discuss Buddhist doctrine, publish research on Buddhist culture and history, and organize professional training and academic conferences. This represents an effort to open up parochial Wenzhou Buddhist circles to the dynamic and cosmopolitan Buddhist traffic found in Shanghai. This initiative also promises to give voice to Wenzhou's local Buddhist culture in larger national and global Buddhist conversations.

The above examples reveal the tremendous grassroots initiative, energy, and persistence for nurturing the "sprouts of religious civil society." Whether the shamanic spark that sacralizes temple space to jump-start new village temples, or secularized Buddhist ethical teachings, the religious element is crucial in rallying people together to organize community life and civil society. The large temple complex of Xianyan Chan Buddhist Temple ritually serves its local residents and, in addition, promotes their connections with the world beyond the locality.

Each of the above cases of temple start-ups involved struggles and negotiations with powerful institutions. The City God Temple had to move the powerful Grain Bureau out to protect a historical site of social memory that was endangered by profit-minded state real estate developers; the Mountain Stream Daoist Temple was fined for expanding their new temple without permission. These examples showcase persistent efforts to loosen the grip and detach from the all-encompassing state body and retrieve physical and social space from both the state and the profit-oriented commercial sphere for religious rituals and community activities.

Despite each family's engagement in private enterprise and the profit economy, the spirit of community ethics remains very strong. Wenzhou society's organizational and fund-raising genius can be seen in the ways people petition local government offices for land purchases, building permits, and temple registrations. Organizational acumen is also evident in the complex work of temple construction and in the mobilization of voluntary labor to put on temple festivals and ritual events that bring the community together. Temple activities and festivals provide a regular social gathering place for the exchange of news and reflections on local issues. All of these temples received virtually no state funding; instead, they relied on grassroots donations. The Celestial Immortal Temple reveals a creative ability to keep its revenue stream flowing with the purchase of "peace and prosperity lamps." This wealth is redistributed to the needy.

Instead of a clear-cut binary between civil society and the state, there is actually a gradation of religious organizations, from more autonomous and self-organizing smaller temples to larger, wealthier, and more state-penetrated organizations. For example, back in 1979–1980, the rebuilding of Xianyan Buddhist Temple was a spontaneous grassroots effort that faced hostile local officials. However, by the time the temple established the Nalanda Buddhist Academy and Charitable Foundation in 2007 and 2009, these efforts had become intertwined with new state agendas to promote traditional Chinese culture, local tourism, and a "harmonious society." Indeed, the Nalanda Charitable Foundation actually joined the local government in celebrating a secular national holiday, the founding of the People's Republic. The academy's course offerings also reflect significant inroads made by the standard secular college curriculum found across China. Both the foundation and the academy are responding to the early twentieth-century reformist monk Taixu's call for a "humanistic this-worldly Buddhism" (人間佛教), a new form of Buddhism that is well positioned to cooperate with the state and be subject to state penetration. At the same time, Buddhism can also be said to have started to operate from *within* the state, since it is bringing a transcendent religious message to a secular national holiday. Furthermore, Xianyan Temple still exhibits a certain religious independence in its meditation classes, Buddhist sermons, Buddhist rituals, and wildlife-releasing ritual outings, all of which construct transcendental communities.

GRASSROOTS TEMPLE MANAGEMENT: EGALITARIAN AND REDISTRIBUTIVE

Temple management differs from one temple to another. Often the members of a temple management committee (廟宇管理委員會) overlap with those managing the local Old People's Association (老人協會); the latter is made up of retired elderly people, usually men. The association usually has a pavilion, often located next to a stream or canal and built in traditional Chinese style, with roof corners curved up, where the senior members of the local community while away their remaining years playing mah-jongg or watching television. Sometimes temple management committee members also overlap with local lineage leaders, cultural station workers, local gazetteer writers, and members of Daoist and Buddhist Associations.

The method of selecting temple committee members and the temple manager often features a democratic element. A slate of nominees is put together from names that people contribute. Then the members of the local Old People's Association and other village members gather to publicly discuss the merits of each nominee. Sometimes a decision is made by public consensus. Sometimes a vote is taken to select a temple committee, which can range from six to thirty members. Occasionally a woman makes it onto the temple committee. The committee members then select the "temple manager" (會長). Sometimes men who have served as a local cadre or accountant before their retirement will be selected, since they have leadership experience. Smaller temples might have a rotating system of temple managers, where each prominent person in the village gets their turn to serve as temple manager. Sometimes the original founders or major investors in the temple will run the temple for years before converting to a temple committee. Small pockets of Minnanese-speaking communities have a "host of the incense burner" (爐主) system, as in Taiwan (Sangren 1987: 55–56), where a local man of means is selected each year to organize a major ritual festival event.

In 2001, the Mountain Stream Daoist Temple was managed by an organization of eleven local elders drawn from three of the four surrounding villages, who formed a temple managerial committee. The temple did not hold formal elections: any current committee member could nominate someone to be a member, and the others would discuss the matter at a meeting. I was told that there were seldom disagreements, and decisions were made by consensus. People generally supported those who commanded prestige (威望) in the local community. I was told, "Everyone just wants to manage the temple well so that local villagers would have a good place to pray to the gods to protect their family and community." In 2016, this loose managerial arrangement was the same, but the managerial committee had reached thirty people, all volunteers representing their villages. The committee head serves for a five-year term. One of the villages sends no representative to sit on the temple committee, so they have no say in the running of the temple. If a volunteer gets involved and attends meetings regularly, then he or she will eventually end up on the committee.

The Celestial Immortal Temple first got the idea for forming a "managerial team" (管理組) in 1993, from the Great Yin Temple to Mother Chen nearby, which was the first temple in the area to do so. The Celestial Immortal managerial committee in the early 2000s was composed of older men who had some formal education and had retired from positions as lower-level cadres, businessmen, factory heads, farmers, and accountants. They told me that decisions were generally made by consensus, with a few more influential leaders swaying the others. Here again, there were supposedly few disagreements. Each time they select new managerial committee members, they report the name(s) to the village government, the township government, and the Daoist Association.

When the construction of the Jinxiang City God Temple was completed in 2004, the original "preparatory committee" that oversaw construction was transformed into an eighteen-member temple "management commit-tee" composed of middle-aged men, including some local retired cadres and Party secretaries, people who possessed wide social networks. At a meeting, they were nominated and selected based on their contribution to the temple restoration effort and their good reputations in the local community. Their work as temple managers earned them no salary or compensation. The head of this committee in 2004 was a man in his sixties, a former worker for the town Grain Bureau. In other temples, such as the Gathering of the Sages Hall in a village outside Wenzhou City, there is an expectation that all village members fifty-five years and older should spend at least five days a year volunteering at the temple. Smaller temples often adopt the principles of rotating temple man-agers, electing or choosing them by consensus.

Sometimes temples select their managerial committee based on income, but this does not necessarily mean that the system *privileges* wealth, for those selected are expected to *lose* some of their wealth in donations to the temples they lead. Indeed, here we see an egalitarian and redistributive aspect of grass-roots Chinese communal religion. For example, the Prosperity Complete Pal-ace, a newly built temple in Cangnan County dedicated to Mother Chen, had a system of leadership in which wealth was a criterion. In this Minnanese-speaking village of three hundred households, the position of "main sponsor" (頭家) is rotated among thirty people in the village who command sufficient wealth to be considered for the post. In order to assume leadership in a given year, one must contribute at least 200,000 yuan ($32,600 in 2014) for the temple. Each year, on the patron deity's birthday, the fourteenth day of the first lunar month, the village members gather in the temple to ask the god-dess to select the right person. Each contestant pulls a divination stick from a bamboo jar, or temple managers present each name to the goddess and then throw two divining crescent blocks to the floor. Thus, the new head is chosen by a combination of divine selection and the willingness to give away part of his wealth. Temple managers are motivated by the prestige the job brings, the protection they will receive from the deity, and the merit they will accrue for the afterlife. Thus, the leadership position often does not enhance wealth but, rather, redistributes it in the community. This brings to mind Pierre Clastres's (1987: 30–31) work among Native Americans of Amazonia, in which he discov-ered that across indigenous South America, the moral authority of the chief depends on his generosity, and the expectation that the chief must give away his wealth to the community amounts to a form of "bondage" or "looting."

Some common temple managerial principles in rural Wenzhou include public discussion and debate of nominees' credentials; decision by consensus;

voting; rotating leadership; the expectation that leaders and wealthy members should donate more personal funds than the rank and file; and divine selection. These principles all suggest that in local communities, rural religious culture harbors a communal, egalitarian, redistributive, and perhaps even democratic ethos. Due to the paucity of historical records on village temple management in late imperial times, it is difficult to know how common this grassroots communalism and egalitarianism was in the past. We do see this redistributive tendency in rural temple societies in twentieth-century North China, where local associations promoting deity cults or organizing temple festivals were open only to those who had donated money or land (Duara 1988: 121). The flexible rule by group consensus or rotation was also observed in rural Taiwan in the 1980s; in discussing this practice Steven Sangren noted, "Arguments that emphasize the presumed inability of Chinese culture to imagine nonauthoritarian patterns of leadership and social relations seem to me overstated" (1987: 58).

ENTER THE DAOIST AND BUDDHIST ASSOCIATIONS

Since 1994, most Wenzhou deity temples belong to a local Daoist Association (道教協會), a quasi-state, quasi-religious, and civil organization that registers and oversees temple activities (M. Yang 2004). In the eyes of the state, popular religion seemed "backward" and their activities were difficult to supervise; therefore, deity temples were pushed to join the Daoist Association, where they could be better monitored and administered. In 1994, the State Council of the central government promulgated Document 145, "Regulations on the Management of Sites of Religious Worship" (Guowuyuan Zongjiao Shiwuju 1994a), signed by Premier Li Peng. Article 2 stipulates that all sites of religious worship must be properly registered with local authorities. In practice, most deity temples were not permitted to register unless they joined the Daoist Association. Unregistered temples risked getting shut down or even physically dismantled by the state. Most local deity temples rushed to convert themselves into Daoist sites. Those that could prove their existence before the Cultural Revolution got registered as Daoist temples in 1993 or 1994. Then, in the late 1990s, there was a second wave of registrations in which newer temples were also accepted into the Daoist Association. Thus, the unintended beneficiary of the state's anxiety about unregulated deity temples was institutional Daoism.

Temple elders told me that they were willing to register as Daoist temples because getting state approval and registration was an insurance against getting summarily dismantled by the state. Registration gave temples certain rights. For example, if the local government should one day need to build a highway right through the site of their temple, then the temple would enjoy state compensation for being dismantled. If temple managers did not have the proper papers, then they would have no right to compensation. Thus, throughout the 1990s and into the new millennium, the temple managers and women's sutra-chanting groups were busy learning Daoist scriptures, ritual pacing, and the Daoist art of writing talismans.

The idea of Daoist Associations across China is that local Daoist temples and Daoist practitioners could govern themselves on religious matters, while being guided by state authority. Daoist Associations would create a communication channel with state agencies to voice local concerns and interests, while also allowing the centralized state to funnel its religious policies and directives down to grassroots levels. Daoist Associations are funded by fees that each Daoist temple under its jurisdiction must turn in every month, a requirement called "delivering payments upward" (上繳). Daoist Associations are composed of local Daoist priests and laypersons who have an enthusiasm for Daoist activities, and this kind of membership provides it with its civil society or religious dimension. However, the state dimension of Daoist Associations is seen in the selection of their leadership, which is managed by the local government. Furthermore, association activities are often dictated from higher state levels. In popular parlance, Daoist Associations are "half folk [minjian] and half official [半民間, 半官方]."

Historically, the traditional mode of Daoist religious organization comprised local and dispersed lineages of Daoist masters who transmitted Daoist self-cultivation methods, scriptural knowledge, and liturgies, usually in secret, to their chosen disciples and apprentices. Quanzhen Daoists transmitted these methods in male and female monastic contexts, where their acolytes were expected to live a life of sexual abstinence. Zhengyi Daoists often transmitted them in the context of their families, from father to son, with daughters excluded, and lessons were also transmitted from master to apprentice. In 1912, a new mode of modern Daoist organization emerged, in the form of two nationwide Daoist Associations established by urban educated Daoist modernizers in Beijing and Shanghai: the Central Daoist Association (中央道教會) and the Republic of China Daoist Main Association (中華民國道教總會). In 1957, following the Communist Revolution, these organizations were replaced by a state-led national Daoist Association. This entity had barely held its first and second national Daoist meetings and established its own national journal before being shut down during the Cultural Revolution. In 1980, the national Daoist Association regrouped and held its third national meeting in the capital, and since then, local Daoist Association chapters have been set up across the country.

The Wenzhou City Daoist Association (溫州市道教協會) was founded in 1986 and established its base offices at the Purple Cloud Daoist Temple (紫霄 道觀) in the Western Mountains of the City. It is composed of eleven chapters, based in Wenzhou City's urban districts (市區), counties (縣), and municipalities (市). The City Daoist Association helps the government administer 1,915 Daoist sites of worship throughout the Wenzhou area, of which 910 were originally deity temples.[1] All Daoist Association branches are linked vertically in an ascending chain to the Wenzhou City level, the Zhejiang Provincial level, and finally the national headquarters: the White Cloud Daoist Temple (中國道教 協會, 白雲觀) in Beijing.

The Beijing Daoist headquarters privileges the Quanzhen sect of monastic Daoism, even though the vast majority of Daoist laypeople and priests across China subscribe to the Zhengyi sect. This may reflect the modern history of Daoism, whereby the Western definition of "religion," based on the Christian church and its clergy (Goossaert and Palmer 2011: 51; M. Yang 2008b, 2011), exerted a profound influence on the Chinese elites who modernized and reformed Daoism. The old Daoist religious capital of Dragon Tiger Mountain in Jiangxi Province has experienced some new life as the carrier of the Celestial Masters lineage, tracing back two thousand years. However, although Dragon Tiger Mountain has won back the power to ordain Daoist Zhengyi priests, it lacks influence, money, and direct access to top-level state and Party authorities. Thus, it cannot compete with the national state-sanctioned Daoist Association in Beijing as the official voice of Daoism in China today.

Moving to Buddhism, the Wenzhou City Buddhist Association (溫州市 佛教協會) is also a quasi-state, quasi-civil and religious organization, overseeing Buddhist temples in Wenzhou. The Buddhist Association is found in the same eleven regions of Wenzhou as the Daoist Association. It also serves as a two-way conduit between civil grassroots religious organizations and state administration. Most of the Wenzhou Buddhist Associations were founded in the 1980s and 1990s. The Wenzhou City Buddhist Association seems the most enmeshed with the state. It sometimes holds meetings and social events with the heads of Wenzhou's United Front Communist Party head and the chief of the local Bureau of Religion. Compared to the Daoist Association, Buddhist temples and Buddhist Associations tend to be wealthier, even though Wenzhou is considered a stronghold of Daoist culture. The reason for its financial strength may be that it enjoys more acceptance and legitimacy by officialdom. Increasingly, some officials in Wenzhou quietly subscribe to the Buddhist faith. Enjoying stronger official support, Buddhism attracts more members of the entrepreneurial class, who rub shoulders with the official class at many Buddhist social functions.

Certainly Buddhism acts as a moderating force on the highly charged commercial culture of contemporary Chinese state capitalism. Buddhist teachings of charity and compassion toward the poor, the weak, and the suffering stand in contrast to the accumulative spirit that drives capitalism. Buddhists' concern for nonhuman forms of sentient beings and "wildlife-releasing" (放生) activities lead them to a ready acceptance of environmentalist messages.

The exception to the requirement that all deity temples must be integrated into the Daoist Associations is found in southern Wenzhou's Cangnan County. Here the Cangnan Popular Religion Connections Office (蒼南民間信仰聯絡處) was set up to administer deity temples in the 1990s. Only in Cangnan County and Fujian Province is "popular religion" officially recognized and accorded this institutional office and self-governing power. However, when I interviewed at this office in 2016, the staff still referred to themselves as "hanging and leaning" (掛靠) on the Daoist Association, implying that they were not fully independent. In 2013, the Wenzhou City Party Committee sent down a directive that Cangnan County must register all of its deity temples, so 1,555 deity temples were registered with this office and the County Bureau of Religion.

The office is made up of representatives from the ten townships and two rural districts (乡) of Cangnan County. An indication of its stronger nonstate "folk" (*minjian*) character is the fact that most of these representatives are actually lineage heads (族長) across Cangnan, a kinship organization not formally recognized by the state but strong in grassroots society, especially in Cangnan. The office also overlaps with two new religious associations in the county: the Chen Jinggu Association (陳靜姑協會), which has three hundred temples, and the Mazu Association (媽祖協會), which has seventy. In 2014–2016, there was talk about upgrading the Cangnan Popular Religion Connections Office into an "association," on an equal footing with the Daoist and Buddhist Associations. However, I was told that "higher levels did not approve it" (上面不同意). I got an inkling of the possible reason when I interviewed a member of the Daoist Association in another county. "We will fight this!" said this Daoist, adding that he and other Daoists had already petitioned higher levels to prevent the Popular Religion Office from upgrading. It seems evident that any independence of a Popular Religion Office would threaten the power and influence of the Daoist Association, since it would lose 1,555 deity temple members currently under its jurisdiction.

Figure 6.3. Wenzhou City Daoist Association headquarters, Purple Cloud Temple in Western Mountains, 1998. Photo by the author.

Figure 6.4. Cangnan County Popular Religion Connections Center, 2016. Photo by the author.

RE-EMBEDDING WITHIN THE STATE:
TWO STATE OFFICES GOVERNING RELIGIOUS LIFE

In Wenzhou there are two important state agencies at the county and munici-pal level that have a direct say in the activities of all religious organizations or ritual sites. The Daoist or Buddhist Associations, the Three-Self Patriotic Movement for Protestants, and the Catholic Patriotic Association are all under their authority. One is the Bureau of Ethnicity and Religion (民族宗教局). This bureau is part of government administration, divided into three "de-partments" (ke): (1) Buddhism, Daoism, and popular religion; (2) Protestantism and Catholicism; and (3) minority ethnic religions. The bureau is in charge of registering temples, and its approval is required for establishing or expanding any temple, church, or monastery and for undertaking religious processions and large-scale religious activities. It also takes an active role in shaping the elections of new temple or association heads. The bureau also transmits direc-tives and religious policies from the national-level State Administration for Religious Affairs (SARA) (國家宗教事務局).

The second office, the United Front Office (統戰部), is more powerful than the Bureau of Ethnicity and Religion because it is part of the Chinese Commu-nist Party. Established during the Chinese Civil War against the Guomindang Party in the 1930s, its task is to transform potentially hostile forces outside the Communist Party into allies and supporters. These outside forces include other political parties, overseas Chinese communities, ethnic minority groups, religious groups, and non-Party intellectuals. The fact that the work of the United Front Office includes reaching out to Sinophone communities in Tai-wan, Hong Kong, and Southeast Asia has an important bearing on popular religion. United Front Policy often deploys the strategy of promoting religious exchanges between the Chinese Mainland and religious Chinese communities in Taiwan and beyond (M. Yang 2008a). In March 2018, SARA was dismantled, leaving religious affairs administered solely by the United Front. This move indicates a new tightening of controls over religion, as SARA used to be more about government administration but is now integrated directly into the Party, which is about ideological conformity.

CONCLUSION

The Émile Durkheim epigraph at the beginning of this chapter is especially apt for our understanding of the link between the resurgence of popular religion in China and the reinvention of indigenous forms of "civil society." Durkheim's classic work *The Elementary Forms of Religious Life*, originally published in 1912, is seldom linked to discussions of civil society, which tend to privilege urban and secular contexts. Durkheim argued that religious impulses and icons are key to the inauguration of societies because they generate the social solidarity that all societies need to maintain and reproduce themselves. In other words, for Durkheim, all societies and social organizations were originally founded as religious entities: the religious impulse gave them both inspiration and the strength to endure.

However, most writings on Chinese civil society leave out the religious dimension of nonstate associations, an especially important dimension when we are examining rural and small-town contexts. When I first started fieldwork in the 1990s, I went in search of secular nonstate organizations, conducting interviews at a private high school, the Wenzhou Literary Federation, a calligraphy society, and a stamp collection association. However, I found that these all had funding from local governments and their way of thinking was not far from state discourse. The truly nongovernmental associations were spontaneous grassroots organizations, all of which had a ritual or religious raison d'être. What galvanized people to organize local associations and strengthen communities was their concern about spiritual redemption and the afterlife, transcendence of temporal desires, and commemorating powerful gods who reside in parallel worlds. The religious impulse spurred the rebuilding of grassroots civil society and self-governance and provided the language through which people understood their efforts to emerge from an era of warfare, impoverishment, and militarization of society.

However, the state is adaptive and can respond to this riotous religious growth to regain control. Once a local temple registers and joins the Daoist or Buddhist Association, it loses a certain independence and becomes the lowest level of a vast state religious administration stretching all the way to Beijing. This attenuates its role as an icon of local community and reduces its self-governing node, since it now answers not only to the local community but also to the Daoist and Buddhist Associations, the state, and the Party. Thus, the reritualized locality becomes partially reembedded within the state bureaucracy.

To sum up, in the initial phase of the restoration of temples that started in the 1980s and 1990s, the grassroots energy revealed an impressive rural Wenzhou propensity for local initiative and community self-governance. However, these dynamic grassroots energies were tamed and somewhat neutralized by the 1994 state requirement that all temples must join and belong to either the Daoist or Buddhist Associations. However, the Popular Religion Connections

Office in Cangnan County is able to preserve more local independence and the "folk" flavor of religious civil society. The encompassing of temples by the quasi-civil and quasi-state Daoist and Buddhist Associations is further solidified by the involvement of the state Bureau of Religion and the Party's United Front, to which the religious associations must answer. As commercialization of the Wenzhou economy intensifies and a younger, better-educated generation starts to exercise power, we wait to see what they will do with the "sprouts" of religious civil society growing from seeds sown by their parents and grandparents.

7 The Rebirth of the Lineage

Creative Unfolding and Multiplicity of Forms

如果利益是給個人, 那就叫'私.' 如果利益是給集體, 或給宗族, 我們叫 '公.' 過去解放前我們不考慮國家的.

If the benefit is for the individual, then it is called "private"; if it is for the "collective," or the whole lineage, then we call it "public." You know, in the past, before Liberation, we did not think about the nation.

—Zhang Chengdu 張成都, Zhang Lineage elder, Yong Zhong Township, Wenzhou, 1993

In China, lineages (*zongzu*, 宗族) are kinship groups that trace their common ancestry through the patrilineal line to a founding male ancestor, many generations in the past. These descent organizations are ritual communities composed of member family units. These families come together a few times each year in ritual sacrifices and tomb-sweeping ceremonies during the Qingming Festival to honor their ancestors. Lineages trace back to archaic China, but they became most prominent in late imperial times, especially in southeastern China, which was an area of frontier settlement by Han Chinese. Here, far from the imperial court, lineage organizations became a form of self-government by local gentry. Along with the anti-Confucian movements of the twentieth century, lineage organizations became targets of attacks and were shut down, their communal lands confiscated, and their rituals banned during the Mao era.

In the new millennium, a Confucian revival has spread across China in the form of both official culture and a grassroots movement (Billioud and Thoraval 2015). However, most studies focus on the Confucian education and Classics movement and do not address lineage revivals. The Confucian Classics devoted great attention to ancestor rituals, filial piety, and the importance of family, kinship, and intergenerational relations. During the Song dynasty, lineages experienced a dramatic revival through the writings of Neo-Confucian scholars, who urged attention to lineage rituals and activities in their efforts aimed at the moral reform of society (Ebrey 1986, 1991). What Peter Bol (2001, 2003) called the Song "localist turn" brought renewed commitment by Confucian gentry to their local places. Throughout late imperial times, lineages established local Confucian academies, charities, ancestor halls, and even deity temples and wrote local histories and lineage genealogies (Szonyi 2002). Given this Neo-Confucian association, today's resurgence of lineages in Wenzhou can be described as popular Confucianism in action.

ANTITRADITIONALIST DISCOURSES ON LINEAGE: WENZHOU AND LOS ANGELES

In the early 1990s, there was considerable animosity toward lineage organizations by officials and educated people in China. On a cold February day in 1991, I joined Zhang Lei, an entrepreneur who shuttled between Hangzhou and Los Angeles, to meet a writer of the Wenzhou Writers' Association, and we told him that we had just interviewed a lineage elder in Yongchang Township. He shook his head disapprovingly, saying,

> Lineages represent the backward, reactionary elements of China. Indeed, they are fascistic! They get involved in lineage rivalries and fight each other during dragon boat races, and people die. Within a lineage, they are authoritarian and not democratic at all, and democracy is what China needs. The lineage head [族長] is like a dictator. Their family regulations [家法] are very strict, there is no freedom. Violation of the rules brings punishment for matters of love and adultery.

After we parted from the writer, Zhang Lei criticized him: "This kind of intellectual just buys into whatever the government feeds him. How can he not see the 'human feelings' [renqingwei, 人情味] in lineage life?" This phrase—which referred to what was regarded as natural, the warmth and care that people have toward their family, kin, and friends—had made a comeback in the 1980s and 1990s. "Human feelings" were thought to have been suppressed during the Cultural Revolution in favor of an austere political correctness that called for drawing lines of separation between oneself and those family members, kin, friends, and coworkers who were not loyal state subjects. By identifying lineages with renqing, Zhang Lei was suggesting that the writer was still ensnared in cold-hearted Maoist-era discourse and had not caught up with the new times of seeking alternative values.

My encounters with living Wenzhou lineages suggest that this writer's description of lineages is an unjust caricature. Lineage rivalries certainly exist, but it is extremely rare that they lead to bloodshed. The major case of interlineage violence occurred during the Cultural Revolution in an area known for the most powerful lineages in Wenzhou. According to local historian Lin Shundao, this was in the area south of the Ao River (鳌江) and Longgang Town (龍港鎮). There had been intermittent violent outbreaks during the Republican era, but it was during the Cultural Revolution that lineage fighting here led to many deaths. People were whipped into a frenzy to attack "class enemies" and Red Guard factions, and "class struggle" was reinterpreted as old interlineage hostilities. Without this violent Maoist political rhetoric, lineage violence might not have broken out. Today's lineages are quite civil with one another and are tied together not only through intermarriage but also through common religious worship and coattendance at each other's major ritual events. Wenzhou lineages today may be male-dominated, but they are far from autocratic. Indeed, I found some "democratic" leanings in the way that lineage leadership and succession were worked out through open public discussion, consensus, rotational selection, and even elections for limited terms. Given recent sexually permissive attitudes promoted by consumer culture and mass media in China, Wenzhou lineages today hardly concern themselves with imposing puritanical sexual mores.

In official discourse of the 1980s and 1990s, a distinctly negative and suspicious attitude toward lineages can be discerned. A 1989 article complained, "These feudal activities seriously hamper the work of agricultural production, strengthen feudal clan thinking and power, and obstruct the dissemination and implementation of our government's policies and law. Lineage genealogical work facilitates factionalism . . . and increases interlineage feuding with bloody consequences" (Li Q. 1989: 29). In the Zhejiang Party School newspaper, a provincial publication intended for Party members only, the author chastises Wenzhou lineages: "New and restored ancestor halls have already replaced the old public buildings of the collectivized era and have become the new centers of public activity in village community life" (Zhu K. 1997: 84). The author goes on to enumerate the problems of lineage revival: They give rise to interlineage conflicts; local officials can no longer get their laws and policies implemented through the government village committees; they must now go through lineage authorities in order to be heard; lineages have their own internal laws, which sometimes conflict with state laws.

This negative evaluation of lineages reflects the contestation between the state and lineages for local authority and legitimacy in Wenzhou. Where lineage autonomy is perceived, official discourse represents lineages as an illegitimate government unto themselves, or prone to violent conflict, which requires state intervention. This overlooks the positive dimensions of lineages, such as charity and welfare provision, scholarship support for students, local infrastructure-building, and their self-initiating and self-governing abilities.

A second negative evaluation of lineages came from *outside* China. Back in the United States, I attended a Chinese Studies conference at UCLA in 1992 that addressed the applicability of Jürgen Habermas's notion of "public sphere" to Chinese history and culture. I presented my paper on reemergent voluntary associations such as temple societies, lineages, and churches in rural Wenzhou and said that they held promise as indigenous building blocks for "civil society" in rural China. One American historian of China asked me how lineages, which are closed and "ascribed" organizations with membership by birth, could be considered a form of civil society, which is supposed to be "open and free." Civil society is supposed to lie in the "public domain," the historian said, while something like lineages belong with the family in the "private domain." I feebly mumbled that the lineages I saw were spontaneously organized by volunteers and activists, and lineages took initiative in addressing local public needs and concerns, not just for their members, but for their local communities.

In hindsight, I should have recited the epigraph at the beginning of this chapter, words uttered by a Zhang lineage elder in Longwan District. Mr. Zhang said that, when referring to corporate lineage matters, lineage members use the term "public matters" (公家的), as distinguished from "private individual matters" or "private family matters" (私人家的). People in rural Wenzhou refer to pre-Liberation corporate lineage lands with the phrase "public land" (公家的土地) or "public fields" (公田), and they use the term "public benefit" (公益) to describe the aim of lineage activities and the work of lineage activists. In his fieldwork in southern Fujian, Wang Mingming found the same terminology of "public" used for lineage affairs, property, and fields, while "private" was used for individual family or household (2004: 73–75). He also found that the peasants used these categories of public and private in a shifting and relational way, and not as fixed abstract categories, so that lineage was "public" in relation to the family, but it was considered "private" or the "self" (我們自己的) when contrasted with the outside world or with other lineages.

This assumption that lineages can only belong to the private domain and should be excluded as modern civil society has also plagued researchers who work in Africa, where ancestors and descent-groups are common (Comaroff and Comaroff 1997a). According to Mikael Karlstrom (1997: 109), most Western scholars of Africa exclude kinship and descent-groups from the definition of civil society in Africa, even though these kinship structures go very deep in African cultural histories. Western scholars focus on voluntary associations as the key to a civil society that can counter the expansionary and predatory modern state in Africa. When they find few voluntary associations, they conclude that Africa has a "weak civil society." However, for many Ugandans, the revival of Bugandan kingship and its associated hierarchically ranked lineage and clan heads have produced "the most stable, cohesive, and responsive political order possible" (1997: 107), in contrast to Western-style political parties, which have been divisive and destructive in Uganda. Karlstrom concludes that we must challenge unexamined Western assumptions that "kinship as an axis of solidarity and association" (1997: 107) belongs only to the private sphere and must automatically be excluded from modern civil society.

Like Africa, kinship in China was also a basic principle of the social order, and descent-organizations and ancestor worship are very deep in Chinese culture. Indeed, so deep are patrilineal kinship structures in China that anthropologists Jack and Sulamith Potter, who conducted fieldwork in rural Guangdong Province in the early 1980s, invoked Lévi-Straussian structuralism. They had to account for how the Communist Revolution in the ownership of the means of production was still not able to change the "deep structure" of cultural categories of kinship belonging (Potter and Potter 1990). Despite the dismantling of private family farms and lineage lands, and the introduction of collectivized agriculture, the Potters found a curious continuity of patrilineal kinship structures: membership in Maoist "production teams" and class categories were both inherited from one's father, and women in a team were married off exogamously outside the team (1990: 251–269). Thus, the old unconscious structures of a group of patrilineally related men owning and managing property and importing wives from outside their kin group was so powerful that it affected how socialist "production teams" and "brigades" were understood and practiced.

I suggest that, contrary to Western ethnocentric assumptions that regard them as "private," lineages fit the definition of "civil society" as a social collectivity in between the state and the private family, an entity that possesses self-organizing abilities, promotes the public good, and understands itself as a public collectivity promoting public interests. Although lineages look out especially for their own kin, we have much evidence that in late imperial and modern China, lineage leaders have been in the forefront of contributing to local charities and temple- and infrastructure-building. It is important that scholars pay attention to how non-Western cultures enter modernity by evolving and adapting their indigenous traditions and organizations. The forms and structures of non-Western civil societies should not be expected to conform to Western categories.

LINEAGES AS GRASSROOTS ORGANIZATIONS IN WENZHOU TODAY

During Land Reform in the 1950s, those Wenzhou lineages that owned communal land had to give up the land for redistribution, and many ancestor halls were converted into schools, storage places, or offices (Lin S. 2002). Throughout the Maoist era, lineage rituals were banned, and local governments increasingly took over lineage functions. However, in areas with more powerful lineage organizations, in Pingyang and Cangnan Counties, the state had a more difficult time displacing lineage power. In general, single-lineage villages produced more powerful lineage organizations than those with several competing lineages. In southern Wenzhou, right after Liberation, northern Communist Party cadres from Shandong and Hebei Provinces came down and displaced local Wenzhou Communist cadres from power. Since the local people did not trust outsiders, they turned to their local lineage organizations for governance, leaving lineages in the South more intact and powerful.

Throughout Wenzhou, lineages began reviving at the end of the 1970s, according to Lin Shundao, and some ventured to construct new ancestor halls, only to see them torn down again by the government. Thus, lineages had to find ingenious ways to get their halls erected. There were cases of two lineages coming together to share a single hall, and some built their halls near the mountains, where there was more available land. In the 1990s, many lineages resorted to building "memorial halls" (紀念堂) by finding a famous ancestor in their lineage history to commemorate. This move represented a safe and secularized approach that did not raise alarm bells in local government offices.

I visited the six-story Ye Shi Memorial Hall in Xin Teng Township, Rui'an City. Built in 2001 with donations from Ye Shi's descendants, it avoids the sensitive term "ancestor hall." It honors Ye Shi (葉適, 1150–1223 CE), a famous philosopher of the Southern Song dynasty who belongs to the Yongjia School (永嘉學派) of Confucianism. Ye Shi advocated a pragmatic Confucianism that was comfortable with a market economy. The hall cost 2 million yuan; most of the money came from member donations, and only 200,000 yuan from the township government. The museum is open to the public and displays busts of Ye Shi, excerpts from his writings, and biographical accounts of his travels and activities, with photographs of the places where he was active. The lineage today offers college scholarships to its promising youth. Lineage youth who test into college receive 1,000 yuan each, while those who get into an MA program receive 2,000 yuan. In 2008, the lineage gave out 10,000 yuan in scholarships.

Around the year 2000, many lineages also started building ancestor halls as "cultural centers" (文化中心), such as the Chen Lineage Ancestor Hall (陳氏宗祠) in Qianku Township in Cangnan County, which I visited in 2004 and 2010. These cultural centers were open to the public regardless of their kinship, and they provided the community with services such as sports and adult education classes. They served as de facto community centers for a local area. Official attitudes started to relax, although legal status for lineages continued to be withheld. This new attitude is reflected in an article about Wenzhou lineages by Ye Dabing (葉大兵), former head of the Wenzhou City Bureau of Culture. Ye outlines the positive contributions of lineages to society: lineages have historical value, and their genealogies supplement official history-writing; they preserve historical relics and develop folk culture; they organize cultural educational activities; they promote scholarship in history, folklore, and archaeology; and they have strong organizational skills and can help local governments in economic development and connecting up with overseas Chinese (Ye D. 1997: 9).

THE GENDER OF THE LINEAGE AND WOMEN'S STATUS

Due to its patrilineal structure (父系制度), in which descent is traced only through the male line, men are implicitly regarded as more valuable than women, who are structurally not full members of a lineage. Rural and small-town Wenzhou culture continues to prefer the birth of a boy. In lineage logic, since women do not carry descent lines, the children they produce are not theirs but belong to their husband's lineage (K. A. Johnson 1983), making divorce perilous for women due to the risk of losing their children. Moreover, the logic is also that women should not be entitled to full inheritance of lineage or family property, despite China's law of equal inheritance. The vast majority of lineage activists and managerial committees are composed of men, giving the impression that lineages are still a men's organization. At the same time, these attitudes have become more self-conscious and less explicit, due to China's brief period of Maoist "state feminism" (M. Yang 1999a).

The state birth controls since 1979 do not seem to have drastically affected this lineage logic of privileging sons in rural Wenzhou.[1] In 2016, I asked Mr. Yang, a college-educated junior high school teacher from a peasant family in Cangnan County, what would happen if a family only has one daughter, and no sons: How would it continue the lineage line, and how would property be inherited? He replied that it is actually rare that a rural family ends up with only one daughter. The law for rural areas is that if the first child is a girl, the family can have one more birth. Most families will give birth a second (or third) time if the first child is a girl, or they will give the girl away to a relative in another part of Wenzhou and not register her birth so that they get another chance at having a boy. Generally, officials are lenient if a family does not work for an official work unit (*danwei*). So most people can get away with having one or two out-of-plan births, or they willingly pay a fine. When the children are grown and it is time to "divide up the household" (分家), the son usually inherits the property and land, while the parents may give 30–40 percent of the family inheritance to the daughter as her wedding dowry. Chinese law requires that the daughter must sign a form to give away her inheritance share to her brother(s), and most women agree to do this.

Theoretically, many lineages now allow daughters to "continue the root" (行根), that is, to transmit descent to their offspring in a bilateral system of kinship descent. This has been possible since late imperial times for lineage daughters who marry men who agree to matrilocal residence—that is, moving in to live with their wife's family. These cases were not common, though, due to the loss of face for the man. My queries about daughters "continuing the root" elicited no consensus on this question. Some lineage activists told me that women could transmit lineage descent; others did not think so. One lineage activist told me that women could continue lineage descent "if a family has no male offspring," implying that most of the time, women could *not* carry the lineage line. Some people thought that when a child reached the age of eighteen years, she could choose whether to belong to her mother's or father's lineage. Others thought that children could also have a double surname (雙姓), adopting the surname of both their father and their mother, like "Ou-Yang." I sensed that this debate had not been fully resolved.

Certainly, women's social position in rural and small-town Wenzhou has greatly improved since the early twentieth century, thanks to the Communist Party's discourse of gender equality (Croll 1985; Friedman 2006; Hershatter 2014; M. Yang 1999a). Women are no longer excluded from public lineage events and can now enter ancestor halls and participate in the annual ancestor sacrifice and other rituals. Their names are now written into the new genealogies, as daughters, wives, and ancestresses. Most lineages have deleted offensive language written in old Ming and Qing dynasty lineage genealogies and charters, which called on members not to listen to their wives. With the recent decline of arranged marriage and of constraints on widows, the patrolling of women's sexuality by lineage organizations has been greatly reduced. Indeed, premarital sex is increasingly common in rural Wenzhou, as in Heilongjiang villages (Y. Yan 2003: 65–72), although it may still adversely affect a woman's social reputation should a marriage not ensue.

During the Maoist era of poverty, most rural families did not provide their daughters with the same amount of formal education as their brothers. However, with post-Mao prosperity, daughters now enjoy equal education and are encouraged to attend high school and get into college, and they are also awarded scholarships by their lineages. Economic prosperity has also meant that many brides and their families now refuse the bride-price offered by the groom, and new married couples prefer to live in nuclear households separate from the groom's parents. This means that young brides are not so beholden to their husbands and in-laws and are able to reduce the old structural tensions between mother-in-law and daughter-in-law. In the Reform era, with so many Wenzhou men fanning out across China in search of business opportunities, their wives, sisters, and adult daughters are the ones keeping the family business running smoothly. Thus, women do not need to leave the domestic sphere, which is also the site of the home factory or business, to gain work and management experience and leadership skills.

THE YINGQIAO WANG LINEAGE OF YONGCHANG

The Yingqiao Wang Lineage (英橋王氏宗族) is based in New Town (新城) in Yongchang Township (永昌鎮), Longwan District (龍灣區). New Town is located inside a walled fortress called Yong Chang Fortress (永昌堡). It was "new" back in the Ming dynasty, built in 1558 by the Wang Lineage to protect the local people against marauding pirates on the coast (Chen and Zhang 2010; Shen Y. 2002; Wang G. 2003;). The town walls enclosed family residences and fields whose crops fed the people inside when besieged by pirates, as well as the imposing Wang Lineage ancestor hall, built in 1542. Today both the fortress wall and ancestor hall still stand proudly.

I first met Wang Qinsheng (王勤生), then the lineage manager, in 1990 on my first visit to Wenzhou. He was in his midfifties, with gray hair, a slightly hunched back and a quiet, hesitant, and self-deprecating manner that revealed he was not used to authority and power. That February day in the sunny courtyard of the Wang lineage ancestor hall, Wang Qinsheng proudly brought out one heavy volume of the new 1981 lineage genealogy and flipped through the pages to show me the beautiful printing job. The names of ancestors were

Figure 7.1. Wang Lineage genealogy being aired in ancestor hall courtyard, 1990. Photo by the author.

printed in black, and thin red lines connected each ancestor with both their forebears and descendants through the patrilineal line. The Wang Lineage's precious Qing dynasty genealogy had been burned during the Cultural Revolution, a devastating loss, so they did research to produce a new one.

At Liberation, the Wang lineage's four thousand *mou* of corporate land, which they called "public land" (公家的地), was rented out to landless peasants. According to Wang Qinsheng, proceeds from the corporate land were spent for the collective benefit of the lineage: maintaining and repairing the ancestor hall and holding sacrificial rituals; updating the lineage genealogy; scholarships for the bright sons of the lineage; local construction projects such as bridges, irrigation and transport canals, and roads; and fees and bribes necessary for lineage members' litigation. Much to Wang lineage members' chagrin, about a hundred years earlier, at the end of the Qing dynasty, an elementary school had been established by the local government in their ancestor hall. There it stayed, well into the 1990s. During Land Reform in the 1950s, the lineage land was taken and divided up among the poor peasants, and the lineage was prohibited from holding further ancestor sacrificial ceremonies in the hall.

In 1991, there were about 40,000 Yingqiao Wang lineage members, including married-in wives, and most of them lived in the neighboring coastal townships of Yong Chang, Yong Zhong, and Yong Xing, known collectively before Liberation as Yong Qiang Prefecture (永強區), with a population of about 220,000 in the early 1990s. The Yingqiao Wangs comprised anywhere from 50 percent to 80 percent of the local population in this area. About 4,000 Wang members lived inside New Town, representing 90 percent of its residents. Lineage members were also scattered in faraway Taiwan, Singapore, Hong Kong, France, and the United States. In 1991, a total of twenty-six generations had carried on the lineage identity since its first ancestor, with ten living generations, from the sixteenth to the twenty-sixth. By 2010, there were over 50,000 lineage members and thirty-two generations since the founding ancestor.

The Wang lineage is divided into nine lineage segments or branch descent lines, called *pai* (派), of which seven are currently active. In the past, when a family became prosperous, its members distinguished their own line of descent from the other lines in the lineage by setting aside funds or land whose proceeds would go toward building a branch ancestor hall. Here branch descendants worshipped their own branch ancestors in addition to joining the rest of the lineage in honoring the founding ancestor. Underneath each Wang lineage branch is a further subdivision into "large houses" (*da fang*, 大房), each of which is further divided into a number of "small houses" (*xiao fang*, 小房). Before Liberation, there were about thirty-five "small houses" branching off from the main descent line or "trunk" of the lineage.

Wang Lineage History

The first ancestor (始祖) of the Wang lineage was Wang Hui (王惠), with a posthumous title of "Eleventh Lord of the Ten Thousand" (萬十一翁). He settled in the Wenzhou area in the Southern Song dynasty in the late twelfth century from the Huangyan area of Fujian province. In Wenzhou, many lineages trace back to the Southern Song, when there was a wave of migration from central and northern China to the coastal areas by people fleeing invaders such as the Khitan from the North, as well as another migration from Fujian Province northward to Wenzhou to repopulate the land after a tsunami hit in the twelfth century, wiping out much of the population. This first ancestor found work as a household manager for the well-to-do Ying family. His third-generation grandsons set up three lineage branches (*pai*, 派) to commemorate their three parents of the second generation. In the fifth generation, there was a further division in one of these branches into seven new branches, making up a total of nine branches in the Wang lineage.

In the Ming dynasty, the Wang lineage became a powerful and wealthy local organization. Sixteen Wang ancestors in the Ming and Qing dynasties attained the highest *jinshi* degree in the imperial examinations, and ninety attained the *juren* and *gongshi* degrees. The two higher degrees generally led to assignment to official positions in the imperial government, granting the Wang lineage power and influence in local affairs. Although their genealogy was burned, a multivolume copy of the *Wang Lineage Family Records* (王氏家錄) was discovered in the Wenzhou City Library, and lineage members quickly had several copies made. In addition, local libraries possessed copies of important local histories such as *Gazetteer of Wenzhou Prefecture: Ming Dynasty Hongzhi Reign Period* (弘治溫州府志) (Wang Z. 2006) and *Gazetteer of Yongjia County* (永嘉縣志; Yongjia 1983), which their ancestors had a hand in writing and which contained information about their lineage. The ancestors Wang Shuguo (王叔果, 1516-1588) and Wang Shugao (王叔杲, 1517-1600) are credited with organizing and financing the building of Yong Chang Fortress. Even back then, this fortress was entirely a local initiative "of the people" (民間), relying on donations, with no imperial state funding.

Wang Lineage Activists in the Post-Mao Era

In contrast to the elitist history of the Wang lineage in the Ming dynasty, most of the lineage activists (*gugan*) who got together in 1978 to reconstruct the Wang genealogy were from poor or middle peasant backgrounds, with little formal education. This reflects the history of the Maoist era, when those with education usually came from landowning families before Liberation; these people experienced a sudden loss of not only their land but also their citizenship rights. Furthermore, in the 1980s and 1990s, the task of reviving a lineage was still not something a person from a "bad" class background would wish to risk. Thus, the two kinds of people who were best positioned to take up the task of renewing lineage culture were peasants and retired local officials. It would be hard to accuse peasants of reviving a lineage in order to restore the "reactionary landowning class," and retired local officials still commanded authority and had their network of former colleagues to protect them in case of political trouble.

Wang Qinsheng, the first lineage manager (總首事) in the lineage revival of 1980, was born in Yong Chang in 1937, the year of the Japanese invasion. I felt a special kinship with him during my fieldwork and benefited enormously from his generous and patient discussions with me. During Land Reform, his father owned only thirteen *mou* of land to provide the whole family's livelihood, so he was labeled a "middle peasant." He only attended primary school for two and a half years before he was needed in the fields. At sixteen he became the brigade leader of the local agricultural cooperative and was promoted to treasurer for his village. He always liked to study and read in his spare time, enjoying history and tales of the past. His reading knowledge led him to participate in the local "Sweep Away Illiteracy" (*saomang*) program for peasants. Over the years, he believes he has attained the equivalent of a high school education on his own. At eighteen, he joined the People's Liberation Army and was sent off to Korea, where he operated antiaircraft missiles against US planes. On August 25, 1958, he took part in a big battle against Guomindang troops on Jinmen Island in the Taiwan Straits. As with many other men in Wenzhou, joining the army enabled him to learn Mandarin. In 1961, he injured his back and returned home to Yong Chang, taking up a position as an accountant. When I met him in the 1990s, he had shifted into more lucrative and formerly banned occupations, such as *Yijing* divination, ritual consultant, and fengshui master siting new tombs. He went through an arranged marriage in 1960, and his wife is a devout Daoist who gave him four children. Toward the end of his life, Wang Qinsheng had a larynx operation for cancer and lost his speech ability, so we communicated through written notes. He passed away in 2015, and the following year I paid my respects at his hillside tomb in Longwan District.

Wang Fuyuan (王福元), another activist in his seventies, came from a poor peasant family of ten children. Growing up, his family ate dried sweet potatoes at breakfast and dinner; they had rice, the preferred staple, only at lunch. They supplemented this with homegrown vegetables, and they seldom tasted meat. At Chinese New Year's, they could not afford leather shoes, so their mother hand-sewed cloth shoes for them. These shoes were useless when it rained, so he devised a contraption to cope with the wet and muddy days: he tied his feet to two bricks which were attached to long strings he tied around his neck. He would tread gingerly on the bricks while using the strings to pull his feet up, one after the other, in the mud. During Land Reform, their family suddenly received land, a house, and furniture, property confiscated from wealthier families. Wang Fuyuan joined the army in 1951, traveled to twenty-three provinces, and learned to speak Mandarin, but he never learned to read or write. After returning home, he headed a local construction gang. He liked to drink Chinese *baijiu*, a fiery rice liquor, and when I once gave him a bottle, he beamed from ear to ear with pleasure.

I asked Wang Fuyuan, "You all come from ordinary peasant families; why do you want to revive the lineage? Wasn't the lineage controlled by wealthy landlords in the old days who did not really care about their poor relatives?" He replied, "Our ancestors did great things. They used their blood and sweat to build the ancestor hall and the town fortress and wall to fight the Japanese pirates. So our generation should honor and remember them. If we did nothing to commemorate them, then how can we lift our heads to face our descendants [後代]? Our descendants will say to us, 'Look at you, you did not live up to your responsibilities'!" At this point, Wang Qinsheng chimed in: "They were not landlords, just people who became officials through their own hard work." Wang Qinsheng added that he appreciated how traditional Chinese culture produced the "emotional feelings" (*ganqing*, 感情) between one generation and another. "One kind of *ganqing* is filial piety [孝]. When my father was dying, I tried all I could to get the best treatment to prolong his life." After decades of "class struggle," the Wangs valorized kinship warmth, human feeling, and the mutual responsibilities that tied one generation to another in the continuity of a lineage line moving through history.

Reviving the Lineage without the Term: 1980s–1990s

When the political winds started to shift in 1978, Wang Qinsheng and other activists took a bold political risk to revive the lineage. This revival proceeded on four fronts: reconstruction of the lineage genealogy; repair of the old tombs of the lineage; repair and protection of their 450-year-old ancestor hall; and revival of the annual springtime ancestor sacrificial ritual. Wenzhou historian Lin Shundao (2002: 53, 69–72) also identifies four key activities in the Chen lineage revival in Shunxi Township, Pingyang County (順溪鎮, 平揚縣); although they are not expressed in precisely the same terms, they are effectively the same activities. These four initiatives support Patricia Ebrey's (1986: 29, 55) text-based findings that rituals were more important than land acquisition in the establishment of organized descent groups in the eleventh to fifteenth centuries. They also reinforce Allen Chun's critique (2000) of Maurice Freedman's overemphasis of Chinese lineages' landed property. Chun found that Hong Kong rural lineage membership was defined first in terms of ritual practices rather than biological origins, so that the performance of ritual can sanction lineage membership where there is no blood relatedness.

Since it could not officially be called a "lineage," the organization formed in 1978 for the Wang genealogy was called "Small Group for the Reconstruction of the Wang Genealogy" (重修王氏族譜小組). In 1993, an official of Ouhai Prefecture told me that he disapproved of the Wangs calling themselves a "committee": "They should not call themselves a committee; that is much too grand. They can only call themselves a small group or a team [*dui*]!" The Small Group was composed of twenty-one lineage activists who were nominated from a larger Genealogy Renewal Committee (修譜委員會) of 122 members. Wang

Qinsheng wanted to ensure good representation, so half of the committee members resided outside the Yong Qiang area. He kept in touch with them by telephone or through periodic visits. I asked why there were twenty-one activists in the Small Group and was told that Wang Lisheng, one of the activists, had read in a magazine that the number 21 was the optimum size for decision-making bodies: surpassing this number would invite too many disagreements.

After finishing the genealogy in 1981, the Wangs found a new justification for their existence as an organization when they discovered that local officials planned to dismantle the 450-year-old Wang Lineage Ancestor Hall, which the officials thought was blocking traffic that would bring economic development. The Wangs renamed themselves the "Team for the Preservation of the Wang Ancestor Hall Historical Relic" (王家祠堂文物保護隊). They petitioned higher authorities to recognize their hall as a historical relic in need of state protection, collected local donations to repair the hall after typhoon damage, and petitioned local school authorities to move the elementary school out of their hall. The team members, all men in their forties, fifties, and sixties, were volunteers who received no financial compensation for their time and effort. Wang Siming confided that sometimes he was exhausted by having to work his regular job and then volunteer for the lineage, but when he thought about the "face" (mianzi) of his lineage, and how other lineages had renovated their ancestor halls, he felt renewed energy.

In the 1980s, serving as lineage leader was taking a political risk. Therefore, Wang Qinsheng approached several Wang lineage members who held local official posts as Party secretaries, seeking their protection should anything go wrong. They told him to go ahead with the genealogy and reassured him that they would cover for him, but asked him not to mention their names. Wang Qinsheng was summoned to appear at the Ouhai Prefecture office four times in the 1980s, and each time he was interrogated for at least two hours. He and the authorities got very angry, and they argued back and forth. Said Wang to me with some bravado, "I was not afraid—I have not committed any crimes." He gave me the gist of these unpleasant encounters.

The official in charge asked him if there was any Party member in his lineage small group, and Wang said no. The official lashed out angrily: "Then how dare you form an organization [zuzhi]?" Wang calmly responded, "Our lineage has over forty thousand members. Among them there must be several hundred Party members. If these Party members all consented to have their names included in our genealogy, then you should go talk to each of them!" The official also challenged Wang about what he would do if the lineage genealogy celebration he was planning attracted the area's "bad people" or the massive gathering led to some terrible accident. Wang Qinsheng reassured the official that he would personally assume all responsibility for the event and that he would assemble the village's old people to direct traffic and ensure safety. The official also accused Wang of "fomenting feudal superstitions" (搞封建迷信). Wang Qinsheng answered, "First, I'm not guilty of factionalism [*zongpai zhuyi*]. I never promote hostilities or conflicts with other lineages, and I do not mistreat nonlineage people." Wang then dared to ask the official if he believed that the souls of his own parents or grandparents were *not* watching over his family and should *not* be honored. Didn't the official wish to respect his own parents too? "Of course he could not reply to that, since he had feelings for his own parents and grandparents," said Wang.

The first major step of lineage revival, revamping the genealogy, started in 1978 and took three years to complete. Lineage volunteers visited every Wang lineage family in the local area, and volunteers were also sent to places outside Wenzhou where lineage members were clustered. They compiled a lineage census, recording the names of each grandparent, parent, and offspring in a household and retracing each family's birth origins and those of their immediate ancestors. The final genealogy was completed in 1981, composed of forty-six volumes, and they printed out thirteen sets, totaling a staggering six hundred volumes.

Second, Wang lineage activists worked on restoring major ancestor tombs. The most important tomb was that of the Song dynasty lineage founder Wang Hui, who first moved to the Wenzhou area from Fujian. His tomb lay just outside the New Town Fortress walls, to the north of the ancestor hall. When I first visited this tomb in 1992, it had already been cleaned up and was a stately grass-covered earth mound enclosed within a walled and gated circular compound. I accompanied three Wang activists to their main Ming dynasty ancestor graves on Half Mountain (Banshan) in Yao Xi Township. We climbed up the mountain on a winding path of stone stairs carved into the rocks. Each of the tombs faced in directions that gave them a sweeping view of the plains below or the opposite mountain, and they were approached along paths with large pairs of stone tomb guardians lined up on both sides. With resentment in his voice, one of the Wangs said, "Our lineage used to own all of this mountain; only Wang lineage graves could be put here. But after Liberation, the land became government land and all sorts of other graves were sited here. They wreak havoc with the fengshui and the original spatial design, and they block the scenic view."

During the Maoist years, they could only attend to their own immediate family graves for the tomb-sweeping festival of Qing Ming. Since the 1980s, they have revived the old practice of organizing the entire lineage to climb up to Half Mountain en masse. On the first day of Qing Ming, usually falling in early April, the key elders of the Wang lineage go to the tomb of their founding ancestor just outside the north wall of New Town Fortress to sweep it and make offerings. On the third day of Qing Ming, individual families sweep the graves of their immediate ancestors. On the fifth day, the Wang lineage organizes a "collective" outing for the whole lineage, with one thousand people climbing boisterously up Half Mountain to sweep the Ming dynasty tombs. It is a joyous occasion, and people bring liquor, food offerings, and incense for the ancestors. They bow and *ketou* in front of the tombs, and later, after the ancestors have eaten, enjoy the offerings themselves.

After repairing the major ancestor tombs and completing the genealogy project, the third item on the Wang lineage agenda was protecting their hall from destruction by officials and gathering funds to repair and restore the ancestor hall. Their efforts paid off: in 1981, their ancestor hall was designated a Wenzhou City Important Cultural Relic Protection Unit. Lineage activists continued their campaign to win protection from higher state authorities. In 1989, their hall won the designation Zhejiang Provincial Cultural Relic Protection Site, and in 2001, after lineage activists personally lobbied officials in Beijing, an archaeological team from that city came down to investigate. Finally the Wang lineage ancestor hall won the highest level of protection: it was designated a National Cultural Relic Preservation Unit (國家文物保護單位).

In 1991, a typhoon caused two walls of the ancestor hall to slide and the roof to slant down. A Main Ancestor Hall Restoration Committee (大宗祠修理委員會) was quickly formed. Its twenty-one members—five retired workers, six local entrepreneurs, and ten ordinary peasants—sprang into action. They quickly called for donations from all Wang lineage members, and by early 1993 they had amassed 200,000 yuan to fix the hall. They also lobbied the Provincial Bureau of Culture and the Ouhai Prefectural government to allocate 20,000 yuan each for the restoration of the hall. They hired artisans and craftsmen to redo the entire hall: the ceiling beams, wooden pillars, large wooden doors, and wooden wall carvings were all repainted in harmonious colors of black and dark brown, relieved by little flourishes of red and green wooden carvings of flowers and auspicious bats. The area outside the imposing front stone gate was also cleaned up, and the old Party propaganda slogans on the front walls were painted over. After the restoration, the Wangs erected a large stone stele commemorating the repair, carved with the names of donors who gave more than 200 yuan to the hall. Even my own donation made it onto the stele.

Figure 7.2. The Yingqiao Wang Lineage of Yongchang Township, when their ancestor hall was designated a Zhejiang Provincial Cultural Relic Protected Site, 1990. Photo by Haibin Arts Photography Studio.

The fourth aspect of reviving the Wang lineage was reconstructing the annual springtime ancestor sacrifice, which was first held on the twelfth day of the first lunar month in 1979. The previous times the Wang lineage had performed their ancestor ritual were in 1948 and 1951. The spring sacrifice of 1979 drew several hundred lineage members to the main ancestor hall, where they lined up in the central courtyard according to descending generations and followed the ritual master's calls to bow, kneel, and *ketou* in unison as food, drink and incense offerings were offered to their ancestors, who were represented in spirit tablets on the front altar or portraits hung up on the walls. The Wang lineage had reconstructed the ritual by studying the written Ming dynasty liturgy and by interviewing a few old people who remembered some of the ritual procedures. A major reform of the late imperial ritual was opening the ritual to lineage women and girls.

From the 1980s to the new millennium, the Wangs struggled to win annual government approval to hold the ancestor ritual. The local government

Figure 7.3. Yingqiao Wang Lineage ancestor sacrifice, Longwan District, February 2012. Photo by the author.

voiced its disapproval of the return of a "feudal" institution and the "corruption of the social atmosphere" (敗壞社會風氣) that public ritual performance would bring. In 1993, I was at first given permission to witness the annual ritual event, but to my great disappointment, the local authorities later changed their minds and would not allow me to attend. I was finally able to see the ritual in 2001 and 2012, and I managed to videotape the performances.

In 2010, I found out that the Wang lineage elders had petitioned to have their ancestor sacrifice recognized as an Intangible Cultural Heritage. Having experienced how intensely nervous local authorities were about traditional public rituals, I felt that a milestone had been reached when, in 2012, Wang lineage elders happily informed me that their ancestor sacrifice had been recognized as a Longwan District ICH, under the category of Folk Custom. Henceforth, their sacrificial ritual would enjoy state protection and the right to be performed annually. With local governments now vying to get more local customs registered as Intangible Cultural Heritage, popular religious culture is finally able to enjoy a respite from the continuous waves of decimation throughout the twentieth century.

The Restructuring of Lineage Social Roles

In May 1993, while making my documentary about the revival of traditional culture in Wenzhou, I videotaped a ninety-minute interview with Wang Qinsheng on the outdoor rooftop of his three-story home (M. Yang 1994b). The reason for choosing the rooftop was that it would protect us from prying eyes, and it provided peace and quiet from the loud street noises below. To my question about the services and activities the Wang lineage organized each year, Wang Qinsheng replied, somewhat primly because he was in front of the camera, "In order to commemorate our senior generations, and to respect and love the elderly [為了紀念長輩, 敬老愛老], we engage in the following activities each year." He then listed them:

1. Ancestor sacrificial ritual on the twelfth day of the first lunar month
2. Sweeping the ancestral tombs at Qingming Festival
3. Drying out the genealogy on the sixth day of the sixth lunar month (晒譜)
4. Resolving internal conflicts of the lineage "so as to help the government administer the local community"

Here I must note that this list of revived lineage activities reveals the centrality of ritual to the coherence of lineage organization. These rituals cluster local people into kinship groupings and provide them with alternatives to identifying solely with the nation, the state, and the Party. The annual drying out of the genealogy volumes is to prevent mold in the hot and humid Wenzhou summers. This careful maintenance also shows its overriding importance for lineage identity and organizational solidarity. In the new millennium, the Wang lineage started giving scholarships to its youth who tested into college and providing financial aid to poor widows and orphans.

The fourth item, resolution of family conflicts within the lineage, reveals both continuity and rupture with late imperial lineage patterns. Now that women are entered into the genealogy and can theoretically "continue the root," new social conflicts have arisen. Having one's name in the genealogy meant that one was a full lineage citizen, implying that henceforth, women also enjoyed the right to a full share of the inheritance on the death of their parents. However, as is often the case, the local culture lags behind formal written policy changes, so there were many disputes centering on a daughter's right to a share of the inheritance. These conflicts often took the form of struggles between a deceased man's paternal nephew (侄子) (his brother's son) and his son-in-law (女婿), and were, according to Wang Qinsheng, the most important kind of family dispute that he regularly had to mediate. Previously, when a man had no sons of his own, either he adopted a son or his brothers' sons would expect a right to the inheritance. Now that daughters have a tenuous right to inheritance, the daughter's husband often steps up to contest the nephews' right. This of course does not sit well with the nephews, who argue that the old ways are better. When asked how he resolved these difficult disputes, Wang Qinsheng replied that he listened sympathetically to both sides and then split the property equally between the nephew and son-in-law.

Wang Qinsheng's list of lineage activities does not include services that late imperial lineages used to provide, including running the local school; organizing the repair and building of local transport canals, roads, and bridges; judging and punishing wrongdoers or criminals within the lineage; or collecting and paying taxes to the state. Lineages in late imperial China were often local organizations for self-government (Freedman 1958; Li S. 2005; Lin S. 2002). They provided assistance to the poor, widows, orphans, and aspiring young scholars of the lineage; organized community rituals and infrastructure-building; and served as bridges between local communities and the imperial state. They generally took care of nonserious crimes and adjudicated internal lineage disputes. People generally feared taking cases to the courts of the imperial state, because of the severe punishment meted out and the high cost of bribes to win litigation or post bail (Freedman 1966: 114–115).

The Wang lineage no longer acts as judge and court for cases of wrongdoing by lineage members. Crimes are always turned over to the local Public Security Office to handle. Nor does the lineage provide much social welfare or economic assistance to poor families, for that is now the provenance of the village government or the township's Civil Affairs Bureau (民政局). Now their lineage can no longer take up most of these burdens, for lack of funds. They can only afford to fund their annual spring ancestor sacrifice and the Qingming Festival and to work on the genealogy about every twenty years. Thus, it is clear that the local government has taken over many of the functions that lineages used to serve.

Wang Wei told me that before Liberation, their lineage activities and financial assistance used to all come out of the rents that the lineage collected from corporate lineage landholdings. Since the lineage lost all its land during Land Reform, it no longer has any regular source of income and can only mount occasional donation drives. The original land deeds were burned or lost, and now most of the lands have buildings on them, so generally it is impossible to remove current occupants. When I asked him why the lineage did not ask for donations to purchase a new piece of land to rent out, he replied, "The state is the biggest landowner and it would never allow the sale of land to a lineage. This is a question of our political system" (制度問題). Lineages, whose existence was already unwelcome in the eyes of the state, would not be given or sold any land. Only individuals or profit-making enterprises could purchase land.

Dual Lineage Leadership: The Lineage's Inner and Outer Face

For the Yingqiao Wangs today, the "lineage head" (族長) is largely a ceremonial position. The officer in charge of the lineage's practical day-to-day affairs is called "general manager" (總首事). Wang Qinsheng held this position from 1981 to 1998, leading donation drives, overseeing ancestor hall repair and genealogy work, and planning for the annual ancestor sacrifice and Qingming Festival tomb-sweeping outing. It may come as a surprise that Wang Qinsheng's leadership role was the outcome of a nomination and election process. Soon after the completion of the genealogy in 1981, 40 of the 122 lineage committee members came together at a meeting to select their leader. Three people were nominated, and the participants debated the pros and cons of each person. The discussion reached a general consensus, and a show of hands was called. The result: 90 percent of those present were in favor of Wang Qinsheng as the head of their lineage. Said Wang Lisheng, a lineage activist, "You see, our lineage is not feudal, it's very democratic [hen minzhu]!"

In July 1998, returning to Wenzhou after an absence of five years, I was informed that since my last visit, the local officials' policy toward their lineage activities had become more relaxed. "Now our lineage activity has become open [gongkaihua]," a Wang lineage member grinned, referring to the fact that they could now carry out lineage business in public. He had recently joined the Communist Party, and when they asked him what he was doing lately, he openly told them that he had been helping his lineage work on their new genealogy. The elementary school had finally moved out of their ancestor hall, and they were now allowed to open their lineage office at the front of the hall.

The lineage managerial committee then numbered 105 people: 103 middle-aged men and 2 women. Even though they could still not officially call themselves a lineage, they now had clear organizational roles and titles: there were twelve lineage managers (首事), including one head manager; eleven advisers; one accountant; one cashier; one storage keeper; and one guest greeter. The selection of people to fill each of these roles was discussed publicly and chosen by group consensus at a lineage meeting. Meanwhile, the lineage had published two volumes about their lineage: a record of major lineage events in the last one hundred years, titled *Record of Great Events* (大事記); and a record of lineage members who had attained higher education or office at the county level and above, titled *Record of Famous People* (名人錄).

The year 1998 was also when the Wang lineage successfully completed their second post-Mao genealogy renovation. After the genealogy celebrations, the Wangs gathered one hundred lineage committee members and selected sixty-five-year-old Wang Yuzhao (王玉昭) as the new lineage manager. Wang Yuzhao used to be a poor fisherman who could barely read or write. Lineage members were not deterred by this, however, because he possessed other advantages: he had the right "family conditions," such as three successful sons and one daughter, all of whom earned high incomes with their family businesses in Wenzhou and Dalian in Shandong Province. As lineage manager, he was expected to dip into his personal family wealth to help cover the public needs of the lineage. Here we see the communal and redistributive aspect of lineage leadership, similar to temple leadership discussed in chapter 6, where leaders were expected to support public activity with their own money. Wang Qinsheng told me that his own modest income hampered his lineage work because he could not set a good example of generosity. Thus, it was not mere wealth that made people look up to a leader, but the bestowing of that wealth for the "public benefit" (公益) of the lineage, that bestowed authority on a lineage head.

In 1999, another lineage manager was selected to help run the Wang lineage, not to replace Wang Yuzhao but to perform different functions alongside him. The new leader was Wang Jinling (王金麟), a retired local official who had shown great zeal in volunteering for the second genealogy in 1998. At a meeting of the 105 members of the Committee to Restore the Wang Lineage Genealogy, ten people were nominated for this new leadership position, and after discussion and debate, Wang Jinling was selected. Like Wang Yuzhao, he had a large extended family and his children had done well economically, so he was financially comfortable. He had donated the giant bronze gong that stood inside the Wang lineage ancestor hall that was used in the annual sacrificial ritual. People described him as politically astute. As a former cadre, he had a high school education and so was better educated than Wang Yuzhao.

Curious about this dual leadership, I asked Wang Yuzhao, "Now that the Wang lineage has two leaders, is there any danger that Wang Jinling, with his higher education, might just take over the leadership by himself?" Wang Yuzhao replied that the danger existed, but "if he tries anything funny [*laishi*], or goes against the interest of the lineage, then all the Wangs will go after him." Wang lineage members look up to Wang Yuzhao first as their lineage leader, as the person who organizes ritual events and solves problems. However, officials and cadres above the township level, such as provincial and central government officials who come down to visit their famous ancestor hall or grant permission for hall matters, will seek out Wang Jinling as the person in charge of the hall. In other words, Wang Yuzhao was the "*internal* leader" (對內領導) for fellow lineage members, while Wang Jinling was the "*external* face" (對外領導) of the lineage to outsiders and to officials.

The "Opening Up" of the Lineage: Public Roles and State Penetration

In June 2001, the Wang lineage ancestor hall was finally recognized as a National Cultural Relic Preservation Site, and the elaborate state-orchestrated celebrations took place onsite in the following month. The Wenzhou City government spent 500,000 yuan for the festivities, which included VIP guests from Beijing; the Zhejiang provincial government; Qian Xingzhong, the mayor of Wenzhou City; two vice mayors; the heads of Wenzhou's Culture, Health, and Tourism Bureaus; and local officials. A colorful procession including twenty-two horses marched down a red carpet first inside, then outside the Yong Chang Fortress.

In 1997, the Bureau of Culture of Zhejiang Province sent down a directive, Document 204, calling for the Wang lineage ancestor hall to become the "Yongchang Museum" and to allow the public to purchase tickets to enter the hall. That same year, the Wenzhou City National Defense Committee designated Yong Chang Fortress as a Base Area for National Defense Education (國防教育基地). Since the fortress town had been built to repel Japanese pirates, local officials thought that it made the perfect place to bring schoolchildren and soldiers to increase their patriotic spirit. The museum's organizational committee numbered eight people receiving regular salaries from the township government. Wang Jinling, the museum head, received 1,000 yuan per month. The museum also employed a secretary, an accountant, a dispatcher, groundskeepers, and a woman librarian for the new public library added in the rear of the hall. Three of the eight were not members of the Wang lineage. By contrast, Wang Yuzhao, the internal lineage manager, and other lineage volunteers continued to receive no salary.

This development for the Wang ancestor hall—winning a designation as national historical relic, being transformed into a public museum, and serving as Base Area for National Defense Education—created, in local parlance, a more "open" (*kaifang*) lineage, meaning that it was opened to the outside world of

Figure 7.4. Wang lineage ancestor hall interior, 2014. Photo by the author.

nonlineage members and also to officialdom. In appreciation for the Wang lineage's willingness to turn their hall into a museum, the Wenzhou City government gave them 600,000 yuan, and the lineage used this money, along with member donations, to build a library and garden open to both lineage members and the public. As Wang Yuzhao told me, "Our generation is low in education; we want our next generation to be better, so we are building the library." Now the Wang lineage would also have a secure and steady source of income, with the township and prefecture governments promising their museum 300,000 yuan every year. This new situation of a more "open" lineage meant that it now needed a more educated person who had experience dealing with officialdom to represent the lineage to the outside world. Thus, lineage work was divided up into two domains: museum and lineage.

The new leader, Wang Jinling, further opened the lineage to the outside world beyond the local village and township authorities. He attended government meetings on how to promote local tourism and interacted with officials at the county, city, and provincial government levels. To lobby for Yong Chang Fortress to become a national-level cultural relic, he even made trips to Beijing to gain the support of central government antiquities agencies. He and others had grand visions for the future of their ancestor hall and fortress town. They wanted virtually all of the families living inside the fortress walls to move out and their modern boxlike multistoried homes to be dismantled. They planned to resettle these families into new high-rise apartment buildings outside the walls. Inside the fortress walls, they would restore the Ming dynasty stone gentry mansions, memorial shrines, and four-hundred-year-old stone bridges. They would clean up the water in the central north–south canal, build picturesque gardens, and try to reproduce the Ming dynasty look of the town for tourism. They needed to accumulate over 200 million yuan and find a business partner. They initially found an Italian preservation company with funding from the European Union, but this cooperation did not bear much fruit. The families living inside the fortress had to be persuaded to move out and be compensated, not always an easy matter in China. Alas, when I talked to Wang Jinling in 2010, he seemed dispirited, acknowledging that they had not managed to persuade people to move.

In short, the outcome of increased openness to the outside world was that many different outside agencies came to wield influence in lineage affairs and decisions. The designation of the ancestor hall as a museum and Base Area for National Defense Education and its recognition as a national-level cultural relic brought them a secure source of annual funding. Their hall and fortress town have been repeatedly profiled in newspapers and on the Wenzhou City and Zhejiang Provincial television stations, greatly strengthening lineage pride. However, these achievements have also come at a price, for the Bureau of Culture, Bureau of Tourism, and the city's military agencies now have a say in how the lineage spends its money.

In 2002, another development also compromised lineage autonomy. A new state agency was set up under the Longwan District government, called the Yong Chang Fortress Managerial Committee (永昌堡管理委員會). It was headed by Longwan District's vice director, a Party cadre who did not belong to the Wang lineage. To quote from its own publication (Chen and Zhang 2010), the duties of this agency were to

1. Supervise the planning, protection, and maintenance of the Fortress
2. Organize the dismantling and moving of buildings and people out of the Fortress

3. Rigorously direct all building and restoration activity within the Fortress according to plans

4. Raise the consciousness of local residents toward the preservation of historical relics

5. Enthusiastically incorporate market mechanisms and open up the Fortress as a cultural resource to tourism

6. Undertake the advertising and propagation of the Fortress to the larger world

One of this agency's first measures was to deny the Wang lineage permission to rent out portions of their ancestor hall for lineage income, in order to protect the historical monument from damage. Many lineages large and small throughout the Wenzhou area rent out their ancestor halls as a way of funding lineage activities. In the 1990s, the Wang lineage rented out a room of their hall to a billiard hall that catered to young men; other lineages rented their halls to a private daycare center and a machine parts factory. Lineages would reclaim their halls once a year, clearing up industrial debris, in order to conduct their ritual sacrifice to their ancestors.

I asked a few Wangs whether they regretted their lineage monument becoming a "national treasure." One person responded, "I do not regret it, because from the start, I was fully opposed to handing our hall over to the care of the government. I knew we would lose our sovereignty [主權]." Wang Fuyuan was more conciliatory: "Everyone seems to regret it, but not me. Neither the government nor us can totally claim this space, so neither side wins nor loses, right?"

Deprived of their ancestral land, the lineage today is without sufficient means to earn income for benefits that their ancestors enjoyed in the late imperial past: poverty relief for poor families, help for widows and orphans, scholarships for the youth, funds for improvement of local infrastructure, and money for lineage and community development. The lineage cannot continuously pester its members for donations. When their hall became a national treasure, the funds came primarily from the state, compromising lineage economic autonomy. State agencies have yet to officially acknowledge that the lineage is an autonomous, living social organization with a clear legal status. They still regard the Wang lineage as a "museum" tended by local elders, and they prefer to deal with Wang Jinling, the "museum head," rather than Wang Yuzhao, the real lineage head. Without a clear legal status, the lineage cannot purchase land, build up lineage financial assets, or fully act as an agent of civil society.

"External Relations" and Social Networking

In 2008, I discovered that the lineage had assumed a new role to serve the local community: it organizes community festivals for the local area. For the Chinese Lunar New Year of 2008, the Wang lineage organized a parade of people dressed in traditional costumes walking on stilts, with floats carrying giant papier-mâché figures of their most prominent ancestors. This joyous event cost 2 million yuan and was paid for jointly by donations from the local community and an allocation from the local government. For the Lunar New Year of 2010, the Wang lineage initiated and organized another procession of a thousand people to celebrate the 450th anniversary of the building of Yong Chang Fortress by their ancestors. This event was described as "initiated by the people on their own" (民間自發), which meant that it was not a project handed down by the local government. The procession began at the Wang ancestor hall, then proceeded through the streets of Yong Chang Town, passing through many villages and the tomb of the first Wang ancestor, before returning to the ancestor hall. The total cost came to 600,000 yuan. Local officials were present at the opening ceremony, including the Wenzhou City Party Propaganda Department, the City Bureau of Culture, Longwan Prefecture, and Yong Chang Street Committee. With pride Wang Jinling said, "We want to promote our lineage culture and expand our social influence."

At the Wang's lineage committee meeting of 2010, a new issue surfaced that revealed the evolving influence of the lineage on local society: discussing how the lineage should conduct its "external relations" (外交), referring to maintaining good social relations with other lineages and temple societies. Whenever a lineage completed their new genealogy or restored their ancestor hall, or when a temple held a public ritual event, a new local custom had developed of sending out invitations to leaders of other friendly lineages and temple committees to join their celebration. These invitations were printed on impressive red velvet covers with gold characters. Wang lineage organizers had to decide whom to send to another lineage's event and what kinds of fancy gifts to bring to the hosts. The fact that these external relations were considered important enough to discuss at the lineage meeting suggested that they were becoming an important feature of the local social landscape, with sociopolitical implications for lineages. It suggested that lineage and temple committees have begun to serve as local social nodes and units of local identity that were knitting together the local society through ritual events, bringing social connectedness and cohesion, without relying on state administration or leadership.

Birth of a Local History Study Association: Lineage as Scholarly Society

In October 2008, I discovered a new and encouraging development involving educated Wang lineage members: a new association had been formed in May 2007, called the Yong Chang Fortress Folk Custom and Cultural Study Society (永昌堡民俗文化研究會) (Yongchang 2007). The society's charter, which was approved by its eighty members, described itself as a "voluntarily formed popular academic nonprofit social organization" (自願結成的學術性民間非營利社會組織). The chief pursuits of this organization were (1) to collect and preserve historical sources and cultural materials on the history and culture of Yong Chang Fortress; (2) to study its folk customs and social relations; (3) to write and edit studies of Yong Chang local history and biographies of important people; (4) to enthusiastically participate in the preservation and restoration of Yong Chang Fortress and its cultural relics; and (5) to participate in other social activities of public benefit (社會公益性事業). Requirements for selection as a member of the society included predictable descriptions: "support for the basic direction and policies of the Chinese Communist Party and nation, as well as those of the Municipal and District governments." However, what was eyebrow-raising was this membership requirement: "having a sense of principle and righteousness, and being willing to speak out on behalf of the people [有正義感, 能為群眾說話], and being concerned with the greater interest of the larger community."

Wang lineage elders wanted their members to better understand their own collective history: "We have such a glorious history, and our young people should know more about it." They sought out a wealthy local industrialist for donations and also roped in a recently retired factory manager, Wang Wei, to serve as vice director of the society, the hands-on manager. The directorship was merely a ceremonial position.

In 2009, the society published a special issue in a local journal (Cao and Wang 2009) to commemorate the 450th anniversary of Yong Chang Fortress. Administratively, the society, a voluntary association, is positioned under the jurisdiction of two bureaucracies and receives dual leadership from the Longwan District Bureau of Culture, Radio, Television, News and Publishing, on the one hand, and the Longwan District Bureau of Civil Affairs, on the other. In one of the society's 2009 publications, it also listed as its "agency in charge" the Propaganda Department of the Longwan District Party organization (Cao and Wang 2009). Although the society was subjected to oversight by two state bureaucracies and one Party Department, its charter provided for a surprisingly democratic internal organization. Any member could stand for election to society leadership, and all members could criticize the society's activities, as well as vote to elect the society's director, vice director, and secretary, who serve three-year terms. These leaders would convene a general meeting once a year to report to the membership. The charter also included provisions for the election and impeachment of society leaders, and for setting up an executive board (常务理事会) of thirteen directors who would advise society leaders. The society's funding sources were several: membership fees, private donations, government assistance grants, services rendered by the society, interest fees, and other legal income. Given the continued lack of formal legal status for lineages in contemporary Wenzhou, the society may be developing into a new public face of the Yingqiao Wang lineage of Longwan District.

SURNAME ASSOCIATIONS AND THE EMERGENCE OF A SELF-ORGANIZING, GLOBALLY ORIENTED LOCAL SOCIETY

Lin Shundao told me of a growing interest in the history of surname groups in Wenzhou, a prelude to the development of surname or clan associations. These associations are much larger than lineages, and they cannot trace detailed genealogies because they have been lost due to population movement. Clans and surname associations were historically more developed in urban centers and in Southeast Asia, where Chinese migrants came together based on shared surname, having no local place-based identities or kinship in common. As head of Pingyang County's Local Gazetteer office, Lin was asked by community elders to start publishing a new research series called Local Surname Gazetteers (地方姓氏志). Local elders wanted to know about the first settlement of each surname group in the area, the historical processes of segmentation (枝派), and their ancestor halls, stele records, literary output, and mythologies in Pingyang and Cangnan Counties. Lin's office agreed to organize the research and writing of forty volumes of the major surname groups in these two counties. The writing of surname group histories may lead to the formation of interlocality surname associations that will overcome the weakness and parochialism of local lineages throughout the Wenzhou area.

In 2012, I visited a Mr. Yang, a local leader of the Yang surname and clan movement in Wenzhou. He told me there are fifty to sixty Yang ancestor halls in Cangnan County. He showed me a group photo taken at the first national-level meeting of Yang clan representatives in 2007, when they rented one hall of the Great Hall of the People (人民大会堂) in Beijing. Only one Wenzhou representative, from Cangnan County, attended that historic gathering, but he came back and shared his experience with other Yangs in Wenzhou. Across the nation, people with the Yang surname have gotten better organized, and communication links have been established between far-flung Yang groups. For example, in August 2006, a severe typhoon made landfall in Jinxiang Township, killing forty-three people in the single-lineage village of Heweiyang, who were mainly Yangs. A representative of the Zhejiang Yang Clan Association came down to donate money to the village. So many Yangs across the nation gave the village survivors "warmth" that today they are living in new homes. There were Yang clan gatherings in Taiwan, Hong Kong, Singapore, Macao, and Malaysia, but Mr. Yang has not been able to afford the trips, so he settled for a clan meeting in Hainan Island, which only cost 8,000 yuan. Thus, lineage logic has been extended to larger kinship identities based on shared surname, and these new associations have discarded the parochialism of local lineages.

In 2010 I had an illuminating discussion with a young Communist Party official on the prospects of lineage development, both in local Wenzhou society and on a national and global scale. College-educated and in his thirties, Xu Jun represented a new breed of youthful cadres who reveal a genuine independence of thought and even crack jokes at the Party's expense. When I asked him why lineages could not purchase land when private families and capitalist enterprises could, he offered several explanations. The first was historical: "Both the Guomindang and Communist Parties have consciously sought to expand the role of the state, so that the government does not recognize lineage as an economic actor. Today, only private businesses and government units can buy land." Second, Xu Jun believes that since the economic reforms of 1978, village governments have developed economic interests that regard the revival of lineages as a threat. Cadres of Village Economic Cooperative Associations, Village Government Committees (村委會), or the Village Party branch all wish to monopolize their own corporate economic opportunities and shut out competition from lineages. Third, Xu Jun pointed to the greater social and geographical mobility that has lured talented people to other parts of China or the globe. Many lineages lost their most capable people, who could have brought strong lineage leadership. Those who stayed tended to be older, less educated, and unable to keep up with the fast-changing times, so they are limited in what they can do to develop their lineage. However, many lineages give out scholarships, and the example of the Wang lineage's Folk Custom and Cultural Study Society shows that many lineages recognize this problem and are making efforts to upgrade their members' educational levels.

On the potential for lineages to go global, Lin Shundao, the Wenzhou historian, said to me, "With more geographic mobility, lineages may now have a new role to play. They are really good at connecting [聯絡], at bringing far-flung kin together. They are always 'searching for roots and debating ancestry' [尋根論祖]." Indeed, Lin's own book on the Chen lineage of Shunxi in western Wenzhou shows recent Chen lineage efforts to pursue long-lost lineage branches and kin networks across the Wenzhou area and beyond, through research into genealogical records, old tomb locations and epitaphs, and visiting far-flung lineage branches and kin (Lin S. 2002: 65–77). Wang Wei also told me that whenever their lineage activists travel, they look for long-lost Wang lineage tombs and branch ancestor halls. These add another piece of the puzzle of their lineage history and reunite lost kin communities. "When we find our kin, we immediately share a common cultural identity [馬上就有文化認同]." Reinforcing this view that with mobility, the role of lineages has been enhanced, Xu Jun also observed,

> In some ways, lineages can be stronger than village governments or Party branches. Lineages are connected with migrant kin in other parts of the country and can call on them to donate money for the latest genealogy revision, ancestor hall repairs, or other social effort. When lineage members are dispersed, they are out of the control of the village authorities. Take a lineage like that of the famous philosopher Ye Shi: he has descendants scattered all over China and even abroad in Australia and Hong Kong, engaged in a wide range of occupations in education, industry, politics, agriculture, and so on. This lineage can be stronger than the village because it is more diversified [多樣化] and it can draw on a much broader support base across the world.

With their college scholarships, Wenzhou lineages are making a sound investment for their future when all those educated professional members will collectively bring to bear their combined leverage from around the world to bolster their hometown kin community.

CONCLUSION

Today, Wenzhou lineages no longer conform to the classic model of landed agricultural lineages described by anthropologists. This is due to various historical conditions of the twentieth century: the great dispersals of population in the wars, conflicts, and famines; the interruption of lineage activities during the Maoist era; and the dramatic shift in Wenzhou from agricultural subsistence to highly mobile industrial and commercial pursuits. Furthermore, in the post-Mao revival of lineages, political and legal constraints on lineage organizations have continued to reshape the form that lineages take today.

A primary constraint is that the category of lineage is still not officially recognized by official mainstream culture, and the term "lineage" cannot be used as an entity enjoying legal rights. Thus, lineages have had to adopt diverse and versatile forms. Another obstacle is the inability of lineages, since Land Reform in the 1950s, to own and manage land and other forms of significant income-generating enterprises or properties, severely limiting lineage activities and their role in local society. Lineages no longer act as the main social welfare agency for disadvantaged kin or the primary agent for community self-government. In these two roles, lineages today are a pale shadow of their former late imperial and Republican-era past.

However, post-Mao lineage organizations in Wenzhou have shown an impressive capacity for shifting forms and creating new structures, including the social network structure. Take the Yingqiao Wang lineage's new Yong Chang Fortress Folk Custom and Culture Study Society, with its surprisingly democratic charter. Established in 2007, it has not only published many local histories and writings by Wang ancestors but also organized ritual events and the procession celebrating the 450th anniversary of the building of Yong Chang Fortress. With time, the Wangs may find that the more educated membership of this organization, with their new mandate to "speak up for the people," may offer more effective lineage leadership and carve out a greater legal legitimacy for their kin community. Another new form of traditional lineage is exemplified by the Chen Family Fortress Cultural and Athletic Activity Center in Qianku Township, which has become a community center catering to anyone who lives in the area, organizing martial arts exercises, games, and leisure activities.

Today, lineages are far from the hegemonic structures of patriarchal state authority that many had become in late imperial China. Lineage authority and social influence in local society today are constrained and even marginalized by new political entities such as village and local Party organizations that answer to an administrative apparatus stretching upward to Beijing. Lineages today mainly devote themselves to organizing ancestor rituals of local identity, community festivals, and ritual processions; exploring local history; building local social memory; and strengthening local social networks among disparate kinship and religious groups. Today the state no longer upholds a normative Neo-Confucian model of lineage that it can control from afar as local nodes of government beyond the formal limits of the state at the county level. Instead, currently the lineage is positioned outside and marginal to the state apparatus, and increasingly with a transnational network that deterritorializes state territory.

In Deleuzian and Guattarian terms (1987), lineages today pose a "rhizomatic" challenge to the "arborescent" central trunk of the state, offering an alternative social organizational growth. The vines of lineage connectedness are often not visible, as they thread through state bureaucracy but are not incorporated as part of the state body. They are shut out of the state and therefore have evaded being linked up vertically to a hierarchical and centralized state bureaucracy. Given their lack of legal status, lineages have had to rhizomatically proliferate in a creative variety of social forms ranging from memorial halls, genealogy renewal associations, ancestor hall repair committees, and cultural and athletic centers to historical study societies and surname associations, while adhering to the basic principles of tracing historical kinship connectedness and committing to the well-being of one's native place. In their efforts to link disparate social groupings together in local ritual events, lineages strengthen horizontal social ties in and across localities. Thus, lineages have begun to "decode" the political and social priorities of the nation-state and to help in "reterritorializing" China into local places of diverse languages, customs, kin identities, and social memories; at the same time, they have begun a globalizing movement of reconnecting with kin transnationally.

8   Of Mothers, Goddesses, and Bodhisattvas

Patriarchal Structures and Women's Religious Agency

In the past, Yongjia [Wenzhou] women did not venture out of the house without good reason. It was shameful if a woman showed her face at the magistrate's office or engaged in business in the market. This was the charm of local customs, and those who observed the rule of women's seclusion were honored in local gazetteers, bringing glory to their families. We do not know when they became mesmerized by Buddhism, so that now, seven or eight out of ten women have fallen under its power. It started out with poor and old women gathering at home with Buddhist nuns to eat vegetarian meals and chant Buddhist scriptures. Now it does not matter whether they are poor or wealthy, young or old, these women transgress all the rules of propriety. They ceaselessly construct altars and shrines to ten thousand buddhas and indulge in extravagant vegetarian banquets. They empty out their purses and spare nothing in generously giving out alms. How can this be proper feminine virtue? Can we find someone in charge of local customs to control these women, and prevent them from widely disseminating this custom? They are violating the law of the "Three Obediences" [to one's father, husband, and son]. Only by prohibiting these customs can we hope to stop them from spreading wildly out of control.

—*Yongjia County Gazetteer*, Qing dynasty, 1879

在昔,永嘉婦女無故不出戶庭,恥向官府與行鬻於市, 此其為 俗之美。載諸邑乘者, 炳若也。夫何邇歲以來, 婦女之耽 溺佛教者, 十居七八。始惟寒 微之家, 哀邁之嫗, 修齋誦經 於室, 或僅招一二尼予往還而已。今則無論貴賤之家, 老少 之輩, 踰閑越度, 匪但修萬佛 之社, 勇伊蒲之筵。抑且傾囊 倒橐, 以事布施, 署不悋惜。是豈婦道之宜然哉。安得司 風化者, 挽其澆俗。有不從者, 罪及三從。設為厲禁, 或 者既倒之瀾。

—(永嘉縣志)清光緒八年

As the disapproving voice of the male gentry writer above reveals, in late imperial Wenzhou there were patriarchal requirements that women stay at home and not venture outside. The Neo-Confucian cults of feminine chastity and virtue to restrain women's dangerous sexuality were especially strong in the Ming and Qing dynasties (Carlitz 1994; K. A. Johnson 1983). The patrilineal kinship structure also had an interest in patrolling women's sexuality and reproduction to ensure correct paternity and descent and avoid disrupting lineage inheritance and unity. Orthodox Confucianism's disdain for Buddhism is also evident in the above epigraph. We also learn that in the late Qing, larger social developments must have triggered a movement by Wenzhou women to exercise religious agency by organizing public Buddhist gatherings and making generous donations (Kang 2016).[1] The result was women eluding the strict Neo-Confucian gender regulations for female seclusion. Thus, it would seem that in the late Qing, Wenzhou women's religious piety offered a countermechanism and relief from the Confucianized kinship system.

Today, 130 years later, after vast social transformations, rural Wenzhou women have a reputation for being a bit more conservative and traditional than in many other areas of China. The older generation of peasant women received much less formal education, and they comprise the vast majority of rank-and-file worshippers and temple volunteers. Religious leaders in Wenzhou, however—the Buddhist and Daoist temple abbots, the lay heads of volunteer temple committees, and of course lineage leaders and secular state officials—are overwhelmingly men, with the notable exception of Abbess Wan Ru of the Taiping Buddhist Temple. Everyone I spoke with agreed that women were more likely than men to be religiously devout (*qiancheng*, 虔誠) and to spend more time engaged in devotional activities, such as chanting Buddhist or Daoist sutras, making offerings or attending temple rituals, and volunteering their labor at temples, monasteries, and religious festivals. Women are also more frequent donors to temples and monasteries, although male entrepreneurs occasionally donate huge amounts.

Given the ubiquity of women's religious participation today, this chapter tackles the question of how to conceive of rural Wenzhou women's religious agency. A key question is: Does women's religious agency contribute to strengthening, adjusting, or transforming patriarchal structures? By "patriarchal structures," I mean social structures, whether discursive or institutional, that regulate and promote social actions that privilege men over women and cause both to valorize men's roles and points of view. The chapter further explores the issue of Wenzhou women's nonconfrontational negotiation of gendered social norms. A related question is whether religious practice today empowers women in a similar way to that described in the epigraph. Finally, what social effects has women's religious agency had within Wenzhou society?

Figure 8.1. Observing Geng Shen Day: women devotees sit through the night in the Town Center Hall Buddhist Temple, Yongzhong Township, 2010. Photo by the author.

GENDERING THEORIES OF STRUCTURE AND AGENCY

The quest for theories of agency emerges out of a sense that many theories of power may be too top-heavy and overbearing, ignoring the role of agency exercised by individuals or social groups. Attention to agency recognizes that human actors do not always carry out the injunctions and regulations of power orders; rather, they calibrate and calculate their behavior according to shifting historical conditions or contingent situations. Thus, while patriarchal structures of social life have long and deep historical legacies, they still need to be implemented, reproduced, and transmitted down through the ages by women and men agents. In other words, structures do not exist except in their instantiation through the performances and actions of myriad social agents in a given time and place. As both Pierre Bourdieu (1977) and Anthony Giddens (1976, 1979) have shown, agency cannot be automatically subsumed to structures of power; it always has a relative independence and contingency.

Agents are always acting in a given situation, historical time, and sociopolitical context; thus, their actions involve strategic calculations about whether, when, and how to operationalize the rules of structures of power. Giddens has emphasized that *"all reproduction is necessarily production . . .* and the seed of change is there in *every act* which contributes toward the reproduction of any 'ordered' form of social life"* (1976: 102). In emphasizing every act of social reproduction, Giddens foregrounds the agency of actors and the dependence of structures on those agents' (often imperfect) implementation of structural rules. Giddens uses the term "structuration" (1979: 61) to draw attention to the temporal, processual, and contingent nature of structures that unfold in real times and places.

Bourdieu counters the formalism and structuralism of Lévi-Strauss and other forms of "objectivist knowledge" by emphasizing "strategy" and "bodily *habitus.*" Bourdieu's notion of habitus, defined as a "system of durable transposable dispositions" or actors' "improvisations" (1977: 72), seeks to bring the body into discussions of agency. Although initially cultivated as part of childhood socialization, in the ritualistic culture of rural Wenzhou habitus is reinforced through frequent ritual performance and customs. Wenzhou women's religiosity is better captured by the notion of bodily habitus, for pious women engage in regular meditation, sutra-chanting, and ritual movements that, on the one hand, impart religious bodily discipline and, on the other, may give rise to unexpected miracles of seeing, or physically sensing, and, in the case of spirit mediums, embodying divinities and gods.

The question of agency has also engaged scholars working at the intersection of gender studies, religious studies, feminist theory, and postcolonial studies. Feminist theorists of religion have grappled with the issue of women's agency in patriarchal religious traditions (Avishai 2008; Burke 2012). Some difficult questions that have emerged include: How do we understand women's religious acquiescence to patriarchal expectations? Does a feminist outlook require secularization? Do current definitions of agency privilege a modern Western autonomous individual subject who resists power? Patriarchal orders are maintained by both male and female agents. Just as the primary agents of footbinding were mothers who pushed their daughters to endure the pain, so also I found that for many older rural women growing up in Maoist China, it was their mothers who prevented them from attending school. Thus, we have to understand how female agency works historically to reproduce, as well as to reconfigure or derail, patriarchal structures.

Compared to urban Chinese women, rural Wenzhou women seem less responsive to discursive exhortations about social behavior in the media, whether by a declining "state feminism" from the Maoist era or by the new consumer sexuality. They continue to cultivate traditional virtues of modesty, deferral to men, and religious piety, virtues that are internalized, then expressed and reproduced more bodily than consciously. For example, back in 1993 I attended a village opera performance of the Buddhist-themed *Journey to the West*. Several people told me that the person who organized the event, collected the funds, and hired the performers was "a very capable strong woman." The phrase "strong woman" (*nüqiangren*) is not really a compliment; most rural women do not wish to earn this title. When I congratulated this woman for her organizational achievement, she immediately denied it, saying, "No, it was not I who organized this—it was all my husband's work!" Having cultivated modesty and been tutored for years to avoid outperforming her husband, her embodied habitus was self-effacement. Nevertheless, without claiming credit, this woman had quietly orchestrated an opera performance that helped in reconstructing local religious civil society.

Here Giddens's distinction between "discursive" and "practical consciousness" (1984: 4–14) is especially relevant in addressing the socially conservative agency of pious Wenzhou women. "Practical consciousness" is a tacit knowledge of social norms and routines that allows agents to carry on with everyday life without having to reflect on or question every act. "Discursive knowledge" develops when social acts and routines must be explained to a non-native, or elicits social reflection or even questioning. For Giddens, agency that is involved in structuration, or the process of reproducing social structures, often works through "practical consciousness." In rural Wenzhou, where Communist inroads were lighter than elsewhere in China, women's conservative agency is informed more by "practical consciousness," the taken-for-granted ways inherited from the past. During this transitional post-Mao period when "discursive" state feminism has declined and the resurgence of an older explicit Neo-Confucian patriarchal discourse has been kept at bay, cultural conservatism has renewed itself. Meanwhile, Western-style "discursive" liberal feminism has appeared in some urban college education, but it has not made major inroads here. Thus, we can see similarities between Giddens's notion of "practical consciousness" and what Bourdieu called habitus, which are both nondiscursive forms of structured agency, although the latter emphasizes bodily inculcation.

Writing about the women's Islamic piety movement in 1990s Egypt, Saba Mahmood (2005) has criticized the narrow definition of women's agency put forth by Western feminists such as Judith Butler. Mahmood suggests that women's agency cannot be understood or defined solely in terms of resistance, counterdiscourse, or rebellious acts, but must also take into account the modesty, self-effacement, and self-sacrificing ethos of pious and socially conservative women such as those in the Islamic piety movement. She shows how social action for these pious women depends on a paradoxical cultivation of docility and submissiveness. Our understanding of women's agency must be broadened to include the ethos of submission to social norms, self-discipline, and religious self-cultivation.

Mahmood's theoretical intervention allows us to account for agency in more traditional cultures and conservative religious practices. Indeed, the majority of rural Wenzhou women today, especially those over thirty, also cultivate modesty, self-restraint, and domesticity and believe that men are more capable than women in the public sphere. They certainly do not engage in the liberal feminist or individualistic discourse of resistance to the patriarchal order. However, unlike the piety movement in Egypt, and perhaps due to the strength of the secular and formerly Revolutionary Chinese state, Wenzhou women today are not exposed to a voluble patriarchal discourse explicitly counseling female subordination. Of course, Chinese patriarchal culture survived the Revolution, but it works less overtly than Islamism. Thus, in rural and small-town Wenzhou, neither an explicit patriarchal nor a feminist discourse is prominent, while the strength of traditional culture means that both male and female agents unconsciously reproduce older gender habitus.

I certainly welcome Mahmood's innovative insight that pious and socially conservative women exercise important agency and that women's agency cannot be defined by resistance. However, in her focus on a critique of Western liberal feminism, her work at times seems to implicitly abandon feminist inquiry into non-Western religiosities. For me, there are different kinds of feminist discourses and multiple paths of postcolonial feminist inquiry. We need to explore and help construct non-Western feminisms or hybrid feminisms that issue from *within* a native culture and align with certain features of native religiosities. The aim is to discover forms of women's agency and their conditions of production that may lead to a native feminist or women-centered religious development (Avishai 2008; Burke 2012). Since these prowomen agencies already exist as potentialities or practices within existing structures, they do not have to be invented wholesale or anew, nor do they have to explicitly reject or belittle native religiosities. That is to say, *non-Western pious women do not need to become secular, nor do they need to become Western-style feminists in order to modify patriarchal structures. Furthermore, the "discursive consciousness" of new hybrid feminisms can build on and expand some already existing forms of women's agency.* Thus, Mahmood's postcolonial critique of Western feminist discourse represents only the first step in our inquiry, not the end. The next step is to identify and explore the different forms of native women's agency, in an effort to help build native feminist discourses from already promising preexisting forms and potentialities.

Perhaps due to her aversion to resistance theory, Mahmood did not sufficiently theorize the paradoxical *social effects* of conservative women's religious agency on gendered power structures. This is evident in her account of Abir, a devout and conservative woman who ignored her husband Jamal, who opposed his wife going out to join the piety movement (Mahmood 2005: 176–180). Although all Muslim wives are, under Sharia law, bound juridically to obey their husbands, Abir was able to skirt her husband by claiming the moral high ground of being more devoted to God than was Jamal, who drank alcohol and prayed infrequently. Thus, Abir's conservative religious agency had the ironic effect of undermining the Sharia institutional privileging of husbands over wives. While Mahmood is keen to focus on the conservative *intentionality* of Abir and other Egyptian pious women, she undertheorized how Abir and pious Muslim women's agency might affect structures of power. Here we could borrow Giddens's idea of "the unintentional consequences of intentional conduct" (1984: 12). Abir and pious women had the intention of perfecting themselves before God through prayer and obedience to Islamic patriarchal social norms. They did *not* set out with the *intention* of opening the public space of the mosque to women, or of challenging their husbands' authority, but these were some structural effects of their religious agency. Similarly, I will attempt to show that "unintended consequences" provide an important window of observation for linking up Wenzhou women's religious agency with the larger structurations of power. We will explore how nonliberal and nonfeminist forms of conservative intentionality and practice among Wenzhou women not only reinforce patriarchal structures but also modify and recalibrate them.

INNER AND OUTER: GENDERED DOMAINS IN WENZHOU TODAY

Returning to the late Qing, we have another account written in a different text—*Nine Sayings about Eastern Ou*—that confirms the importance of Wenzhou women's religious agency:

甌俗婦女入廟燒香及出門游覽，略不避人，習以爲常。
溫忠翰 (東甌九説).

According to local customs in Ou [Wenzhou], women can go out to temples to burn incense and outdoors for leisure and travel, without having to avoid people. This practice is so common it is normal. (Wen 1879: 17, cited in Hu 2000: 105)

Vincent Goossaert (2008) has shown that in the Shanghai and Jiangnan region, local writers in the late Qing were also describing similar women's religious outings as a new trend. As in Wenzhou, large numbers of women were quietly violating Neo-Confucian prohibitions against women venturing outside the home. Goossaert detects a tension between the disapproval of Confucian officials and gentry, and the larger "moral consensus" of local commoners, ordinary peasants, Buddhist and Daoist clerics, and spirit mediums, who had no problems with women visiting temples (2008: 234). We can surmise that, perhaps due to discourses of reform flowing into China from Japan and the West, traditional power structures in nineteenth-century Jiangnan and Wenzhou were being shaken. As they started to lose their authority and rigidity, these conditions enabled a movement of devout women going on religious outings in groups. Ironically, just as women were starting to exercise religious agency more frequently in public spaces, thereby unintentionally resisting Confucian patriarchal culture, the winds of secular nationalism started to shut down the religious arena, with its potentials for religious forms of women's public engagement (M. Yang 2008b).

When women went out to crowded festivals or enjoyed outdoor operas, late imperial texts often sounded an alarm that "men and women mingled together indiscriminately" (*nannu hunza*, 男女混雜). This gender mingling defied the strictures of Neo-Confucian controls over women's sexuality and its promotion of female chastity and sexual fidelity. I submit that women's display of religious devotion allayed male concerns about women's sexual purity. There is something pure and nonthreatening in women's devoutness and service to the gods and buddhas. A single unescorted woman wandering public streets filled with men can be read as a sexual provocation. However, when women travel in groups to temples with a devout mission, their sexuality is diminished by their religiosity. Devout women are thought less likely to indulge in adulterous liaisons, and they are associated with notions of purity and sacrality, an association that helps women overcome their status as polluting elements in traditional Chinese notions of menstruation and blood from childbirth as defiling (Ahern 1975). Thus, women in late Qing Wenzhou and Jiangnan were able to deploy their religiosity and piety to carve out a public space for themselves in local temples. This is an important path through which the nonoppositional agency of pious women can gradually reshape the power structure of gender relations.

In rural Wenzhou today, Maoist state feminism did not penetrate deeply. Women who grew up in that era received only one or two years of formal education, if any. Most older women do not speak Mandarin, and they had arranged marriages. Today, they run family businesses and easily leave the home to go shopping and visiting with friends. Living in prosperous times, younger women are much better educated and have many opportunities to work in the public sphere and experience upward social mobility. However, the traditional gendered division between the "inner domain" (*nei*, 内), or women's domestic sphere, and the "outer domain" (*wai*, 外), where men should dominate, along with the phrase "inner and outer should be differentiated" (*neiwai youbie*, 内外有别), continue to resonate. There is still a public zone beyond which women are discouraged from going. Women who travel out of town by themselves, spending nights away from home, are looked down on as "immoral," and gossip may belittle their husbands as cuckolds. Several women entrepreneurs said this cultural restriction posed professional difficulties, and they have either avoided travel or quit their occupations in order to conform to social mores. If they have to travel, they will often go with a relative or female friend. In family enterprises, it is usually the husband or adult son who travels on business, and the wife who stays at home attending to the family business. While both pre- and extramarital sex relations have greatly increased, the negative consequences for women far exceed those for men. However, as in the opening epigraph, women today can get around this spatial restriction by traveling in groups with their "sisters" to visit temples across the land, and by gathering funds to support temples and religious events.[2]

FIVE MODES OF WENZHOU WOMEN'S RELIGIOUS AGENCY

In my fieldwork, I uncovered five different modes of women's religious agency, which are presented below. These modes are not mutually exclusive, for they wax and wane through time, and different modes can combine in the actions of a single individual. Since most rural Wenzhou women now live in a society undergoing "re-enchantment," sometimes their religious agency is porous to forces of supernatural agencies, or interacts with or models itself on them. Even though Wenzhou women usually have no intention to change or challenge patriarchal structures, sometimes their religious agency can lead to unintended social and religious consequences. That is, women's religious and ethical pursuits, their modesty, self-cultivation, and self-sacrifice, may ironically lead to shifts in the patriarchal structures of power.

1. Women's "Conservative" Agency and Their Contribution to Patriarchal Structures

The first kind of agency generally stays within the strictures of patriarchal structures, serving to reproduce and sometimes even strengthening them. For example, in rural Wenzhou there is a common understanding that women are more religious than men because of their "lack of will or decisiveness." In January 2012, I asked Tao Fengqiao, a lay Buddhist woman, why it seemed that women in Wenzhou were more devout and active in religious worship than men. Tao answered that women's personalities are more "soft and flexible in nature" (*rouxing*, 柔性), while men tend to be "hard and firm" (*gangqiang*, 剛強), so women need to rely on the gods more than men, who are more independent. Here women are believed to turn to the gods and bodhisattvas for help in bolstering their weak will or lack of self-confidence. I would also add that women seek help from the gods when they encounter difficulties conforming to the requirements of patriarchal structures, and the gods often counsel forbearance with regard to patriarchal power.

Zhou Xiulan, a middle-aged woman who separated from her husband but could not bring herself to divorce him for fear that people would gossip, often seeks solace in the gods. Her fate has not been good. Her husband sometimes beat her, and debt from his uncontrollable gambling resulted in a family catastrophe: they lost their house. As a single woman, she must now work as a live-in caretaker of an elderly man to send her daughter to technical school and to save money for her son to get married and pay for the bride-price and house. But whenever she meets with a setback in her life, she said, she never blames the gods. Instead, she thought that maybe in a previous life she had done something bad to incur punishment in this life. "The gods give me spiritual support [神給我精神支柱。]," she told me. She prays to the highest god, the Jade Emperor, and his mother, and also to Bodhisattva Guan Yin, the Three Great Officials (*sanguan dadi*, 三官大帝), and lower local gods.

Sun Xiaohua, a sixty-five-year-old Buddhist lay woman, explained to me that women are more devout than men because women are more "compassionate" (*cibei*, 慈悲), self-sacrificing, and filial than men. She told me the story of Guan Yin's selfless compassion and unwavering filial piety:

> Guan Yin went against her father's wishes and refused to marry the man he chose for her. She wanted to go become a nun in the monastery, and

this enraged her father, who had her killed. Even though her father was brutal and she suffered at his hands, she was still so filial. In the Nether World [yinjie, 陰界], when Guan Yin heard about her father's illness, she rushed back to her father's side. She noticed that he had a big boil on his face. She knelt down and used her mouth to break open the boil and suck out the pus. When she spit the pus out, a beautiful lotus flower came out of her mouth! Guan Yin also gouged out her own eyeball to help her father see better, and she cut off her own hand to feed him. She was so filial!

Ms. Sun reveals her conservative female agency by clearly identifying with the self-sacrificing agency of a filial daughter instead of with Guan Yin's marriage resistance, which appeals to feminist scholars who discuss her story (Yü 2001: 333–338).[3] Indeed, one could say that Guan Yin's initial resistance to being incorporated into the patriarchal marriage system is neutralized or repaired later by her return to her father and her reincorporation into the patriarchal family. Here we can see that religious culture can certainly be a conservative force in steering women to identify with self-sacrificing agency and persuading them to stay in unhappy marriages.

2. Self-Cultivation and Transcendence

Instead of trying to fit within patriarchal structures, some women seek release and escape by checking out of society and family and engaging in religious "self-cultivation" (xiuxing, 修行). In the dormitories of the Auspicious Efficacy Buddhist Monastery in Cangnan County live about thirty lay Buddhist women, ranging in age from their midforties to their seventies. Each had paid 10,000 yuan to purchase a room in the monastery dormitories, which they now called their permanent home. I asked Ms. Su and Ms. Lai why they wanted to live in the monastery. They replied that they wanted to escape "the endless Wheel" (lunhui, 輪迴) of Birth, Life, and Death:

> This temple environment is very good for us to engage in cultivation so that we can become buddhas [xiuchengfo, 修成佛]. Through constant meditation, chanting of sutras, crying out the Buddha's name, and doing good deeds, we will rid ourselves of all the dirt in our hearts. Then we can become pure and float up to the top like a lotus rising out of the mud.

These women engaged in a highly disciplined regimen of Buddhist self-cultivation. Every morning they got up between three and four in the morning to meditate for forty-five minutes to an hour, followed by the chanting of a Buddhist sutra—often the Amitabha Sutra (阿彌陀經), a key text of the

Pure Land sect (*Jingtuzong*, 净土宗) of Mahayana Buddhism. They then ate their breakfast and then spent the day performing their chores: laundry, food shopping, cleaning, and so forth. If the monastery was preparing for a Buddhist ritual or festival, they helped with preparations. They also participated in charitable activities and on wildlife-releasing trips (*fangsheng*, 放生). Around five in the afternoon, they cooked and ate their dinners, and then some went out in small groups for a leisurely walk in the park next door. Others retired to their rooms to read or watch a little television. Around eight, they engaged in the "evening session" of meditation and sutra-chanting. They led a simple life both materially and emotionally, attempting to free themselves from the distractions of family and the pursuit of wealth.

Ms. Su and Lai both observed that life is harder for women. "Everyone wants to be a man in their next life. We no longer want to be a woman, because the life of women is too hard," said Ms. Su, the older woman, with a hint of bitterness. I asked the two women what aspects of being a woman were especially difficult for them, and they offered these examples: giving birth, raising children, dealing with their husbands, and not being able to leave the house as much as they wanted because household chores tied them down. "Sometimes we just wanted to leave our unhappy lives!" said Ms. Lai. They said that they envied women who could go to college. They believed that they were women in this lifetime as a punishment for neglecting self-cultivation in a previous (male) life. Moreover, Ms. Su explains, "if you do not cultivate yourself, then you will not become a man in your next life. You might not even come back as a human being! You know, in the Western Paradise, all souls will become male." Ms. Lai recounted how her friend personally saw the corpse of a recently expired woman when he attended a relative's funeral. It had only been about a day since she had died, and he was startled to see a mustache growing around her mouth. "He saw it happen on her face!" marveled Ms. Lai. "She was becoming male because she will soon be entering the Pure Land!"

There may be a certain gender appeal for Ms. Lai and Ms. Su in the way that Buddhism sometimes invokes gender neutrality or fluidity. Indeed, in the Amitabha Buddha's *Forty-Eight Vows*, Vow 35 is that Amitabha would not attain buddhahood until all women who wished to renounce womanhood and attain Enlightenment could be reborn as men after death. Here, Pure Land Buddhism seems to explicitly acknowledge the unique sufferings of women in this world. It offers a path of liberation quite different from a modern secular sensibility toward gender injustice: through gender reversal in one's next life. Similarly, in the Lotus Sutra (妙法蓮華經), the key scripture of the Tiantai Sect of Buddhism, centered just north of the Wenzhou area, we have a passage about a girl attaining buddhahood. Manjusri, or Bodhisattva Wenshu (*Wenshu pusa*, 文殊菩薩), tells another bodhisattva named Wisdom Accumulation how the eight-year-old daughter of the dragon king Sagara has attained enlightenment due to her meditation, understanding of the dharma, and compassion. Wisdom Accumulation protests that he does not believe that a girl could achieve enlightenment. Even when the girl appears before him to assert her attainment of Bodhi, he still refuses to believe, saying,

> A woman's body is filthy, it is not a dharma receptacle. How can you attain unexcelled Bodhi? The path of the Buddha is remote and cavernous. Throughout incalculable *kalpas*, by tormenting oneself and accumulating good conduct, also by thoroughly cultivating the perfections, only by these means can one then be successful. . . . How can the body of a woman speedily achieve Buddhahood? (Hurvitz 2009: 184)

Whereupon, before the assembled multitude, the dragon girl immediately turns into a man. With perfected bodhisattva conduct, she sits "on a jeweled lotus blossom, and achieve[s] undifferentiating, right, enlightened intuition." All those who witness her buddhahood are "overjoyed at heart."

From a secular feminist perspective, one feels uncomfortable with this Buddhist teaching that the only way for women to gain enlightenment is to become men; it implies that women are inferior or innately impure or immoral. Even when Buddhist teachings seek to be inclusive, with messages about gender equality, the "soteriological inclusiveness presupposes (and reinforces) gender discrimination" (Faure 2003: 94). Nevertheless, until the divine arrival of radically new scriptures that are women-friendly, Ms. Su and Ms. Lai must work within the parameters of Buddhist teachings handed down for centuries. What is crucial is their particular interpretation of Buddhist teachings, the form that their agency takes, and its structural effects. The religious agency of Ms. Su and Lai is one of recognizing gender inequality and acting on that knowledge by adopting a pathway available to Buddhist women seeking release and salvation. They engage in self-cultivation as a technology for transcending both the suffering of this temporal life and Buddhist constructions of female gender.

On another occasion, I asked Ms. Lin whether she identified with Guan Yin because this Buddhist deity was female. She answered, "We women do not pray to Guan Yin just because she is female. We pray to all of the buddhas. The buddhas and bodhisattvas are beyond male and female. They are both genders, or they are neither, or they are a thousand genders [又可以是男性女性, 又是没有性, 又是一千個性]." Pure Land Buddhism seems to harbor another kind of gender fluidity or neutrality, a transcendence of the gender binary on which patriarchal structures depend. While scholars have focused on the gender transformation undergone by the Bodhisattva Avalokitesvara from a male image into a maternal Buddhist deity in tenth-century China, there are very few studies on the gender transformation of ordinary lay Buddhists, or of Buddhist teachings on gender reversal or gender fluidity across lifetimes. This is an important area of inquiry that awaits further fieldwork and textual studies.

Ms. Lai and Ms. Su are painfully aware that their parents' denial of an education for them has disadvantaged them in their adult lives. They experienced difficult married lives and struggled to cope with the traditional female duties of caring for children, husband, parents, and parents-in-law. The strategy they have chosen for cultivating their piety is to leave the patriarchal family, their husbands and children, to live a sex-segregated life with other women in pursuit of personal salvation—what Albert O. Hirschman (1970) has called the strategy of "exit," over "voicing" their complaints, or remaining "loyal" to marriage and family. While their intentions and actions neither challenge nor overturn existing patriarchal structures, their religious agency can be understood in a number of ways. First, toward the end of a difficult life, these women finally have time to attend to their own spiritual quest for salvation through self-cultivation practices that seem also therapeutic. Second, by removing themselves from patriarchal family and kinship structures yet not inserting themselves as nuns into a different patriarchal order, the Buddhist sangha, these women gain a certain self-direction in their lives. Third, in voting with their feet and distancing themselves from the ordinary pursuits of the temporal world, these women's religious pursuits have allowed them to transcend the burden of female gender, providing entry into those realms of Buddhist cosmology that are gender neutral or third gender, or that can lead to gender reversal.

This lay Buddhist women's community resembles the medieval Christian institution of *beguinage*, one of whose building complexes I visited in Antwerp, Belgium. *Beguinage* were lay Christian women's communities housed in dedicated buildings, which started in the twelfth century in the Low Countries and persisted across Europe into the early twentieth century (Swan 2014). Like *beguinage* women, these lay Buddhist women carried out charity work and lived segregated from the wider society, but were able to move in and out of their walled compound.

3. Constructing Religious Sisterhoods and Women's Community

A third mode of women's religious agency is the construction of lay women's communities. These women live with their families but form "sisterhoods" through their shared spiritual attachment to Mother Chen or Bodhisattva Guan Yin. These rural women "form into groups or federations" (*jiebai jiemeng*, 結拜結盟) of ten, named "Worshipping with Ten Sisters" (*bai shijiemei*, 拜十姐妹) (Chen Q. 2014). These sisterhoods were likely inspired by the immortal sisterhood alliances that Goddess Mother Chen (陳靜姑) formed with other female deities when she finished her Daoist martial arts and shamanic training and descended from Lü Mountain (Yu B. 2007: 40). This process is described as "forming friendships to promote the Way" (結友行道). Mother Chen's two main sister deities are Mother Lin the Ninth (Lin Jiuniang, 林九娘), whom she saved from the Lake of Blood in the deeper recesses of Hell, and Mother Li the Third (Lin Sanniang, 李三娘). Together with Mother Chen, they comprise the cult of the "Three Mothers" (Sannai, 三奶), as shown in figure 8.2, where the three goddesses lead a spirit army battling demons. Brigitte Baptandier (2008: 46–53, 123–141) also describes Mother Chen's thirty-six "sister assistants" (*pojie*, 婆姐), who were concubines at the ancient court of the Kingdom of Min in Fujian. Some of these sisters were saved from misfortune by Mother Chen, while others were demons that she converted to the correct path. They endured hardship and fought alongside Mother Chen as her spiritual army.

As a Party member and former Women's Federation cadre in her seventies, Ms. Tang said that she does not completely believe in the gods. Nevertheless, she belongs to one of these sisterhoods. She first joined her group in the early 1960s, when she was twenty, and her "sisters" all worked together in the kitchen of a giant communal canteen during the Great Leap Forward. At that time, they dared not voice allegiance to Goddess Mother Chen. Over the years, she and her sisters took turns sending each other off to their weddings. Before the wedding day, the sisters would get together to "drink wedding wine" (吃囍酒) and enjoy a banquet at the bride's natal home (娘家). If one member was in need, the others would lend money to her, visit her in the hospital, or even help her take care of her ailing mother-in-law. The sisters have stayed together for over four decades, although three of them have passed away. These sisterhoods continue to be formed among teenage girls today, said Ms. Tang.

Wenzhou folklore scholar Chen Qiu (2014) describes a group initiation ritual of these sisterhoods in rural Yueqing in 2013, which took place in Mother Chen's temple on her birthday, the fourteenth of the first lunar month. The head Daoist priest wrote down each sister's name on a piece of yellow paper,

Figure 8.2. Scroll painting (dated 1892) depicting Mother Chen and her two sisters charging on horseback with drawn swords, leading their spirit army to battle demons. Photo by Thomas Pavia, who donated painting to UC Santa Barbara University Art Museum.

and he enjoined the sisters to help each other throughout life. The women swore to support each other like blood sisters. Then the paper was burned in the incense burner, and firecrackers were released to announce this sisterhood oath. The ten sisters took turns each year hosting a banquet, called "drinking the wine of prosperity" (吃福酒), to celebrate Mother Chen's birthday.

Younger-generation rural women continue this sisterhood tradition today, but some have become more secular, as reflected in their new term for sisterhoods: "*identifying* with ten sisters" (認十姐妹), instead of "*worshipping* with ten sisters" (Chen Q. 2014). Some younger sisterhoods have even changed their annual banquet from Mother Chen's birthday to the Lunar New Year, when their far-flung sisters outside Wenzhou return home. Another generational difference is that younger women may go on collective excursions to places much farther from home. Older sisterhoods generally traveled to Mother Chen temples within the Wenzhou area or, at most, to Buddhist temples on Putuo Island (普陀山). In the current era of commercialization and globalization, younger women generally have jobs and extra spending money, so they can travel farther away with their sisters. This travel is sometimes more leisure than religious travel, to major scenic and historical sites across China or to Southeast Asia, Taiwan, or Europe. Their husbands often encourage them to go out, since they do not feel threatened when their wives are in the company of other women. Thus, continuing a pattern from late imperial times, Mother Chen lends legitimacy for younger women to travel far from home and even outside China.

I heard of a similar rural sisterhood devoted to the worship of Bodhisattva Guan Yin, called "Walking the Forty-Eight Vows" (走四十八願). This phrase commemorates the Scripture of the Buddha Speaking of Infinite Longevity (佛說無量壽經), where the Amitabha Buddha swears forty-eight oaths to save myriad souls and build a virtuous and beautiful Buddhist state. Buddhist lay sisters rent a van or truck and "go to eight Buddhist temples" (過八寺), trying to visit all eight in one or two days. They usually go on a major Buddhist festival day, such as Sakyamuni Buddha's birthday on the eighth day of the fourth lunar month.

These religious sisterhood associations enable women to construct a women's community around worship activities, allowing women to give each other emotional as well as material support in times of need (Chen Q. 2014). When women get together to enjoy periodic banquets, they can confide in each other about their family problems and share information about important resources and opportunities in the changing market economy. The sisterhoods also allow women to travel together without worrying about people gossiping. They carve out a public space for women, strengthening women's public activities.

4. The Divine and Defiant Agency of the Warrior Goddess Mother Chen

It goes without saying that the divine agency of gods and goddesses is much more powerful than that of ordinary mortals. Gods are omnipotent beings who intervene in the cosmic movements of the universe, fate, and human existence, while human beings are weak and dependent on the gods' whims and favors. Most patriarchal cultures seem to have no problems with harboring powerful and assertive female deities, such as Guan Yin in Chinese Buddhism, Kali in Hinduism, the Catholic saint Joan of Arc, and Goddess Mazu in southeastern China (Sangren 1983; Yü 2001). This may be because most women do not serve as mediums for channeling these powerful goddesses or seek to model their own agency after the goddesses, so the goddesses pose no big threat to patriarchal power. Yet goddesses and their cults may sometimes undermine or transcend male-dominant social orders. Such was the case, I argued, of Goddess Mazu and her Taiwan pilgrims who crossed the Taiwan Straits to her ancestral temple in Fujian, a journey that compromised the male-dominated spatiality of the triumphant nation-state by foregrounding the matrifocal regional and local spatiality of temples descended matrilineally from the ancestral temple on Meizhou Island (M. Yang 2008a).

I wish now to examine Goddess Mother Chen's (陳十四娘娘) supernatural agency: How is this divine agency expressed, and how does it inform or shape the female agencies of her religious subjects? A goddess's human subjects may interpret and identify with the goddess in multiple ways. Historically, women mainly adopted the first mode of agency discussed above, identifying primarily with those aspects of a goddess that did not challenge patriarchal power; Ms. Sun, for example, was inspired by Guan Yin's filial self-sacrifice rather than her mischievous or commanding agency. Thus, the fourth mode of women's religious agency involves women identifying with and partaking of the boldness and rebelliousness of a goddess such as Mother Chen. This fourth mode of agency remains a potentiality rather than actuality, for I met almost no women in rural Wenzhou who explicitly adopted this mode.

The Wenzhou tales of Mother Chen present this goddess with distinctly *un*feminine qualities that depart from traditional notions of women's virtue as being soft-spoken, retiring, and ladylike (賢惠). This is a feisty goddess who proves herself much more capable than her shaman father and two brothers Faqing and Fatong, all of whom failed to slay the two snake demons harassing the local people. Like the Bodhisattva Guan Yin and Goddess Mazu, Mother

Chen also resisted an arranged marriage to a man chosen by her father. When her parents insisted on this marriage, she fled far from home, to the legendary Lu Mountain (閭山), apprenticing herself to Daoist masters of the Lushan School, where she learned martial arts fighting skills and exorcistic and magical technologies. On returning home and finding her parents very ill, she relented and married the man they had chosen for her, out of filial piety. However, her marriage and pregnancy did not cramp her style. She continued to gallivant around the countryside, riding on clouds and doing battle with demons and monsters to help the weak and needy across Fujian and Zhejiang. With her generous spirit of helping others and upholding justice, she even defied the higher gods. In a move reminiscent of the rebellious Monkey King God or "Great Sage Who Is Equal to Heaven" (Qitian Dasheng, 齊天大聖), Mother Chen dared to challenge the highest divine sovereign, the Jade Emperor himself.

In the following passage from *Marvelous Tales*, Goddess Mother Chen learns that the community of Dingzhou in Fujian Province has experienced a terrible drought and needs a shaman to perform rituals to bring down rain. To protect her unborn fetus from the exhausting rain ritual she is about to perform, she takes charge of her own body's reproductive process, performing a magical ritual to remove the fetus from her body so she can leave it in a safe place:

> [She] perform[ed] the magical technique of "cutting open the womb and extracting the fetus." Shaking the divine bell in one hand, she grasped the divine knife in the other, and then gently sliced into her abdomen with one stroke. Her flesh and muscles automatically split and opened up. Gently she reached into her womb, took out the fetus, and placed it into a basin. Her flesh and muscles then automatically closed and fused together, leaving no scar. Mother Chen put the fetus in the basin on the bed and covered it with the dustpan. She shut the bedroom door. (Ye Z. 1985: 286–287)

Mother Chen then flies to Dingzhou to ritually summon the rain, but two Thunder Gods order her to stop, on orders from the Jade Emperor himself. Ignoring this imperial edict, Mother Chen demands an audience with the Jade Emperor. She flies up to Heaven and forces her way into the Jade Emperor's court.

> In a great rage, Mother Chen demanded, "You are the Jade Emperor; you say that you protect the people of All-under-Heaven; why is it that Dingzhou has not seen a drop of rain for three years? . . . How can you see death

all around and not try to save people?!" The Jade Emperor said, "The people of Dingzhou cursed and swore at Your Highness, so I am punishing them for their irreverence." Mother Chen retorted, "This three-year drought, in which parents witness their own children die of exposure to the sun, and children watch their parents die of thirst, and husbands gaze at their wives dying of hunger, how can this human tragedy *not* drive a person to blame Heaven and chastise Earth? In my opinion, Heaven, you are not at all just! You *should* be chastised! You Earth, you are not moral, you *should* be cursed! You ruler, you are not humane or upright, why do you keep on punishing the people?" This angry tirade left the Jade Emperor speechless, and he sputtered, "Chen, the Fourteenth! How dare you . . . ! You have violated Heaven's Regulations, and I will punish you by decreasing your life span by nine years . . . !" Mother Chen replied, "If you still do not bring down rain, I will again slash your Thunder Gods . . . I, the Fourteenth, don't care if you reduce my life span to nothing!" (Ye Z. 1985: 290–291)

Since the Jade Emperor has nothing else to threaten her with, he reluctantly sends down to Dingzhou a hard, driving rain for three days and nights, bringing salvation to the people.

Unfortunately, the cunning snake demon, alerted to Mother Chen's aborted fetus, sneaks into her room and swallows the baby. Furious, Mother Chen chases the snake demon back to its cave lair in Gutian County (古田縣), Fujian. Sadly, as she rides astride the snake demon's head and finishes him off, her body, weakened by exposure to the cold rain, collapses from overexertion. Before she dies, she vows, "After I die and become a god, I will save all those women undergoing difficulties in childbirth!" After her death, she was immortalized (羽化) and ascended to Heaven (Pan E. 2001: 115).

There is a significant contrast between the unladylike image of Mother Chen as a fierce, sharp-tongued goddess and the way she is worshipped today by most rural Wenzhou women, who focus on Mother Chen's dying utterance about helping women in childbirth. In the early 1990s, when I first started conducting fieldwork in Longwan District, many temples devoted to Mother Chen were quite small. Mothers who wished to conceive or were expecting a baby would place a small clay figurine of a baby in front of Mother Chen so that the goddess would grant them a baby or ensure a successful birth.

I asked many women what they admired about the goddess, and whether they saw in her adventurous spirit a model that would inspire them to defy social convention and change society for the better. Their answers brought me down to earth from my unrealistic feminist flights and longings: they looked to Mother Chen to protect their children and families. One woman in her thirties thought about my question and frowned, saying, "Not really, Niangniang does not make me want to change society. It's more like I look up to her spirit of sacrificing for others [為他人的奉獻精神]." Most women, that is, identified with her maternal and self-sacrificing qualities, adopting the first mode of female agency. They did not approach her as an assertive female model after whom to fashion themselves. Mother Chen's daring and militant prowess are seen as part of her supernatural power, not as a power that ordinary mortal women might imitate. Thus, the fourth mode of women's religious agency, identifying with Mother Chen's defiance of power structures and her battles for social justice, exists, for now, mainly as a potentiality in the local religious culture.

5. Pious Women's Initiative, Temple-Building, and Leadership

Had I simply accepted everyone's declaration that women worship Mother Chen or Guan Yin by seeking divine protection for their babies and families, I would have concluded that these goddess cults were irremediably embedded in patriarchal structures that tied women to reproduction and domestic life. However, further exploration turned up an unexpected way in which women exercised agency through their worship of deities. Some women take the initiative to accumulate funds and lead the establishment or restoration of temples and religious organizations. Sometimes their initiative is triggered by divine inspiration in a dream or a visitation from a deity. At other times, it is in gratitude for a god's divine assistance. In this process, women come to assume a leadership role in local religious communities. However, once the organization or temple grows larger and more socially prominent, the tendency is for men to take over the reins of leadership. I stumbled on a significant number of women who displayed initiative and leadership qualities in their piety. Just as women shamans often assume the role of resacralizing abandoned small temples (see chapter 6; M. Yang 2015) as the "initial spark" that brings down the gods and reactivates temple and community religious life, pious women's agency plays a significant role in initiating the construction of new temples and founding new religious associations. Below are three examples of this fifth mode of women's religious agency.

Building a Statue of Mother Chen

Nanjiang Village in Cangnan County had an old Qing dynasty deity temple built around the incense ashes brought back from Mother Chen's ancestral temple (祖廟) in Gutian, Fujian Province. It was a rare distinction to have a direct connection with the pilgrimage center, but the temple was abandoned after the Communist Revolution. It was a diminutive sixty-eight-year-old woman, Huang Jianying, who in 1979 brought the dilapidated old temple back to life. Back then, the old wooden Qing temple was tiny and decrepit, with only an image of the goddess painted on the temple wall. Although illiterate, Ms. Huang, along with six other village women, thought that the villagers needed a proper statue to embody Mother Chen's spirit, so they took the initiative to collect funds to erect a new statue of Mother Chen and, later, to restore the Qing temple.

That year, 1979, was not far beyond the religious destruction of the Cultural Revolution. "Wasn't that a politically risky thing to do, to build a goddess statue back then?" I asked Ms. Huang. "Maybe Mother Chen's example of killing the snake demon gave you courage?" She nodded proudly and said, "Yes, I was very bold back then, and Mother Chen's example gave me courage. So I mobilized [發起來] the other women to build the statue together." They each donated their own money and went from house to house collecting additional donations. Only the Christian families declined to donate. A few years later, a fierce typhoon hit Wenzhou, so she got up in the middle of the night and made her way to the temple, amid howling winds. There she threw the one-hundred-pound statue on her back and brought Mother Chen home to protect the goddess from the rain running through the leaky roof. Later, she even made a complete set of silk robes for Mother Chen to wear.

I asked Ms. Huang what gave her the idea of erecting a new statue of Mother Chen. She replied that her husband was a shaman (僮生) and that one night, as he slept quietly next to her in bed, she saw a female figure standing beside his bed, leaning over him. "Mother Chen entered his body, right in front of my eyes," said Ms. Huang. This divine possession caused him to jump up and start shaking and uttering words she could not understand. This miracle motivated her to build the goddess statue, but it was a long time before she dared speak openly of what she had seen.

The seven village women who erected the statue and restored the tiny temple went on to manage the temple for many years. Later, however, the gender balance of power shifted. In 2014, when the old Qing temple was torn down and renovated, the new temple committee (廟宇委員會) composition was changed to fourteen male villagers, with a rotating leader for managing the temple and ritual festivals. Indeed, it seems that although women often initiate construction of a new temple or statue, afterward, as the temple membership and finances expand, male temple committees step in to take over the management. When a temple reaches a certain size and wealth, it inevitably attracts the attention of local state agencies, who require that the temple be absorbed into the state system of temple governance. Men are better positioned to negotiate with officialdom, because local state bureaucracies are dominated by men. Nevertheless, it is often a group of uneducated women who start up a new temple or statue building, and their bold initiative emerges paradoxically out of their pious wish to honor a god or goddess's spirit of self-sacrifice.

A Charismatic Buddhist Peasant Leader

Ms. Chen was a sixty-one-year-old peasant woman who led a Buddhist grassroots revival movement in a town in Cangnan County. Ms. Chen had a broad honest-looking face, and her frequent smiles had etched deep wrinkles around her eyes. She did not receive much formal education, and her Mandarin Chinese was hard to follow. She was not raised Buddhist, and for much of her life she did not believe in the Buddha. In her late twenties, she fell gravely ill, and the doctor told her that her illness was very difficult to treat. In despair, she wanted to "pray to the Christian gods," but as chance would have it, a visiting family friend who was a vegetarian persuaded Ms. Chen and her mother to pray to the buddhas instead. Once Ms. Chen prayed to the buddhas, she started feeling better, and the abbot of a nearby Buddhist Temple also conducted a ritual of sutra-chanting for her. After the ritual, Ms. Chen experienced the miracle of full recovery and became a devout Buddhist.

In order to spread Buddhist teachings, in 1984 Ms. Chen "mobilized" (發動) everyone around her, her kin network, her fellow villagers, and surrounding villages to gather to chant and study Buddhist sutras. She relinquished her role in the family grocery business, giving it to her husband so she could devote herself full-time to starting up her sutra-chanting association. She opened up her home to anyone who wanted to join her in chanting. At first they had a small group of only about forty to fifty people who could all fit into her house. Later, the numbers grew rapidly and they had to gather in several neighboring houses. Soon they had to "accumulate funds" (集資) to purchase a new house dedicated to their sutra-chanting meetings. In 2004, they purchased a large house under her name for 100,000 yuan (over $16,200). The majority of their members had peasant household registration, but they also included people who lived in nearby towns. The new house had a couple of rooms that could accommodate long-distance visitors, sleeping overnight on cushions laid out in tight rows on the floor. Today their gatherings attract 300 to 500 people for each meeting, and their total membership has reached over 800 people. The Buddhist Study Group meets on the first, eighth, fifteenth, eighteenth, and twenty-eighth days of each lunar month, plus on any buddha's or bodhisattva's birthday.

As Ms. Chen told me, "If you sincerely practice 'self-cultivation' (修行), for one day or seven days, your mind will quiet down or attain stillness, and then you can be assured of rebirth in the Pure Land." The three sutras they chant the most often are the Amitabha Sutra, the Great Compassion Dharani (大悲咒), and the Universal Gate of the Bodhisattva Guan Yin (觀世音菩薩普門品), which is the twenty-fifth chapter of the Lotus Sutra (妙法蓮華經). Interspersed with the sutra chants are frequent interludes in which the name of the Amitabha Buddha, "O-mi-to-fo!" (阿彌陀佛), is repeatedly invoked. When I asked Ms. Chen what Buddhists feel as they chant, she replied,

> When we chant continuously, it often results in "a spiritual response" [心靈感應]. It's like two good friends who have not seen each other for many years, and then one thinks about the other fondly, and at that very moment, the other person also happened to be thinking of her. This sort of spiritual connection is what we can get with the buddhas and bodhisattvas when we chant. We can often reach them and feel the response from the bodhisattva.

The Buddhist Study Group members dress in the black or coffee-colored robes with wide sleeves, called "ocean blue/green" (海青), worn by Buddhist lay initiates when engaged in Buddhist rituals. At each meeting, they cook together to provide two or three meals for the Buddhist worshippers. Occasionally they hold a special kind of gathering called "abstinence from the eight openings" (八關齋戒), in which they close all doors, windows, televisions, and cell phones, ending all communication with the outside world to focus inward on their spiritual path. They often invite a Buddhist monk to lecture on the Buddhist sutras.

Cai Weiming, a lay Buddhist man, extolled Ms. Chen's selfless spirit. He said that she frequently offers assistance at people's deathbeds. She will sit next to the dying person and chant sutras, and after the person dies, she will bathe the corpse and change the bedding. This is considered a great act of kindness (善良心), compassion (慈悲心), and self-sacrifice, since death is regarded as highly polluting. "In our area, often not even a person's own son or daughter is willing to wash the dead body," observed Mr. Cai. He went on to say that Ms. Chen never accepts any "red package" (紅包) or monetary reward for her services. "She is a Buddhist who has a lot of prestige and authority [威望] among the people, because she sacrifices herself for others. She is respected by everyone, so she has the charismatic authority [號召力] to rally people around her," he said enthusiastically.

In Ms. Chen we have an example of a pious saintly female agency. We can see how her dedication, self-sacrifice, and bold initiative have made her a religious leader in the eyes of most Buddhists in her area. Far from plunging Ms. Chen into a retiring domestic role, her modesty and selflessness ironically propelled her to assume community leadership with the charismatic authority to command followers. Her religious agency was crucial in her ascent to leadership because she was not competing with men on men's terms, which are usually secular. She commanded religious authority by outsanctifying and outsacrificing men. Although her intention was religious, to be a devout Buddhist who could help disseminate Buddha's wisdom for the salvation of others, the unintended structural consequence was that a local female religious leader emerged, thanks to grassroots forces. When I visited their Buddhist Study Group's prayer hall in 2016, I found that Ms. Chen had already started grooming her daughter, a Buddhist nun, to inherit her leadership role. Having recently graduated from a Buddhist Academy, Ms. Chen's thirty-year-old daughter was much better educated than her and had the further advantage of being a fully ordained nun. Thus, Ms. Chen's female religious agency and leadership seemed destined for successful transmission to the next generation.

Building a Temple to Mother Chen: Divine Visitations and a Link to Taiwan

My third example of women's religious agency in the form of female initiative and leadership is a peasant businesswoman who founded a temple to Goddess Mother Chen, called the Sacred Palace of Mountain and Water (山水聖宮), in Cangnan County. In September 2014, I talked with Zeng Jinglian (Golden Lotus), the founder of this temple, while her silent and smiling husband sat nearby. Golden Lotus was a self-assured but modest woman in her fifties. She grew up in a small, impoverished mountain village dating back to the Qing dynasty. One year their tiny old temple to Mother Chen was destroyed by a typhoon. They did not have any money to rebuild it, and she resolved that one day she would work to rebuild it. When she was in her twenties, she left the mountain village and went down to the lower plains to become a businesswoman trading in dried foods, and she also ran a food-processing factory.

Golden Lotus told me about how she met her husband and how they joined together to construct the large temple to Mother Chen. When her husband was only three years old, he refused to eat seafood, the basic food in a coastal fishing village. In rural Wenzhou, refusing to eat meat or seafood is often taken as a sign that one is either destined to become a Buddhist monk or nun or has been selected by the gods for a special destiny. Due to his crossed eyes, rare utterances, and slow movements, people often mistook her husband

Figure 8.3. Ms. Chen and her daughter (seated on her right) and the author (seated on her left) in the new Buddhist Recitation Hall, Cangnan County, 2016. Photo by passerby.

for an "idiot" (傻子). Golden Lotus however, was drawn to the strength of his dedication to the gods. She marveled at his sensitivity to the presence of the gods and his accurate premonitions of miracles and events of ritual efficacy (他感念很靈). Before they ever met, he had a dream in which Mother Chen appeared and asked him to find a woman to help him build a temple to honor her. He looked everywhere for this woman without success.

One day he passed by Golden Lotus's store and said to her, "I have been looking for you for two years. Where have you been all this time? Let's work together to build Mother Chen a new temple." At that time, Golden Lotus was ill and not feeling energetic. However, while visiting her home village, she entered the restored village temple and begged Mother Chen, "Do you think I am without ability? Do you find me capable of carrying out this mission? If you can heal me, then I promise I will build you a wonderful temple." The goddess restored her to health, so she embarked on the long journey with this man to build a temple together. The partnership was a perfect match between a man whose body was very receptive to divine inspiration, but who was not effective in the practical world, and a businesswoman who, while observing the norms of feminine modesty and piety, also possessed a knack for hard-nosed negotiations and could engage the male world of officialdom.

Golden Lotus has now been married to her husband for twenty years. To build the temple, she sold her house and borrowed 400,000 yuan, using a second house as a deposit on the loan. Bit by bit, she and her husband bought parcels of land from farmers in these mountains. One *mou* of land cost 50,000–60,000 yuan. The village government had to approve each sale of a piece of land, which I took to mean that she had to use all sorts of tactics to persuade and cajole these cadres. She assured me that her temple was entirely privately financed: they did not take any money from any level of government for this temple. Her two daughters gave up all their money for this temple, and her two brothers also each donated 1 million yuan. They used up over 6 million yuan in building the temple, and she and her husband are in debt by over 1 million yuan. Golden Lotus asserts that they have never gone to wealthy entrepreneurs to ask for donations because they did not want other people to accuse them of profiting from the gods. "We only want people to donate if they sincerely want to give on their own, and not out of pressure," she said. Her friends and relatives have scolded them for not being practical, for going into debt, and for not leaving their hard-earned money to their children. We see in Golden Lotus an intractable will to take a financial risk in the pursuit of a higher divine end. To my question of why she would take this great risk, she replied, "So that the masses can come to burn incense."

When they started celebrating Mother Chen's birthday at the temple in 2008, they only had enough attendees—ten—to sit around one round banquet table. In 2016, they put out sixty-five tables, seating 650 people, a dramatic increase in the number of worshippers coming up the mountain to participate in the daylong Daoist ritual (法事). They come to beg the goddess to help them conceive a child, have a safe birth, or gain success in business. In return, they promise that they will volunteer to work on her temple construction or assist at festivals. This is called "giving back for a wish fulfilled" (還願), and it can add up to over a hundred hours of donated labor per person.

In 2012, a Taiwanese man visited her temple. He marveled at her hard work and urged her to visit the ancient ancestral temple of Mother Chen in Gutian, Fujian Province. When Golden Lotus went to Gutian, it happened that a large group of Taiwanese worshippers were visiting, so she struck up a conversation with them. This led to their proposing that her temple play host to a Cross-Strait Cultural Exchange Festival. She came back to her town and reported to

Figure 8.4. Golden Lotus with her husband in their Sacred Palace of Mountain and Water Temple, Cangnan County, 2014. Photo by the author.

Figure 8.5. In this mural at Sacred Palace of Mountain and Water Temple, Mother Chen seeks apprenticeship from Lord Xu, with the help of Guan Yin, who casts a spell on him. Photo by the author.

the Bureau of Ethnicity and Religion (民族事務宗教局) that Taiwanese people wanted to organize a festival to honor Mother Chen, but she did not know how to make it happen. The bureau gave her permission to organize this large-scale event, which took place at her temple in 2013, 2014, and 2016.

I interviewed Tang Shengxi, who attended the first festival in 2013 and took colorful photographs of the event, which he posted on his blog.[4] The daylong event started in the morning with the opening ceremony, a secular ritual presided by the mayor of the town, who welcomed the thirty or so guests from Taiwan. Next came the main ritual, the Requesting Prosperity Ceremony (祈福大典), conducted in the temple courtyard by local Daoist priests, along with a few priests from Taiwan. The altar featured life-sized statues of Mother Chen, flanked on both sides by her two divine sisters, Mothers Lin and Li. The male priests were dressed in elaborate Daoist garb, some with "skirts" made of hemp cloth, which I had never seen before, and blew on "dragon horns" (龍角), a symbol of the Lu Mountain Sect of Zhengyi Daoism. The fact that these priests were called *saigon* (司公), whirling around in their "skirts" and blowing on horns that were much thinner than elsewhere I have seen in Wen-zhou, suggested to me the influence of Fujian culture that had crossed over the provincial boundary. At noon, there was a long ritual procession in which the goddess and her two divine sisters were carried on palanquins (花轎) through the streets of the town.

This was the first time that I heard about any "cross-strait" festival to celebrate Mother Chen with Daoist priests and worshippers from Taiwan. I had heard about cross-strait pilgrimages made by Taiwanese to Fujian Province, such as the visits to the "ancestral temple" (祖廟) of maritime Goddess Mazu and the Monkey King (M. Yang 2008a). However, I had never heard of such pilgrimages to the Wenzhou area from Taiwan. Evidently, seeing how cross-strait religious exchanges were able to stimulate the economy in Fujian, Wenzhou local officials were also starting to promote religious events to link up the Wenzhou economy with Taiwan's. On the temple wall of the Sacred Palace of Mountain and Water, a giant poster advertised the second festival in 2014 with the secular title "Zhejiang-Taiwan-Cangnan-Chen-Jinggu Folk Cus-tom Cultural Festival." The sponsoring units listed were the Cangnan County Government; the Taiwan Affairs Office; the Ethnic Affairs and Religion Bu-reau; the Bureau of Culture, Radio, Television, Journalism, and Publishing; the Township People's Government; and the Office of Popular Religion. The organizing unit was listed as the Cangnan County Chen Jinggu Belief Cultural Association,[5] a new nongovernmental organization of worshippers. With local government participation, the secularized festival seemed to be implementing a recent saying: "Religion provides the stage, so that the economy can perform the opera" (宗教搭檯，經濟唱戲). However, for Golden Lotus it was the other way around: promoting business links with Taiwan helps justify and expand her religious goals. The 2014 festival was on a larger scale than the previous year, bringing three hundred Taiwanese visitors instead of thirty. It featured a three-day Daoist *jiao* (醮) community-blessing ritual, to promote harmonious families, good health, and academic success for the people of Cangnan, and good fortune for local industry and business. The poster called on all individuals faithful to Mother Chen, as well as economic enterprises and government offices, to donate to the temple.

Although the poster left out Golden Lotus's name, it was clear that her handiwork was crucial throughout the first and second festivals. In 2014, she was elected to the position of vice director of the new Cangnan County Chen Jinggu Belief Cultural Association, made up of 170 member Mother Chen temples in the county, most of which were represented by men. The festivals were a brilliant move by Golden Lotus that produced two returns: increasing the religious visibility of the temple to worshippers far and wide, all the way to Taiwan; and promising to increase trade between Cangnan County and Taiwan. Golden Lotus reveals herself as a savvy and ambitious woman, able to build up a whole new giant temple from scratch and launch a series of annual religious festivals–cum–business encounters across the Taiwan Straits. Golden Lotus seemed to be holding her own as a leader of the nongovernmental Chen Jinggu Association, and she and her husband continue to manage their temple themselves. One thing was clear to me: in her diminutive and modest feminine way, Golden Lotus exerted a strong female religious and economic agency in building a local religious institution. She credited Mother Chen's daring adventures for inspiring her, so perhaps the fourth mode of female religious agency, that of modeling oneself after a goddess, may be developing into an actuality.

CONCLUSION

We started this chapter with the question of whether Wenzhou women's religious agency contributed to strengthening, adjusting, or transforming patriarchal structures. Having examined the religious agency of many Wenzhou women, we can now conclude that they can produce *all* of these structural effects. In the first mode of conservative female religious agency, certain women believe themselves to be weak and must rely on the gods to help give them strength. They may see, in the exemplary hagiographies of goddesses, certain feminine self-sacrificing virtues that they respect and choose to model themselves after. Here female agency approaches the gods for relief from their suffering, which is sometimes an outcome of reconciling themselves to patriarchal structures. When women take the gods' advice to be forbearing and accept abusive husbands or unhappy marriages, they enact the first mode of agency, which helps to reproduce patriarchal structures.

The second mode of female agency accomplishes a spiritual release and transcendence from worldly attachments to patriarchal structures, such as the traditional marriage and patrilineal kinship system. By focusing on the work of self-cultivation, pious women remove themselves from both domestic family role expectations, as well as from the distractions of mass media's sexualized images of women in the consumer economy. It may be that Buddhist cosmology, with its features of gender fluidity, gender neutrality, and gender reversal, offers a special escape from the patriarchal structure predicated on the gender binary required for marriage and reproduction. The third mode of female religious agency is the formation of women's sisterhoods and communities that last a lifetime. This form of female agency strengthens women's social bonds, increases women's public space, and provides a refuge for women seeking each other's emotional and material support.

The fourth mode identifies with and incorporates the supernatural agency of forceful female deities for social action in the temporal world. In Wenzhou, this mode remains a potentiality rather than an actually existing form of women's agency. If, one day, this mode were to become prevalent in the re-enchantment of society, it would not require secularization nor a rejection of female piety, but merely a crucial shift in women's approach to interpreting and interacting with goddess figures. This form of female agency would work from *within* the indigenous religious culture to modify patriarchal structures for gender equality, and it would not necessitate conversion to Christianity or secular culture. The key ingredients and resources for a female agency that would help to produce gender equality are already there; they are as yet culturally unrecognized and untapped in the current practices of indigenous religiosity.

Finally, I was surprised to discover an important fifth mode, whereby a pious self-sacrificing female religiosity led to women taking social initiatives and adopting leadership roles in the public sphere. Ms. Huang, who initiated the construction of a statue of Mother Chen and revived the old Qing dynasty temple in her village, practiced this form of agency. The charismatic authority of the living saint Ms. Chen enabled her to start up a local Buddhist study and meditation society of over eight hundred members. Ms. Zeng (Golden Lotus), who founded a large temple dedicated to Mother Chen and launched a series of religion-and-trade festivals connecting Taiwan with Cangnan County, managed to position herself in the world of men. Often emboldened by divine inspiration, devout women have built new temples or restored old ones, thus launching new religious communities. However, our examples also reveal that it is easier for women to initiate and lead the building of smaller local temples than it is for them to preside over them once these organizations grow larger. Once temple membership and fame grow, the temple must win state approval, register with the local Daoist or Buddhist Association, and accept the guidance of male-dominated state offices. Thus, once a temple becomes successful, it becomes difficult for women to hold on to its leadership. The contrast between Ms. Chen and Golden Lotus is instructive. Ms. Chen's organization, including mainly rural peasant and lower-class faithful, is denied state recognition and, thus, further expansion. Golden Lotus, on the other hand, is better educated than Ms. Chen and is able to participate in the world of male officialdom and religious managers. For now, Golden Lotus and her husband continue to control the temple they founded, but we do not know how long she will prevail in a man's world.

Except for the fourth mode, these ethnographic examples of women's piety in Wenzhou do not show resistance to patriarchal structures, yet they are clearly examples of women's religious agency. Here we follow Saba Mahmood's point that our understanding of agency cannot be restricted to examples of resistance, but must instead encompass nonliberal forms of agency guided by conservative religiosities. Since all processes of social structuration depend on the myriad agents whose actions, beliefs, and discourses reproduce and instantiate structures of power, we also follow Bourdieu's practice theory argument that it is not sufficient to merely analyze structures in terms of their rules, ideals, and expectations. We must also scrutinize the manifold ways in which these structural regulations are implemented or modified through the exercise of human agency in contingent historical conditions. What we have observed is that changes in social structure do not rely solely on the agency of resistance, confrontation, or explicit disobedience; they may also be engineered *from within* a structure of power, through loyal adherence to its ideals and rules. Thus, the women who initiated the building of a deity statue or temple, or founded religious associations or institutions, did so by being exemplars of patience, dedication, and self-sacrifice, which have traditionally been more strongly associated with ideals of femininity.

This unexpected linking of the agency of conservative religiosity with women's religious leadership may be understood in a number of ways. First, power structures are internally complex, diversified, and contradictory, thus the predominant form of normalized agency often does not exhaust the possibilities of agency in given structures. If historical conditions allow, new interpretations of structural ideals and rules may develop, and new habitus and new forms of agency that do not rely on resistance may bring about structural modifications. This was the case in the increasing tendency for pious women in the late Qing dynasty to leave the domestic sphere to worship in temples. Second, one institutional structure may produce forms of agency that may counterbalance the power of other institutional structures. When religious institutions allow women's participation or spiritual transcendence, women's religious involvement can often compensate for women's disadvantages in the patrilineal institutions of marriage and kinship. Through her loyal agency of selfless acts that endowed her with religious authority, a pious woman like Ms. Chen was able to establish the Buddhist Study Society and deflect patriarchal expectations of women as followers, rather than leaders.

By initiating and leading the rebuilding of temples and religious communities of worship, women's agency has helped open up a realm of religious civil society that negotiates with and counterbalances male-centered state institutions. Here I share Mahmood's postcolonial approach of recognizing multiple forms of female agency, so that resistance does not dominate our understanding of agency. However, her postcolonial critique of Western feminism runs the danger of implicitly closing off feminist inquiry into non-Western religious cultures. We have seen that whatever the intentionality of agency, we cannot always assume that the structural effects automatically align neatly with the conservative intentions of women's agency. That is why we must study not only women's agency but also the unexpected structural effects of their power. The modes of female agency explored here may serve as a basis for the development of alternative forms of feminism that build on and issue from native institutions, traditional culture, and women's religious practices. These forms of female agency may help construct a postsecular and re-enchanted society of both gender difference and equality.

9 Broadening and Pluralizing the Modern Category of "Civil Society"

A Friendly Quarrel with Durkheim

According to the Qing Dynasty author Xu He, "a gathering" [*jihui*] refers to a one-time coming together, to celebrate some occasion. "Forming an association" [*jieshe*] has a permanent nature, belonging to the category of getting things accomplished or discussing issues. We can see that "a gathering" is a temporary alliance, and "an association" has a more lasting nature. In ancient China, whenever the popular folk came together to welcome the spring, or give thanks in autumn, they often held public competitive rituals of welcoming the gods. Therefore, "association" and "gathering" can be brought together, and so we have the phrase "associational gathering" [*shehui*, modern term for "society"].

—Chen Baoliang, *China's "She" and "Hui"*

根据清人徐珂所載，...集會爲一時之聯合，歡迎歡送之類屬之。結社有永久性質，辦事討論之類屬之。可見, ..."會"爲臨時的聯合，而"社"則有永久之性質。然在中國古代，每當民間社日舉行春祈秋報之時，通常會舉行一些迎神賽會的儀式，爲此社與會又可并稱，隨之衍生出"社會"一詞。

—陳寶良著。《中國的社與會》

Arborescent systems are hierarchical systems with centers of significance and subjectification, central automata like organized memories.... An element only receives information from a higher unit, and only receives a subjective affection along pre-established paths.

—Gilles Deleuze and Félix Guattari, *A Thousand Plateaus*

[In egalitarian Amerindian societies], power exists . . . totally separate from violence and apart from any hierarchy. [To understand them], one has to solve the riddle of a "powerless" power.

[These societies exercise] the refusal of [a] separate political power [and] the refusal of the State.

—Pierre Clastres, *Society against the State*

It is not clear why society needs to be projected on to arbitrary objects if those objects count for nothing. Is society so weak that it needs continuous resuscitation? So terrible that, like Medusa's face, it should be seen only in a mirror? And if religion, arts or styles are necessary to "reflect," "reify," "materialize," "embody" society—to use some of the social theorists' favourite verbs—then are objects not, in the end, its co-producers? Is not society built literally—not metaphorically—of gods, machines, sciences, arts, and styles? . . . Maybe social scientists have simply forgotten that before projecting itself on to things, society has to be made, built, constructed?

—Bruno Latour, *We Have Never Been Modern*

Back in the 1990s, a group of American scholars debated whether a similar process to what Jürgen Habermas (1989) called the emergence of the "public sphere" in early modern Europe, also occurred in late imperial and modern China (P. C. C. Huang 1993; Madsen 1993). Although they adopted Habermas's term, since their discussions focused on Chinese associational life rather than public discourse, debate, or media, they were actually addressing the question of "civil society." I will limit my discussion in this chapter to the question of civil society, addressing issues of changing social structure, rather than discourse. Can a concept that emerged out of the modern West be deployed for understanding China, which has a long and quite different religious and institutional history of its own?

William Rowe (1993) and Mary Rankin (1993) both suggested that after the Taiping Rebellion in the late nineteenth century, there was increasing gentry social activism and local autonomy in China. They argue that Chinese trade guilds, charities, benevolent halls, and native-place associations at this time represented a nonstate Chinese "public sphere." Writing against them, Frederic Wakeman (1993) pointed out that Chinese guilds, merchant organizations, and native-place associations have never been free of state penetration, intervention, financing, or monitoring, whether in late imperial or twentieth-century China. Zhao Dingxin later also suggested that in none of the three periods of intensive gentry voluntarism and local activism (Southern Song, late Ming, and late Qing dynasties) did the Chinese gentry "undermine the Confucian-Legalist political framework consequentially or for the long term" (D. Zhao 2015: 339, 340–342), compared with the modern Western bourgeoisie. The Neo-Confucian gentry were ideologically aligned with the imperial state, and they never developed an independent political or military power base that allowed them to institutionalize their local organizations. Zhao came of age in China during Mao Zedong's "Criticize Lin Biao, Criticize Confucius" campaign of 1973–1976, when he was first exposed to the Legalist classical texts. Thus, projecting backward in time, for Zhao the state desire for total control has been strong throughout Chinese history, down to the present.[1]

Also resisting the term "civil society" are Robert Weller (1999) and Kenneth Dean (1997). Weller points out that temples, lineages, and nonstate associations in postwar Taiwan did not fit the Western connotations of the term. Weller's approach is to focus on the Western concept of civil society, rather than Chinese culture or the imperial past. For Weller, whereas the Western term emphasizes voluntary participation, the Taiwanese counterparts are based on ascription, such as kinship and locality; whereas the Western version valorizes individual choice in membership, in Taiwan communalism is important; and whereas the Western term implies the ability of "broad-based horizontal institutions" to organize democratic transitions across local areas, the Taiwan examples were too localistic. Finally, for Weller, the term emphasizes a clear-cut opposition between society and the state, which is not often found among Taiwanese voluntary associations (Weller 1999: 14–16).

The above objections to the mechanical application of a Western dualism to Chinese contexts are useful precautions. I certainly would not apply the notion of "civil society" or "public sphere" to late imperial China, before modernity, when waves of new Western discourses swept across China and sowed the seeds for reform, nationalism, and revolution. "Civil society" does not apply well before the dramatic state expansion of modernity, which subsequently made civil society discourse important and attractive for so many around the world.

Moving in a countercurrent, I will instead suggest that "civil society" is indeed useful as a category of modern societies, including China. All modern societies have been touched by shared forces of modernity; thus, their differences from modern Western societies have diminished, and therefore a category that emerged in the modern West can also apply in other modern experiences. However, instead of expecting Chinese conditions to live up to a predetermined Western definition and ideal of "civil society," we need to adapt the term to fit Chinese historical and cultural conditions and their modern transformation. In the next section, I offer a few proposals on how and why the modern category of "civil society" can indeed be relevant in examining Wenzhou's re-enchantment of modernity.

THE IMPORTANCE OF HISTORICITY
AND SEMICOLONIAL MODERNITY

In addressing the relevance of the category of civil society to Chinese contexts, it is important to have a strong sense of processual historical unfolding and contingency. We cannot posit an essentialized Western culture of civil society as compared with an ahistorical Chinese despotism, for both cultural zones are subject to historical vicissitudes. To ignore historical flux and change is to run the risk of Orientalist binarism, whereby the Others of the modern West serve to further a Western self-gratulatory project. While Alexis de Tocqueville (2000: 489) marveled at the rich associational life in early nineteenth-century America, there were later periods in Europe that Carl Schmitt (1985) and Giorgio Agamben (1998) have called the reassertion of "sovereign power," such as Nazi Germany and fascist Italy and Spain, during which civil society was eclipsed. In modern China, the semicolonial status of the late Qing empire and Japanese occupation gave rise to anticolonial Chinese nationalism. These colonial encroachments led to the rapid buildup of a stronger, deeper, and more centralized modern nation-state, and the abandonment of late imperial China's flexible and indirect state rule at the grassroots level.

In his study of rural North China villages in 1900–1942, Prasenjit Duara (1988) was still able to find much evidence of late imperial local self-governance. Duara identified cultural mechanisms such as deity cults, local temples, lineages, irrigation societies, and ritual-organizing societies, and the gentry social networks, that constructed a public realm which Duara calls the "cultural nexus of power." At the same time, this very period was the point at which the Chinese state started its modern expansion and deep penetration of grassroots society. The Republican state chose to work entirely *outside* this cultural nexus, regarding it as "backward" and "superstitious," and the state opted instead for a new system of political brokers or "local bullies" who extracted taxes and subverted local cultural authorities without the traditional moral obligations to local communities (Duara 1988). After the Communist Revolution, local self-governance was replaced by cadres, who were usually more loyal to higher levels of state administration than to the local community, as seen in their behavior that resulted in the tragic famines of the Great Leap Forward (J. Yang 2012). In this process, late imperial flexibility and negotiated relations between local society and the state gave way to direct state reterritorialization of local society, firmly embedding it into the state bureaucratic hierarchy. Thus, a potent anticolonial Chinese nationalism and the modern expansionary state together decimated older graduated identities and loyalties woven around three key vectors of traditional China: kinship, religious worship, and locality.

As Chinese historian Qin Hui has argued, when China was buffeted about by Western and Japanese imperialism, the "major community" (大共同體) or nation-state seemed very weak and in need of strengthening. In order to save the nation and "liberate the individual," twentieth-century Chinese political activists attacked the "small communities" (小共同體), such as local lineages, guilds, temples, voluntary associations, and village communities, which came to be regarded as centers of "feudal" oppression (Qin 1999). With the Communist Revolution, and its twin drives of agricultural collectivization and state secularization, virtually all local temples, lineages, and voluntary associations across the land also came to a halt.

The late Qing reformer and journalist Liang Qichao (梁啟超, 1873–1929) lamented that the Chinese people were too disunified and insufficiently nationalistic, like a "plate of loose sand [一盤散沙]" (Liang 1901). However, by the height of the Maoist era, the Chinese nation had severely overcompensated: it was now intensely molded into a single political body with only one voice, that of the leader. This modern state was more powerful and penetrating than the late imperial state, because now Heaven, the transcendent divine power, and the intermediary checks on it, such as traditional Chinese religious, kinship, and community organizations, as well as local gentry and religious activists and leaders, had all been systematically removed. Modern technology also bequeathed a new communication and transportation infrastructure that facilitated direct state control and monopoly that had only been a far-off fantasy in the ancient imagination of Legalist discourse.

As Li Xiangping (2010) has observed, although "freedom of belief" is no longer an issue in post-Mao China, a looming "crisis of religion" lies ahead: the formal organizations and institutions of religion are weak and undeveloped, lacking in both religious independence and popular legitimacy. It remains to be seen whether China, under the new historical conditions of economic development, globalization, and growing national confidence, will continue its (hesitant) movements toward increasing tolerance for diverse organizational principles and grassroots initiatives.

ARBORESCENT MAOISM: THE "MONO-ORGANIZATIONAL SOCIETY" AS TRIGGER FOR CIVIL SOCIETY DISCOURSE

The radical state expansion of the previous Maoist era that systematically removed the "cultural nexus" and the "small communities" of late imperial and

Republican times makes it appropriate to examine today's Wenzhou's temple societies and lineages as modern indigenous Chinese rural "civil-society-in-formation." We are no longer talking about late imperial China or China's initial encounter with modernity, but about *post-Mao China*, after Chinese modernity has greatly "outmodernized" Europe and North America, in the radical expansion and penetration of state power. China during the Maoist era witnessed the consolidation of state power in *all* domains of life.

"Mono-organizational society" was a term coined by T. Harry Rigby about the Soviet Union, where "nearly all social activities are run by hierarchies of appointed officials under the direction of a single overall command" (1976, 1977: 59–60). Maoist China was a Soviet-type social structure in which no social organization or institution was external to or independent of state organization, where all domains of life belonged to and were administered by a single state body whose parts were interconnected hierarchically. This is an example of what Gilles Deleuze and Félix Guattari called "arborescent structures" par excellence. The basic units of Maoist society were "work units" (單位), which in rural areas were "production teams" and "production brigades" of agriculture run along military lines, while in urban areas, they were the factories, offices, schools, hospitals, and neighborhood committees. Work units were attached to the chains of command sent down the Party-state administrative bureaucracies, and all were linked to a single unified organization, the state apparatus. It was not possible to have independent self-funded groups or grass-roots organizations; all organizations had to be under or attached to a state office. This swallowing up of society by the modern state was a severe departure from late imperial China, where localities loosely shared in a neo-Confucian culture but were flexibly self-governed by local gentry and community elders. Just as writings on civil society became common in the late Soviet-type societies of Eastern Europe (Arato 1981; Hankiss 1988; Keane 1988a: 2–5; Pelczynski 1988), Maoism so dramatically altered the traditional social landscape that the modern category of "civil society" can now be justified as both a tool of analysis as well as a stimulus to social change in China. Despite the spontaneous and destructive mass mobilization of youthful Red Guards and the later private sectors of market economy, state arborescence remains largely intact today (Zhonggong Zhongyang Weiyuanhui 2018). Thus, in contrast with the hesitancy of some Western academics, there has been a proliferation of civil society discourse in both late Soviet Eastern Europe and post-Mao China.

Having lived through the radical fusion of state and society in the Maoist era, many Chinese intellectuals have, since the 1990s, embraced the notion of "civil society." Thus, state penetration in China today can be understood not as *precluding* civil society analysis, but as the particular context which triggered the invoking of civil society, and in which an ongoing fitful and contested process of emerging civil societies is taking place. Very rapidly, the proliferation of nonstate associations in post-Mao China has outpaced the ability of academic discourse to keep up with social developments on the ground. Already in 2005, Chinese political scientist Yu Keping (俞可平) estimated that there were 8 million registered nongovernmental and nonenterprise associations across China (Yu K. 2011a: 91).

Gao Bingzhong (2008: 246) divides Chinese civil associations into three types: legally registered associations, "hanging and leaning" (挂靠) associations, and not legally recognized associations. This classification reveals the inordinate power of the state to control, constrain, and shape the civil society process. The majority of associations are eager to be legally recognized and registered with the state, because that way they can avoid state harassment and enjoy the right not to be closed down without warning. Since the state will not allow all to register, some can only live a furtive existence through the unique Chinese system known as "hanging and leaning" (挂靠), in which they latch onto a legal entity, whether government office, work unit, or business enterprise, as a dependent or subsidiary, so as to come under an umbrella of protection. The third group are associations that are entirely outside the legal state administrative purview, so they are exposed and constantly under threat of closure. Most of the ritual and religious associations I have discussed in this book are legally registered, but a large number, especially lineages and smaller temples, exist precariously as the second and third types.

CIVIL SOCIETY AS A PERFORMATIVE

Much of the English-language discussion on whether the notions of "civil society" or "public sphere" are applicable to China rests on a simple empirical project, the quest to measure late imperial or contemporary China against a certain fixed definition of an ideal Western civil society. This effort is conceived solely as a descriptive project, a scientific task where the observer stands fully outside that which is described or measured. However, as J. L. Austin (1962) has reminded us, language is not simply an inert symbolic system that makes descriptive statements of truth-value, representations of reality, or assertions of fact. Languages are highly dynamic, and their speakers are often engaged in what they are describing, and concerned about the social consequences of descriptions. There is often an overlooked dimension of language that eludes the empirical mind-set: language that behaves as *performative utterances*. Here language does not merely describe, represent, or symbolize, but accomplishes real social effects through speech acts. Thus, the very act of writing about civil society is part of the effort to increase social awareness, engage in social reflection, and work to bring civil society into existence.

There have been official attacks on the notion of civil society, such as an article by Zhou Benshun (2011) arguing that the notion is a "trap or pitfall" (*xianjin*) laid by the West for China and that China has a totally different political system, wherein the Party must strengthen, not loosen, its management of society. However, this article attracted counterarguments, both sarcastic and well-reasoned, on the Chinese internet and blogosphere, dismissing it as too "hardline" and "Leftist" (Cao G. 2011; Huangcheng 2015; Yu K. 2011).[2] Despite an official media ban on the term, a few online discussion groups on this topic were still hanging on in 2019 on social networking website Douban.com (豆瓣),[3] and a Civil Society Development Institute at Zhejiang University (浙江大學公民社會研究中心) was still in operation in 2016.[4] Thus, to persist in discussions of civil society is to continue the long negotiation with state power. State authorities need to be persuaded that giving looser rein to civil societies is not promoting opposition to the state, but opening up to the Chinese creative organizational genius and social dynamism of grassroots community self-help efforts. In the words of my friend Wang Qinsheng, of the Wang Lineage in Longwan District, "We help the government to take care of our people and to solve social problems."

TWO MEANINGS AND CONSEQUENCES OF CIVIL SOCIETY

The literature on "civil society" is vast, and we need to distinguish between two understandings of civil society.

First, civil society can be understood as producing a plurality of organizational principles that both diversifies and knits together the social fabric of a society without relying on state organs. This pluralization enables self-initiating and self-governing groups and communities to form, interact, and stimulate each other, while being motivated by different social, religious, or educational ideals. Examples in contemporary China include calligraphy societies, alumni associations, lineages, temple associations, religious organizations, nonstate Confucian schools, native-place associations, and occupational and hobby groups.

Second, civil society can also be understood as social or political activism and critique, propelled by a modern reflexive social awareness and opposition to existing power structures. Here civil society is the conscious will of nongovernmental organizations (NGOs) to actively work for social change through explicit agendas, strategies, and targets. Goals include trying to change public discourse and social values, transforming state laws and properly implementing them, or influencing government officials. Examples in China today include environmental NGOs, migrant worker rights groups, homeowners associations, and feminist, human rights, and labor activist groups.

In contemporary China, the first kind of civil society has seen great gains and dynamism in the post-Mao era; the second kind has emerged but is not thriving, for it is subject to state surveillance and periodic crackdowns. The presence of foreign NGOs exacerbates state insecurities and surveillance. Christian and Muslim religious organizations, although usually not activist, are also subject to intense scrutiny. In this book, I am clearly only addressing the first understanding of civil society, focusing on the organizing principles of religiosity, kinship, and locality as reemerging ways of diversifying Chinese rural and small-town social structure.

THE PROBLEM OF ELITIST AND URBAN PERSPECTIVES ON CIVIL SOCIETY

Many writings on Chinese civil society see it arising in large urban areas, in the form of secular nongovernmental organizations. Indeed, one of the Chinese translations for "civil society" is "city people's society" (市民社會). Another Chinese translation for civil society translates as "citizens' society" (公民社會), seemingly to promote the idea that ordinary citizens can feel a sense of social responsibility to participate in building society through their voluntarism, local activism, and self-governance.[5] My own preferred Chinese term to describe what I observed in rural and small-town Wenzhou is "people's society" (民間社會) (M. Yang 1994a: 287–311), where "the people" has the connotation of "the folk," at the grassroots.

There is also a tendency to focus on the elite, such as late imperial gentry or contemporary entrepreneurs and intellectuals, as the primary agents of civil society. However, civil society construction requires building from the ground level up, and the participation of a broad swath of occupations, classes, and social statuses. In their early influential essay on civil society first published in 1992 in Hong Kong, Deng Zhenglai and Jing Yuejin preferred the term "city society [市民社會]" (2008: 9–10; 2011: 34–35). Indeed, they specifically *excluded* peasants from consideration in building Chinese civil society!

Peasants self-sufficiently relying on lands are also excluded. In Chinese civil society, entrepreneurs and intellectuals are the backbone. . . . Entrepreneurs are the chief force for the building, development and improvement of market economy. . . . The economic strength and status thus possessed endow them the leadership in organizing and sponsoring all forms of groups, organizations and interest groups. Chinese intellectuals generally have the awareness of modernity and knowledge on modernization. . . . [They] have been the source of knowledge and energy for the progress and development of Chinese civil society. (Deng and Jing [1992] 2008: 7)

Such confident elitism was typical of Chinese intellectual discourse in the 1990s. Today wealthy big entrepreneurs depend on the patronage of state officials, and there is a "revolving door" between the state and business. Family members of currently serving officials go into private business, using their official connections, and retired officials move into business, calling in the debts that people owe them from their term in office. Thus, it is hard to imagine how the large business owners and the state could extricate their mutually vested interests enough for big entrepreneurs to lead a civil society movement.

In many Chinese writings on civil society it is clear how much the authors have been reading American or Western sociologists and political scientists—hence their frequent emphasis on contractual relations, individuals, and urban contexts. China's population was 73 percent rural in 1990, when I first visited Wenzhou, and 43 percent of its people were still living in rural areas in 2016.[6] Since a significant proportion of town residents in China were peasants who only recently moved there, or peasants whose entire physical environment was dramatically built up into towns, most Chinese still subscribe to a peasant culture to varying degrees. As I showed in my discussion (chapter 7) of how Western scholars dismiss African lineage organizations as a form of civil society, the assumptions of sociologists and political scientists in the United States, where the rural population is minuscule, need to be questioned in thinking about emerging civil societies in the non-Western world.

INDIGENIZING MODERN CHINESE CIVIL SOCIETY

While individual contractual membership, NGOs, and politicized civil society can be found in large cosmopolitan cities in China, the majority of Chinese people still live in rural or small-town settings, places where extended families, lineages, temples, native-place associations, and religious associations and their charities are more intact or recently reinvented. These indigenous associations were embedded within late imperial structures of *indirect rule* by the state, or the civilizational mode of governance, which often entailed a de facto local autonomy. Thus, we need to pay special attention to the native precursors or emergent indigenous forms of Chinese civil society, and not just imagine civil society in terms of existing Western urban forms. Civil society construction will be more effective and enduring if this process builds on pre-existing cultural and institutional configurations and taps into the deep cultural unconscious of the social order.

Lineages often operated as the self-governing strength of local societies. They were often engaged in charitable activities. Take the case of the famous Fan Lineage's charitable estate (范氏義田), lineage corporate land donated by Fan Zhongyan (范仲淹, 989-1052 CE) in the eleventh century for his lineage members and descendants. The wealth generated from the estate was used for distributions among lineage members, family ritual expenses such as funerals and weddings, charity for poor lineage members, and educational and examination expenses of poor families. Since the Song dynasty, there has also been a common practice of setting aside lineage "sacrificial fields" (祭田), or corporate land whose rental income would pay for a lineage's ancestor sacrificial ceremonies and community feasting (Twitchett 1959: 111), and "school fields" (學田), used for financing boys' education.

Indeed, the extent of lineage communal ownership of land in areas of southern China was phenomenal. Zheng Zhenman's (1992: 258) research shows that in Fujian beginning in the mid-Ming dynasty, lineage public "sacrificial fields" started to grow in size, attaining equivalence with privately owned land by the late Qing. In Land Reform records of the 1950s, public lineage land represented over 50 percent of total cultivated land in western Fujian, and 20-30 percent in coastal areas. In the Pearl River Delta of Guangdong, 30-50 percent of local agricultural production was from lineage communal land. In Pujiang County, Zhejiang, it was one-third, and in some villages in Yiwu County, Zhejiang, it reached an astonishing 80 percent (Qin 1999: 361). One could say that Marx's "primitive communism" already existed in parts of southern China before the Revolution. So it was a great historical irony that during Land Reform, these public communal lands were confiscated and turned over into the hands of the modern state apparatus, which in the post-Mao era transformed them into capitalist real estate.

Lineages also made donations that benefited their local community, sometimes including people of other kinship groups. True to their Neo-Confucian values, gentry lineage leaders established local schools that were often open to nonlineage members. In the Wenzhou area, in 1092 CE, an ancestor of the

Chen Lineage in Pingyang County donated fifty *mou* of land on which to construct a school open to all male youth in the county. To express its appreciation, the county magistrate bestowed on the Chen Lineage sixty *jin* of sacrificial meat twice a year. The magistrate also exempted Chen students from paying tuition and granted the Chens reduced taxes in bad harvest years. This arrangement persisted until the early Republican era (Lin S. 2002: 25). On this land, the Confucian school has lasted in different forms for over nine centuries. In 1901, a later Chen lineage descendant, Chen Shaowen (陳少文), established the Benefit Intellect Senior Girls School (益智高等女學校) with his own personal funds in Shunxi, Pingyang County (Lin S. 2002: 26–28; Zhang Q. 2003: 61–62). The school recruited both lineage and nonlineage girls, giving them tuition-free education.

In chapter 7, I noted the recent rise of new surname and clan associations in Wenzhou. These broader kinship associations send local representatives to annual national meetings in such places as a rented hall in the Great Hall of the People in Beijing, and thus are increasingly breaking the boundaries of localism in their construction of national and even global networks. Similarly, many lineages now reach out to expatriate kin living outside China, establishing the beginnings of a transnational network that strengthens the lineage at its local origins. Indeed, James Watson's (1975) early fieldwork on the Man lineage—how it organized the emigration of its members from Hong Kong to London and maintained transnational kin connections—was an early innovation in multisited fieldwork. We can see that these contemporary Wenzhou lineages and temple societies are modern public associations that have reinvented themselves from indigenous late imperial forms. Although they are based on traditional principles of kinship, religiosity, or native place, they are quite capable of overcoming what Robert Weller (1999) cited as "localism" when he excluded them from considerations of civil society.

How did the West build up modern civil society, if not from its own past cultural forms, such as local Christian churches, guilds, village or town councils, and ladies' reading and quilting societies? In the same way, modern rural Chinese civil societies must also arise from indigenous forms. Instead of dismissing Chinese temple associations and lineages as obstacles to modernity, one could describe them as Chinese-inflected forms of religious civil society. They may not follow the modal forms familiar in the West, but they are able to adapt themselves to the needs of a modern state-dominated society. At the Jinxiang City God Temple (Jinxiang 2007), the temple committee stressed that their transparent accounting of all expenditures was to further "democratic financial accounting and strengthen public monitoring" (民主理財，強化監督).

Similarly, the Charter of the Yong Chang Fortress Folk Custom and Cultural Study Society in chapter 7 called on its members to participate in "social activities of public benefit," and its requirement for membership was "having a sense of principle and righteousness, and being willing to speak out on behalf of the people, and being concerned with the greater interest of the larger community." Instead of rigidly imposing Western expectations and assumptions about what civil society should look like, we need to examine the huge modern civil society potentials in indigenous grassroots formations. Thus, we need to broaden and diversify our definitions of modern civil societies to accommodate non-Western and rural forms.

THE RELIGIOSITY AND LOCALIZATION OF INDIGENOUS CHINESE CIVIL SOCIETY

Two key features can be detected in the building of an indigenous rural civil society in contemporary Wenzhou. First, this rural civil society is both ritually and religiously inspired and driven. Second, rural grassroots civil society is tied up with the ritual expression of locality and community. The notion of locality means that temples are generally tied to a geographical space or delimited territory, and their constituencies tend to form local identities and collective memories. As we saw from chapter 6, deity temples and Daoist and Buddhist temples serve their local villages, township, county, or town neighborhood. They bring together local people for periodic ritual performances, deity or Buddha birthday celebrations, or lunar calendar festivals. People not only pray and make offerings to the gods in temples, but also socialize over banquets and renew their local social networks and community identities through the auspices of their temples. Some temples bring out their deity statues once or twice a year in palanquins and parade them around the locality, and the god is said to "inspect the boundaries" of their community.

Like local temples, lineages are also locality-based: their ceremonies remind their members of their earliest ancestors who first settled in the local area, and the waves of lineage demographic growth and expansion in a certain territory over the centuries. In Yongchang Town, where the Yingqiao Wang Lineage organizes periodic ritual processions with papier-mâché effigies of their ancestors, the route generally traces out the boundaries of the old Republican-era geographic/administrative area called Yongqiang District (永强區), where their Wang Lineage ancestors lived. Although this area has been disaggregated, geographically and administratively reconfigured, and renamed at least two or three times since the Communist Revolution, it would seem that in terms of ritual memory, older spatial designations and imaginaries die hard. Ancestors hover around the native place (家鄉), attracting their diasporic descendants to come back to their native place to renew ties and donate money.

Indeed, scholars of Chinese popular religion have generally noted that "there is a direct relationship between popular religion . . . and local history [地方歷史], . . . and [its] ritual activities are the symbols of a village's self-governance and solidarity [鄉村自治的凝聚符号]" (Ye T. 2009: 287; see also Zhu H. 2008: 12). Just as in late imperial China, one finds a revival of interest in writing local histories, and new local gazetteers written today share many features with their precursors, such as describing the histories of local temples and lineages, along with their ritual and charitable activities. The main difference is that contemporary gazetteers proudly describe local industries, incomes, and entrepreneurs. Today many older and retired men who have some education often volunteer to join three different efforts to preserve local memory: temple managerial committees, lineage managerial committees, and local gazetteer-writing groups. They may also help to run the local Old People's Association, which actively solicits donations to establish and run temples and lineages.

The connection between popular religion and the ritual marking of territory and native place has been noted by many anthropologists. Taiwanese anthropologist Lin Meirong (1989) made a classic distinction between "ritual circles" (祭祀圈), the bounded space of a localized community's ritual activities, and "belief circles" (信仰圈), the larger regional territory of pilgrimage devoted to a single deity. Fiorella Allio (2003) has also shown how places in the rural Tainan area are ritually marked in the *koah-hiu* processional system, and how collective ritual produces both the community and its self-identity. Steven Sangren (1987: 52) has also noted how "territorial cults" of deities in rural Taiwan construct a "cosmic nested hierarchy" of community identities of different geographical scales: the neighborhood, the village, and the multivillage level. Lin Weiping (2015) has also stressed the importance of understanding the ritual embedding of deities (their statues) and their "sons," the spirit mediums, in the local territory of a village or larger space. Taiwan spirit mediums openly go into trance in public outdoor ceremonies; their bodies, like their gods, represent, protect, and ritually construct the village space and local identity.

These periodic rituals of local identity bring to mind the work of spatial theorist Henri Lefebvre. He critiqued capitalist "abstract space," the rationalized and instrumentalized space that is conceived, planned, and built by capitalist urban planners around the world. Capitalist space is made homogeneous, repetitive, interchangeable, and easily reproducible, no matter what specific culture, history, or natural landscape the built space is imposed upon (Lefebvre 1991: 396). Think of the endlessly same parking lots, shopping malls, skyscrapers, or highways around the globe. We can also imagine the history of Chinese state spatialization efforts to turn natural tribal or peasant villages, settlements, and towns into the orderly lower administrative units in a vast bureaucratic hierarchy. In contrast with these top-down spatializing, administrative, and commercializing plans are the periodic movements of people deploying their bodies to ritually "mark" their local spatial identities, places of kinship, and pilgrimages in constant efforts to insist on local *difference*. These ritual markings of the body into the earth, such as the deity processions of City Gods in small-town Wenzhou, can be seen as various ways of preserving local cultures against assimilation into uniform state-capitalist subjects. Against the overpowering nationalism in twentieth-century China that sought to sweep away these "superstitious" local spatial differences, the resurgence of community rituals and the active building of new and old ritual sites would seem to be an effort in recuperating communal space at the expense of state-capitalist space.

THE EARTH GOD AND THE MODERN NOTION OF "SOCIETY"

The Chinese term for the imported modern notion of "society" is *shehui* (社會), a term also found in the phrase for "civil society" (公民社會; 民間社會). By an intriguing coincidence, *shehui* is made up of two characters that were originally ancient terms with strong religious connotations. In twentieth-century modernity, the term *shehui* underwent a significant modern semantic shift. Lydia Liu calls this modern term an example of "return graphic loans" (1995: 302, 336), a phrase referring to classical Chinese characters (kanji) that were used by the Japanese to translate modern Western terms and that were then later reintroduced back into China with the new modern meaning.

As Chen Baoliang (2011) has shown, the ancient term *she* (社) originally had the same meaning as "earth" or "soil" (*tu*, 土), which is a component of this character. When a *shi* (礻) radical, which signifies "divine being," was added to the left of the character for "earth," the resulting character (社) referred to the Earth God, a god who watched over a local territory, protected its human inhabitants, and received sacrifices from the local people (Xu S. 1963: 7; Zheng 1998). Today the Earth God is commonly called *tudigong*, or "God of the Soil" (土地公). In ancient times, *she* was often paired with Ji (稷), the God of Grains, who ensured good agricultural harvests, so we have Sheji (社稷), "Gods of Soil and Grain." When a group of people come together to form a group or community, it is called "forming an association" (結社), which entailed sacrifices to the Earth God as their protector. Thus, the original meaning of *she* had a geographic and territorial component of group identity, as well as a religious engagement with a territorial protector-god. With the commercialization of the Song dynasty, new and diverse deity cults came to replace many Earth God cults, providing new sources of place and community identification (Hansen 1990; Katz 1995: 25–28).

The other ancient term (*hui*, 會), which meant "gathering," "assembly," or "association," was often paired with the term *she*, because the members of each *she* or association periodically gathered together for a ritual or festival event to renew their social ties and common identity. At these ritual gatherings, there were often competitive feasting events, sports, and ritual performances, hence the term "competitive meets" (賽會). Thus, composed of two ancient characters (社 and 會), the modern term for "society," as in "civil society," harbors within it the ancient ritual and religious features that are no longer in our modern secular understanding of "society."

In ancient times, before the empire was established in 221 BCE, sacrifices to the Earth God started out as a bottom-up assertion of spatiality.

就原始意义而言，社并非上層規定下的行政機構，。。而是產生于民間的自發組織。。對于認識中國社會的下層構造不無裨益。社作為一種社神崇拜與地域性的祭祀組織，自先秦出現以來，秦漢兩朝，猶有遺存。

In the original meaning of *she,* it did not designate an administrative unit imposed from above by higher levels of authority . . . , but was produced by the folk as a spontaneous organization. . . . Therefore, it is of great advantage in helping us understand the construction of the lower levels of Chinese society. As the worship of the Earth God and a territorially based organization for ritual sacrifice, the term *she* first emerged in pre-Qin times, and it is also found in the Qin and Han Dynasties. (Chen B. 2011: 7)

In later imperial times, at the pinnacle of the Chinese empire, the emperor and his court took to making sacrifices to the Gods of Soil and Grain to ensure good crops and harvests for his people across the empire. However, the court did not monopolize sacrifices to territorial gods, as it did with sacrifices to Heaven, the supreme deity. There developed a graduated and nested hierarchy of descending sacred territorialities. Any social entity, from the emperor, nobility, temples, and fields to local communities, villages, and families, could set up a *she* altar or shrine to protect their local territory.

With modernity and the secularization of the modern bureaucratic state, the central, provincial, and county governments no longer bother with the Gods of Earth and Grain, and for a while during the Maoist period it was able to suppress them at the grassroots level. However, these grassroots territorial and organizational energies could not be subjugated for long. Local Earth Gods, deity cults, and lineages have reasserted their local territories, community identities, and collective memories. Once again, the gods (and ancestors) create and protect a patchwork of myriad sacred localities across the land. They produce sacred terrains that often do not replicate or align with secular state administrative units or with capitalist geographic "target audiences" for marketing and advertising.

QUERYING DURKHEIM: PLURALIZING AND REHYBRIDIZING THE MODERN CATEGORY OF "SOCIETY"

Having pointed out, in chapter 6, Durkheim's relevance to the ritualized and religious reconstruction of indigenous civil societies in Wenzhou, I must now also part company with him on three issues. The first has to do with the way that Durkheim in his classic *Elementary Forms of Religious Life* always referred to "society" in the singular, as an abstraction, and as having a natural higher unity and integration: "If the totem is the symbol of both the god and the society, is this not because the god and the society are one and the same?" ([1912] 1995: 208). The inspiration for Durkheim's profound insight about the original role of religious force and the category of the sacred in any construction of "society" was Australian aboriginal cultures and their use of "totems" (sacred animals or plants) to establish and symbolize their "clans" or kin units of social identity and belonging.

The irony is that, while Durkheim himself noted that "totemism is basically a federative religion that cannot go beyond a certain level of centralization without ceasing to be itself" ([1912] 1995: 199), he set aside this observation about Australian acephalous structure in making his leap from "clans" to the modern category of "society." For Durkheim, both clan and modern society, such as that launched by the French Revolution ([1912] 1995: 212–216), share the same religious force in their establishment and maintenance. However, Australian clans are structured as plural and flexible, occasionally joining together in loose, decentralized confederations on a continent that did not experience state formation before its colonization by Westerners. Durkheim was one of the "fathers" of the modern notion of "society," but despite his Australian examples, he formulated this concept as something unified and totalizing. He usually referred to "society" in the singular, rather than plural form. In the modern Chinese and Wenzhou contexts, gods who occupy the central altar and Earth Gods in local village or town temples, and the spirit tablets of founding lineage ancestors are similar to the dispersed Australian clan totems. The gods and ancestors dotting the countryside are always plural, residing in multiple temples, fields, ancestor halls, and shrines. They represent local communities and identities based on kinship, religious affiliation, and native place. They may come together in cooperative ritual or charity events, as we see in chapter 7 in the increasing considerations for "external relations," but they retain their separate plural identities and spaces.

Second, Durkheim's synchronic structural functionalism prevented him from examining how religio-social formations develop historically or become absorbed into larger formations. He did observe that the Australian notion of a universal "mana" had the potential of imagining a higher social unity, but "a religion of the tribe" did not develop to transcend their clan cults ([1912] 1995: 199). What he did not consider was how so many local indigenous religions and small-scale societies in human history were subordinated or integrated into more powerful religio-social formations, such as Axial Age religious movements (Buddhism, Christianity, Islam, Hinduism, etc.), and of course, monarchical state formations that often aligned or merged with them. In the case of China, shamanism and popular religion were repeatedly enfolded into the "three religions" (Confucianism, Buddhism, and Daoism) and the imperial state through what I call a process of "hierarchical encompassment" that sought not to eliminate them but to absorb and subordinate their gods to lower ranks. Moving to later times, missing in Durkheim's discussion of modern society is the modern state. Modern societies cannot be understood without thinking about the modern "state" that holds a society together, by orchestrating its rituals and discourses of religio-moral unity, protecting its territorial boundaries, enforcing its laws, and repressing individual or sectarian divisive forces. Indeed, one could say that the French Revolution provided one important launching pad for the modern state and modern secular nationalism. By conflating Australian "clans" with modern "society," Durkheim has obscured significant differences between them. The multiplicity of aboriginal clans contrasts with modern society's integrated "organic solidarity" and the modern state. Thus, implicitly, what Durkheim really had in mind when he wrote about "society" in the singular was society-writ-large as the equivalent of the monolithic nation-state. When he made Australian totemic clans examples of religiously constructed "society," he downplayed their plurality, autonomy, and structural equality, and instead reimagined "society" as a singular integrated modern nation-state. Thus, I would like to build on Durkheim's precious insight: If religiosity constructs society, and all modern societies have a state, then how does religiosity position itself or adjudicate the sometimes tense relations between state and society?

My third issue with Durkheim was taken up by Bruno Latour in the epigraph at the beginning of this chapter. Here Latour seems to grapple with Durkheim head-on, asking why social scientists commonly write that "objects," such as a statue of a god or totem, merely serve to reflect, represent, or embody "society," but at the same time also deny the god or totem any agency or materiality in this process. By suggesting that the object (the god, statue, or image) must be understood in a new way as an active "coproducer" of society, he is not only returning agency to the gods and ancestors but also mediating and blurring the boundaries between human and divine, and renegotiating the relationship between the object (god or ancestor) and the subject (human society). The epistemology of modern social science grants these objects only the weak role of reflection, symbol, and representation, not the active processes of production and construction, because modern humans must be separated from both nature and the supernatural and understood as the only agent of history. By adopting the term "quasi-objects," Latour suggests that gods are active subjects and agents too, and not overdetermined by society and its forces. In Latour's "actor-network theory," gods, along with machines, ritual, and art, all contribute as society's "coproducers" (1993: 54). Thus, a "postsecular society" breaks down the separations between religion and economics and among gods, humans, machines, and nature. It recognizes that gods and ancestors help humans construct alternative forms of society within a modern nation-state and enable communities to transgress state administrative territorialities. Since Chinese modernity drastically delegitimized traditional Chinese religiosities, their important role in constructing modern civil societies has been greatly hampered. Today, China's many civil societies must work toward mutual respect and tolerance for cultural difference (Gao 2008: 290). That is to say, they must move toward a new postsecular society that recognizes the religious and ritual coproduction of civil society by local residents and their gods and ancestors.

CONCLUSION

Just as the rise of the absolutist state in modern Europe presaged a discourse of civil society in the eighteenth century, the experiences of modern state saturation in China and other places have now made a once Western category relevant. This has led two anthropologists to declare, "The dominant Western models of civil society are the ones we wish to challenge, but we must also recognize they are also [in turn] *challenging* models [of power around the world], [and have] great appeal throughout the world" (Hann and Dunn 1996: 19). Indeed, "civil society" has now become a global category, applied to non-Western contexts by native intellectuals and Western observers alike (Comaroff and Comaroff 1999). The term has joined notions such as "capitalism," "class," "democracy," and, more recently, "governmentality" in being applied to modern non-Western societies.

Thus, our task is not to avoid adopting the term "civil society," but to ensure that what Dipesh Chakrabarty (2000) called "provincial European" narratives of civil society do not get rigidly universalized. Certainly, the term carries European cultural baggage, such as the liberal discourse of the individual's rights, contract theory, or civil society's indebtedness to the "free market." However, if we can broaden the meanings and usages of the term, it can encompass the modernizing movements of native cultures and institutions, such as temple societies and lineages in contemporary Wenzhou. Instead of measuring non-Western social formations against an idealized European definition of civil society, it would be better to broaden the modern category of civil society to accommodate non-Western cultural genealogies.

In his critique of Western liberal assumptions of civil society, Partha Chatterjee adopts both a Marxist and a postcolonial studies perspective. Chatterjee challenged Charles Taylor's liberal focus on "freedom," the individual, and contractual relations, equating it with the "narrative of capital." For Chatterjee, this liberal promotion of a civil society that wrests control from the state merely furthered the interests of private property, predicated on the individual (1993: 234). Here Chatterjee follows Western Marxists, notably Antonio Gramsci, in conflating civil society with bourgeois society (Bobbio 1988), a conflation that I find problematic because it gives too much weight to the profit economy. Civil society may overlap with bourgeois society, but the latter is not boundless and should not be overinflated. Among civil society's many forms, one must acknowledge the forms that are noncapitalist or even countercapitalist.

On the other hand, Chatterjee's critique of postcoloniality echoes a point I would like to drive through in this chapter. Indian intellectuals have been better able to confront the "condition of postcoloniality," where postcolonial native elites unconsciously adopt the categories and prejudices of their former colonial rulers when dealing with their own society. The exclusion of peasants, and rural and religious culture, from the ability to create forms of civil society in modernity is an example of this "postcolonial complex" that I have also critiqued (M. Yang 2004, 2011). When communal *Gemeinschaft* societies are excluded from any effort in building modern civil society, there are unconscious assumptions that the Western model is the measure of modernity. Although Chatterjee's argument relies too much on Hegel rather than Chatterjee's own Indian society, the call to uncover the "suppressed narrative of community" (1993: 231) is worth considering in addressing civil society in contemporary China.

Although China has had a long history of the archaic state, and social hierarchies of aristocracy, officials, and educated gentry have dominated the peasantry for several millennia, I still found, in rural Wenzhou, elements of an egalitarian communal culture that shares some features with primitive societies. These elements seem to have been stubbornly preserved and reproduced through all these centuries of hierarchy and state coercive power. In the epigraph by Pierre Clastres at the beginning of this chapter, he observes that indigenous Amerindian societies in South and Central America have managed to "ward off" the state from developing within their societies through the mysterious mechanisms of a "powerless" power (1987: 22, 216). His book seeks to turn the tables on Western social evolutionism, which assumes backwardness in societies without a state. He shows the sophistication of Amerindian mechanisms of "noncoercive" power that allows them to govern themselves without a state. These include belittling and impoverishing the chief through laughter and making him share his wealth; systems of social exchange of food; exogamous marriage that cement ties with other kin groups; and denying skillful hunters the means to translate their skills into wealth or position. In Wenzhou's religious community–building, I found similar social mechanisms of self-governance and social integration in lieu of the state: a developed "ritual economy" of gifts and exchange between humans and gods (see chapter 10); expectations that temple or lineage leaders give away personal wealth; rituals of family development and kinship connectedness; and the return of governance through ritual performance. Both the ancient Confucians and Roy Rappaport (1999) found ritual performances were effective and noncoercive means of encoding social ethics, without relying on coercive state laws and punishment (M. Yang 1994a: 225, 228, 232). Thus, in thinking through the task of indigenizing modern Chinese civil society, Clastres's work inspires us to examine the rich corpus of Chinese community religio-social forms, some of which may have genealogies that stretch back to an archaic China before the state.

In Chinese modernity, the *longue durée* process of "hierarchical encompassment" of a multitude of sacred local spaces, communities, gods, and ancestors by the imperial state was completely abandoned as the modern state positioned itself outside traditional religiosity. This modern state not only ceased to recognize and bestow honorific titles upon the gods but also banned the old ritual constructions of local communities. In the post-Mao period, gods and ancestors have again been producing multicentered indigenous communities and sprouts of civil societies that pose as alternative spatialities to the singularity of the nation-state. As chapter 6 showed, the secular state responds by launching a new process of secular penetration and bureaucratic integration of temples and lineages into its secular administration. After their initial breaking off, these temples were later "recaptured" by the state, when in 1994 they were required to register and submit to the management of the Daoist and Buddhist Associations; likewise, lineages have been required to accept the leadership of local governments. These in turn are linked to the Bureau of Civil Affairs and the Bureau of Religion, and all come under the guiding and restraining hand of the Party's United Front Office. These sacred territorialities may be penetrated and constrained by the state, but at the same time, they are grassroots-initiated, self-governing, and self-funded, and they continue to negotiate with the state. They frequently invoke higher transcendent authorities and values that allow people to put earthly desires and temporal powers in relative perspective.

The ritual and religious spatialities of local Wenzhou lineages and temple societies initially ruptured from the Maoist state apparatus in the 1980s and 1990s, relying on donated funds and voluntary labor. The local people's surplus wealth that were plowed into these ritual sites could only have been possible with the commercial movement out of the Maoist state command economy. Today in Wenzhou, we are in a similar period of commercial upswing that China earlier experienced in the Song, Yuan, and mid-Ming dynasties. Just as those periods brought about religious and social dynamism with commerce carving out a space of autonomy from state and official extractions, we also find, today, a process of breaking partially free and negotiating with the state for local autonomy.

In these examples of religious associational life, we find efforts to construct "subnational" loyalties and commitments to localities and regions, and sometimes even "transnational" identities, as when lineages reach out to their diasporic kin around the world, or when a deity cult such as the members who worship Mother Chen reach out to fellow worshippers in Taiwan and Southeast Asia. Both subnational and transnational invocations can work toward moderating or subduing the hegemonic "national identity" that has taken over everywhere in modernity.

What's Missing in
the Wenzhou Model?

The "Ritual Economy" and
"Wasting of Wealth"

The local custom of people in Wenzhou is to support spirit mediums and access spirits and ghosts. They hold elaborate Buddhist and Daoist rituals, engage in extravagant expenditures, and exhaust their energies. Unconcerned with heavy-duty wastefulness, each year in the first lunar month, they have a lantern festival that lasts over ten days. These attract festivalgoers day and night, the men mixing freely with the women. They also hold dragon lantern competitions, each with fine detailed craftwork. Tens of gold pieces are wasted on a single lantern. Gongs and drums are beaten thunderously; the boisterous din is insane. In just a few days, the dragon lanterns are then put to the torch. This sort of reckless wastefulness must be immediately prohibited!

温郡之俗好巫而近鬼，大舉佛事道場，靡不盡心竭力以为之。不惜重費，乃若正月初旬，以至燈市十余日，晝夜游觀，男女雜沓，競制龍燈，极其精工，大龍燈一條，所費不下數十金，鑼鼓喧闐，舉國若狂，不數日間，付之一炬，此種妄費，亦當急為禁革者也。

一勞大與著。
《甌江逸志》。（清）

  —Lao Dayü, *Leisurely Trip Down the Ou River*
  (Qing dynasty, eighteenth century)

Classical economy imagined the first exchanges in the form of barter. Why [does it think] that in the beginning, a mode of . . . exchange [only] answered the need to acquire, [instead of] the contrary need to lose and squander? The classical conception is now questionable. . . .

Religion is the satisfaction that a society gives to the use of excess resources, or rather to their destruction. . . . This is what gives religions their rich material aspect, . . . when . . . spiritual life withdraws from labor a time that could have been employed in producing.

  —Georges Bataille, *The Accursed Share*, vol. 1

One might represent economic practice as comprising a rich diversity of capitalist and noncapitalist activities and argue that the noncapitalist ones had until now been "invisible" because the concepts and discourses that could make them "visible" have themselves been marginalized and suppressed.

—J. K. Gibson-Graham, *The End of Capitalism (as We Knew It)*

The conventional account of the Wenzhou Model is favored by economists, political scientists, and sociologists—but it only acknowledges the four features outlined in chapter 2. The focus of this chapter is to show what is missing in the conventional description of the Wenzhou Model, to examine the intersection of Wenzhou's rich ritual life, religious material culture, and famous economic development. Generally overlooked by commentators on the Wenzhou Model is a fifth feature, what I call a "ritual economy" (禮儀經濟) (M. Yang 2007, 2009), which is predicated on ritual expenditures that circulate wealth in a parallel economy that is threaded through the profit-driven market economy. This chapter responds to Gibson-Graham's call in the epigraph above, to show "the rich diversity of capitalist and noncapitalist activities" in Wenzhou, and to make visible the ritual economy that counterbalances and restrains the profit economy.

In recent years, many publications have argued that there is a Chinese version of what Max Weber has called the "Protestant Ethic" ([1904] 1958) of deferred gratification and reinvestment of profits back into expanding capitalist enterprises. They suggest there is a "Confucian Ethic" or family ethics that propels Chinese to work hard and save their earnings (Horn, n.d.; Redding 1995; Tu 1996), and this explains the success of Chinese businesses across China and the Chinese diaspora. Against this current, I will try to show that the Wenzhou Model is propelled by something quite different from both the "Protestant Ethic" and the putative "Confucian Ethic." The genealogy of the Wenzhou Model is not the Protestant Reformation; rather, it traces back much further in indigenous time, to the "Chinese commercial revolution" of the Song dynasty, if not before.

Wenzhou family firms are not only units of production but also units of worship and ritual consumption, as well as nodes in larger kinship and ritual networks. Starting up a new enterprise entails consultation with diviners and fengshui masters to determine the most propitious time and place for the business start-up. To ensure the health of the firm and its members, one needs to propitiate the gods and buddhas, and make sacrifices to them. Since the business is embedded in social and business networks, gifts and banquets must be given out to maintain good social standing, and offerings must be made to the ancestors. Thus, family firms pay for a variety of ritual services that are conducted inside deity temples and Daoist and Buddhist temples, and if they are Christian, inside churches. These are all the normal costs of doing business.

In family enterprise production, the principles of thrift, asceticism, discipline, and antagonistic stinginess with suppliers, hired laborers, and sometimes clients are the operational rules. However, in family and community ritual activities, often a very different ethos of exaggerated generosity and almost feverish ritual expenditure takes over. Whether rich or poor, family corporations in rural and small-town Wenzhou feel the urge to conduct rituals, festivities, and banquets lavishly—even if it sometimes requires depleting their savings. The surplus gained from productive activity is not only saved for economic accumulation, reinvestment, and the expansion of the firm; just as importantly, it is also expended on *nonproductive* and *nonaccumulative* activities, such as family and community rituals. In this tension between productive and nonproductive expenditures, thrift and generosity, asceticism and festive release, the Wenzhou Model posits a very different model of economic development from the austere rationalism of the Protestant Ethic that propelled the history of Western capitalism. In the midst of economic privatization in the post-Mao Reform era, there was a remarkable commitment to community development and the construction of public ritual spaces.

I define "ritual economy" as expenditures of wealth on ritual, religious, ethical, and social bonding practices, forms of consumption that do not directly lead to profit accumulation and indeed often eat up profits and savings for nonutilitarian ends. A ritual economy involves human transactions and economic exchanges with the divine world of gods, ancestors, nature spirits, and ghosts. It diverts a segment of wealth from the material economy. Unlike the profit economy, which stresses accumulation of wealth and the intake of profit, the ethos of ritual economy is generosity and self-abnegation and the willingness to give out or part with one's material wealth. An important aspect of the ritual economy is the spirit of private donations by ordinary people of all walks of life. No less than the building of infrastructure, the ritual economy is part of the Wenzhou Model and the growth of its thriving markets and rural towns. It deploys the gods in its redistribution of wealth, reconstruction of community, and promotion of the public good. Thus, its internal logic of "giving out" often acts counter to the capitalist logic of accumulation, or "taking in."

However, in Wenzhou's official discourse, the ritual economy was dismissed or condemned in the 1980s and 1990s as "ignorant" and "superstitious" behavior, and as "wasteful" (*langfei*, 浪費) and not contributing to economic development. Despite undergoing a modern revolution, these local officials strangely echo earlier Qing dynasty Neo-Confucian gentry condemnations of the ritual economy, as seen in the epigraph at the beginning of this chapter. Here expenditures for the Lantern Festival are condemned as "heavy-duty wastefulness" or "reckless wastefulness" (重費, 妄費).

Wenzhou's ritual economy resonates with Georges Bataille's notion of "excessive ritual expenditures" and supports his call for a vision of the "general" rather than "restricted economy" (1985, 1989, [1947] 1991). In the above epigraph, Bataille takes issue with the "restricted" vision of classical economics, which only focuses on narrow barter and production. Instead, he envisions a much broader "general economy" that reaches beyond accumulation and production to take into account "wasteful" and "gratuitous" consumption practices, such as ritual and religious expenditures, which from a utilitarian point of view only wastes and destroys wealth. Indeed, part of Bataille's definition of "religion" is the drive to divert time from productive labor to the "destructive" activity of expending wealth to become more "intimate" with divine forces.

THE FEATURES OF WENZHOU'S "RITUAL ECONOMY"

I have mapped out the main divisions of the ritual economy: (1) sacrifices and offerings; (2) rituals and festivals; (3) donations and charities; (4) construction of ritual sites; (5) gift circulation; and (6) ritual services: ritual performances, spirit possession, divination, geomancy, and scriptural chanting.

Wenzhou's Ritual Economy

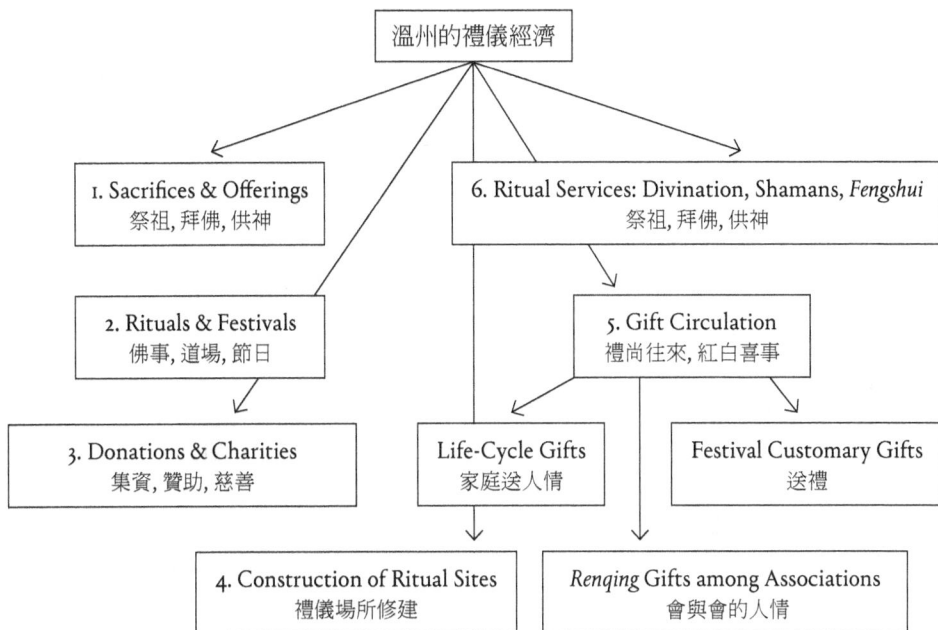

溫州的禮儀經濟

1. Sacrifices & Offerings
祭祖, 拜佛, 供神

6. Ritual Services: Divination, Shamans, *Fengshui*
祭祖, 拜佛, 供神

2. Rituals & Festivals
佛事, 道場, 節日

5. Gift Circulation
禮尚往來, 紅白喜事

3. Donations & Charities
集資, 贊助, 慈善

Life-Cycle Gifts
家庭送人情

Festival Customary Gifts
送禮

4. Construction of Ritual Sites
禮儀場所修建

***Renqing* Gifts among Associations**
會與會的人情

Figure 10.1. Wenzhou's ritual economy.

WENZHOU'S RITUAL ECONOMY

Sacrifices and Offerings

In sacrifices and offerings, gifts move from the human world to the divine one of the gods, nature spirits, buddhas, ancestors, demons, and ghosts. These are transfers of wealth whereby human beings petition or thank divinities for their assistance and protection, or placate and "bribe" demons and ghosts to spare them from misfortune or punishment. Sacrifices serve to connect and embed individuals and communities within the larger cosmic realm of natural/divine forces.

Henri Hubert and Marcel Mauss saw sacrifice as "establishing a means of communication between the sacred and the profane worlds through the mediation of a victim, . . . a thing that in the course of the ceremony is destroyed" (1964: 97). Thus, sacrifice is a ritual-economic transaction that allows the mundane human and divine worlds to come closer together. These two worlds are mutually interdependent: the divine world expects nourishment and respect from the human world. In turn, the human world gains access to the divine world through gifts of animal victims, food offerings, incense, candles, alcoholic beverages, paper spirit money, and prayers. Here I shall also follow Mauss and Hubert's distinction between sacrifice and offerings: "The difference between a simple offering and a sacrifice is that in offerings, . . . no victim is destroyed; in sacrifice, the degree of solemnity and efficacy is higher, and 'the religious energy released is stronger' and the havoc it could cause is greater" (Hubert and Mauss 1964: 11–12). In rural Wenzhou, formal ancestor sacrifice is designated with the archaic term "to sacrifice" (jisi, 祭祀), but the traditional practice of slaughtering live animal victims as part of ritual performance is less common. What we find more often are offerings, designated by the verb gong (供), "to offer [to divinities]." These are generally cooked food and rice grain alcohol offered to gods and ancestors on ceremonial occasions and then later consumed by the humans themselves. When the Wang Lineage of Yongchang Township celebrated the historical completion of their genealogy in 1998 with live animal sacrifices, it was a special year. The animals were slaughtered not during the ritual, but one day *before* the sacrifice. Ordinarily, the Wangs' annual ancestor sacrifices are observed with only cooked meat offerings.

The generic term "to worship" (bai, 拜) is used to describe everyday worship of the gods. On a daily basis at local temples, worshippers offer cooked meat dishes (pork, duck, fish, or chicken) for deities of popular religion and Daoism, fruit and vegetarian dishes for buddhas and bodhisattvas, and sometimes lit cigarettes for male gods. In the 1990s, the offerings were carried in the traditional round or square wooden or bamboo decorated "gift containers" or "gift boxes" (lisheng, 禮盛; lihe, 禮盒).

Worshippers also offer incense and candles, which are sold at the temple entrance and contribute to temple coffers. This temple income can be quite significant. For example, during the New Year Festival of 2009, the Daoist Temple of the Sacred King Who Disseminates Spiritual Efficacy (宣靈聖王廟), Yongxing Township, managed to sell 17,400 yuan ($2,547) worth of candles (Zhengxie Wenzhou Shi Longwanqu Weiyuanhui 2011: 57). Giant candles as tall as human height, with a diameter of thirty to thirty-six inches, can fetch up to 10,000 yuan each. In 2008 at the Temple Curator Daoist Temple in Shacheng Township (沙城太保觀), the recycled wax from burnt candles alone fetched the temple 25,667 yuan ($3,696; Zhengxie Wenzhou Shi Longwanqu Weiyuanhui 2011: 57).

A third nonfood offering is paper "spirit money" (冥幣, 冥錢), which comes in many different forms and shapes and generally must be first folded or stamped before being burned as wealth offered to divine beings. Gold

Figure 10.2. Ritual gift containers or gift boxes with food offerings to the gods, Celestial Immortal Deity Temple, Longwan District, 1993. Photo by the author.

paper money is reserved for the gods. Silver paper money is burned to placate ghosts. There is also a rough earth-brown paper money, produced using traditional handicraft techniques, which is often stamped with a design using a metal press and collected into large bamboo baskets. Paper money can be folded into shapes of lotuses or golden ingots (金寶), or printed to look like real *renminbi* legal tender, but with images of the Jade Emperor and the words "Bank of Hell" (地獄銀行). Burning paper money is discouraged by monks and nuns in Buddhist temples, who say it is a local custom that is not Buddhist.

At funerals, a rich array of other paper gifts are burned: giant paper flower wreaths mounted on thin bamboo stands; giant paper and bamboo mansions, complete with garages, kitchens, bedrooms, and living rooms with televisions and air conditioners; paper clothing; paper gold ingots, watches, jewelry, and mobile phones. These items symbolize the luxury items that people imagine the deceased would cherish using in the afterlife. All of these items cost real money to purchase for burning.

Rituals and Festivals

The range of rituals is quite broad, from the large Daoist communal blessing ceremony called the *jiao* (醮), which can last several days and brings out a whole village or several villages; to ordinary family life-cycle rituals commemorating birth, marriage, death, and house construction; to Buddhist temples' "opening of the light" (開光) ceremonies to activate the miraculous efficacy of newly installed Buddha statues. There are communitywide banquets celebrating temple deities' birthdays, and small-scale therapeutic and exorcistic rituals for individual psychological or medical maladies. The organizers of these rituals generally pay for the services of ritual experts, including Daoist or Buddhist monks and nuns, spirit mediums, and diviners, and they may also pay musicians, ritual organizers, opera performers, cooks, artisans and craftspeople, and workers. Expenses mount up for large-scale public rituals and street processions, where organizers must hire videographers, costume-makers, traffic police, and craftspeople to make the wooden palanquins that carry the gods or buddhas.

Festivals are celebrated according to the lunar calendar. One major festival is the Daoist Festival of Universal Salvation (中元普度), held on the fifteenth day of the seventh month, to appease the wandering ghosts and orphan souls. The Buddhist equivalent is called Yulanpen Festival (盂蘭盆節), which occurs at the same time and also takes care of the wandering souls. The Lunar New Year's Festival is perhaps the most important, when far-flung family members return home to Wenzhou to be with their family and kin. Wealth is expended in purchasing new clothes, throwing banquets, and giving New Year's gift money to the children. Each religious tradition has their own special festivals. The Buddhist calendar includes festivals to mark the birthdays (聖誕) of various buddhas and bodhisattvas, or their day of attaining enlightenment. These include the buddhas Sakyamuni (釋迦穆尼佛) and Amitabha (阿彌陀佛), and the bodhisattvas Guanyin, Wenshu, Mi-le, Puxian, Dizang (觀音, 文殊, 彌勒, 普賢, 地藏), and others. Daoist temples organize festivals and banquets to celebrate the birthdays of the Three Purities (三清), the Three Officials (三官大帝), the Jade Emperor (玉皇大帝), the Queen Mother of the West (西王母), and lower-level gods.

In addition, almost every local village or town temple holds a ritual and community banquet two times a month, on the first or second, and the fifteenth or sixteenth day of each lunar month. These ritual activities all entail large expenditures of income, but they also provide temples with worshippers' donations and an opportunity to recruit new worshippers.

Wenzhou temple activities confirm Adam Chau's (2006) observation that temple "folk event productions" reveal the business or enterprise character of temples.

Donations and Charities

In the spring of 2005, I chatted with Tang Weiwen, a woman in her thirties who studied at a vocational college and was trying her hand as an entrepreneur in the steel sheeting business. She asserted, "People are now more superstitious than ever. A lot of people are willing to spend money supporting superstitious habits of worshipping gods." She knows several old women who look deceptively poor, wearing tattered clothes, but were willing to donate tens of thousands of *renminbi* in hard-earned savings to build deity temples. As if exasperated with herself, she declared, "It's in our genes! Even though we don't believe, it's still inside us. When the time comes, we still feel like we should give some money!"

Throughout my fieldwork, I was struck by the pervasiveness of an ethic of generosity in community donations among the local people. They referred to these fund-raising activities as "accumulating funds among the people" (*minjian jizi*, 民間集資) or "sponsorship and support" (*zanzhu*, 贊助), the latter usually reserved for larger, more prominent donations of money. The notion of "public benefit" (*gongyi*, 公益) was often invoked by people explaining the local spirit of donations. Wenzhou entrepreneurs who had made money in far-flung places in China, or who lived outside Wenzhou and only returned for visits at New Year's, said that they were happy to donate money for their "hometowns" (*jiaxiang*, 家鄉). People gave money to public community projects, regardless of whether they were ordinary pedicab drivers or wealthy local industrialists, although there was community pressure and higher incentive for the wealthy to give much more generously. According to the Party secretary of a town in Longwan District, Mr. Wu, whom I interviewed in 1993, the practice of "collecting funds among the people" was conducted in secret in the 1970s, but in the 1980s, peasants began doing it openly to raise money for the erection of temples and churches. Fund-raising started in the late Mao era as a way of reestablishing religious-ritual community spaces to connect with divine forces, but then it widened to secular community projects, such as building and repairing local roads, bridges, and schools.

The religious funding drives were so successful that many local governments also started conducting their own fund-raising activities. When he was township head, Mr. Ling held many fund-raisers among wealthy families to build a new elementary and middle school. He invited them to banquets and made speeches impressing upon them the importance of education for their children and the future of their community. He received considerable contributions, many donations as high as 5,000 yuan, a large sum back then. He also went to Catholic and Protestant churches, carefully timing his visits to follow church services, so he could speak to the congregation about donating to their local schools. He estimates that about 75 percent of the Christian congregations gave him money.

Mr. Jiang established his medical instruments factory in 1988, and by 1993 his business was flourishing, with twenty-eight employees. In 1992, he paid 15,000 yuan in taxes to the state and contributed 14,000 yuan to various community causes, including 5,000 yuan toward the construction of the Zhennan Village Community Center; 1,000 yuan for relief aid to poor mountainous areas of Wenzhou; 3,000 yuan for the Hope Project (Xiwang Gongchen), a Taiwanese charity to help poor families send their children to school; another 3,000 yuan toward building an Old People's Pavilion in his village; and, finally, 2,000 yuan for the renovation of his 120-year-old Jiang Lineage Ancestor Hall. Although he received no government tax breaks for his donations, he said that, like most Wenzhou entrepreneurs, he just wanted to help out his hometown.

The organization that most often initiated and led these funding drives was the Old People's Association (*laoren xiehui*, 老人協會). In 1993, I interviewed Mr. Zhang, who headed a village Old People's Association established in 1984 in Yongzhong Township. The main purpose of these associations was to engage in "works for the public good" (公益事業). Old people are the most effective in soliciting donations, he said, because their seniority wins them respect and trust. Mr. Zhang's association was housed in an Old People's Pavilion (*laorenting*, 老人亭) built in 1989 with a funding drive that collected 130,000 yuan. They also collected donations to replace dirt roads with paved roads, and public toilets to replace the smelly and unsanitary "outhouses" (*maokeng*) that families kept along the roadside. The old people volunteered their labor (義務勞動), going door-to-door collecting money, hiring a technical expert, supervising construction, and even lugging rocks for the road foundation.

Religious organizations also actively participate in collecting donations. In temples, money is anonymously tossed into wooden donation boxes. The local people have also revived the practice of erecting carved stone tablets, or steles (石碑), commemorating the establishment or restoration of a temple or ancestor hall, on which names of major donors, and sometimes amounts contributed, follow a short introduction of the origin and history of the site. These steles recount an alternative history of localities and grassroots initiative, and the legendary history and powers of the gods or ancestors housed within.

Table 10.1. Donations to Wenchuan Earthquake Victims Made by Longwan District Buddhist Association Temples and Individuals in 2008 (in RMB yuan)

AREA OF LONGWAN DISTRICT	TEMPLE DONATIONS	INDIVIDUAL DONATION	TOTAL
Area 1: 浦州，狀元，瑤溪	143,193	46,700	189,893
Area 2: 海濱，靈昆，外地	207,248	31,252	238,500
Area 3: 永興，沙城，天河，海城	199,015	43,750	242,765
Total	549,456	121,702	671,158

Source: *Zhengxie Wenzhou Shi Longwanqu Weiyuanhui* 2011: 68.

In 2008, six hundred members of the Daoist Temple of the Sacred King Who Disseminates Spiritual Efficacy (宣靈聖王廟) in Yongxing Township contributed a total of 200,000 yuan ($29,200); about half of this sum was donated during the New Year's festival alone. Nearby, five hundred members of Shacheng Town's Temple Curator Temple (沙城太保觀) together donated 20,000 yuan ($2,920). That same year, the prominent City God Temple in Ning Village (宁村城隍廟), Longwan District, collected a total of 200,000 yuan (*Zhengxie Wenzhou Shi Longwanqu Weiyuanhui* 2011: 56). In 2008, after the Wenchuan earthquake in Sichuan, the Buddhist Association of Longwan District (龍灣佛教協會) quickly collected 671,158 yuan ($97,989) from member temples and individuals to help the earthquake victims.

There are different individual motivations to give generously to public or religious causes. First, there is the deep-seated Buddho-Daoist idea that one accumulates spiritual merit from doing good deeds and demerits from doing evil deeds. Giving away money might mean a loss of material wealth, but one earns spiritual capital for this life or the next. According to Cynthia Brokaw (1991: 25–26, 31–52), the notion of accumulating merit and demerit points for one's moral behavior traces back to the fourth century CE in China, developing out of both Daoism and Buddhist traditions. In late imperial China, keeping personal ledgers of merit points became widely popular among the gentry and literati. Although I did not encounter anyone in Wenzhou who actually tracked their merits and demerits, people frequently employed the language of "accumulating merit" (集功德) when praising others for good deeds or when they chanted sutras repeatedly.

A second motivation for donating money is to repay the spiritual debts one has incurred from one's sins. In urban China, I almost never heard people talk about sin or contrition for sins, but in rural Wenzhou, the religious notions of "sin" (罪) and "repentance" (懺悔) are quite common. Many Daoist and Buddhist sutras are called "repentance sutras" (懺). The notion of repentance for sins is also a connotation of two words used to describe Daoist and Buddhist funerals, "to transcend and cross into" (*chaodu*, 超度), which suggests that funeral participants help the deceased to "expiate for his or her sins." Through the burning of incense and paper spirit money, the chanting of sutras and prayers, and the ritual performance, the funeral attendees help to "dissolve the sins" (化罪) of the dead so that they may receive lighter sentences in the afterlife. These rituals of penitence hark back to the Song dynasty, when, according to Richard von Glahn, the ubiquity of "rituals of redemption attests to the profound preoccupation with sin that suffused Song religion" (2004: 139–141). In both the Song dynasty and today, religious culture in a highly commercialized society came to quantify sin and merit.

On their path to wealth, many Wenzhou entrepreneurs employed morally questionable methods, stepping on weaker and less cunning people. So they feel they must make amends by giving large sums away in support of community ritual events. In some ritual processions, the largest donors and benefactors of the event are honored with the role of "prisoner"—they dress up as "criminals" locked up in cages and pulled on wheels as they repeatedly whip themselves for their crimes. Committing sins is understood as "being indebted" and "owing money" (*qianzhai*, 欠債), so there is the notion that before one dies, one must settle one's accounts and give out wealth so as not to be in moral arrears. In the Buddhist tradition, when people are on their deathbed, they are haunted by images of their "debtors" (*zhaizhu*, 債主), people whom they treated unjustly or verbally maligned.

A third reason to give away wealth is to express gratitude to the gods. A pervasive relationship with gods and buddhas is one of humans "requesting divine assistance" (許願) and "repaying the divine for granting their prayers" (還願). Often people will go to a temple and offer incense and light candles, beseeching the gods for help and promising to repay with donated money or voluntary labor to help with temple maintenance, ritual events, or charities. The grateful person may also repay by hiring ritual masters to perform a ritual thanking the gods, and provide generous food and drink offerings.

Finally, a fourth rationale for making donations is not a spiritual but a worldly one: to gain social prestige or "face" (*mianzi*, 面子) in the community. Wealthy families feel more social pressure to give generously than families of modest means, and they are also expected to spend more money on life-cycle rituals and to invite the community to their banquets and ritual events. In return for their loss of material wealth, they increase their social standing or cultural capital. When their names are carved into stone steles for their impressive donations, the world will know about their generosity. Rivalry among wealthy families or between village communities provides another motivation to give generously.

Construction of Ritual Sites

Beginning in the 1980s, there was a frenzy of building ritual sites, including temples, monasteries, lineage ancestor halls, churches, and family tombs. This followed upon the 1980 promulgation by the Bureau of Religion in the State Council of Document 188, *Report on the Implementation of the Policy on the Buildings and Properties of Religious Communities*, which paved the way for the return of religious sites and properties that had been confiscated by the state during the religious persecutions of the Maoist era (Guowuyuan Zongjiao Shiwuju 1980). Whenever I returned to Wenzhou after one or two years, it seemed that new or restored ritual sites had popped up during my absence (N. Chen 2016; M. Yang 2004). Obtaining permits for building new religious sites is much more difficult than for building industrial or commercial sites, partly because officials believed that religious sites did not add to the local economy and therefore would not show up in the records as an accomplishment that could help in their official promotions. The building frenzy was so acute in Wenzhou that in 1994 the city's Bureau of Religious Affairs decried the "uncontrolled building of Buddhist and Daoist temples" (Guowuyuan Zongjiao Shiwuju 1994b).

The size and space of most new temples far exceeded the size of older late imperial or Republican-era religious buildings. These new or restored religious constructions, too, should be considered part of the local economy, for they provide jobs to artisans, folk architects, wood carvers, ritual experts, decorative wall and mural painters, bricklayers, and so forth.

The sums expended on these sites can be quite high. For example, chapter 5 discussed the 2004 rebuilding of the great Taiping Buddhist Temple (太平寺) in Wenzhou City, a collective labor of love funded by 30 million yuan ($3.65 million) in donations. That same year, another Buddhist complex of seven temple and monastic buildings, the Mei Feng Everlasting Spring Chan Buddhist Temple (梅峰永泉禪寺), also took off in the Mei Feng Mountains above Jin Shan Township, Cangnan County. Dating back to the Northern Song dynasty, the old complex had been entirely dismantled during the Cultural Revolution. Mr. Fu, the local village head and a leader in the rebuilding effort, told me in 2004 that the new buildings, along with large outdoor Buddha statues, were projected to cost 4 million yuan ($487,800). Inside the main hall,

Figure 10.3. Beautiful craftmanship in the wooden ceiling of a deity temple in Rui'an City, 2005. Photo by the author.

gazing up at the giant five-story wooden statue of a still-unpainted Bodhisattva Guanyin, I envisioned large crowds of worshippers making the long trek up to this mountain temple to pay homage to Guan Yin's "compassion and mercy" (慈悲).

In 2008, I interviewed a Daoist priest at the Great Sage Who Equals Heaven Temple (齊天大聖宫) in Linxi Town in Cangnan County, which honors the Monkey King God. The two-hundred-year-old original temple was expanded that year. The new hall and interior courtyard alone cost 4 million yuan ($571,428) to build. A single stone post carved with a spiraling dragon cost 100,000 yuan ($14,285), and there were about twenty posts, all shipped from Quanzhou in Fujian to the south of Wenzhou. The head of the temple managerial committee, who had retired from the shipping industry, where he made a lucrative living, donated large sums to the temple construction. Most of the other members of the temple managerial committee also donated impressively.

Table 10.2. Table of Jinxiang City God Temple Reconstruction Finances (in RMB), 2001–2004

INCOME		EXPENDITURES	
Donations	1,061,424	Fixed property	30,635
Incense sales	874,432	Regular expenditures	1,039,725
Candle & oil sales	61,460	Construction costs	1,496,129
Erecting statues	24,600	Deposits	500
Renqing fr. temples	531,298	Available cash	23,921
Qingming Festival	27,790	Bank savings	630
Trad. costume rentals	11,760	Storage	1,224
Total	2,592,765 ($313,514)	Total	2,592,765

The Jinxiang City God Temple Committee (Jinxiang Chenghuangmiao Bianji Weiyuanhui 2007) reconstructed its temple from 2001 to 2004. In table 10.2, we see that this City God Temple accumulated funds in three ways: individual donations; renqing gifts from other temples or lineages; and temple business, such as incense and candle sales and renting of temple costumes.

In 2014, the White Cloud Daoist Temple (白雲道觀) in South White Elephant Street Committee (南白象街道) put out a poster soliciting donations to pay for various temple statues and furnishings, with this pricelist for donors:

Gold statue of the God of Wealth	280,000 yuan ($44,800)
God of Wealth divine seat	220,000 yuan ($35,200)
God of Wealth offering altar	38,000 yuan ($6,080)
Gold statue of the Medicine King	280,000 yuan ($44,800)
Medicine King divine seat	220,000 yuan ($35,200)
Medicine King offering altar	38,000 yuan ($6,080)

The poster promised donors spiritual rewards with these words: "Gather Records of Virtue and Good Karma from Far and Wide; Accumulate Countless Spiritual Merit" (廣紀善緣，無量功德).

The eagerness of today's Wenzhou entrepreneurs to support temple-building resonates with the fourteenth-century description of the rebuilding of the main temple dedicated to goddess Mother Chen in Gutian, Fujian, which in the Yuan dynasty was under the same provincial administration of Jiangzhe Province (江浙省) as Wenzhou:

Figure 10.4. Gold-plated statues of Daoist immortals awaiting their placement in Hong Yan Daoist Temple, Chashan Township, Ouhai County. In 1998 each donor paid 6,000 yuan per statue. Photo by the author.

正七年邑人陳遂 ... 致力廟宮, 祇迓殊渥, 帥諸同志請于監邑承務公觀. 由典史魏某薛某上下翕合, 抽俸倡先. 雄資鉅産聞義悅從. 檜禳祈禱, 遠邇來者懽忻樂施. 遂斥金楮, 鳩工徒.
(張以寧著. "古田縣臨水順懿廟紀") in 《四庫全書》

In 1347, Chen Sui . . . devoted all his efforts to making the temple even more beautiful. He gathered together people of generous spirit, all sharing a common purpose. He requested the prefectural official for the Inspection of Public Affairs to organize people of high and low stations [to rebuild her temple], and each competed in generosity by bringing contributions. Having learned of this righteous cause, the great landholders and rich merchants happily supported and donated to it. A religious service was arranged; everyone near and far took part and eagerly contributed funds. A large sum was thus raised, and builders were able to begin work to renovate the temple. (Zhang Yining, "Memorial on the Shunyi Temple in Linshui, Gutian County," in *Siku Quanshu*, quoted in Baptandier 2008: 6–7)[1]

Figure 10.5. Illegal family tombs (called "sofa tombs") in the traditional Wenzhou style, Yaoxi Township, 2010. Photo by the author.

Despite the great span of time between the fourteenth century and today, there is a similar willingness among people of economic means to support temple-building and expansion, and a similar eagerness to win state approval and recognition for a locality's patron deity and temple.

Family tombs are either legal or illegal. The illegal ones are secretly built on hillsides with good fengshui but are subject to unpredictable local government campaigns to demolish them. In recent years, the local government has encouraged people to house the ashes of their dead in new legal "public cemeteries" (公墓). These cemeteries generally cover a whole side of a mountain and are owned by a private company that builds endless rows of stone or marble tombs to sell to families. In 2008 and 2010, I accompanied my friend Wang Qinsheng, who was conducting fengshui siting of tombs in several public cemeteries. Tombs can cost a family anywhere from 50,000 to 2 million yuan ($7,142 to $285,714). Since tomb expenses are high, families start saving up early and often have the tomb ready years before their elders pass away.

These temples, churches, ancestor halls, and family tombs are ritual sites where local entrepreneurs can go to access higher cosmic powers and beg them to help in their family businesses. Thus, entrepreneurs have deposited some of their surplus into developing a ritual economy that accompanied the growth of the industrial profit economy. Investments in this supernatural economy rose in tandem with investments in the material economy, and the two cannot be separated. Wealth generated in the material economy spilled over into the ritual economy and propelled it forward. At the same time, the desire to expand and build up the supernatural economy, for divine protection and community pride, for personal salvation or gratitude for divine help, spurred on the growth of the material economy.

Gift Circulation

There are three kinds of gift circulation, and rural Wenzhou people make an explicit distinction between the first two. First, there is "giving renqing" (*song renqing*, 送人情), literally "giving human feelings," in which families give gifts or throw banquets to renew social relationships at life-cycle events. These gifts or banquets are understood as voluntary gifts to relatives and friends at birth celebrations, engagements and weddings, housebuilding, funerals, and dragon boat races at the springtime Duanwu Festival. The amount of expenditure is not fixed; rather, it depends on the closeness of relations between giver and recipient and their relative income levels. Second, "giving gifts" (*song li*, 送禮) are smaller courtesy presents that local custom requires of everyone around the time of lunar calendar festivals. The type of gifts, their value, and whom to give them to, are said to be fixed according to local custom. However, with economic prosperity in recent years, local custom has experienced the inevitable gift inflation. Third, in the new millennium, once so many temple associations, lineage organizations, and lay and clerical Buddhist societies had been established, there emerged a new custom of renqing gift- and banquet-exchange *among* organizations and associations during each other's temple festival or lineage ritual events. These interorganizational exchanges were also called renqing.

"Giving Renqing" (送人情): Giving Gifts of Human Affection

An important occasion for "giving renqing" is a wedding engagement. In the 1980s, engagement presents were simply a slab of raw pork, rice cakes, and modest cash brought from the groom's family to the bride's family. The presents were brought in stacked "gift containers" (*lisheng*, 禮盛) balanced as a pair on a bamboo shoulder pole. By the late 1990s, I chuckled at encountering a wedding procession in which the bride's family had stuffed an outsized cassette player boom box into a lisheng made of woven bamboo strips. The boom box was so large and heavy that it teetered dangerously as the bamboo container creaked and swung from side to side on the shoulder pole. With increased gift inflation, I noticed the rapid decline in the usage of lisheng. By 2001, when Wang Zhaorong got engaged, she received a diamond ring, a watch, and a pearl necklace from the groom's family, and no lisheng was used.

Weddings involve the exchange of bridewealth (caili, 彩禮) paid by the groom's family and dowry (jiazhuang, 嫁妝) offered by the bride's family. Generally, the groom's family makes the major financial outlays for the wedding: the house that the couple will live in, the furniture, and the motorcycle or even automobile. In 1993, I learned from a cook that an average expenditure by the groom's family ran about 50,000 yuan, not including the house. The bride-price may include 4–5 liang of twenty-four-karat gold, worth over 20,000 yuan, and about 20,000 yuan cash (40,000 yuan = $5,714). Following custom, the bride's family returns a portion of this sum back to the groom, called the "return gift box" (huihe, 回盒), the amount of return depending on her family's economic means. In the 1990s, there was a new trend for the bride's family to equal the wedding expenditures of the groom, either by giving back more of the bride-price (over 50 percent), or by rechanneling it into the dowry, so that dowries exceeded the traditional modest household bedding and utensils. Thus, increasingly a bride moved to her husband's home with more financial independence and enhanced social status, since her family had spent almost as much as her husband's, if not more.

The wedding is an occasion for the couple to receive renqing gifts and money from relatives, friends, neighbors, and even local officials. At the gift table on the day of the wedding, each gift and its donor's name is recorded, so that the couple will know the people whom they owe at future weddings and life-cycle ritual occasions. In the 1980s and 1990s, weddings were modest, with just a few banquet tables at the groom's home, spilling over into a neighbor's borrowed space. The labor of cooking and serving dishes was generally provided by relatives and neighbors. Nowadays, families pay large sums to stage the wedding at a fancy restaurant, seating hundreds of people, with hired performers and a master of ceremonies speaking over a microphone. In 2004, a businessman said that he spent 500,000 yuan ($60,000) for his son's wedding, and 1 million yuan ($120,000) for their apartment. The wedding costs included a new car and car permit, the wedding banquet, furniture and interior decor for the house, jewelry and clothing for the bride, and studio

Figure 10.6. Daoist funeral banquet, Yong Chang Township, Longwan District, 2001. Photo by the author.

photography. These expenses illustrate the ritual inflation that comes with increasing prosperity.

Funerals are often more important than weddings, and people are willing to spend more hard-earned money on renqing gifts, usually money. Costs of funerals include hiring experts to perform the funerary ritual, which lasts at least one full day; hiring musicians; hosting many tables of guests for the funerary banquet; and consulting with divination masters to establish propitious dates for starting the funerary procession and lowering the coffin into the ground. A plot of land must be purchased and a tomb built on it. Skimping on funerals will bring nasty gossip about the lack of filial piety and how one is shortchanging the dead.

House-building celebrations provide another opportunity for giving renqing. In the 1980s and 1990s, most homes were built by family members themselves, with the help of kin and friends. The host would provide a big banquet to thank the volunteer laborers. The blessings of the new home's resident Earth God were invited during the ceremony. The project of house-building usually involves a consultation with a geomantic master who is paid to provide advice on the most auspicious location and direction for the new residence. The placement of the home must be in accord with the movements of the natural qi (氣), or "primal energy force," that circulates around the landscape. A good geomantic placement will bring the family good fortune for generations to come. Thus, a new home must be consecrated by the dual ritual procedures of geomantic placement and invoking the resident Earth God.

Renqing-giving is also evident at dragon boat rowing events for the spring Duanwu Festival. Villages or rowing societies organize rowers to bring incense burners from their village temple to pay courtesy visits to the villages where their married-out daughters now reside. They are received by the daughters and in-laws with long offering tables with food for their visiting god. In the 1990s, the issue of dragon boats was hotly contested, with local governments seldom granting permission to row, for fear of stirring up intervillage and interlineage rivalries that might break out in violence. Dragon boat rowing was also regarded as "superstitious," since it invoked and propitiated patron gods. The local people sent teams to local government offices to allay their fears and campaign for permission, but still they were often denied permission. Since about 2008, many local governments have changed their negative attitudes toward dragon boat rowing, and some even organize their own races.

In May 1993, New Town Village in Longwan District (新城村, 龍灣區) was granted permission to sponsor a dragon boat rowing event. Three kinds of renqing were circulated for this event: (1) married-out daughters living in other villages returned to their natal village and gave money to the village Old People's Association to support the event; (2) direct relatives of rowers in the dragon boats gave personal gifts to the rowers; and (3) parents of a daughter in her first year of marriage gave gifts to her and her husband. For the first kind of renqing, a standard money gift was 100–200 yuan, for which the donor would receive a briefcase that the village organizers had prepared. Those giving higher amounts would receive more valuable gifts. The organizers expected to receive a total of 300,000 yuan from the village's married-out daughters living in neighboring villages, and since they expected the event to only cost them 100,000 yuan, they planned to use the extra money to build a village park and an Old People's Pavilion for elders. The second kind of renqing could involve very expensive gifts, depending on the financial status of the donor. These are generally household items for the rower's family, including big gifts like color televisions and even motorcycles. If the rower's family was wealthy, then the "return gift box" (huihe, 回盒) would be 70–80 percent of the gift, and if they were poor, it was only a 30 percent return.

Renqing gifts and banquets are offered by wealthy families at any time of the year. Lavish hospitality overwhelms the recipients and strengthens social bonds. One evening in 2014, a Daoist priest dragged me to a fancy new seafood restaurant where a rich woman entrepreneur was hosting over one hundred guests. She owned a successful aluminum mine in Yunnan Province. Returning to her native Wenzhou for a visit, she invited the priest, her local relatives, neighbors, friends, and business associates to an eye-popping feast of seafood delicacies. The dishes included raw lobster, frog brains in sweet soup, fish that cost 400 yuan per *jin* (about $62.50 per pound), crab that cost 200 yuan per *jin* ($31 per pound), abalone, and liberal amounts of French red wine and Chinese grain liquor. I was seated next to her neighbor, a local schoolteacher, and a pedicab driver who worshipped at her favorite Daoist temple. As the hostess came to each table to toast her guests, I could see social redistribution in action.

"Giving Gifts" (送禮): Small Customary Gifts

In the local understanding, "giving gifts" (*songli*) is distinguished from "giving renqing" (*song renqing*) in that the former is not voluntary, but constrained, and the kind of gift, amounts given, and lunar calendar festival occasions for giving are all fixed by local custom. In the 1990s, these small courtesy gifts for special occasions were said to be a custom that originated long before Liberation, and were also borne in traditional round decorated wooden or bamboo gift containers (禮盛). In the 1990s, I found the following customary forms of giving, which, having evolved out of an agricultural society, now seem quite modest:

1. New Year's (春節)—married-out daughters return to natal homes with gifts of pork, rice cakes (*songgao*), liquor, and money
2. New Year's—apprentices visit the masters who taught them their trade with pork, rice cakes, and liquor; their teachers reciprocate with small gifts of money
3. New Year's—the younger generation gives gifts to their family elders, the older generation gives money to the children of the household
4. Qingming Festival (清明節)—fathers visit married-out daughters' homes bearing white rice cakes: maternal uncles visit nephews' (sister's sons') homes bearing the same items
5. Duanwu Festival (端午節)—nephews go to homes of maternal uncles with *zongzi*, sticky rice and meat wrapped in bamboo leaves; sons-in-law (daughters' husbands) go to fathers-in-law's homes with the same item
6. Qiqiaohui Festival (乞巧會節), when the Shepherd Star moves across the sky to visit the Embroidering Maiden on the seventh day of the

seventh month—fathers-in-law and maternal uncles visit sons-in-law and nephews with white rice cakes or nine-layer cakes (*jiucenggao*)

7. Mid-autumn Festival (中秋節)—sons-in-law and nephews visit fathers-in-law and maternal uncles with rice vermicelli (*fengan*); married-out daughters in another village return to natal homes bearing moon cakes, clothing, chickens, or ducks

8. Winter Solstice (冬至)—sons-in-law and nephews visit fathers-in-law and maternal uncles with sweet sticky rice flour balls (*tangyuan*)

In the 1990s, these gift-giving customs were standardized and applied equally to rich and poor families. These customs had declined in the Maoist era, especially during the Cultural Revolution, when they had to be conducted in secret because they were considered "feudal superstition" and "wasteful." It was also during the Cultural Revolution's "Smash the Four Olds" (破四舊) campaign that the traditional round gift containers (lisheng) were ordered to be destroyed. Each family was ordered to destroy them themselves, which was especially difficult when the containers were family heirlooms passed down through generations. This gifting custom and the containers resurfaced openly in the late 1970s, but in the new millennium, I noted a second disappearance of the containers. With increasing prosperity, these customary gifts have also become more flexible, prone to heavy gift inflation and thus no longer adhering to custom.

Renqing Gifts between Ritual Associations

In the new millennium, a new custom of renqing prestation between lineages, deity temples, Daoist and Buddhist temples, and religious or scriptural study associations took shape. These exchanges of renqing took place on the occasion of ritual events and festivals being celebrated by each organization. For example, when the Yingqiao Wang Lineage held their 1998 celebration for the updating of their genealogy, other friendly lineages made gifts of a live pig and goat as sacrifice to their ancestors. When a new deity temple invites Daoist temple management committees to their "opening the light" celebrations, they print out elaborate invitations, and their guests bring renqing gifts or cash. Likewise, Buddhist temples invited other Buddhist temples to their religious festivals, and their guests would come bearing gifts. These courtesy visits followed the principle of reciprocity, so that the renqing would be repaid at a later date when the donors held their own ritual celebrations. This ritual circulation of renqing gifts among religious and ritual organizations suggests that a dense religious network and civil society are in the process of formation.

Ritual Services and Occupations

Divination masters (算命師) operate from their homes or in temples and can be consulted on many important questions: auspicious dates and times for holding a ritual, opening a new business or new temple; one's personal fortunes in the future; the health of the family; and so on. Wang Qinsheng, an old diviner, told me that in the first five months of 2010, he made 50,000 yuan ($7,400), while Fragrant Orchid, a female medium he took me to visit, made about 200,000 per year ($29,600). Divination technologies are generally variant forms of the ancient *Classic of Changes* (易經), employing tools such as coins shaken in a turtle shell and the eight trigrams (八卦). Spirit mediums (靈姑僮, 神僮) also operate from their homes or small temples; they are hired to communicate with the deceased or with a god or wandering ghost. Geomantic masters (風水師) provide expertise on the best direction and location for siting a new home, tomb for the dead, or factory. A correct siting brings good fortune to several generations of family members.

Different ritual masters can be hired to conduct ritual services, including grassroots "hearth-dwelling Daoist priests" (火炬道士) of the Orthodox One sect of southern Daoism; formally ordained Quanzhen sect Daoist monks and nuns and Buddhist clergy; and ritual fixers, who serve as a sort of middlemen, assembling a full team of grassroots Daoist priests, Buddhist monks, and folk musicians to conduct rituals for clients. Although they themselves do not command ritual authority like the priests, they do possess the ritual knowledge to help priests set up the ritual site properly, light candles and incense at the proper moments, help with calligraphy for the written ritual petitions and talismans, and arrange offerings in the correct configuration. For the most part, these ritual services cannot command excessive prices, which would violate the ethical teachings of religious traditions. Since one's religious power is granted by the gods, being venal and greedy will incur doubts about how one received divine selection.

Although spirit mediums and shamanistic healers are popular and in much demand in Wenzhou, they come under special scrutiny by state discourse. In 2001, I heard several people referring to a national television show called *Focus Interviews* (*Jiaodian fangtan*, 焦點訪談) that presented an exposé of rural Wenzhou's "feudal superstitions." I was able to obtain a copy of this half-hour show, which first aired on Central Chinese Television in 2000. The show targeted the village Party cadres of Yandang Village in the mountains of Yueqing City (樂清市) for colluding with a spirit medium in the village deity temple to "cheat people out of their money." The village cadres entered into a "contract"

(承包) with a woman medium whereby she would "get possessed" (跳僮身) and communicate with spirits on behalf of her village clients in the temple. In return for being allowed to run her lucrative operations in the temple, each year she would deliver (上繳) to the village government 500,000 yuan ($75,700) out of her earnings. The show accused the medium of faking possession in order to cheat the "superstitious masses" and decried the village cadres' violation of Party principles. It condemned them for having the audacity to assist the medium at her ritual performances, chanting mantras and writing calligraphy, when they were Party members sworn to atheism.

Although the show admitted that the money collected from the medium did not end up in the private pockets of the cadres, but *did* go toward public expenditures such as local infrastructure and schools, it nevertheless claimed that the village reliance on "superstitious earnings" inhibited the village's "economic and scientific development." The show ended with a stern warning for other "absurd businesses" (荒唐的經營), informing the audience that the cadres involved had been "punished." Here we see that in the state discourse on popular religiosity that was dominant at the turn of this century, the basic assumption of a structural opposition between religion and economic development still held sway and was unchanged from the Republican and Maoist eras. This thinking assumed that "superstitions" could only obstruct rational economic development. However, most rural and small-town people in Wenzhou understood this relationship between ritual/religiosity and economy quite differently.

A local woman cadre surnamed Liu told me in February 2001 that most people she knew in Wenzhou were very "turned off" (很反感) by this official television program in which big-city people chastised Wenzhou "superstition." They lamented that the village cadres and even the township official lost their positions over this incident. According to Ms. Liu, many Wenzhou village governments do indeed enter into contracts with mediums who operate in deity temples:

> It's common in Wenzhou. If the village government doesn't do this, then all the money earned in the temple would just remain in the private hands of the mediums. If the village takes a cut from the medium's earnings, that's doing something for the collective. This should be called "collective spirit" [集體精神]; it should not be treated like a crime, because those cadres actually benefited their village. It makes sense, it's good for the economy, it provides a source of revenue and spurs on the economy. Lots of people really believe in mediums, and every year in the eighth lunar

month, many people flock to that area. The "incense fire is thick and abundant" [香火很盛] then. In fact, the village became so prosperous, the show itself said that the village kept on being chosen "Advanced Unit" [先進單位] [by higher officials] year after year!

Here we see that at the grassroots level, there is an entirely different understanding of the role of spirit possession for local communities from that presented in the television show. The locals have no issues with their cadres supporting mediums and taxing the mediums' incomes. In the local understanding, the presence of mediums in local temples brings in more worshippers and therefore more money, which the temples then use to help fund community development, such as building roads, bridges, and schools, and to support local charities. Thus, in stark contrast to the urban television discourse about mediums cheating ignorant rural people and holding back economic development, mediums are actually seen to help stimulate the local economy! Although they derive personal profits, they are also catalysts of generosity and spearheads of community funding drives.

In addition to ritual experts, a panoply of occupations provide technical services required for rituals and temple-building. Before the 2001 banning of earth burials in rural Wenzhou, I saw many coffin-maker shops. Today there are makers of funeral wreaths, paper houses, and spirit money. Temple wall mural painters, casters of bronze deity statues and bells, porcelainware producers, and wood carvers of deity and Buddhist statuary all supply temples and home altars. Folk musicians, whether playing traditional Chinese instruments or Western-style trombones and drums, are in demand for ritual and funeral processions. Printers supply the many lineages with multiple copies of their lineage genealogies and invitations to renqing events. Ritual offering foods must be made by specialists. Candle- and incense makers supply the faithful with the basic tools they need to communicate with the gods. Needless to say, all these services for the rich ritual life of Wenzhou contribute to economic growth and the GDP.

RITUAL AND MARKET ECONOMIES:
BLURRED BOUNDARIES, DIFFERENT LOGICS

From the official point of view, the wealth that is plowed into the ritual economy by Wenzhou people is misused. It could be reinvested into expanding family businesses and industries, but instead it is "squandered" in ritual expenditures. However, as we can see in the examples above, Wenzhou's ritual economy is not separate from the market economy, but overlaps with, inter-penetrates, and extends it; profit and ritual economies rely on and stimulate each other. It is also through the ritual economy that people gain the motiva-tion, meaning, and rewards of working in the market economy. Competitive production for the market is often fueled by competitive religiosity. Here indi-viduals, families, lineages, and local communities rival each other in generosity and depleting their wealth to put on more lavish banquets, rituals, and festivals or to build more expensive ancestor halls, temples, tombs, and churches.

At the same time, people with ritual occupations cannot derive unseemly profits, or else their greed may diminish their spiritual efficacy, showing that they lack the sincerity required to move the gods. In this section, I explore the blurred boundaries between these two economies and make the argument for their conflicting internal logics. The ritual economy harbors the countermar-ket logic that the more one gives away wealth and labor, the more one accu-mulates spiritual merit for one's afterlife. Thus, although the ritual economy interpenetrates with and stimulates the market economy, it retains a certain independence in harboring an older religious logic that refuses to submit to the maximization and cost-benefit logic of the market economy.

The mother of Tang Weiwen is a sutra-chanter who provides a ritual ser-vice at home for people who do not have time to chant themselves to accumu-late merit. For a modest fee, Tang Weiwen's mother will chant the appropri-ate sutra for clients, using a calligraphy brush to cover a deity image with red dots. The images are printed on envelopes, and the dots indicate how many ten- to twenty-minute intervals she has chanted. The client then burns them in a temple, which is said to dissolve people's sins (化罪), grant wishes, and protect one's family.[2] Clients may also choose another paid ritual service that is performed by a group of twelve to fifteen middle-aged women called "re-pentance and worship groups" (懺拜團). For about 600–1,000 yuan per family ($89–$148), a client can ask one of these groups to chant or sing three sutras for the family, providing the name of the person they wish to help and the nature of the assistance they wish to obtain. With a presiding Daoist priest, the chant-ing group will hold a Daoist ritual service in their temple for the client. Tang's mother chanted in her local deity temple about five or six times a month and derived great satisfaction in helping others gain the gods' protection.

In 2017, when I mentioned this ritual service of chanting scriptures for clients during a lecture at the University of Antwerp in Belgium, a scholar in the Faculty of Theology and Religious Studies at the Catholic University of Leuven observed that these ritual services reminded him of the old "indul-gences" sold by the Catholic Church to lighten sinners' punishment. Indeed, five hundred years ago Martin Luther launched the Protestant Reformation with a passionate critique of the Church's practice of selling indulgences. Similarly, as we observed in chapter 3, both Catholic saints and Chinese gods were human beings who sacrificed themselves or made great contributions to humanity, becoming divine beings after death (Overmyer 1997)—and giving rise to cults and pilgrimages that generated high ritual consumption and expenditures. Indeed, Bataille ([1947] 1991: 120; 1989) harked back to the lavish ritual expenditures of medieval Catholicism, when giant cathedrals and idle monks absorbed so much of Europe's excess wealth.

In talking with Tang and her mother, I was struck by the economic language they employed to discuss these ritual services. Tang called the dotted paper records "cash" (鈔票), saying that they are like purchased presents for the buddhas or gods, as well as "currency" (貨幣), which implies that they are convertible, from economic value to spiritual credit or the ritual investment of wealth. Others also used religious and economic language interchangeably. Local people often said that "giving renqing" is like "making investments" (投資), because later one can reap benefits when the recipient does one a favor. It is also like "giving loans" (貸款), because what one gives away at a wedding for a neighbor may be recouped later, with interest, when that neighbor attends the funeral of one's own family member. Here we see the blurring of boundaries between economic and religious ideas.

However, the local people also recognize that the profit economy and ritual economy may also follow different logics, such as when people make donations and offerings to temples, ancestor halls, festivals, and charities. In the native classification, these actions belong to a separate category because, in the words of Tang Weiwen, "one cannot recoup one's money" (錢是拿不回來的). Even though the gods may grant people's wishes, the wealth that is given away to them is transferred permanently from our temporal world to the divine realms. As a middle-aged woman in a temple explained to me, "With renqing exchange, you get paid back the next time your own family has a wedding or funeral. They will give your gift back, so there is basically no 'trade imbalance' or 'trade deficit' [貿易逆差] here. However, with donations to temples and offerings to gods, you do not see that money again [錢就見不到了]." I will say more about the significance of this distinction between renqing as loan, and the permanent loss of wealth given to gods, buddhas, and charities, at the end of the chapter.

This ease with which an economic language and logic can be employed to discuss matters of the religious realm should not surprise us. Popular religious practice in southeastern China is deeply imbricated and familiar with the logic of a market economy that stretches back a thousand years, to at least the commercial revolution of the Song dynasty (960–1279 CE). Indeed, popular religion as we know it today in southeastern China and Taiwan took shape and crystallized during the Song, which witnessed thriving handicrafts industries, specialized commodities markets, long-distance trade, and rapid urbanization (Edward Davis, personal communication; Hansen 1990; von Glahn 2003, 2004: 130–179, 2016: 242–254).

This religio-economic tradition can be seen today in the use of paper "spirit money," an even more direct expression of wealth lost in giving it away to divine beings than food offerings. Spirit money is offered to gods at their temple birthday festivals or when a plea is entered; to ghosts, appeasing their tendencies to prey on the living, at the Universal Salvation festival (*pudu*, 普度); to ancestors on their birthdays, at the Qingming Festival of tomb-sweeping, or at annual ancestral sacrifices; and to the souls of the recently dead at funerals, to repay the gods for the debts incurred during the deceased's life span and for the dead to use on their long journey through the Underworld. Spirit money offerings to the gods reveal the deep familiarity and savvy of these supposed rural "peasants" with a money economy and the intertwined logic of profit, indebtedness, accumulation, and a balancing of one's accounts. Julie Chu (2010: 171–184) has also shown how Fuzhou peasants plotting their illegal migration to New York City have introduced a global element into medieval Chinese spirit money, with new printed currencies in US dollars, Japanese yen, and Hong Kong dollars. At the same time, paper money ritual offerings also express a willingness to part with material wealth in pursuit of higher ends in the divine world and the afterlife.

In Hou Ching-lang's (1975) masterful French-language study of the history of Chinese spirit money, he describes two Daoist rites in which a transfer of funds is made to the Celestial Treasury in Hell. Anna Seidel writes that these rites "reveal the basic concept of life as a financial loan which has to be repaid. To be born is to receive an advance payment, to die is to have exhausted one's loan from the Celestial Treasury" (1978: 421). Today in rural Wenzhou Buddho-Daoist popular funerary rituals, the medieval notion of "reimbursing the Treasury" (填庫 or 交庫) is still kept alive when the surviving family members repay the treasury for the specific life span of the deceased. The preoccupation with the ritual storing and payment of money is seen today in three towns in Cangnan County, whose names date back to the Song dynasty: Money Storehouse (錢倉鎮 Qian Cang Town), Money Treasury (錢庫鎮 Qianku Town), and Gold Native Town (金鄉鎮 Jinxiang Town). What is revealed by the use of paper spirit money, economic language, and commercial logic in the realm of religion and ritual is the deep interpenetration of religion and economy in this culture. It shows not only the embeddedness of religious activity in both the Song commercial revolution and the recent economic development of Wenzhou today, but also the mutual embeddedness of religious logic in indigenous economic rationality.

Here, much as I agree with what Hill Gates called China's "petty capitalist mode of production" (1996), I must demur from her Marxist analysis of money offerings to the gods (1987). Gates sees offerings of spirit money to the gods as merely a "penetration," a "reflection," or an "expression" of the petty capitalist economy (1996: 168–176). For Gates, spirit money produces "models of, and for human behavior, which [implies] that the creation of human life itself depends on capitalist-like principles" (1996: 170). She proposes that two practices of Chinese money offerings can be understood as parallel to Marx's distinction between money as mere medium of exchange of commodities (C-M-C), and "capitalist money," where money takes on a life of its own as "interest-bearing capital" (M-C-M) (1996: 174–175). Somehow she understands the money used by humans when they pay for their life spans as the former "unproductive" kind of money, whereas the spirit money presented to the gods is the latter capital-bearing, profit-inducing kind of money. In Gates's analysis, the gods are like capitalists who make profit, and they serve as models for human emulation of capitalist rules. For Gates, Chinese popular religion merely spurs on the "petty capitalist mode of production."

The Chinese use of spirit money extends back much further than Song dynasty commercialism, which puts Gates's argument for their merely derivative role as the "reflector" of Chinese "petty capitalism" in doubt. The first historical record indicating the use of spirit money dates to the early Tang period of the sixth century CE, fully "four centuries *before* the first use of paper money as legal tender" (Seidel 1978: 425). Paper money as legal currency appeared much later, in Sichuan Province during the late ninth century CE, when Certificates of Deposits or paper bills of credit known as *jiaozi* (交子) were issued by rich merchants and financiers of Chengdu, and the first legal banknotes were printed by the Song imperial state in Sichuan only beginning in 1024 CE (Gernet 1985: 324–326; von Glahn 2016: 233).

The problem of seeing ritual money as a mere reflection or expression of material economy is that it grants no autonomy to religious logics and practices; it sees them as mere epiphenomena or "superstructures" of the economic. Many religious practices historically *preceded* commercial and monetary cultures, not to speak of modern capitalism. For example, archaeologist K. C. Chang (1983: 108) pointed out that the arrival of bronze metallurgy in ancient China was applied not to the making of agricultural implements and tools to develop the economy but to the religio-political technology of the archaic ritual-state: in manufacturing bronze ritual vessels and weapons of war. Since spirit money used in religious rituals emerged *before* Song commercialization and *before* the invention of paper currency as legal tender, we must expect that spirit money will bear the traces of a much older religious logic of animal sacrifice and food offerings for the gods and ancestors—as a shorthand to express a sacrifice or removal of material wealth from this-worldly life and its redeployment for higher ends in the divine world.

Here we can ponder the significance of Ms. Tang's words above: "With donations to temples and offerings to gods, you do not get that money back." Unlike the contractual exchange principles of renqing gifts, in which one's wealth given away is reciprocated with interest, sacrifice and donations to divinities are a temporal loss; they remove wealth from reinvestment and economic circulation. This means that they represent a cost to the dynamism and growth of the market or capitalist economy, and this is probably why local officials had a dim view of ritual expenditures as "waste." Furthermore, the divine world is not merely an extension or repetition of this world: it sits higher, on a transcendent plane, an expression of human ideals and aspirations, as well as fear and awe. Thus, far from what Gates views as a mere affirmation of the capitalist market, what is being expressed in making large offerings to divine beings is a willingness to sustain a material loss in this world for the pursuit of higher transcendent aspirations. This is a very different sort of reinvestment in the divine world, not for material profit, which would only bind people to this world, but for spiritual transcendence, communication with divinities, and access to eternity. The ritual action of burning spirit money to send wealth upward acknowledges a transcendent realm above and beyond this fleeting mundane life.

I have sought to show how the ritual economy parallels and threads through the market economy, yet has a relative independence. It subscribes to a different principle of operation and logic from the market or profit economy. Gift-giving, donations, sacrifices, and ritual site construction are all based on the *logic of generosity* and *the giving away of wealth* and conflict with the *logic of profit and accumulation of wealth*. Indeed, diverting funds into the ritual economy means a loss of material wealth and a slowdown in the growth of the profit economy. While these offerings may harbor a sublimated principle of interested exchange and "investment," the returns on the investment are primarily social and spiritual, not direct, predictable, or primarily material.

Social returns come in the form of the strengthening of social and kinship ties and obligations and the building up of social reputation and prestige in the community through one's generosity. Spiritual returns include the improvement of one's moral stature and the buildup of spiritual merit for that journey into the great unknown after death. The divestment of one's material wealth in this life increases one's spiritual credit and expresses a willingness to sacrifice material aspects of this-worldly life in pursuit of higher, more eternal goals.

Thus, the category of ritual economy in Wenzhou derives from its contrast with the profit-driven, accumulation-oriented market or capitalist economy, which focuses on expanding material production. Through the channeling of wealth into the ritual economy, today's rural Wenzhou residents not only construct and maintain a higher cosmic order but also keep in check the ravages of the runaway predatory modern capitalist market economy. Through such practices as "squandering" family and community wealth on ritual expenditures, rural Wenzhou people are carving out a social-ritual space and protecting it from the insatiable and ever-expansionary logic of the market that has elsewhere taken over all of social life.

THE PROTESTANT ETHIC AND THE SPIRIT OF SACRIFICE: RITUAL ECONOMY AS BOTH INVESTMENT AND DIVESTMENT FROM CAPITALISM

For Max Weber, in the Protestant Ethic that gave rise to modern Western capitalism,

> man is dominated by the making of money, by acquisition as the ultimate purpose of his life. Economic acquisition is no longer subordinated to man as the means for the satisfaction of his material needs. This reversal of what we should call the natural relationship is . . . a leading principle of capitalism, as it is foreign to all peoples not under capitalistic influence. ([1904] 1958: 53)

In modern capitalism, we witness a decline in sacrificing to the gods or displaying generosity to the community. Economic acquisition has become an all-consuming end in itself. The Calvinist spiritual anxiety about Predestination was allayed by the feverish activity of erecting material signs (factories, houses, heavy bank accounts) that proved that one was chosen by God for salvation. Ironically, it was the very pursuit of spiritual salvation that led Western civilization on the path to economic acquisition as the primary end of existence. This new end has become extremely contagious across the globe and has arrived belatedly in post-Mao China, where capitalist accumulation has become all-consuming.

However, in pockets across China, especially in rural areas, an older indigenous market economy intertwined with ritual economy still persists. This discussion on Wenzhou's "ritual economy" has sought to answer Gibson-Graham's call in the epigraph above for retrieving "noncapitalist" practices from the peripheries and making them more visible. I suggest that the flourishing ritual economy in the Wenzhou Model actually represents *a reversal* of Max Weber's Protestant Ethic, not destroying the commercial ethos but acting as a check on its socially destructive impetus. In rural Wenzhou, good works, deferred gratification, and material success in this world are not sufficient to mitigate the deep sense of isolation and risk in the highly competitive world of state capitalism in China or to allay one's anxiety about one's spiritual destiny. Here it is not just by working hard that one gains a sense of security about one's supernatural destination. Instead, one must be willing to sacrifice a portion of one's material wealth in the ritual economy to gain social recognition in this life, assure a better future in the afterlife, and improve one's standing with the gods, ancestors, and buddhas.

In Wenzhou, the movement of wealth is different from the Protestant Ethic of raking in and accumulating wealth. One accumulates wealth, but then one must give out and release part of that wealth, circulating it in the ritual economy and investing in divine worlds. It is not so much that productive work brings family honor; rather, it is how one *spends and consumes* that wealth in social giving and ritual activities. While we can say that in Wenzhou the market economy produces wealth that feeds the ritual economy, we can also say that the need to assuage one's anxiety about the afterlife galvanizes people to *diminish* and even *deplete* their material wealth in ritual consumption to please the gods. Wenzhou people excel at amassing material wealth, but they also ritually consume much of it to ensure social well-being in this world and spiritual security in the afterlives to come.

When urban "boss" Protestants in Wenzhou City declare that their entrepreneurial prowess is somehow due to their "Protestant Ethic" or Calvinist doctrine (N. Cao 2011: 165–166), it immediately triggers questions about this causality. China's Song dynasty commercial revolution a thousand years ago had already demonstrated that Chinese culture is capable of producing and amassing wealth through commerce. This venerable heritage of entrepreneurial culture may also explain why, once the modern Chinese state's Economic Reform policies opened the floodgates in 1979, the Chinese economy took off, propelled especially by private businesses, while large state-owned enterprises tended to languish. Economic growth took off just as much among non-Christian communities as among Christian ones. Since about 85–90 percent of the Chinese population is not Protestant, it is questionable that the Protestant Ethic can explain economic growth.

As we face global climate change and species extinction from industrial overproduction, it seems pressing to examine how diverse religious systems may exercise checks and restraints on an ever-expanding profit economy. We can take seriously Weber's critique of capitalism's elevation of "acquisition as the ultimate purpose of . . . life" ([1904] 1958: 53). Beginning in the Song, Chinese culture embarked on a path to material prosperity that did not open the floodgates to an unfettered capitalism, and the ritual economy seems to play an important protective role in this regard. Meanwhile, centuries of Neo-Confucian chastisement of excessive ritual waste did not close down the ritual economy until the twentieth century—and even then only temporarily. The difficult task before us is no longer the accumulation of wealth but how to "give away" wealth, which is entirely different from Marx's exhortation to better distribute wealth.

My fieldwork in 1990s Wenzhou revealed that local governments actively discouraged what they called "wasteful" (浪費) investment in the ritual economy, represented by lavish weddings, funerals and tombs, and temple rituals and festivals. Local state actions in rural Wenzhou were designed to capture much of the profits from industries. Taxes and local fees levied on enterprises in the 1990s ranged from about 35 to 55 percent of profits, depending on how each enterprise was able to elude such levies. In addition, for joint-stock enterprises, many local governments instituted a procedure called "standardization" (guifanhua), spelling out how each enterprise must spend their profits. In the early 1990s, Yongzhong Township government's Structural Reform Committee required all joint-stock enterprises to allocate their earnings after taxes thus:

50 percent expansion and reproduction
25 percent profit division to each stockholder
15 percent accumulation
10 percent public and worker welfare

This state formula attempted to channel surplus profits back into capital accumulation, the economic growth of firms, and the widening of the taxation base. Thus, the modern secular state attempted to capture the wealth generated from the local economy. While the state continued the late imperial Confucian castigations of ritual extravagance, much wealth at the grassroots in Wenzhou today again eludes state capture to end up in the ritual economy.

In "the spirit of capitalism," no penny should be wasted, and every penny must produce and expand wealth. According to Benjamin Franklin, "Money is of the prolific, generating nature. Money can beget money, and its offspring can beget more, and so on. . . . The more there is of it, the more it produces every turning, so that the profits rise quicker and quicker. He that kills a breeding-sow, destroys all her offspring to the thousandth generation" (quoted in Weber [1904] 1958: 49). In rural Wenzhou today, this kind of profit motive is not at all alien. However, it competes with two other indigenous economic logics. Earlier in this chapter, I noted how rural Wenzhou people distinguish between the reciprocal and contractual nature of renqing-exchange among humans one the one hand, and the loss of material wealth when humans make offerings to the gods on the other. In renqing reciprocity between humans, one's gift is like a social "loan" that will be repaid, while the social bond is strengthened. The end here is not profit but bond-strengthening through moral obligation to repay, as noted by Marcel Mauss (1967). In human-divine transactions, material wealth is thought not to return, or its return is so indirect or unpredictable that it must be put into a separate category from human-to-human reciprocity. In this sense, the indigenous logic of sacrifices and offerings to divinities in rural Wenzhou resonates with what Bataille (1985, 1989, [1947] 1991) wrote about sacrifice and religious expenditures as *pure* expenditure, something that involves a true "wasting" or "loss" of wealth, rather than a utilitarian investment with monetary returns. Both kinds of expenditures—gift reciprocity or social loan, and sacrifice to divinities—would earn Franklin's scorn and disapproval, given his utilitarian logic of saving.[3]

Unlike the Protestant Ethic, which launched a process of "disenchantment," deritualization, and radical iconoclasm or erasure of saints and their divine power, in rural Wenzhou economic development and commerce are brought back *along with* and even perhaps *because of* the reinstallation of gods, ancestors, buddhas, and immortals and the lavish rituals performed for them. In this movement, a portion of wealth is diverted away from production and accumulation and invested into the ritual economy that connects this world with divine realms. The ritual economy harbors a collection of ethics and logics that diverge from those found in the profit economy. Its ethics of generosity and giving out—its penitential sacrifice for sins—accumulates spiritual rather than material merit and delays material gratification in favor of investment in the afterlife.

CONCLUSION

When the market economy roared back to life in rural Wenzhou in the 1980s, it was not the deritualized Protestant kind, but an older indigenous late imperial Chinese market economy that was interwoven with a ritual economy. The market economy here had not disembedded itself fully from traditional institutions of kinship and religiosity. In the Wenzhou Model, *acquisition* is still not always the endgame, but often a means to public and community *ritual spending and consumption*. Here *giving away wealth* and conspicuous ritual consumption are sometimes just as important a means to power as accumulating wealth. In the Wenzhou Model, the ritual economy has managed to survive late imperial Neo-Confucian condemnations and subsequently the Republican and Maoist state secularization of society, which can be seen as attempts to create a Protestant Ethic in China.

Whereas the productivist profit economy widens the gap between rich and poor families, community ritual organizations reduce this gap, redistribute wealth, and provide community services, not least of which is attending to the spiritual yearnings for transcendence. This balanced model of economic growth means that in Wenzhou, more than in other places, economic development is better able to strengthen the horizontal ties of kinship and community and to reduce the alienation and individual isolation of competitive capitalism. Religious revival and ritual expenditure provide the basis for the reconstruction of an indigenous form of "civil society," the society of localism and community, which was been decimated with the rapid expansion of the modern state throughout the twentieth century.

The Wenzhou Model has relaunched China's "petty capitalist mode of production" through a reverse process of *reritualization* that often undercuts capitalist accumulation by promoting the "waste" of capital. Thus, although there is still profiteering and exploitation of migrant workers, the Wenzhou Model represents a quite different approach to capitalism from the Protestant Ethic version. It is the reinvention of an older indigenous model of market economy that possesses a built-in break, what Deleuze and Guattari (1987) called a "line of flight," or escape from both the relentless teleological principles of capitalism and the ever-expanding modern state.

Conclusion

We started this book with a discussion of modernity as a "purification" process whereby a hard wedge is driven between the categories of culture and nature, natural and human sciences, nature and "the supernatural," and divine beings and human beings (Latour 1993). Already in the European Reformation, purification involved the hardening of the boundaries separating the human from the divine, so that human beings no longer attained sainthood and only Jesus could cross the boundary between human and divine. The Reformation paved the way for subsequent purifications that made possible modern capitalism, nationalism, and science.

In China, the radical shift from divine imperial authority and the civilizational mode of governance to modern nation-state and centralized planned economy was also enabled by various purification campaigns. Given China's late development, its anxiety about being left behind in modernity, and the condensed timeline of China's speedy modernization, purification was more radical and intense. The powerful agencies of gods, ancestors, and cosmic-divine-natural forces had to be diminished or removed, so that purely human agency could rise up to construct the nation-state, engage in social engineering, and fuel the economic engine of development. This meant that traditional Chinese religiosities and their human-to-divine transformations, such as rebirths in the afterlife, self-cultivation and transcendence, human-to-god miracles, and attaining enlightenment and buddhahood all had to be actively combated and forgotten. The old transgressing of purifying boundaries had to be radically curtailed. Whether the transformation from human to Daoist immortal, deity, Bodhisattva, or Buddha, or the communications between humans and divinities, or rebirths from humans to animals or gods, they all had to be vehemently denied so as to block all passages to transcendence from this-worldly attachments and, instead, facilitate earthly commitments and projects.

This book examined Wenzhou, a region of China that had managed to partially insulate itself from some of these purification and separation campaigns, due to its relative geographical isolation and its unique language, which kept outsiders from exerting undue influence on local culture. These same conditions also helped Wenzhou become one of the earliest in the country to undergo the recent resurgence of "hybridization" or "mediation" movements to transgress these boundaries. In 2008, after witnessing an exquisite performance of a Buddho-Daoist funerary ritual in a Pingyang village, I chatted with Mr. Dong, one of the ritual specialists. He said that he was struck by the great difference between Chinese religiosity and Christianity:

> In Buddhism, everyone can cultivate themselves and become a Buddha [自修成佛]. This is the most radical equality: when a human being can become like a god, and humans, gods, and buddhas can be interchangeable. . . . In Christianity, however, people believe in a higher god above everything. Worshippers and believers can go to Heaven, but they can never become God themselves. [For Christians,] if a human being should ever *become* a god, it would be an alarming event!

For Dong, the strict Christian dualism between the human world and God in Heaven was too simplistic and fixed. The Buddho-Daoist religiosity that was familiar to Dong offered him a more complex and fluid cosmos, one in which sentient beings come in multiple forms and can transform themselves or be reborn into animal life or divine beings, through a vast array of different universes in unimaginable spans of time.

What difference does this rehybridization of separate realms, and return of divine-human interactions make, for both the faithful and nonbelievers alike? Why call for a postsecular society when China's radical modern purification and secularization seems to have helped propel its astounding economic development? This book has focused on a few reasons.

The first reason is that divine beings like gods, ancestors, immortals, buddhas, and bodhisattvas are most effective in galvanizing community-building efforts; they prevent local people from falling deeper into the state-capitalist disciplinary machinery and its mysterious logic. This book has shown how they have helped people to reconstruct local communities. These divinities have given the divine sparks and inspiration for the production of a multiplicity of "sprouts of religious civil society"—temples, ancestor halls, monasteries, churches, sutra-chanting and study associations, and deity-worshipping sisterhoods. They have helped the Wenzhou area stand out in its impressive ability for grassroots community initiative and local self-governance, moving away from a twentieth-century "mono-organizational" state-arborescent society. These religious organizations foster the social skills needed for activating civil society: community and transnational fund-raising; traditional arts and crafts and architectural skills for temple-building; skills for enhancing organizational cohesion; protocols in selecting and replacing organizational leadership; and skills in organizing ritual events and processions, while negotiating with state religious, sanitation, and traffic administrations. Thus, divine beings are helping to rebalance the relationship between society and the state, which in Chinese modernity has been asymmetrically developed, or one could even say distorted, into a thoroughly state-dominated and state-penetrated top-down system. Remarkably, some of these lay religious practitioners and leaders have even started to make their way into the halls of local government and to religiously convert some officials, meaning that they now operate from *within* the state. They pave the way for the possible "societalization" of the state, and the "re-enchantment" of not only modern Chinese society but even, perhaps, the modern state.

In November 2016, I chatted with Mr. Wang, an entrepreneur based in western China, who was visiting his hometown. He complained about how the local government took over the task of renovating the Cultural Heritage site of the Yingqiao Wang Lineage walled fortress to promote tourism. They formed a government Yongchang Fortress Restoration Committee to build new apartment blocks outside the fortress walls, so as to relocate most residents from inside the walls. The aim was to tear out the newer boxlike concrete buildings inside the walls and preserve the older heritage structures for a tourist experience of going back in time to the Ming dynasty. Mr. Wang has been frustrated with the slow pace of this state committee. It has taken sixteen long years to resettle the families outside the walls. He complained to the committee that, back in 1558, his Wang ancestors took only eleven *months* to build the entire fortress, without modern machinery. "There are over thirty people on this committee," said Mr. Wang. "They collect salary, but they have no sense of public service, no motivation, and they just drag their feet." The residents inside the walls were impatient to move out into new apartments, but they had to wait endlessly for the new buildings to be built. Once built, the buildings sat empty for years, waiting for the installation of interior plumbing, electricity lines, and windows. Meanwhile, the government was losing 6 million yuan annually from rents it could have been earning, and spending money to house residents elsewhere. Mr. Wang was convinced that if the job had been given to his own lineage, it would have been completed in no time. He concluded, "If you do not rely on the *minjian* [realm of the people], you cannot get the job done! [没有民間是搞不起來的!]." One could also add that it is the higher purpose of serving the ancestors that makes the *minjian* more efficient and motivated than the secular bureaucratic committee.

Second, in these sprouts of a religious and ritualized civil society, we must pay attention not only to the agency of gods and ancestors, and male organizers and leaders of religious associations and lineages, but also to women's religious agency, including goddesses. Women comprise the majority of pious worshippers, dedicated volunteers, sutra-chanters, and generous donors in Wenzhou's popular religion and Daoist and Buddhist cultures. Women's agency is also responsible for a significant number of start-up temples, shrines, and religious associations, although they have much less involvement in lineage organizations. Divine visitations and communications with the gods persuade many women to take the initiative to accumulate funds and erect a new deity statue, or to launch or restore a temple. However, these small start-up temples are often rejected for registration as officially recognized temples, and they tend to fall victim to occasional waves of temple destruction by local officialdom. Even when a start-up temple survives and grows in membership and social influence, its troubles are not over. Lucrative temple finances and social influence tend to attract the notice of locally influential men, who may soon take over a temple on the upswing and purge the women founders. We can also see that while the traditional Chinese patrilineal kinship system favors men, women's agency has found more favorable opportunities in religious activities.

Third, the gods and ancestors have even been resettled into the Wenzhou economy. The "ritual economy" of expenditures for ritual performances, religious events and services, renqing gifts, and the building of ritual infrastructures and religious material culture have together dissolved the modern purification and artificial separation between "religion" and "economy." In stark contrast to the modernist discourse (whether orthodox Marxism or modernization theory) arguing that traditional religiosities are obstacles to economic development, we have seen throughout this book that in the Wenzhou Model's impressive rural economic development, religion and economy are inseparable and intertwined forces that mutually support and stimulate each other in a circular movement of cause and effect. The motivation to get rich is just as much about pleasing the ancestors, providing for descendants, and having enough surplus funds to make offerings to thank the gods and secure their protection as it is for the material comfort and social pride and rivalry of each family. When launching a new business, building a retail outlet or industrial plant, and maintaining enterprise or business health and success, Wenzhou people try to align themselves with larger cosmic movements by consulting divination and fengshui masters and making ample offerings to the gods. The health and longevity of the family firm is also a source of uncertainty, so divine protection is sought. Firm expenditures thus include generous sacrifices and rituals to propitiate gods and ancestors, and donations to temples and local communities to maintain the spiritual creditworthiness of the firm.

The ritual economy has a venerable genealogy that traces back to at least the commercialization of the Song dynasty, when religious and economic production were intertwined, and this religio-economic culture catapulted China into an economic power in the globe at that time. Indeed, religious products such as deity cults, printed scriptures and liturgies, religious statuary, and lineage genealogies and territories developed and spread along trade routes, linking up both domestic and foreign lands. It may be true that a modern secular economy can grow radically faster by cutting down ritual expenditures, stressing only the pursuit of profits, and forcing the reinvestment of surplus wealth back into expanding the economy. However, it does so by ignoring and suppressing the astute social mechanisms that the ancestors worked out over the centuries through the ritual economy: social reciprocity to strengthen social bonds of kinship and associations; the social redistribution of wealth through religious and lineage charities that counter the concentration of wealth; lineage funding of local schools and academies; temple and lunar festivals to maintain and reconstruct local community identity and commitments; deity cults to renew social memory and community history and cohesion; and the promotion of grassroots social initiatives of community-building and self-governance, so that the state bureaucracy and its officials do not need to run everything.

The ritual economy provides what Deleuze and Guattari called "a line of flight" (1987). Flight from what? From the modern capitalist economy's competitive self-aggrandizement that makes us forget our social obligations and responsibilities. From the teleology of nation-state expansion and penetration that have diminished the integrity, autonomy, and self-governance of local communities and civil societies. From our narrow and singular pursuit of material consumption in the temporal world, which creates an ever-expanding and environmentally unsustainable industrial productivism. From the constant deterritorialization of both the state and capitalism, which makes us forget our groundedness and dependency on the earth and a healthy natural environment. In Wenzhou we see how the ritual economy has made it possible for some people to turn inward in self-cultivation and work toward enlightenment about the transience of life. The significance of making sacrifices to gods and ancestors, and donations to temples and charities, lies in people's readiness to sustain a material loss—a loss that helps one to detach from worldly obsessions and pursue higher cosmic ends. The re-enchantment of modernity in Wenzhou has much to teach us.

Chronology of Chinese Dynasties

DATES	DYNASTY	
ca. 2000–1500 BCE	Xia	夏
1700–1027 BCE	Shang	商
1027–771 BCE	Western Zhou	西周
770–221 BCE	Eastern Zhou 770–476 BCE: Spring and Autumn period 475–221 BCE: Warring States period	東周 春秋時代 戰國時代
221–207 BCE	Qin	秦
206 BCE–9 CE	Western Han	西漢
9–24 CE	Xin (Wang Mang interregnum)	新
25–220 CE	Eastern Han	東漢
220–280 CE	Three Kingdoms	三國
265–316 CE	Western Jin	西晉
317–420 CE	Eastern Jin	東晉
420–588 CE	Southern and Northern Dynasties	南北朝
581–617 CE	Sui	隨
618–907 CE	Tang	唐
907–960 CE	Five Dynasties	五代
960–1279 CE	Song 960–1127 CE: Northern Song 1127–1279 CE: Southern Song	宋 北宋 南宋
916–1125 CE	Liao	遼
1038–1227 CE	Western Xia	西夏
1115–1234 CE	Jin	金
1279–1368 CE	Yuan	元
1368–1644 CE	Ming	明
1644–1911 CE	Qing	清
1911–1949 CE	Republic of China (in mainland China)	中華民國
1949– CE	People's Republic of China	中華人民共和國

Note: Gaps in time between one dynasty or period and the next result from periods of disunity before a new emperor and royal family claims the throne to found a new dynasty.

Notes on Currency, Weights, Measurements,
and Chinese Romanization and Pronunciation

In 2017, the exchange rate between Chinese yuan (or *renminbi*) and the US dollar averaged between 0.145 and 0.155 US dollars for 1 Chinese yuan. Throughout the book, I try to give the currency conversions for the year that the figure was quoted in, instead of the year of writing.

One Chinese *jin* (斤), a unit in weight measurement, is roughly equivalent to 1 US pound (actually 1.1 pounds), so I simply convert 1 Chinese *jin* to 1 US-Anglo pound or 0.5 kilograms.

One Chinese *li* (里) is 500 meters or 1,640 feet, or about one-third of a Anglo-American mile.

One Chinese *chi* (尺) is 0.33 meters—i.e., 33⅓ cm or 1.094 feet.

NOTES ON MANDARIN CHINESE ROMANIZATION AND PRONUNCIATION

The Romanization of Chinese characters in this book follows the pinyin system. Certain pinyin pronunciations may pose difficulties for readers who do not speak Mandarin Chinese, so here is a guide:

"C" is pronounced with a hard "ts" as in the consonant ending in "heigh<u>ts</u>"

"Ch" has no English equivalent sound but is close to the "ch" in the word "<u>ch</u>ai," plus an "r" sound, or retroflex curling of the tongue

"Q" is pronounced "ch," as in "<u>ch</u>ange"

"Sh" has no English equivalent sound, but is close to the sound "shr" in the word "<u>shr</u>iek" plus an "r" sound, or retroflex curling of the tongue

"X" is pronounced "sh," as in "<u>sh</u>ake"

"Zh" has no English equivalent sound but is close to the sound "dr" in the word "<u>dr</u>ink" with an "r" sound, or retroflex curling of the tongue

Religious Sites in Wenzhou
Visited by Author 1990–2016

ANCESTOR HALLS

Chen Shi Zongci (陳氏宗祠) Chen Lineage Ancestor Hall, 蒼南縣, 錢庫鎮. Cangnan County, Qianku Township.

Chen Shi Zongci (陳氏宗祠) Chen Lineage Ancestor Hall, 龍灣區, 永昌鎮, 前街村. Longwan District, Yongchang Township, Qianjie Village.

Hu Shi Zongci (胡氏宗祠) Hu Lineage Ancestor Hall, 龍灣區, 永昌鎮, 前街村. Longwan District, Yongchang Township, Qianjie Village.

Jiang Shi Citang (姜氏祠堂) Jiang Lineage Ancestor Hall, 龍灣區, 永中鎮, 鎮南村. Longwan District, Yongzhong Township, Zhennan Village.

Jin Shi Zongci (金氏宗祠) Jin Lineage Ancestor Hall, 龍灣區, 永昌鎮, 城北村. Longwan District, Yongchang Township, Chengbei Village.

Li Shi Zongci (李氏宗祠) Li Lineage Ancestor Hall, 龍灣區, 永興鎮, 大塘村. Longwan District, Yongxing Township, Datang Village.

Lin Shi Zongci (林氏宗祠) Lin Lineage Ancestor Hall, 龍灣區, 永昌鎮, 殿前村. Longwan District, Yongchang Township, Dianqian Village.

Wangshi Jiamiao (王氏家廟) Wang Lineage Family Temple, 龍灣區, 永昌鎮, 殿前村. Longwan District, Yongchang Township, Dianqian Village.

Xianjü Chen Shi Dazong (仙居陳氏大宗) Residence of the Immortals Chen Lineage Ancestor Hall, 蒼南縣, 錢庫鎮. Cangnan County, Qianku Township.

Ye Shi Jinianguan (葉適紀念館) Ye Lineage Memorial Hall, 瑞安市, 莘塍鎮. Rui'an City, Xincheng Township.

Yang Shi Zongci (楊氏宗祠) Yang Lineage Ancestor Hall, 龍灣區, 沙城鎮, 八甲村. Longwan District, Shacheng Township, Bajia Village.

Yingqiao Wang Shi Zongci (英橋王氏宗祠) Yingqiao Wang Lineage Ancestor Hall, 龍灣區, 永昌鎮, 新城村. Longwan District, Yongchang Township, New Town Village.

Zhang Shi Citang (張氏祠堂) Zhang Lineage Ancestor Hall, 龍灣區, 永興鎮, 下垟街道, 六村. Longwan District, Yongxing Street Committee, Six Village.

Zhang Shi Zongci (章氏宗祠) Zhang Lineage Ancestor Hall, 龍灣區, 永興鎮, 康一村. Longwan District, Yongxing Township, Kangyi Village.

Zhang Shi Zongci (張氏宗祠) Zhang Lineage Ancestor Hall, 龍灣區, 永中鎮, 普門村. Longwan District, Yongzhong Township, Pumen Village.

Zhu Shi Zongci (朱氏宗祠) Zhu Lineage Ancestor Hall, 龍灣區, 永中鎮, 上金村. Longwan District, Yongzhong Township, Shangjin Village.

BUDDHIST SITES

Ba Cao Nianfotang (芭曹念佛堂) Ba Cao Buddhist Recitation Hall, 蒼南縣, 芦莆鎮, 芦頭村. Cangnan County, Lupu Township, Lutou Village.

Fuhu Si (伏虎寺) Prostrating Tiger Buddhist Temple, 瑞安縣, 仙岩鎮. Rui'an County, Xianyan Town.

Fushan Chansi (福善禪寺) Prosperity and Kindness Chan Buddhist Temple, 龍灣區, 永興鎮, 康二村. Longwan District, Yongxing Township, Kang-er Village.

Guo-an Si (國安寺) Peaceful State Buddhist Temple, 龍灣區, 永昌鎮. Longwan District, Yongchang Township.

Haiyun Buddhist Temple (海雲寺) Ocean Clouds Buddhist Temple, 蒼南縣, 蘆浦鎮, 監後垟村. Cangnan County, Lupu Township, Jianhouyang Village.

Jiangxin Si (江心寺) River Center Buddhist Temple, 溫州市, 江心島. Wenzhou City, Jiangxin Island.

Jingxin Si (淨心寺) Pure Heart Buddhist Temple, 龍灣區, 永昌鎮, 度山村. Longwan District, Yongchang Township, Dushan Village.

Meifeng Yongquan Chan Si (梅峰湧泉禪寺) Plum Peak Eternal Spring Chan Buddhist Temple, 蒼南縣, 金鄉鎮. Cangnan County, Jinxiang Township.

Miaoguosi (妙果寺) Miaoguo Buddhist Temple, 溫州市. Wenzhou City.

Qianyuan Si (乾元寺) First Hexagram Buddhist Temple, 龍灣區, 永中鎮, 普門村. Longwan District, Yongzhong Township, Pumen Village.

Qingshan Chan Si (慶善禪寺) Celebrate Virtue Chan Buddhist Temple, 龍灣區, 永中鎮. Longwan District, Yongzhong Township.

Richuan Tang (日川堂) Sun River Hall, 龍灣區, 沙城鎮, 七甲街. Longwan District, Shacheng Township, Qijia Street.

Taiping Si (太平寺) Taiping Buddhist Temple, 溫州市. Wenzhou City.

Tianzhu Si (天柱寺) Heavenly Pillar Buddhist Temple, 甌海区, 永昌鎮, 天柱峰. Ouhai District, Yongchang Township, Tianzhu Peak.

Xianglin Si (香林寺) Fragrant Forest Buddhist Temple, 蒼南縣, 龍港鎮, 徐家庄村. Cangnan County, Longgang Township, Xujiazhuang Village.

Xiangling Si (祥靈寺) Auspicious and Efficacious Temple, 蒼南縣, 靈溪鎮. Cangnan County, Lingxi Town.

Xianyan Si (仙岩禪寺) Temple of the Cliff of Immortals, 瑞安縣, 仙岩鎮. Rui'an County, Xianyan Town (also called 聖壽禪寺 Sacred Longevity Chan Buddhist Temple).

Yanxia Si (延霞寺) Prolonging the Evening Glow Temple, 溫州市, 南白象鎮. Wenzhou City, South White Elephant Township.

Yicheng Si (一乘寺) One Ascent Buddhist Temple, 龍灣區, 永中鎮, 石浦陡門. Longwan District, Yongzhong Township, Shipu Canal Lock.

Yongfu Si (永福寺) Forever Prosperous Temple, 龍灣區, 華盖山. Longwan District, Huagai Mountains.

Yunyuan An (雲源庵) Source of the Clouds Nunnery, 平陽縣, 錢倉鎮, 錢倉村. Pingyang County, Qiancang Township, Qiangcang Village.

Zhenzhong Tang (鎮中堂) Middle of Town Hall, 龍灣區, 永中鎮, 鎮北村. Longwan District, Yongzhong Township, Zhenbei Village.

DAOIST SITES

Baiyun Daoguan (白雲道觀) White Cloud Daoist Temple, 甌海區, 南白象鎮. Ouhai District, South White Elephant Township.

Chenghuang Miao (城隍廟) City God Temple, 龍灣區, 寧村. Longwan District, Ning Village.

Chenghuang Miao (城隍廟) City God Temple, 蒼南縣, 金鄉鎮. Cangnan County, Jinxiang Town.

Chenghuang Miao (城隍廟) City God Temple, 平陽縣, 昆陽鎮. Pingyang County, Kunyang Town.

Chenghuang Miao (城隍廟) City God Temple, 蒼南縣, 魚熬村. Cangnan County, Yu-ao Village.

Chenghuang Miao (城隍廟) City God Temple, 平陽縣, 錢倉鎮. Pingyang County, Qiancang Town.

Dongan Daoguan (東安道觀) Eastern Peace Daoist Temple, 蒼南縣, 炎亭鎮. Cangnan County, Yanting Township.

Dongcheng Daoguan (東城道觀) East Wall Daoist Temple (formerly 楊陳二府), 永昌堡, 龍灣區. Yongchang Fortress, Longwan District.

Dongyue Daoguan (東岳道觀) East Mountain Daoist Temple, 平陽縣, 昆陽鎮. Pingyang County, Kunyang Town.

Fengmen Daoguan (峰門道觀) Gate to the Peak Daoist Temple, 龍灣區, 永中鎮, 前街村. Longwan District, Yongzhong Township, Qianjie Village.

Hongya Daoguan (洪崖道觀) Immense Cliff Daoist Temple, 甌海縣, 茶山鎮. Ouhai County, Cha Shan Township.

Jinlong Daoguan (金龍道觀) Golden Dragon Daoist Temple, 蒼南縣, 龍港鎮, 江口村. Cangnan County, Longgang Township, Jiangkou Village.

Kuixing Ge (魁星閣) Pavilion of the Big Dipper Stars, 溫州市, 翠微山東首. Wenzhou City, Cuiwei Mountain, Eastern Peak.

Lingshan Daoguan (靈善道觀) Efficacious and Charitable Daoist Temple, 蒼南縣, 炎亭鎮. Cangnan County, Yanting Town.

Sanguan Tang (三官堂) Three Officials Hall, 龍灣區, 永興鎮, 大塘村. Longwan District, Yongxing Township, Datang Village.

Shisheng Daoguan (石勝道觀) Stone Victory Daoist Temple, 龍灣區, 雙嶴村. Longwan District, Shuangao Village.

Taibaoguan (太保觀) Temple Curator Temple, 龍灣區, 沙城鎮. Longwan District, Shacheng Township.

Xuanling Daoguan (宣靈道觀) Broadcasting Efficacy Daoist Temple, 龍灣區, 永興街道, 沙園村. Longwan District, Yongxing Street Committee, Shayuan Village.

Xuanzhen Daoguan (玄真道觀) Profound and Perfected Daoist Temple, 龍灣區, 瑤溪山. Longwan District, Yaoxi Mountain.

Zhonglie Daoguan (忠烈道觀) Daoist Temple of the Loyal Martyr, 龍灣區, 永中鎮, 石浦村. Longwan District, Yongzhong Township, Shipu Village.

Zixiao Daoguan (紫霄道觀) Purple Cloud Daoist Temple, 溫州市, 西山東路, 234 弄. Wenzhou City, West Mountain East Road, Lane 234.

DEITY TEMPLES

Baima Shengwang Miao (白馬聖王廟) White Horse Sacred King Temple, 蒼南縣, 靈溪鎮. Cangnan County, Lingxi Town.

Baogong Dian (包公殿) Lord Bao Temple, 溫州市, 西山東路 116 号. Wenzhou City, Xishan East Road, #116.

Damen Wuxian Miao (大門五顯廟) Temple to the Five Apparitions at Big Gate, 蒼南縣, 靈溪鎮, 大門村. Cangnan County, Lingxi Township, Damen Village.

Fuquan Gong (福全宮) Prosperous and Complete Temple, 蒼南縣, 靈溪鎮, 鎮江村. Cangnan County, Lingxi Township, Zhenjiang Village.

Guandi Temple (關帝廟) Guandi Temple, 龍灣區, 永昌鎮, 新城村, 永昌堡南門. Longwan District, Yongchang Township, New Town Village, Yongchang Fortress South Gate.

Jingtou Yangfu Dian (鯨頭楊府殿) Temple to Yang Family Elder, 蒼南縣, 龍港鎮. Cangnan County, Longgang Township, Jintou Village.

Jüsheng Tang (聚聖堂) Gathering the Sages Temple, 溫州市, 南白象鎮. Wenzhou City, South White Elephant Township.

Kunde Palace (坤德宮) Female Virtue Palace, 龍灣區, 永昌鎮, 新城村. Longwan District, Yongchang Township, New Town Village.

Qi Tian Dasheng Miao (齊天大聖廟) Temple of He Who Is Equal to Heaven, 蒼南縣, 靈溪鎮. Cangnan County, Lingxi Town.

Sangang Shengwang Miao (三港聖王廟) Temple of the Sacred King of the Three Ports, 蒼南縣, 錢庫鎮. Cangnan County, Qianku Township.

Shanshui Shenggong (山水聖宮) Sacred Palace of Mountains and Water, 蒼南縣, 靈溪鎮, 浦尾村. Cangnan County, Lingxi Township, Puwei Village.

Shengjingshan Shidian (聖井山石殿) Sacred Well Mountain Stone Temple, 瑞安市, 聖井山. Rui'an City, Sacred Well Mountain.

Shuixian Gong (水仙宮) Water Immortal Palace, 龍灣區, 永昌鎮, 鄭宅村. Longwan District, Yongchang Township, Zhengzhai Village.

Taiyingong (太陰宮) Palace of the Great Yin, 龍灣區, 沙城鎮, 七甲村. Longwan District, Shacheng Township, Seven Jia Village, Liangshan Pavilion (凉山閣).

Taiyingong (太陰宮) Palace of the Great Yin, 蒼南縣, 龍港鎮, 江口村. Cangnan County, Longgang Township, Jiangkou Village.

Taiyingong (太陰宮) Palace of the Great Yin, 溫州市, 鹿城區, 蒲鞋市街. Wenzhou City, Lu City District, Puxieshi Street Committee.

Taiyingong (太陰宮) Palace of the Great Yin, 瑞安市, 湖岭鎮, 黃林村. Rui'an City, Huling Township, Huanglin Village.

Taiyingong (太陰宮) Palace of the Great Yin, 蒼南縣, 藻溪鎮, 盛陶村. Cangnan County, Zaoxi Township, Shengtao Village.

Tianhou Shengmu Niangniang Miao (天后聖母娘娘廟) Celestial Queen Mother Temple, 靈昆島. Lingkun Island.

Tianxiangong (天仙宮) Celestial Immortal Palace, 龍灣區, 永中街道, 青山. Longwan District, Yongzhong Street Committee, Pumen Village.

Wutong Shengwang Miao (五通聖王廟) Temple to the Sacred King of the Five Passages, 龍灣區, 永昌鎮, 殿前村. Longwan District, Yongchang Township, Dianqian Village.

Yangfu Miao (楊府廟) Lord Yang Temple, 瑞安市, 湖岭鎮, 黃林村. Rui'an City, Huling Township, Huanglin Village.

Yangfu Miao (楊府廟) Lord Yang Temple, 蒼南縣, 錢庫鎮, 雲岩鄉. Cangnan County, Qianku Township, Yunyan Xiang.

Yuhuang Dadi Miao (玉皇大帝廟) Jade Emperor Temple, 龍灣區, 永中街道, 青. Longwan District, Yongzhong Street Committee, Green Mountain.

Yuhuang Dian (玉皇殿) Jade Emperor Pavilion, 龍灣區, 永昌鎮, 坦頭山. Longwan District, Yongchang Township, Tantou Mountain.

Yuhuang Lou (玉皇楼) Jade Emperor Temple, 溫州市, 翠微山. Wenzhou City, Cuiwei Mountain.

Zaowang Dian (灶王殿) Kitchen God Temple, 瑞安市, 莘塍鎮, 下村. Rui'an City, Xincheng Township, Lower Village.

Zhangyu Shan Guan (嶂嶼山觀) Cliff Island Mountain Temple, 溫州市, 梧埏鎮. Wenzhou City, Wuyan Township.

Zhenan Tudi Gong (浙南土地宮) Southern Zhejiang Earth God Temple, 蒼南縣, 靈溪鎮. Cangnan County, Lingxi Town.

1. FROM "SUPERSTITION" TO "PEOPLE'S CUSTOMS"

1　Unless otherwise specified, all translations from Chinese are my own.

2　"温州：浙江省地級市" (Wenzhou: A Regional City in Zhejiang Province), in 《百度百科》 (*Baidu: Online Encyclopedia*), accessed September 10, 2019, https:// baike.baidu.com/item/%E6%B8%A9%E5%B7%9E/212091.

3　"市文廣新局考察龍灣非遺傳承基地" (Wenzhou City's Bureau of Culture, Broadcast, and News Pays a Visit to Longwan District's Intangible Cultural Heritage Sites), in 《龍灣民俗》 (*Longwan Folk Culture*), September 30, 2016, http://lwms .wzlib.cn/msdt/201706/t20170611_217911.htm.

4　See my essay suggesting a common "deep structure" of millenarian peasant rebellions with the modern Chinese Communist Revolution (M. Yang 2018).

5　In 1949, Zhang Enpu, the sixty-third-generation descendant of Celestial Master Daoist leaders, fled to Taiwan with his family (Li L. 2014: 1–5).

2. THE WENZHOU MODEL OF RURAL DEVELOPMENT IN CHINA

1　See *Wenzhou Business News* (温州商報), April 15, 2016, http://www.gywb.cn/content /2016-04/15/content_4809657.htm.

2　Kellee Tsai (2002: 107) found that Fujian women's participation in credit societies ranged from 64 percent to 90 percent.

3　According to a person who had inside knowledge of Premier Wen Jiabao's visit to Wenzhou in 2012, even the premier of China could not be told the actual numbers of Wenzhou business people who had committed suicide due to the crisis. There is a Chinese law that if over ten people die due to problems with the running of the city, then the leading officials of the city must take responsibility and step down. Since the report writers did not wish to compromise their city leaders, they withheld the suicide figures from the premier. I pressed my source about the suicide numbers, asking him, "Was it about a hundred?" He shook his head. "How about three hundred?" He reluctantly nodded and said, "That's more like it." Now that the city leaders have changed, I can include this information.

3. POPULAR RELIGIOSITY

1　The numbers do not total 100 percent because some households claim more than one religious adherence.

2　See Roger S. C. Lo (2012) for a discussion of the Qing dynasty court's conferral of an imperial title on Lord Yang in 1867. Space does not allow me here to disagree with his interpretation.

3 The first two editions in 1982 and 1983 sold 570,000 copies. There was a first printing of the 1985 third edition, and then another printing that same year of 104,000
copies, with a total of about 1 million copies sold by 1985 (Ye Z. 1985: 300). As of
July 2013, one can download the book in PDF from the Chinese internet.

4 See Adam Chau's (2006) delightful discussion of "red-hot sociality."

4. DAOISM

1 十大洞天 (Ten Daoist Caverns), 三十六小洞天 (Thirty-Six Grottoes), 七十二福地
(Seventy-Two Blessed Lands)。The four Daoist Blessed Lands located in Wenzhou
are Nantian Mountain in Wencheng County, Da Ruo Yan in Yongjia County, the
Three Emperor Well in Ouhai County, and Tao Mountain in Rui'an City (blog
.wzdsb.net/space-16961294-do-blog-id-414204.html).

2 Personal communication with Master Li (pseudonym).

3 See the website honoring Huang Gongwang and his painting and Daoist devotion:
www.znhs.org/News_L_show.asp?id=465&classid=10&lb=8.

4 北京白雲觀道教學院 (Beijing White Cloud Temple and Daoist Academy), 上海道
教學院 (Shanghai Daoist Academy), 武當山道教學院 (Wudang Mountain Daoist
Academy in Hubei Province), 青城山道教學院 (Qingcheng Mountain Daoist Academy in Sichuan), 南岳坤道院 (Southern Peak Women's Daoist Academy in Heng
Mountain, Hunan).

5 "First, you must have good vocal chords [嗓子要好]. Second, you must have good
writing and calligraphy skills [筆要好]. Third, you must have good musician skills
[吹打要好]."

6 "No killing [不殺生]; no stealing or robbing [不偷盜]; no indulging in illicit sex
[不奸淫]; no stirring up conflict among neighbors through gossip [不挑撥臨間]; no
ingesting meat or alcohol [不吃葷酒].

7 《太上玉皇心印妙經》(Exquisite Scripture of the Jade Emperor for Imprinting on
the Heart); 《雷公威靈懺》(Great and Efficacious Scripture of Lord Thunder);
《太上玄靈北斗本命延生真經》(True Scripture of the Mysterious and Efficacious
Northern Dipper on High That Prolongs Life); 《太上靈華寶懺》(Scripture of
the Efficacious and Beautiful); 《太上文昌消劫行化寶懺》(Precious Scripture of
Wenchang on High for Dissolving and Transforming Misfortunes).

8 "[His] consciousness must attain a high level": 意念要達到上層.

9 Other terms used for written paper communications sent up to the gods include
guan 關, gao 誥, die 牒, bangwen 榜文, and tie 帖. The word chiwen 敕文 is used for
messages sent down from the gods to the human world, the same phrase used in
imperial times for edicts or decrees sent down by the emperor.

5. BUDDHIST RELIGIOSITY

1 My translation of Scripture of the Lotus Blossom of the Fine Dharma is adapted from
Hurvitz 2009.

2 When I first met Abbot Hong Guang in 2010, he called himself Abbot Nengxian
(能顯方丈).

3 KTV refers to karaoke TV electronic entertainment systems that originated in Japan in the 1960s and 1970s and subsequently took consumerist Asian societies by storm. The equipment allows amateur singers to sing along with the music, words, and images moving across a video screen. In China, KTV lounges often cater to groups of men, providing alcohol, snacks, cigarettes, and pretty hostesses.

4 Taiping Buddhist Temple website, accessed December 29, 2013, www.wztps.org /ShowArt.asp?ID=1620.

6. SPROUTS OF RELIGIOUS CIVIL SOCIETY

1 See the Wenzhou City Daoist Association website, http://www.wzdjxh.com/About .asp?ComID=252 (accessed September 2016).

7. THE REBIRTH OF THE LINEAGE

1 See Greenhalg and Winckler (2005: 218–231) for a useful discussion of peasant responses to the state population policies.

8. OF MOTHERS, GODDESSES, AND BODHISATTVAS

1 See Kang Xiaofei (2016) for a useful grand survey of developments in women and religious practice against the backdrop of modern Chinese history, including Western missionary activity, modern education for some women, nationalist and revolutionary denigration of women clinging to traditional religiosity, and so forth.

2 The prevalence of older women's voluntary activism in rural temples has been observed by Kang Xiaofei (2009) in fieldwork in Shaanxi Province and by Sun Yanfei (2014) in Zhejiang Province.

3 See Yü 2001: 333–338 for a useful discussion of the Chinese feminization of Bodhisattva Avalokitesvara during the Song dynasty and her marriage resistance and filial self-sacrifice.

4 For photographs of the 2013 Zhejiang-Taiwan Cangnan Chen Jinggu Custom Cultural Festival (浙台蒼南陳靖姑信俗文化節), see the blog of Tang Shengxi (唐升溪), http://blog.voc.com.cn/blog_showone_type_blog_id_841521_p_1.html (accessed June 10, 2016).

5. 蒼南縣陳靖姑信俗文化協會, Cangnan County Chen Jinggu Xinsu Wenhua Xiehui.

9. BROADENING AND PLURALIZING THE MODERN CATEGORY OF "CIVIL SOCIETY"

1 See my early discussion of the Confucian-Legalist struggle in ancient China as a "history of the present" in contemporary China (M. Yang 1994a: 209–244).

2 Zhou Benshun was the former head of the Party's Central Political and Legal Affairs Commission. In 2015, the Party Central Commission for Discipline Inspection announced Zhou's arrest for corruption.

3 See https://www.douban.com/group/search?cat=1019&q=%E5%85%AC%E6%B0%9 1%E7%A4%BE%E4%BC%9A (accessed September 17, 2019).

4 Institute of Civil Society Development, Zhejiang University. http://icsd.zju.edu.cn /group.php (accessed August 7, 2016). The Beijing University Civil Society (北京大學公民社會研究中心) was established in 2005 but seems to have become inactive in recent years.

5 See Yu K. 2011 for a detailed discussion of the terminology used in Chinese civil society discourse.

6 See Statista.com, the German online statistics portal, for figures on China's rural-urban population proportions. https://www.statista.com/statistics/278566/urban -and-rural-population-of-china/ (accessed May 3, 2018).

10. WHAT'S MISSING IN THE WENZHOU MODEL?

1 I have benefited from and slightly revised the translation by Brigitte Baptandier (2008: 6–7).

2 The similar red dots in figure 8.2, on a painting of Goddess Mother Chen (dated 1892) charging on horseback with her two deity sisters, illustrate the continuity of such ritual services.

3 See my essay in Chinese (M. Yang 2019b).

an 庵　Buddhist nunnery

bai 拜　to worship or honor (divinities)

baichantuan 拜懺團　"worship and penance groups"—usually composed of women who chant scriptures for Daoist and Buddhist rituals

baifo shaoxiang 拜佛燒香　"worship the Buddha and burn incense"—implies that worshippers pray for favors without understanding Buddhist doctrines

baijingchan 拜經懺　"worshipping and chanting scriptures"—Wenzhou term for popular religion, and popular Daoism and Buddhism, which emphasize doing rituals more than religious teachings and self-cultivation

bai shijiemei 拜十姐妹　"Worshipping with Ten Sisters"—rural women's groups who worship Goddess Mother Chen and go on outings to her temples

baorongxin 包容心　tolerance toward other religious faiths; encompassing rather than excluding other religious practices or ideas

biqiu 比丘, **biquiuni** 比丘尼　Buddhist monk; Buddhist nun

bugang tadou 步罡踏斗　"pacing through the Big Dipper handle and treading across the Star's dipper"—the ritual pacing of Daoist priests

buzheng zhifeng 不正之風　"crooked wind"—devious, immoral actions; corruption

caili 彩禮　bride-price; bridewealth

chanbaituan 懺拜團　"repentance and worship group"—sutra-chanting groups (usually middle-aged women who chant together in temple rituals)

chanhui 懺悔　to do penance; to regret committing a sin

Chanzong 禪宗　Chan Buddhist Sect (called Zen in Japanese)

chaodu 超度　"to seek release from" Purgatory or punishments in the afterlife through proper funerary ritual

chaogong 朝貢　to give tribute to the court; tributary trade between imperial China and its tributary states

chaopiao 鈔票　cash; banknotes

Chenghuangye 城隍爺　City God who protects a walled town

chenghui 呈會　"petition society"—grassroots credit society

chijiu 吃酒　eat at a banquet (with alcoholic beverages)

chujia 出家　"to leave the family"—to enter a monastery and practice celibacy

cibei 慈悲　compassion; Buddhist notion most associated with Bodhisattva Guanyin

cishan 慈善　compassion and charity

citang 祠堂　ancestor hall, where lineage rituals are conducted to offer sacrifices to the ancestors

daochang 道場　Daoist rituals

Daofo heyi 道佛合一　"combining Daoism and Buddhism into one"

daoguan 道觀　Daoist temple

Daojiao Xiehui 道教協會　Daoist Association—a quasi-state, quasi-civil-society organization found at the county or urban district government level

Daozang 《道藏》　*The Daoist Canon*—compilation of Daoist writings through the ages; the latest compilation was by the Ming dynasty court

difangzhi 地方志　local gazetteers—records of local geography, historical personages, buildings, customs and festivals, published by local areas in late imperial China, now revived in China

diyu 地獄　Purgatory, Hell, where the souls of deceased people go in the afterlife, to be judged, sentenced, and punished before rebirth into the next life

diyu yinhang 地獄銀行　Bank of Hell; bank or treasury in the afterlife

Dizang Pusa 地藏菩薩　Bodhisattva Kitsigarbha, who presides over the Underworld

facai 發財　to get rich; to experience sudden wealth

fangsheng 放生　"releasing life" or "releasing wildlife"—Buddhist ritual to release captured wildlife; to practice compassion with nonhuman sentient beings

fangzhang 方丈　abbot or abbess of a Buddhist or Daoist temple or monastery

fei jingji 非經濟　noneconomic

feiwuzhi wenhua yichan 非物質文化遺產　Intangible Cultural Heritage; UNESCO program to designate and protect the world's important cultural heritages

fengshen 封神　to enfeoff or bestow a divine title on a deity, whereby the imperial court incorporates a local deity into the imperial pantheon

fengshui 風水　"wind and water"—Chinese geomancy for siting propitious locations of graves and homes

fengshuishi 風水師　fengshui or geomancy master

fengsu 風俗　local customs; traditional Chinese category that includes ritual, religious, kinship, and festival practices

fenxiang 分香　"dividing incense"—taking incense ash or incense burner from one temple and installing them in another, a process whereby the older temple gives birth to a new temple

fo 佛　Buddha

foshi 佛事　Buddhist rituals

fozhu 佛珠　Buddhist prayer beads

fu 符　Daoist talismanic writing—sacred writing in which the characters do not so much represent a concept or entity as possess a performative function of exerting sacred powers to ritually heal and protect, bestow good fortune, or exorcise demons

ganqing 感情　"emotional feelings" (often associated with kinship bonds)

getihu 個體户　individual enterprise; private or family enterprise

gong 供　to make an offering (to divinities or ancestors)

gongde 功德　merit, good conduct that is often quantified with a point system to ensure a good afterlife

gongjiade 公家的　belonging to the public or the community

gongmin shehui 公民社會　"citizens' society"—a contemporary Chinese term for "civil society"

gongyi 公益　the public good or community benefit

guanfang 官方 official; officialdom; contrasted with *minjian*

guanfang Daojiao 官方道教 "official Daoism"—Daoism that accords with secular state values; shorn of "superstitions" and made compatible with secular nationalism

guanliao 官僚 bureaucracy; bureaucratic

guanxi 關係 social connections involving obligation, reciprocity, and gift-giving

guanxiwang 關係網 social network of obligations and repayment of favors

guci 鼓詞 "drum chant"—Wenzhou ritualized storytelling, usually about the miracles of goddess Mother Chen the Fourteenth

gufen qiye 股份企業 joint-stock enterprise—families combining capital and labor to run larger private enterprises; started in the 1990s

guhun yegui 孤魂野鬼 "orphan souls and wild ghosts"—ghosts who are lonely, without descendants, and resentful and who prey on the living

gui 鬼 ghosts; demons that need to be placated

guijie 鬼節 Ghost Festival, fifteenth day of seventh lunar month, when offerings are made to wandering ghosts

guiyi 皈依 "to seek refuge" in the Three Treasures; to go through a ceremony to become a proper lay Buddhist

Guojia Zongjiao Shiwuju 國家宗教事務局 Bureau of State Administration for Religious Affairs (SARA)—government bureaucracy in Beijing that oversees implementation of Party and state policies on religion

haijin 海禁 Maritime Prohibitions banning private trade with foreigners (during Ming and Qing dynasties)

haiyang wenhua 海洋文化 maritime culture; coastal culture

hongbai xishi 紅白喜事 wedding and funeral rituals

houdai 後代 descendants (in a family or lineage)

huansu 還俗 to leave monastic life and return to a lay person's life

huanyuan 還願 repaying divinities for granting one's requests

huazui 化罪 to dissolve sins through acts of repentance

hui 會 social gathering or association

huihe 回盒 "return gift box"—a proportion of the value of a gift that is given back to the donor; a Wenzhou custom

hukou 戶口 "household registration"—system of state controls over population movement, starting in the 1950s; each person in China is registered legally at birth with the local government; they cannot change their permanent residence without official permission

huobi 貨幣 currency; cash

huoju daoshi 火居道士 "hearthside Daoist priest"—priests who live with their families in local communities and belong to the Orthodox Unity sect

huzhuhui 互助會 mutual aid credit society

jiao 醮 large-scale Daoist communal blessing ceremony

jiaoku 交庫 "depositing in the Bank of Hell" or "delivering to the Divine Storage"—ritual segment in funerals, where spirit money is paid to the Underworld, according to the number of years that the deceased lived

jiating qiye 家庭企業 family enterprise; household industry; family business

jiaxiang 家鄉 native place; hometown

jiazhuang 嫁妝 dowry brought by the bride

jielü 戒律 Buddhist prohibitions and regulations for moral conduct

jieri 節日 lunar calendar festival

jingshu 經書 sutras or scriptures; sacred texts sent down by the gods

Jingtuzong 淨土宗 Pure Land Buddhist Sect or Teachings

jisi 祭祀 to sacrifice (to ancestors); sacrificial ritual

jizi 集資 "accumulating funds"—fund-raising

jushilin 居士林 "forests of reside-at-home lay Buddhists"—modern lay Buddhist societies whose members get together to study scriptures, meditate, and listen to monks' sermons

kaiguang 開光 "opening the light"—ritual dabbing of deity statue's eyes to prepare for the deity to inhabit a new statue

kanpo hongcheng 看破紅塵 "seeing through the red dust"—seeing that life is transitory and filled with suffering, and therefore aspiring to transcendence

langfei 浪費 to waste; to be wasteful

laoban 老闆 a boss, someone who owns and runs his or her own business

laobanniang 老闆娘 a female boss who owns and runs her own business; or wife of a male boss

laorenting 老人亭 Old People's Pavilion, where retired local elders play mah-jongg and watch television

laoren xiehui 老人協會 Old People's Association; voluntary association of retired elders, who help raise funds for building temples or public infrastructure

linggutong 靈姑童 Wenzhou term for shamaness or female spirit medium

lingyan 靈驗 divine efficacy, or the power of gods to grant wishes

lisheng 禮盛 gift containers (made of wood or bamboo, round and multilevel, with lids); also called "gift boxes" 禮盒

liudao lunhui 六道輪回 Six Paths of Reincarnations

liyi jingji 禮儀經濟 "ritual economy"—author's term for an economy of ritual expenditures and services, religious charities, *renqing* gifts and banquets, sacrifices, festivals, and rituals to the gods, ancestors, and ghosts

Longhu Shan 龍虎山 Dragon Tiger Mountain in Jiangxi Province; established as the religious capital of the Daoist Church during the Yuan dynasty

lunhui 輪迴 wheel of transmigration or reincarnation—of birth, suffering, death, and rebirth (Sanskrit: *samsara*)

lunhui 輪會 rotating credit society

Lüshanpai 閭山派 Lu Mountain Sect—Daoist sect in Fujian Province and southern Zhejiang; shamanistic and exorcistic Daoist order believed to be founded by Goddess Mother Chen

luzhu 爐主 "host of the incense burner"—sponsor of ritual or temple festival; term found in Minnanese areas of Cangnan County

Lüzong 律宗 Buddhist Sect of Regulations

manyue 滿月 "full month"—ritual celebration for newborn baby who has reached thirty to forty days

maoyi nicha 貿易逆差　trade imbalance or trade deficit

mianzi 面子　"face"—one's sense of dignity, self-respect, and social standing

miaochan xingxue 廟産興學　"converting temple property into schools"— movement in early twentieth-century China that started the secularization process

miaohui 廟會　temple festival

miaoyü guanli weiyuanhui 廟宇管理委員會　temple managerial committee

ming 命　life or lifetime; predestination; fate

mingbi, mingqian 冥幣, 冥錢　spirit money; paper money burned as offerings for gods, ancestors, and ghosts

minjian 民間　"realm of the people"—of the folk (as contrasted with "realm of officials," *guanfang*)

minjian jizi 民間集資　accumulating funds among the people; grassroots fund-raising

minjian shehui 民間社會　"society of the realm of the people," or "folk society"— another contemporary Chinese term for "civil society"

minjian xinyang 民間信仰　popular beliefs, popular religion

minjian zifa 民間自發　"initiated by the people on their own"—spontaneous bottom-up grassroots initiative

minsu zongjiao 民俗宗教　"folk custom religion"—new term proposed by author to translate the English term "popular religion"

minzu zongjiaoju 民族宗教局　Bureau of Ethnicity and Religion—local government office that overseas Daoist and Buddhist Associations, usually selects their directors

mixin 迷信　superstition (modern Chinese neologism); pejorative term imported from the modern West, referring to folk customs and beliefs that are regarded as "backward" and "ignorant"

neidan 內丹　"inner elixir"—Daoist self-cultivation techniques like meditation, breathing, and yogic exercises

Oujü 甌劇　opera from the region of Ou (Wenzhou)

ouxiang chongbai 偶像崇拜　idolatrous worship; idolatry (usually pejorative)

pingan facaideng 平安發財燈　"peace and wealth lamp"—a lamp that one purchases in a temple to honor the gods and receive good fortune

po sijiu 破四舊　"Smash the Four Olds"—political campaign of the Communist Party from 1966 to 1968 to destroy "Old Customs, Old Culture, Old Habits, and Old Ideas," including religion

pudu 普度　Universal Salvation Festival—Daoist festival held on the fifteenth of the seventh lunar month to save the suffering souls of the deceased

pusa 菩薩　bodhisattvas—those who attain enlightenment but stay in this life to help others

qi 氣　"vital energy" or "primary breath"—in Daoist thought, the primary breath that created the cosmos, flows through the earth, and is found in every newborn baby

qian 籤　thin bamboo divination sticks

qianhui 錢會 money association; grassroots credit society

qianzhai 欠債 to owe a debt

qian zhuang 錢莊 "money shops"—private banks or lenders

qingguan 清官 "clean official"—an honest, uncorrupted official

qinglian 清廉 "clean," especially in the sense of an honest, uncorrupted official

Qingming Jie 清明節 springtime lunar festival when families and lineages go to sweep ancestral tombs and offer food and incense to ancestors

Qitian Dasheng 齊天大聖 Great Sage Who Equals Heaven (Monkey King god)

qiushen 求神 to beg or pray to the gods for help

Quanzhenpai 全真派 Complete Perfection Sect of Daoism, founded in Yuan dynasty, practiced more in northern China; its priests and nuns live in monasteries and practice sexual abstinence

quguixie 驅鬼邪 exorcising demons and evil spirits from a local area or from the human body

renjian fojiao 人間佛教 humanistic this-worldly Buddhism—modern Buddhist movement that pays more attention to the world we live in and its social problems

renqing 人情 "human feelings"—gifts given and received between people, families, and associations

San Bao 三寶 "Three Treasures" of Buddhism—the Buddha, the Dharma (Buddhist teachings), and the Sangha (clergy)

sangai yichai 三改一拆 "Three Reforms and One Demolition"—state campaign in Zhejiang Province to demolish small unregistered temples or Christian churches, 2013–2016

Sanguan Dadi 三官大帝 "Three Officials and Great Emperors"—ancient Daoist gods: Heaven Official, Earth Official, and Water Official; still worshipped today

Sanjiao 三教 "Three Teachings" of Daoism, Buddhism, and Confucianism

Sanjiao heyi 三教合一 "Three Teachings Combining into One"

Sanjie 三界 "Three Worlds"—Upper, Middle, and Lower Worlds; can refer to three rankings of gods in the Daoist tradition, or to three realms of beings: Heaven (realm of gods), Earth (realm of humanity), and Hell (the Yin World of souls)

Sanqing 三清 "Three Purities"—highest gods of the Daoist pantheon, tracing back to natural forces in the origins of the cosmos: Lord of the Primal Origin and Jade Purity (玉清原始天尊); Lord of the Numinous Treasure and High Purity (上清靈寶天尊); and Lord Laozi of Great Purity (太清道德天尊)

shamen 沙門 "Buddhist monastic community" (Sanskrit: *sangha*)

shami 沙彌 young Buddhist novice, not yet ordained

Shanghui 商會 chamber of commerce

shangjiao 上繳 "delivering payments upward"—the monthly fees that temples must pay to the Daoist or Buddhist Association

shashen 煞神 baleful spirit; fearsome god who punishes humans

shehui 社會 modern term for "society"; from ancient term for "ritual association to honor the earth god"

sheji 社稷 "altar for the worship of the spirits of Earth/Soil and Grain"—traces back to ancient times, but was a state-imposed early Ming dynasty cult

shejishen 社稷神　Earth and Grain Gods worshipped since ancient times

sheli 舍利　"sacred relics"—translucent beads left behind after a revered Buddhist monk or Buddha is cremated

shen 神　deity, god, goddess, spirit

shenmiao 神廟　deity temple, associated with Chinese popular religion

shentong 神僮　shaman or spirit medium or ritual healer

shi 氏　"clan"—larger in membership and less genealogically precise than a lineage, but smaller than a surname association

shibei 石碑　stone stelae; used to commemorate the establishment or restoration of a ritual site, to present a brief hagiography of the god, and to record major donors

Shida Dianwang 十大殿王　Ten Great Judges of Purgatory

Shijiamunifo 釋迦穆尼佛　Buddha Sakyamuni

shimin shehui 市民社會　"city people's society"—a contemporary Chinese term for "civil society"

siyouhua 私有化　economic privatization

siyouzhi 私有制　system of private ownership

songli 送禮　to give gifts

song renqing 送人情　to give "human feelings" or gifts, especially at life-cycle rituals

suangua 算卦　divination by the eight trigrams

suanming 算命　fortune-telling; divination

Sunan moshi 蘇南模式　"Sunan Model" of rural economic development in Jiangsu Province, based on village- and township-owned enterprises

taihui 抬會　"elevation society"—grassroots credit society that engages in risky speculative pyramid schemes

taiji quan 太極拳　a system of exercise with flowing motions of the body in tune with the breath; associated with Daoist practice

Taipingjing 《太平經》　*Scripture of the Great Peace;* second-century CE Daoist millenarian sacred text that preached the coming of an era of "Great Peace" and egalitarian society

Taishang Laojün 太上老君　Lord Lao, the Daoist god who is the apotheosis of Laozi

tiangan dizhi 天干地枝　"Heavenly Stems and Earthly Branches"—ancient Chinese calendrical system

Tianshidao 天師道　Celestial Masters tradition of Daoism

Tiantaizong 天台宗　Tiantai Buddhist Sect

tiaotongshen 跳僮身　to be possessed by a god or demon; to dance while the body is possessed or in trance

tongshen 僮身　"servant-body"—Wenzhou term for shaman or spirit medium

Tongzhanbu 統戰部　United Front Office of the Chinese Communist Party; local branches at county and municipal levels

toudeng 頭燈　"first candle" in a temple—whoever lights the first candle of the New Year is said to have good luck

Tudigong 土地公　Earth God

Tudi niangniang 土地娘娘　Earth Goddess; Earth Mother

waidan 外丹 "outer elixir"—Daoist self-cultivation practices that include ingesting substances from outside the body: herbs and chemical compounds roasted or boiled on stoves

Weixin 微信 WeChat; popular messaging, social media, and payment app for cell phones in China

Wenchangye 文昌爺 God of Literature; Daoist god who can help worshippers excel in examinations

wenhua yiliu 文化遺留 "cultural remnants" of traditional society (usually pejorative, implying "backwardness")

Wenzhou moshi 溫州模式 the Wenzhou Model of rural economic development, based on private household enterprises

Wokou 倭寇 "Japanese dwarf pirates" who raided the eastern China coast in the Ming and Qing dynasties (many were actually Chinese)

wu 巫 spirit medium or shaman; shamanism

wudao 悟道 to intuit, to gain enlightenment (in Daoist and Buddhist traditions); also *kaiwu* 開悟 and *juewu* 覺悟

Wudoumidao 五斗米道 "Five Pecks of Rice"—Daoist religious movement, also called Celestial Masters, of the second century CE whose followers contributed a tithe of five pecks of rice

wushenglun 無神論 atheist; atheism

wuwei 無為 "nonaction"—Daoist notion that the best governance is through nonintervention, eschewing force, and following what seems natural

wuxing 五行 "Five Elements"—the basic physical components of matter that made up the ancient Chinese universe: water, fire, metal/gold, wood, and earth; invocations of these elements are part of Daoist rituals and fengshui

xian 仙 Daoist immortals—ethical persons who have engaged in self-cultivation, becoming light and divine beings

xiangan 香案 incense and food offering tables

xianghuo hensheng 香火很盛 "incense fire is very strong"—when people flock to a popular temple to burn incense to the gods

xiao 孝 filial piety; showing affection and care for parents and elders

Xifang jile shijie 西方極樂世界 "The Western Paradise"—Pure Land Buddhist notion of the wonderful afterlife that rewards those who cultivate themselves and engage in moral conduct

xinggen 行根 "to continue the root"—to carry the descent line in a lineage, which, in a patrilineal society, is the right of men

xingshizhi 姓氏志 surname and clan local gazetteers

xinsu 信俗 "customary belief"—recent Chinese neologism to translate the notion of "popular religion"

xiuchi fojiao 修持佛教 "self-cultivation Buddhism"—emphasizes scriptural studies, Buddhist doctrines, and meditational practices

xiulian 修練 practicing self-cultivation: meditation, chanting of scriptures, physical and breathing exercises; also *xiuxing* 修行 and *xiusheng* 修身

xiusheng liandan 修身練丹 "cultivating one's body and exercising one's 'cinnabar fields'"—Daoist practice of self-cultivation, meditation, and exercise of qi around the body's energy fields

xungeng lianzong 尋根聯宗 "searching for roots and connecting the lineage"—lineages looking for long-lost kin, reconnecting with missing lineage branches

xuyuan 許願 requesting divine assistance, with a promise to repay the deity

yaomo guiguai 妖魔鬼怪 monsters and demons

ye heshang 野和尚 "wild monks"—Buddhist monks who are not properly ordained, are secretly married with children, or eat meat

yigong 益工 volunteered labor

yinguo baoying 因果報應 "cause-and-effect repayment and response"—(Sanskrit: *karma*); also *yinyuan* 因緣

yinjie 陰界 the Underworld, where the souls of the deceased go

yinju 隱居 to practice seclusion from the temporal world in Daoist and Buddhist traditions

yishi xingtai 意識形態 "official ideology"—what all citizens are supposed to adhere to and study, in line with Communist Party leadership

yiwu laodong 義務勞動 voluntary labor

yuanshi jilei 原始積累 "primitive accumulation"—gathering start-up capital

yuhuang dadi 玉皇大帝 Jade Emperor, highest god in the pantheon of popular religion; also a high-ranking Daoist god

Yulanpeng jie 孟蘭盆節 "Ullambana Festival"—Buddhist festival celebrated on fifteenth day of seventh lunar month; people make offerings to monastics to get their ancestors' sins absolved

yümei 愚昧 ignorant

zanzhu 贊助 to support financially; to sponsor an event or project with donations

zhai 債 debt, often thought to be the product of sin; must be repaid before death

Zhang Daoling 張道陵 founder of religious Daoist tradition in the second century CE in Sichuan

Zhengyipai 正一派 Orthodox Unity Sect of Daoism, prevalent in southern China; it descends from the original Celestial Masters movement of the second century CE; priests can marry and have families, live in local communities

Zhengzhi yundong 政治運動 political campaign coordinated by the Chinese Communist Party

zhongtang 中堂 "central hall"—the central point of each home, marked by a low wooden pole, which is the residence of the guardian Earth God

Zhongyuan pudu 中元普渡 "Mid-primordial Universal Salvation Festival"—Daoist festival which takes place on fifteenth of seventh lunar month and in which worshippers ask Earth Official to descend to Earth to absolve the sins of ghosts

zhuan 傳 written hagiography of a god or biography of a human

zhuchi 主持 religious leader or abbot or abbess of a temple or monastery; head priest who presides at a ritual

Zhujiang sanjiaozhou moshi 珠江三角洲模式 "Zhu River Triangle Area Model" of industrialization in Guangdong Province based on foreign and overseas Chinese direct investment and joint ventures

ziran 自然 "self-so"—that which is a certain way on its own, without human intervention or artifice; often translated as "natural"

zixiu chengfo 自修成佛 to engage in self-cultivation to become a Buddha

zongjiao 宗教 religion (modern Chinese neologism)

zongshoushi 總首事 lineage manager, person in charge of day-to-day lineage or temple affairs

zongzu 宗族 lineage, kinship, and descent group tracing patrilineal ancestry and genealogy back many generations

zui 罪 sin—both Buddhist and Daoist notion

zumiao 祖廟 ancestral temple; usually the oldest or highest-ranking temple in an interconnected hierarchical network of temples sharing the same deity cult

zuzhang 族長 lineage head

Agamben, Giorgio. 1998. *Homo Sacer: Sovereign Power and Bare Life*. Translated by Daniel Heller-Roazen. Stanford, CA: Stanford University Press.

Ahern, Emily. 1975. "The Power and Pollution of Chinese Women." In *Women in Chinese Society*, edited by Margery Wolf and Roxanne Witke, 193-214. Stanford, CA: Stanford University Press.

Ai Lan 愛瀾著. 2013. "玉蒼之南有遺韻： 訪道教正一派科儀音樂代表性傳承人梁月生" [Interview with Orthodox Unity Daoist Master Liang Yuesheng]. In 《浙江民族與宗教,》第二期, no. 2, 27-30.

Allio, Fiorella. 2003. *Spatial Organization in a Ritual Context: A Preliminary Analysis of the Koah-hiu Processional System of the Tainan Country Region and Its Social Significance.* Taipei: Institute of Ethnology, Academia Sinica.

Anonymous. 1992. "溫州市經貿代表團過洛" [Wenzhou trade and commerce delegation passes through Los Angeles]. In 《世界日報,》August 21, C1.

Anonymous. 2009. "溫州佛教史" [The history of Buddhism in Wenzhou]. In 《溫州佛教》. 第一期, no. 1: 64-66.

Anonymous. 2011. "怎對溫州老闆跑路潮和中小企老闆自殺風波？" In 《騰訊評論》. http://view.news.qq.com/a/20111014/000014.htm.

Arato, Andrew. 1981. "Civil Society against the State: Poland 1980-81." *Telos*, no. 47: 23-47.

Asad, Talal. 1993. "The Construction of Religion as an Anthropological Category." In *Genealogies of Religion: Discipline and Reasons of Power in Christianity and Islam*, 55-79. Baltimore: Johns Hopkins University Press.

Austin, J. L. 1962. *How to Do Things with Words: The William James Lectures Delivered at Harvard University*. Edited by J. O. Urmson and Marina Sbisà. Oxford: Clarendon.

Avishai, Orit. 2008. "'Doing Religion' in a Secular World: Women in Conservative Religions and the Question of Agency." *Gender and Society* 22, no. 4: 409-433.

Ba Jin 巴金著. (1933) 1982. 《家》[Family]. 成都： 四川人民出版社.

Baptandier, Brigitte. 2008. *The Lady of Linshui: A Chinese Female Cult*. Translated by Kristin I. Fryklund. Stanford, CA: Stanford University Press.

Bataille, Georges. (1947) 1991. *The Accursed Share: An Essay on General Economy*. Vol. 1. Translated by Robert Hurley. New York: Zone.

Bataille, Georges. 1985. "The Notion of Expenditure." In *Visions of Excess: Selected Writings, 1927-39*, edited and translated by Allan Stoekl, 116-129. Minneapolis: University of Minnesota Press.

Bataille, Georges. 1989. *Theory of Religion*. Translated by Robert Hurley. New York: Zone.

Billioud, Sebastien, and Joel Thoraval. 2015. *The Sage and the People: The Confucian Revival in China*. Oxford: Oxford University Press.

Bobbio, Norberto. 1988. "Gramsci and the Concept of Civil Society." In *Civil Society and the State: New European Perspectives*, edited by John Keane, 73–100. London: Verso.

Bol, Peter. 2001. "The Rise of Local History: History, Geography, and Culture in Southern Song and Yuan Wuzhou." *Harvard Journal of Asiatic Studies* 61, no. 1: 37–76.

Bol, Peter. 2003. "The 'Localist Turn' and 'Local Identity' in Later Imperial China." *Late Imperial China* 24, no. 2 (December): 1–50.

Bourdieu, Pierre. 1977. *Outline of a Theory of Practice*. Translated by Richard Nice. Cambridge: Cambridge University Press.

Bradsher, Keith. 2013. "Easy Credit Dries Up, Choking Growth in China." *New York Times,* August 15.

Brokaw, Cynthia J. 1991. *The Ledgers of Merit and Demerit: Social Change and Moral Order in Late Imperial China*. Princeton, NJ: Princeton University Press.

Brook, Timothy. 1993. "Rethinking Syncretism: The Unity of the Three Teachings and Their Joint Worship in Late-Imperial China." *Journal of Chinese Religions* 21 (Fall): 13–44.

Burke, Kelsey C. 2012. "Women's Agency in Gender-Traditional Religions: A Review of Four Approaches." *Sociology Compass* 6, no. 2: 122–133.

Buswell, Robert E., and Donald S. Lopez, eds. 2014. *The Princeton Dictionary of Buddhism*. Princeton, NJ: Princeton University Press.

Cai Kejiao 蔡克驕著. 1998. 《甌越文化史》 [A cultural history of Ouyue]. 北京: 作家出版社.

Cai Yu 蔡榆著. 2011. "探秘楊府爺" [Exploring the cult of Lord Yang]. In 《溫州日報》. 七月六, 十三日 (上下).

Cao Guoxin 曹國星著. 2011. "俞可平回應周本順: '應鼓勵、支持公民社會發展'" [Yu Keping responds to Zhou Benshun: "We should encourage the development of civil society"]. In 《360 doc》. http://www.360doc.com/content/11/0616/17/6441751_127410217.shtml.

Cao Linyun and Wang, Zhang 曹凌雲, 王璋, 主編. 2009. 《永昌堡建堡 450 週年紀念專輯》. Special Issue Commemorating the 450th Anniversary of the Establishment of Yong Chang Fortress. 《大羅山: 夏卷》 Great Luo Mountains (Summer Issue). 溫州市龍灣 區永昌堡文化研究會. Wenzhou City Longwan District Yongchang Fortress Cultural Studies Association.

Cao, Nanlai. 2011. *Constructing China's Jerusalem: Christians, Power, and Place in Contemporary Wenzhou*. Stanford, CA: Stanford University Press.

Cao, Nanlai. 2013. "Renegotiating Locality and Morality in a Chinese Religious Diaspora: Wenzhou Christian Merchants in Paris, France." *Asia Pacific Journal of Anthropology* 14, no. 1: 85–101.

Carlitz, Katherine. 1994. "Desire, Danger, and the Body: Stories of Women's Virtue in Late Ming China." In *Engendering China: Women, Culture, and the State*, 101–124. Cambridge, MA: Harvard University Press.

Casanova, José. 1994. *Public Religions in the Modern World*. Chicago: University of Chicago Press.

Central Chinese Television (CCTV) 中央電視台. 2000. "荒唐的經營" ("An Absurd Economy") in 《焦點訪談》 (*Focus Interviews*). 北京 Beijing.

Chakrabarty, Dipesh. 2000. *Provincializing Europe: Postcolonial Thought and Historical Difference*. Princeton, NJ: Princeton University Press.

Chang, Kwang-chih. 1983. *Art, Myth, and Ritual: The Path to Political Authority in Ancient China*. Cambridge, MA: Harvard University Press.

Chao Zhongchen 晁中辰著. 2005. 《明代海禁與海外貿易》 [The Maritime Prohibitions and overseas trade during the Ming dynasty]. 北京： 人民出版社.

Chatterjee, Partha. 1993. *The Nation and Its Fragments: Colonial and Postcolonial Histories*. Princeton, NJ: Princeton University Press.

Chau, Adam Yuet. 2006. *Miraculous Response: Doing Popular Religion in Contemporary China*. Stanford, CA: Stanford University Press.

Chen Baoliang 陳寶良著. 2011. 《中國的社與會》. [China's "she" and "hui"]. 北京: 人民大學出版社.

Chen Duxiu 陳獨秀著. 1918. "偶像破壞論" [On the smashing of idols]. In 《新青年》, 第五卷, 第二號.

Chen Guocan and Xi Jianhua 陳國燦, 席建華 著. 2003. 《浙江古代城鎮史》 [The history of ancient towns in Zhejiang]. 合肥: 安徽大學出版社.

Chen Huangeng 陳煥庚著. 2010. "溫州的鎮壓反革命運動" [The movement to suppress counter-revolutionaries in Wenzhou]. In 《溫州六十年》. 李丁富主編. 溫州： 中共溫州市委黨史研究室出版.

Ch'en, Kenneth. 1964. *Buddhism in China: A Historical Survey*. Princeton, NJ: Princeton University Press.

Chen, Ningning. 2016. "Governing Rural Culture: Agency, Space and the Reproduction of Ancestral Temples in Contemporary China." *Journal of Rural Studies* 47: 141–152.

Chen Qiu 陳秋著. 2014. 《屋理與屋外： 溫州農村女性民俗生活及其主體性建構》 [Inside and outside the house: Folk customs, rural women's lives, women's agency in Wenzhou]. 中央民族大學博士論文.

Chen Xiaoming and Zhang Xudong 陳曉明，張旭東編輯. 2010. 《永昌堡： 建堡 450 週年特刊》 [Yongchang Fortress: 450th anniversary of its construction]. n.p.

Chen Xiren 陳錫仁著. 2010. "'文革'初期溫州市區的破四舊和文物搶救" ["Destroy the Four Olds" and the saving of antiquities during the Cultural Revolution in Wenzhou]. In 《溫州六十年》. 李丁富主編. 溫州： 中共溫州市委黨史研究室出版.

Chu, Julie Y. 2010. *Cosmologies of Credit: Transnational Mobility and the Politics of Destination in China*. Durham, NC: Duke University Press.

Clart, Philip. 2014. "Conceptualizations of 'Popular Religion' in Recent Research in the People's Republic of China." In 《研究新視界： 媽祖與華人民間信仰國際研討會論文集》 [*Studying from New Perspectives: Conference Volume on Mazu and Chinese Popular Religion*], edited by Wang Chien-chuan, Li Shiwei, and Hong Yingfa, 391–412. Taipei: Boyang Wenhua.

Clastres, Pierre. 1987. *Society against the State*. Translated by Robert Hurley. New York: Zone.

Comaroff, John, and Jean Comaroff. 1997. *Of Revelation and Revolution: The Dialectics of Modernity on a South African Frontier*. Vols. 1 and 2. Chicago: University of Chicago Press.

Comaroff, John, and Jean Comaroff. 1999. "Introduction." In *Civil Society and the Political Imagination in Africa: Critical Perspectives*, edited by John Comaroff and Jean Comaroff, 1–43. Chicago: University of Chicago Press.

Croll, Elisabeth. 1985. *Women and Rural Development in China: Production and Reproduction*. Geneva: International Labour Office.

Dean, Kenneth. 1993. *Taoist Ritual and Popular Cults of Southeast China*. Princeton, NJ: Princeton University Press.

Dean, Kenneth. 1997. "Popular Religion or Civil Society: Disruptive Communities and Alternative Conceptions." In *Civil Society in China*, edited by Timothy Brook and B. Frolic, 172–195. Boulder, CO: Westview.

Dean, Kenneth. 2010. "Part I: The Gods Return." In *Ritual Alliances of the Putian Plain*. Vol. 1, *Historical Introduction to the Return of the Gods*, 3–282. Leiden: Brill.

Dean, Kenneth, dir. 2011. *Bored in Heaven*. 《天堂無聊》. Documentary.

DeBernardi, Jean. 2006. *The Way That Lives in the Heart: Chinese Popular Religion and Spirit Mediums in Penang, Malaysia*. Stanford, CA: Stanford University Press.

Deleuze, Gilles. 1994. *Difference and Repetition*. Translated by Paul Patton. New York: Columbia University Press.

Deleuze, Gilles, and Félix Guattari. 1987. *A Thousand Plateaus: Capitalism and Schizophrenia*. Translated by Brian Massumi. Minneapolis: University of Minnesota Press.

Deng Zhenglai and Jing Yuejin 鄧正來, 景躍進著. (1992) 2008. "建構中國的市民社會" [Constructing Chinese civil society]. In 《國家與社會：中國市民社會研究》. 北京：北京大學出版社.

Duara, Prasenjit. 1988. *Culture, Power, and the State: Rural North China, 1900–1942*. Stanford, CA: Stanford University Press.

Duara, Prasenjit. 1991. "Knowledge and Power in the Discourse of Modernity: The Campaigns against Popular Religion in Early Twentieth-Century China." *Journal of Asian Studies* 50, no. 1: 67–83.

Duara, Prasenjit. 1995. "Linear History and Nation-State." In *Rescuing History from the Nation: Questioning Narratives of Modern China*, 17–50. Chicago: University of Chicago Press.

Duara, Prasenjit. 2015. *The Crisis of Global Modernity: Asian Traditions and a Sustainable Future*. Cambridge: Cambridge University Press.

Durkheim, Émile. (1912) 1995. *Elementary Forms of Religious Life*. Translated by Karen E. Fields. New York: Free Press.

Ebrey, Patricia. 1986. "The Early Stages in the Development of Descent Group Organization." In *Kinship Organization in Late Imperial China, 1000–1940*, edited by Patricia Ebrey and James L. Watson, 16–61. Berkeley: University of California Press.

Ebrey, Patricia. 1991. *Confucianism and Family Rituals in Imperial China: A Social History of Writing about Rites*. Princeton, NJ: Princeton University Press.

Eliade, Mircea. 1989. *Shamanism: Archaic Techniques of Ecstasy*. Translated by Willard R. Trask. London: Penguin Arkana.

Fan Enjun, Zhang Xingfa, and Liu Jun 范恩君, 張興發, 劉軍, 編著. 1996. 《道教神仙》 [Daoist gods and immortals]. 北京：中國道教學院.

Fan, Lizhu, and Na Chen. 2016. "The Revival and Development of Popular Religion in China." In *Modern Chinese Religion II, 1850-2015*, vol. 1, edited by Vincent Goossaert, Jan Kiely, and John Lagerwey, 923-948. Leiden: Brill.

Fang Zhou 方舟著. 2012. "它是浙南民間影響最大的本土信俗—千年楊府爺" [Southern Zhejiang's most influential deity cult—a thousand years of Lord Yang]. In 《溫州日報》, August 26, 1.

Faure, Bernard. 2003. *The Power of Denial: Buddhism, Purity, and Gender*. Princeton, NJ: Princeton University Press.

Fava, Patrice, dir. 2005. *Han Xin's Revenge*. Produced by École francaise d'Extrême-Orient.

Fei Xiaotong 費孝通著. 1992. "溫州行" [Journey through Wenzhou]. In 《行行, 重行行—鄉鎮發展論述》. 費孝通主編. 潁川: 寧夏人民出版社.

Fei Xiaotong 費孝通著. 1997. "家地勢, 創新業—再訪溫州" [With family as the base, establishing new enterprises]. In 《行行, 重行行—續集》. 費孝通主編. 北京: 群言出版社.

Feuchtwang, Stephan. 2001. *Popular Religion in China: The Imperial Metaphor*. Richmond, UK: Curzon.

Fisher, Gareth. 2014. *From Comrades to Bodhisattvas: Moral Dimensions of Lay Buddhist Practice in Contemporary China*. Honolulu: University of Hawai'i Press.

Foucault, Michel. 1979. *Discipline and Punish: The Birth of the Prison*. Translated by Alan Sheridan. New York: Vintage.

Foucault, Michel. 1991. "Governmentality." In *The Foucault Effect: Studies in Governmentality*, edited by Graham Burchell, Colin Gordon, and Peter Miller, 87-104. Chicago: University of Chicago Press.

Freedman, Maurice. 1958. *Lineage Organization in Southeastern China*. London: Athlone.

Freedman, Maurice. 1966. *Chinese Lineage and Society: Fukien and Kwantung*. London: Athlone.

Freedman, Maurice. 1979. "The Handling of Money: A Note on the Background to the Economic Sophistication of Overseas Chinese." In *The Study of Chinese Society: Essays by Maurice Freedman*, edited by William F. Skinner, 22-26. Stanford, CA: Stanford University Press.

Friedman, Sara L. 2006. *Intimate Politics: Marriage, the Markey, and State Power in Southeastern China*. Cambridge, MA: Harvard University Press.

Gao Bingzhong 高丙中著. 2008. 《民間文化與公民社會》 [Folk culture and civil society]. 北京: 北京大學出版社.

Gates, Hill. 1987. "Money for the Gods." *Modern China* 13, no. 3 (July): 259-277.

Gates, Hill. 1996. *China's Motor: A Thousand Years of Petty Capitalism*. Ithaca, NY: Cornell University Press.

Gernet, Jacques. 1985. *A History of Chinese Civilization*. Cambridge: Cambridge University Press.

Gibson-Graham, J. K. 1996. *The End of Capitalism (as We Knew It): A Feminist Critique of Political Economy*. London: Blackwell.

Giddens, Anthony. 1976. *New Rules of Sociological Method*. New York: Harper and Row.

Giddens, Anthony. 1979. *Central Problems in Social Theory*. Berkeley: University of California Press.

Giddens, Anthony. 1984. *The Constitution of Society*. Berkeley: University of California Press.

Goossaert, Vincent. 2008. "Irrepressible Female Piety: Late Imperial Bans on Women Visiting Temples." *Nan Nü* 10, no. 2: 212–241.

Goossaert, Vincent, and David A. Palmer. 2011. *The Religious Question in Modern China*. Chicago: University of Chicago Press.

Greenhalgh, Susan, and Edwin Winckler. 2005. *Governing China's Population: From Leninist to Neoliberal Biopolitics*. Stanford, CA: Stanford University Press.

Guanghua, Fashi 廣化法師. n.d. "素食的利益" [The benefits of vegetarianism]. In 《放生功德甘露妙雨》 [The merits of "releasing life" are like the drops of rain]. 索达吉堪布著. 莆田：福建莆田廣化寺印.

Guowuyuan 國務院. 2005. 《關於加強文化遺產保護的通知》 [Instructions on strengthening the protection of cultural heritage]. http://baike.baidu.com/view /3290811.htm.

Guowuyuan Zongjiao Shiwuju 國務院宗教事務局. 1980. 《關於落實宗教團體房產政策等問題的報告》 [Report on problems in implementing the policy of religious properties]. 北京：中國法制出版社.

Guowuyuan Zongjiao Shiwuju 國務院宗教事務局. 1994a. 《宗教活動場所管理條例》 [Regulations on the administration of sites of religious activities]. 國務院 145 號文件. 北京：中國法制出版社.

Guowuyuan Zongjiao Shiwuju 國務院宗教事務局. 1994b. 《關於製止建佛道教寺觀的通知》 [Communiqué on stopping the construction of Buddhist and Daoist temples]. www.law110.com/law/zongjiao/27002.htm.

Guowuyuan Zongjiao Shiwuju 國務院宗教事務局. 2004. 《宗教事務條例》 [Regulations on religious affairs]. 國務院426 號文件. http://www.sara.gov.cn/zcfg/xzfg/531.htm.

Habermas, Jürgen. 1989. *The Structural Transformation of the Public Sphere*. Cambridge, MA: MIT Press.

Habermas, Jürgen. 2008. "Secularism's Crisis of Faith: Notes on Post-secularist Society." *New Perspectives Quarterly* 25: 17–29.

Hankiss, Elemer. 1988. "The 'Second Society': Is There an Alternative Social Model Emerging in Contemporary Hungary?" *Social Research* 55, no. 1: 13–42.

Hann, Chris, and Elizabeth Dunn. 1996. *Civil Society: Challenging Western Models*. Oxford: Routledge.

Hansen, Valerie. 1990. *Changing Gods in Medieval China, 1127–1276*. Princeton, NJ: Princeton University Press.

Hardacre, Helen. 1989. *Shinto and the State, 1868–1988*. Princeton, NJ: Princeton University Press.

Hendrischke, Barbara, trans. 2006. *The Scripture on Great Peace: The Taiping Jing and the Beginnings of Daoism*. Berkeley: University of California Press.

Hershatter, Gail. 2014. *The Gender of Memory: Rural Women and China's Collective Past*. Berkeley: University of California Press.

Hirschman, Albert O. 1970. *Exit, Voice, and Loyalty: Responses to Decline in Firms, Organizations, and States.* Cambridge, MA: Harvard University Press.

Horn, Ivan. n.d. "Max Weber, Confucianism, and Modern Capitalism." www.academia.edu/7792004/Max_Weber_Confucianism_and_Modern_Capitalism (accessed June 2, 2016).

Hoskins, Janet. 2015. *The Divine Eye and the Diaspora: Vietnamese Syncretism Becomes Transpacific Caodaism.* Honolulu: University of Hawai'i Press.

Hou Ching-lang 侯錦郎著. 1975. *Monnaies d'offrande et la notion de trésorerie dans la religion chinoise.* Paris: Collège de France, Institut des Hautes Études Chinoises.

Hu Zhusheng 胡珠生著. 2000. 《溫州近代史》 [Modern Wenzhou history]. 沈陽: 遼寧人民出版社.

Huang, Julia C. 2009. *Charisma and Compassion: Cheng Yen and the Buddhist Tzu Chi Movement.* Cambridge, MA: Harvard University Press.

Huang, Philip C. C. 1993. "'Public Sphere' and 'Civil Society' in China? The Third Realm between State and Society." *Modern China* 19, no. 2: 216–240.

Huang Xiuqing 黃秀清主編, ed. 2011. 《龍灣民俗》 [Longwan folk customs]. 北京: 中國炎黃文化出版社.

Huangcheng Muyang 皇城牧羊著. 2015. "說公民社會是陷阱，周本順落入了誰的陷阱?" [If civil society is a trap, whose trap has Zhou Benshun fallen into?]. In 《皇城牧羊的博客》, http://blog.sina.com.cn/s/blog_593a902c0102vuvb.html.

Hubert, Henri, and Marcel Mauss. 1964. *Sacrifice: Its Nature and Functions.* Translated by W. D. Halls. Chicago: University of Chicago Press.

Hurvitz, Leon, trans. 2009. *Scripture of the Lotus Blossom of the Fine Dharma.* New York: Columbia University Press.

Ji Zhe, Daniela Campos, and Wang Qiyuan 汲喆, 田水晶, 王启元, 編著. 2016. 《二十世紀中國佛教的兩次復興》 [*The two Buddhist revivals in twentieth-century China*]. 上海: 復旦大學出版社.

Jin Bodong 金柏東著. 2009. "《現存最早活字印刷品的發現和研究》" [The discovery and study of the oldest extant movable-type printed text]. In 《溫州文物論集》. 杭州: 浙江人民出版社.

Jin Ze 金澤著. 2008. "關於'轉型時期民間信仰的地位與作用'的幾點認識" [The status and function of popular religion during the Transitional Period]. In 《漢學研究與中國社會科學的推進國際研討會論文集: 民俗文化與鄉村社會》, 杭州市.

Jinxiang Chenghuangmiao Bianji Weiyuanhui 金鄉城隍廟編輯委員會, ed. 2007. 《金鄉城隍廟》 [Jinxiang City God Temple]. 金鄉鎮非物質文化遺產保護辦公室出版.

Johnson, Ian. 2014. "Church-State Clash in China Coalesces around a Toppled Spire." *New York Times,* May 29.

Johnson, Ian. 2017. *The Souls of China: The Return of Religion after Mao.* New York: Pantheon.

Johnson, Kay Ann. 1983. *Women, the Family and Peasant Revolution in China.* Chicago: University of Chicago Press.

Kaltenmark, Max. 1979. "The Ideology of the T'ai-p'ing Ching." In *Facets of Taoism: Essays in Chinese Religion,* edited by Holmes Welch and Anna Seidel, 19–52. New Haven, CT: Yale University Press.

Kang Xiaofei. 2009. "Rural Women, Old Age, and Temple Work." *China Perspectives* 4: 42–52.

Kang Xiaofei. 2016. "Women and the Religious Question in Modern China." In *Modern Chinese Religion II, 1850-2015*, vol. 1, edited by Vincent Goossaert, Jan Kiely, and John Lagerwey, 491–559. Leiden: Brill.

Karlstrom, Mikael. 1997. "Civil Society and Its Presuppositions: Lessons from Uganda." In *Civil Society and the Political Imagination in Africa: Critical Perspectives*, edited by John Comaroff and Jean Comaroff, 104-123. Chicago: University of Chicago Press.

Katz, Paul R. 1995. *Demon Hordes and Burning Boats: The Cult of Marshal Wen in Late Imperial Chekiang*. Albany: State University of New York Press.

Keane, John, ed. 1988a. *Civil Society and the State: New European Perspectives*. London: Verso.

Keane, John. 1988b. "Despotism and Democracy." In *Civil Society and the State: New European Perspectives*, edited by John Keane, 35–72. London: Verso.

Keane, Webb. 2007. *Christian Moderns: Freedom and Fetish in the Mission Encounter*. Berkeley: University of California Press.

Kleeman, Terry F. 1994. *A God's Own Tale: The Book of Transformations of Wenchang, the Divine Lord of Zitong*. Albany: State University of New York Press.

Kleeman, Terry F. 2016. *Celestial Masters: History and Ritual in Early Daoist Communities*. Cambridge, MA: Harvard University Press.

Kohn, Livia. 1993. "Koshin: A Daoist Cult in Japan. Part I: Contemporary Practices." *Japanese Religions* 18: 113-139.

Kohn, Livia. 1995a. "Koshin: A Daoist Cult in Japan. Part II: Historical Development." *Japanese Religions* 20, no. 1: 34–55.

Kohn, Livia. 1995b. "Koshin: A Daoist Cult in Japan. Part III: The Scripture." *Japanese Religions* 20, no. 2: 123-142.

Kohn, Livia. 2009. *Introducing Daoism*. New York: Routledge.

Kong Linghong 孔令宏著. 2008. "浙江道教史發凡" [The development and history of Daoism in Zhejiang]. In 《天台山暨浙江區域道教—國際學術研討會論文集》. 連曉鳴, 孔令宏編. 杭州: 浙江古籍出版社.

Lagerwey, John. 1987. *Taoist Ritual in Chinese Society and History*. London: Collier Macmillan.

Lagerwey, John. 1999. "Questions of Vocabulary or How Shall We Talk about Chinese Religion?" In 《道教與民間宗教研究論集》 (*Studies of Taoism and Popular Religion*), edited by Lai Chi Tim, 165-181. Hong Kong: Xuefeng Wenhua.

Lao Dayü 勞大與著. n.d. 《甌江逸志》 [Leisurely trip down the Ou River]. 嚴一萍選輯. 台北: 藝文印書館 (乾隆： Qing Dynasty facsimile).

Latour, Bruno. 1993. *We Have Never Been Modern*. Translated by Catherine Porter. Cambridge, MA: Harvard University Press.

LeClair, Edward E., and Harold K. Schneider, eds. 1968. *Economic Anthropology: Readings in Theory and Analysis*. New York: Holt, Rinehart and Winston.

Lee, Richard C. Y., Alan K. L. Chan, and Timothy Y. H. Tsu 李焯然, 陳金樑, 祖運輝, 著. 1994. 《道教簡述》 [*Taoism: outlines of a Chinese religious tradition*]. 新加坡道教總會 Singapore: Taoist Federation.

Lefebvre, Henri. 1991. *The Production of Space*. Translated by Donald Nicholson-Smith. Oxford: Blackwell.

Lewis, Ivan Myrddin. (1971) 2003. *Ecstatic Religion: A Study of Shamanism and Spirit Possession*. 3rd ed. London: Routledge.

Li Ji Jinzhu Jinyi. 《禮記今註今譯》. 1987. 王夢鷗註譯 [The book of rites]. Translated by Wang Meng'ou. 王雲五主編. 臺北：商務印書館.

Li Liliang 李麗涼著. 2014. "六十三代天師張恩溥在台灣二十年" [Twenty years in the life of Zhang Enpu, sixty-third generation Celestial Masters leader in Taiwan]. 《道教文化研究中心》, 第三十三期 33: 1–5.

Li Qiude 李秋德著. 1989. "姓氏問題對社會的危害不可忽視" [The harm that is brought by the problem of surnames cannot be ignored]. 《社會》, 第四期, no. 4.

Li Renqing 李人慶著. 2004. "溫州模式的意義和價值" [The meaning and significance of the "Wenzhou Model"]. 北京：中國社會科學院農村發展研究所.

Li Xiangping 李向平著. 2010. 《信仰但不認同：当代中国信仰的社會學詮釋》 [Believing without identifying: The sociological interpretation of spiritual beliefs in contemporary China]. 北京：社會科學文獻出版社.

Li Yuanhua 李元華著. 2002. 《溫州民間融資及開放性資本市場研究》 [Grassroots finance in Wenzhou and the study of the open capital markets]. 北京：中國經濟出版社.

Li Yunhe and Zheng Zigeng 李雲河, 鄭子耿著. 1991. "溫州模式" [The Wenzhou Model]. In 《城鄉發展協調研究》. 周爾鎏主編. 南京：江蘇人民出版社.

Liang Qichao 梁启超著. 1901. 《十種德性相反相成論》 [On the ten types of virtues, in contrast and complementarity]. http://www.my285.com/xdmj/lqc/018.htm (accessed November 10, 2017).

Liao, Christine. 2014. "China's Housing Bubble Is Bursting—Finally the Whole Country Is Turning Wenzhou." http://weichristineliao.blogspot.com/2014/03/chinas-housing-bubble-is-bursting.html.

Lin Meirong 林美容著. 1989. "從祭祀圈到信仰圈: 建構台灣民間社會" [From ritual circle to circle of belief: The construction and development of folk society in Taiwan]. In 《人類學與台灣. 台北: 稻鄉出版社.》

Lin Qiwen 林琦文采訪. 2014. "訪 《溫州鼓詞系列叢書》作者湯振東" [An interview with Tang Zhendong, author of the *Series on Wenzhou Drum Chants*]. In 《永嘉網》, 五月八日. http://www.yjnet.cn/system/2014/05/08/011658379.shtml.

Lin Shundao 林順道. 2002. 《順溪陳族》 [The Chen Lineage of Shunxi]. 平陽: 平陽縣順溪陳少文故居陳列館.

Lin Shundao 林順道著. 2003. "浙江溫州民間念佛誦經結社集會調查研究" [Fieldwork on folk Buddhist scriptural chanting societies in Wenzhou]. In 《世界宗教研究》, 第四期, no. 4, 59–68.

Lin Shundao 林順道著. 2007. "摩尼教傳入溫州考" [Investigation into the transmission of Manicheanism into Wenzhou]. In 《世界宗教研究》, 第一期, no. 1, 125–137.

Lin Shundao 林順道著. 2013. "論蒼南道教文化" [On Daoist religious culture in Cangnan County]. In 《蒼南歷史文化》, 第十期, no. 10, 83–92.

Lin Weiping. 2015. *Materializing Magic Power: Chinese Popular Religion in Villages and Cities.*
Cambridge, MA: Harvard University Asia Center.

Lin Yixiu 林亦修著. 2009. 《溫州族群與區域文化研究》 [The study of Wenzhou's
ethnic and regional culture]. 上海: 三聯書店.

Lin Yixiu 林亦修著. 2011. "論溫州楊府侯王信俗文化研究的意義" [On the value of studying folk religion of Lord Yang in Wenzhou]. In 《蒼南文化資訊》. 溫州市蒼南縣政
府. http://www.cncn.gov.cn/www/wenhuaju/2011/08/06/51008.htm.

Lin Yixiu and Guo Chongmeng 林亦修, 郭重孟著. 2016. 《陳靖姑宮廟境社研究》
[A study of Chen Jinggu temples and communities]. 上海: 三聯書店.

Lin Yixiu 林亦修整理校注, ed., and Chen Deqi 陳德其記述, transcriber. 2011.
《靈經大傳》 [Efficacious scripture and great biography]. 北京: 學苑出版社.

Linshui Pingyaozhuan 《臨水平妖傳》. n.d. History of the Pacification of the Demons
of Linshui. [Ming Dynasty orig. facsimile].

Liu, Lydia. 1995. *Translingual Practice: Literature, National Culture, and Translated
Modernity—China, 1900-1937.* Stanford, CA: Stanford University Press.

Liu, Yaling. 1992. "Reform from Below: The Private Economy and Local Politics in the
Rural Industrialization of Wenzhou." *China Quarterly,* no. 130 (June): 293–316.

Liu Zhongyu 劉仲宇著. 2000. "道教對民間信仰的收容和改造" [The absorption and
transformation of popular religion by Daoism]. In 《宗教學研究》, vol. 4, 41–43.

Lo, Roger Shih-Chieh. 2012. "Local Politics and the Canonization of a God: Lord
Yang (*Yang Fujun*) in Late Qing Wenzhou (1840–67)." *Late Imperial China* 33, no. 1:
89–121.

Longwanqu Feiwuzhi wenhua yichan bangongshi, ed. 龍灣區非物質文化遺產辦公室
編. (Longwan District Intangible Cultural Heritage Office, ed.). 2009. 《守望記憶:
龍灣區非物質文化遺產選粹》 [*Guarding memories: Selected gems of Longwan District's
intangible cultural heritage*]. 溫州: 龍灣區圖書館 Wenzhou: Longwan District Library.

Lu Guimeng 陸龜蒙著. n.d. 《野廟碑》 [Stele inscription for a temple in the wilds]
(唐; Tang Dynasty). http://skqs.guoxuedashi.com/wen_2778e/61076.html (accessed
February 17, 2018).

Lu Zongli 吕宗力, 欒保群著. 2001. 《中国民間諸神》 上下 [Multitudinous gods of
China]. 石家莊: 河北教育出版社.

Lunyu 《論語》. (1893, in Chinese and English) 1971. *The Confucian Analects.* Translated
by James Legge. New York: Dover.

Luo Jianjian 駱建建著. 2008. "變遷之神: 一個鄉村寺廟重建的社會解讀" [A god in the
midst of change: A deconstruction of a village temple's restoration]. In 中國宗教與
社會高峰論壇論文集》 下. 北京大學中國宗教與社會研究中心, 美國普渡大學中國宗
教與社會研究中心.

MacInnis, Donald E. 1989. *Religion in China Today: Policy and Practice.* Maryknoll, NY:
Orbis.

Madsen, Richard. 1993. "The Public Sphere, Civil Society, and Moral Community."
Modern China 19, no. 2: 183–198.

Mahmood, Saba. 2005. *Politics of Piety: The Islamic Revival and the Subject of Feminist Subjects*. Princeton, NJ: Princeton University Press.

Mauss, Marcel. 1967. *The Gift: The Forms and Functions of Exchange in Archaic Societies*. Translated by Ian Cunnison. New York: Norton.

Nedostup, Rebecca. 2008. "Ritual Competition and the Modernizing Nation-State." In *Chinese Religiosities: Afflictions of Modernity and State Formation*, 87–112. Berkeley: University of California Press.

Nedostup, Rebecca. 2010. *Superstitious Regimes: Religion and the Politics of Chinese Modernity*. Cambridge, MA: Harvard University Press.

Nolan, Peter, and Dong Fureng, eds. 1990. *Market Forces in China: Competition and Small Business. The Wenzhou Debate*. London: Zed.

Overmyer, Daniel L. 1997. "Convergence: Chinese Gods and Christian Saints." *Ching Feng* 40, nos. 3–4 (September–December): 215–232.

Pan Ende 潘恩德編, ed. 2001. 《民間信仰諸神譜》 [Gods in Chinese popular religion]. 成都: 巴蜀書社.

Pan Yiheng 潘貽衡著. 2000. "重修仙岩山聖壽禪寺記" [The rebuilding of Sacred Longevity Chan Temple in Xianyan Mountains]. In 《浙南瑞安佛教志》 上冊 vol. 1. 潘貽鎔主編. 瑞安市佛教協會編印.

Pan Yirong 潘貽鎔主編, ed. 2000. 《浙南瑞安佛教志》 上冊 [Southern Zhejiang Rui'an Buddhist Gazetteer], vol. 1. 瑞安市佛教協會編印.

Pelczynski, Z. A. 1988. "Solidarity and the Rebirth of Civil Society." In *Civil Society and the State*, edited by John Keane, 361–380. London: Verso.

Pickering, Andrew. 1994. "Book Review of *We Have Never Been Modern*." *Modernism/Modernity* 1, no. 3 (September): 257–258.

Pittman, Don A. 2001. *Toward a Modern Chinese Buddhism: Taixu's Reforms*. Honolulu: University of Hawai'i Press.

Polanyi, Karl. 1957. "The Economy as Instituted Process." In *Trade and Market in Early Empires*, edited by Karl Polanyi and Conrad Arensberg, 243–269. Glencoe, IL: Free Press.

Potter, Jack M., and Sulamith Potter. 1990. *China's Peasants: The Anthropology of a Revolution*. Cambridge: Cambridge University Press.

Putnam, Robert D. 2001. *Bowling Alone: The Collapse and Revival of American Community*. New York: Simon and Schuster.

Qin Hui 秦暉著. 1999. "從大共同體本位到公民社會: 傳統公民社會及其現代演進的再認識" [From large community to civil society: Reconsidering traditional civil society and its modern evolution]. In 《問題與主意》. 長春: 長春出版社.

Rankin, Mary. 1993. "Some Observations on a Chinese Public Sphere." *Modern China* 19, no. 2: 158–182.

Rappaport, Roy. 1999. *Ritual and Religion in the Making of Humanity*. Cambridge: Cambridge University Press.

Raz, Gil. 2012. *The Emergence of Daoism: Creation of Tradition*. London: Routledge.

Redding, Gordon. 1995. *The Spirit of Chinese Capitalism*. Berlin: De Gruyter.

Reinders, Eric. 2004. *Borrowed Gods and Foreign Bodies: Christian Missionaries Imagine Chinese Religion*. Berkeley: University of California Press.

Ren, Daniel. 2013. "Good Times and Easy Cash Long Gone in Wenzhou." *South China Morning Post,* November 4.

Richburg, Keith. 2011. "Some See China's Future in Debt-Ridden City of Wenzhou." *Washington Post*, October 27.

Rigby, T. Harry. 1976. "Politics in the Mono-Organizational Society." In *Authoritarian Politics in Communist Europe: Uniformity and Diversity in One-Party States.* Institute for International Studies, no. 28, University of California, Berkeley.

Rigby, T. Harry. 1977. "Stalinism and the Mono-Organizational Society." In *Stalinism: Essays in Historical Interpretation*, edited by Robert C. Tucker, 53–76. New York: Norton.

Rosenthal, Elisabeth. 1999. "They Don't Sell Bridges. Tunnels, Yes." *New York Times*, February, 20.

Rowe, William. 1993. "The Problem of 'Civil Society' in Late Imperial China." *Modern China* 19, no. 2: 139–157.

Sahlins, Marshall. 1972. *Stone Age Economics*. New York: Aldine.

Sahlins, Marshall. 1976. *Culture and Practical Reason*. Chicago: University of Chicago Press.

Sangren, P. Steven. 1983. "Female Gender in Chinese Religious Symbols: Kuan Yin, Matsu, and the Eternal Mother." *Signs* 9: 4–25.

Sangren, P. Steven. 1984. "Traditional Chinese Corporations: Beyond Kinship." *Journal of Asian Studies* 43: 391–415.

Sangren, P. Steven. 1987. *History and Magical Power in a Chinese Community*. Stanford, CA: Stanford University Press.

Schipper, Kristofer. 1990. "The Cult of Pao-Sheng Ta-Ti and Its Spreading to Taiwan—A Case Study of *Fen-hsiang*." In *Development and Decline of Fukien Province in the 17th and 18th Century*, 397–416. Leiden: Brill.

Schipper, Kristofer. 1993. *The Taoist Body*. Translated by Karen Duval. Berkeley: University of California Press.

Schmitt, Carl. 1985. *Political Theology: Four Chapters on the Concept of Sovereignty*. Cambridge, MA: MIT Press.

Scott, James C. 1998. *Seeing Like a State: How Certain Schemes to Improve the Human Condition Have Failed*. New Haven, CT: Yale University Press.

Seidel, Anna K. 1978. "Buying One's Way to Heaven: The Celestial Treasury in Chinese Religions." *History of Religions* 17, nos. 3–4 (February–May): 419–432.

Shahar, Meir. 1996. "Vernacular Fiction and the Transmission of Gods' Cults in Late Imperial China." In *Unruly Gods: Divinity and Society in China*, edited by Meir Shahar and Robert P. Weller, 184–211. Honolulu: University of Hawai'i Press.

Shanghai Renmin Chubanshe 上海人民出版社编, ed. 1982. 《破除迷信問答》 [Smashing superstitions: Questions and answers]. 上海：上海人民出版社.

Shen Yeming 沈葉鳴著. 2002. 《抗倭英雄湯和》 [Tang He: Hero who fought the Japanese pirates]. 北京：華齡出版社.

Sheng Aiping 盛愛萍著. 2004. 《溫州地名的語言文化研究》 [The language and culture of Wenzhou place-names]. 杭州：浙江大學出版社.

Shi Jinchuan, Jin Xiangrong, Zhao Wei, Luo Weidong, et al. 史晉川, 金祥榮, 趙偉, 羅衛東, 等著. 2002. 《制度變遷與經濟發展：溫州模式研究》 [Structural transformation and economic development: Studies of the Wenzhou Model]. 杭州： 浙江大學出版社.

Si-ma Qian 司馬遷著. 1982. 《史紀》 [Records of the Grand Historian]. 北京： 中華書局 [漢 Han Dynasty].

Smith, Joanna Handlin. 1999. "Liberating Animals in Ming-Qing China: Buddhist Inspiration and Elite Imagination." *Journal of Asian Studies* 58, no. 1 (May): 51–84.

Song, Ping. 2008. "The Zheng Communities and the Formation of a Transnational Lineage." *Journal of Chinese Overseas* 4, no. 2: 183–202.

Sun Yanfei. 2014. "Popular Religion in Zhejiang: Feminization, Bifurcation, and Buddhification." *Modern China* 40, no. 5: 455–487.

Swan, Laura. 2014. *The Wisdom of the Beguines: The Forgotten Story of a Medieval Women's Movement.* New York: Blue Bridge.

Szonyi, Michael. 2002. *Practicing Kinship: Lineage and Descent in Late Imperial China.* Stanford, CA: Stanford University Press.

Tam, Wailun. 2011. "Communal Worship and Festivals in Chinese Villages." In *Chinese Religious Life*, edited by David Palmer, Glenn Shive, and Philip Wickeri, 30–49. Oxford: Oxford University Press.

Tang Zhendong 湯鎮東收集整理, comp. 2008. 《溫州鼓詞南游傳》 [Wenzhou drum chant: Journeys through the South]. 蘭州： 甘肅人民出版社.

Taylor, Charles. 1995. "Invoking Civil Society." In *Philosophical Arguments*, 204–224. Cambridge, MA: Harvard University Press.

Taylor, Charles. 2007. *A Secular Age.* Cambridge, MA: Belknap Press of Harvard University Press.

Teiser, Stephen F. 1988. *The Ghost Festival in Medieval China.* Princeton, NJ: Princeton University Press.

Teiser, Stephen F. 1994. *The Scripture on the Ten Kings and the Making of Purgatory in Medieval Chinese Buddhism.* Honolulu: University of Hawai'i Press.

Thomas, Keith. 1971. *Religion and the Decline of Magic: Studies in Popular Beliefs in Sixteenth and Seventeenth Century England.* Oxford: Oxford University Press.

Tocqueville, Alexis de. 2000. *Democracy in America.* Translated by Harvey Mansfield and Delba Winthrop. Chicago: University of Chicago Press.

Tsai, Kellee S. 2002. *Back-Alley Banking: Private Entrepreneurs in China.* Ithaca, NY: Cornell University Press.

Tu, Weiming, ed. 1996. *Confucian Traditions in East Asian Modernity: Moral Education and Economic Culture in Japan and the Four Mini-Dragons.* Cambridge, MA: Harvard University Press.

Twitchett, Denis. 1959. "The Fan Clan's Charitable Estate." In *Confucianism in Action*, edited by David S. Nivison and Arthur F. Wright, 97–133. Stanford, CA: Stanford University Press.

van der Loon, Piet. 1977. "Les Origines rituelles de théâtre chinoise." *Journal Asiatique*, no. 265: 141–168.

van der Veer, Peter. 1994. *Religious Nationalism: Hindus and Muslims in India.* Berkeley: University of California Press.

van der Veer, Peter. 2013. *The Modern Spirit of Asia: the Spiritual and the Secular in China and India*. Princeton, NJ: Princeton University Press.

von Glahn, Richard. 2003. "Towns and Temples: Urban Growth and Decline in the Yangzi Delta, 1100–1400." In *The Song-Yuan-Ming Transition in Chinese History*, edited by Paul Smith and Richard von Glahn, 176–211. Cambridge, MA: Harvard University Press.

von Glahn, Richard. 2004. *The Sinister Way: The Divine and the Demonic in Chinese Religious Culture*. Berkeley: University of California Press.

von Glahn, Richard. 2016. *The Economic History of China: From Antiquity to the Nineteenth Century*. Cambridge: Cambridge University Press.

Wakeman, Frederic, Jr. 1993. "The Civil Society and Public Sphere Debate: Western Reflections on Chinese Political Culture." *Modern China* 19, no. 2: 108–138.

Wang Chunguang 王春光著. 2000. 《巴黎的溫州人》 [Wenzhou people in Paris]. 南昌: 江西人民出版社.

Wang Guo-en 王國恩. 2003. 《永昌堡》 [Yongchang Fortress]. 香港: 天馬圖書有限公司.

Wang Ka 王卡, 主編, ed. 1999. 《中國道教基礎知識》 [Foundational knowledge of Chinese Daoism]. 北京: 宗教文化出版社.

Wang Mingming 王銘銘著. 2004. 《溪村家族: 社區史, 儀式與地方政治》 [The lineage of Xicun: Community, rituals, and local politics]. 貴陽市: 貴州人民出版社.

Wang Xiaoqiang, Bai Nansheng, Song Lina, and Zhao Xiaodong 王小強, 白南生, 宋麗娜, 趙小東著. 1985. "農村商品生產發展的新動向" [New trends in rural commodity production]. In 《農村, 經濟, 社會》 第三卷. 北京: 知識出版社.

Wang Zan 王瓚著. 2006. 《弘治溫州府志》 [Hongzhi Reign Wenzhou gazetteer]. 上海: 上海社會科學院出版社. [Ming Dynasty, 15th c.].

Watson, James L. 1975. *Emigration and the Chinese Lineage: The "Mans" in Hong Kong and London*. Berkeley: University of California Press.

Watson, James L. 1985. "Standardizing the Gods: The Promotion of T'ien Hou ('Empress of Heaven') along the South China Coast, 960–1960." In *Popular Culture in Late Imperial China*, edited by David Johnson et al., 292–324. Berkeley: University of California Press.

Watson, James L. 1988. "The Structure of Chinese Funerary Rites." In *Death Ritual in Late Imperial and Modern China*. Berkeley: University of California Press.

Weber, Max. (1904) 1958. *The Protestant Ethic and the Spirit of Capitalism*. Translated by Talcott Parsons. New York: Scribner's.

Weber, Max. (1919) 1946. "Science as a Vocation." In *From Max Weber: Essays in Sociology*, edited and translated by H. H. Gerth and C. Wright Mills, 129–156. New York: Oxford University Press.

Wei, Yehua Dennis, Wangming Li, and Chunbin Wang. 2007. "Restructuring Industrial Districts, Scaling Up Regional Development: A Study of the Wenzhou Model, China." *Economic Geography* 83, no. 4: 421–444.

Welch, Holmes. 1968. *Buddhist Revival in China*. Cambridge, MA: Harvard University Press.

Weller, Robert P. 1987. *Unities and Diversities in Chinese Religion*. Seattle: University of Washington Press.

Weller, Robert P. 1999. *Alternate Civilities: Democracy and Culture in China and Taiwan.* Boulder, CO: Westview.

Weller, Robert P., and Meir Shahar. 1996. "Introduction." In *Unruly Gods: Divinity in Society in China,* edited by Robert Weller and Meir Shahar, 1–36. Honolulu: University of Hawai'i Press.

Wen Zhonghan 溫忠翰著. 1879. 《東甌九説》 [Nine sayings about the eastern Ou region]. Woodblock print book; n.p.

Wenzhou Wenwuchu 溫州文物處. 2009. 《溫州市北宋白象塔清理報告》 [Report on the clean-up of the Northern Song White Elephant Pagoda in Wenzhou]. In 《溫州文物論集》. 杭州：浙江人民出版社.

Wenzhoushi Feiwuzhi Wenhua Yichan Baohu Zhongxin 溫州市非物質文化遺產保護中心編, ed. 2009. 《東甌遺韵：溫州市非物質文化遺產大觀》 [Heritage rhythms of eastern Ou: A survey of Wenzhou City Intangible Cultural Heritage]. Vol. 1. 杭州：西泠印社出版社.

Wenzhoushi tongjiju, Guojia tongjiju 溫州市統計局, 國家統計局. 2015. 《2014 年溫州市國民經濟和社會發展統計公報》 [Report on Wenzhou's economic and social development in 2014]. http://www.sogou.com/link?url=DSOYnZeCC_p7aij5MkEgFHdqlC JuMHzJM7OuAJyBolE4xF5Xwh9iVl-UKe2D-vON5_gnldi93T7BaNicQGzLwT2z KoQLvCWY&query=%E6%B8%A9%E5%B7%9E%E7%BB%8F%E6%B5%8E%E5% 8F%91%E5%B1%95%E7%BB%9F%E8%AE%A1.

Whyte, Martin K. 1988. "Death in the People's Republic of China." In *Death Ritual in Late Imperial and Modern China,* edited by James L. Watson and Evelyn Rawski, 289–316. Berkeley: University of California Press.

Wolf, Arthur P. 1974. "Gods, Ghosts, and Ancestors." In *Religion and Ritual in Chinese Society,* edited by Arthur Wolf, 131–182. Stanford, CA: Stanford University Press.

Wu Cheng-en 吳承恩著. 2010. 《西遊記》 [Journey to the West]. 北京：人民文學出版社.

Wu Zhen 吳真著. 2009. "從封建迷信到非物質文化遺產：民間信仰的合法性歷程" [From feudal superstition to Intangible Cultural Heritage: The path to legality for Chinese popular religion]. In 《中國宗教報告》. 金澤, 邱永輝主編. 北京：社會科學文献出版社.

Xiang Biao. 2004. *Transcending Boundaries: Zhejiangcun—the Story of a Migrant Village in Beijing.* Translated by Jim Weldon from the Chinese: *Kuayue Bianjie de Shequ.* Leiden: Brill Academic.

Xu Hongtu 徐宏圖著. 2005. "平陽縣的陳靖姑信仰及其降妖儀式" [Chen the Fourteenth worship and its exorcistic rituals in Pingyang County]. In 《平陽縣蒼南縣傳統民俗文化研究》. 北京：民族出版社.

Xu Hongtu and Xue Chenghuo 徐宏圖, 薛成火, 著. 2005. 《浙江蒼南縣正一道普度科範》 [Pudu rituals performed by Orthodox Unity Daoists in Cangnan County, Zhejiang]. 香港：天馬出版有限公司.

Xu Qihua 徐啟華著. 1992. "溫州市長貿易團訪問美國" [Mayor of Wenzhou leads a trade delegation to visit the US]. In 《天天日報》, August 21, 1992.

Xu Shen 許慎著. 1963. 《說文解字》 [Explaining and analyzing characters]. 北京：中華書局. [西漢 Western Han Dynasty].

Xu Yaoge 徐姚格著. 2001. 溫州鼓詞 《南遊傳》 [Wenzhou drum lyrics: "Journey to the South"]. In 《古今談》, vol. 3. http://trs.hzlib.net:8080/was40/detail?record =65&channelid=1844.

Yan, Yunxiang. 2003. *Private Life under Socialism*. Stanford, CA: Stanford University Press.

Yang, C. K. 1961. *Religion in Chinese Society: A Study of Contemporary Social Functions of Religion and Some of Their Historical Factors*. Berkeley: University of California Press.

Yang Cengwen, ed. 楊曾文主編. 1999. 《中國佛教基礎知識》 [Chinese Buddhism: Foundational knowledge]. 北京 : 宗教文化出版社 Beijing: Religious Culture.

Yang, Der-Ruey. 2012. "Revolution of Temporality: The Modern Schooling of Daoist Priests in Shanghai." In *Daoism in the Twentieth Century: Between Eternity and Modernity*, edited by David Palmer and Liu Xin, 47–81. Berkeley: University of California Press.

Yang, Jisheng. 2012. *Tombstone: The Great Chinese Famine, 1958–1962*. New York: Farrar, Straus and Giroux.

Yang, Mayfair. 1989. "Between State and Society: The Construction of Corporateness in a Chinese Socialist Factory." *Australian Journal of Chinese Affairs*, no. 22: 31–60.

Yang, Mayfair. 1994a. *Gifts, Favors, and Banquets: The Art of Social Relationships in China*. Ithaca, NY: Cornell University Press.

Yang, Mayfair, dir. 1994b. *Public and Private Realms in Rural Wenzhou, China*. 50-minute documentary video produced at UC Santa Barbara. Formerly distributed by University of California Extension Media Center, Berkeley.

Yang, Mayfair. 1996. "Tradition, Traveling Anthropology, and the Discourse of Modernity in China." In *The Future of Anthropological Knowledge*, edited by Henrietta Moore, 93–114. New York: Routledge.

Yang, Mayfair, dir. 1997. *Through Chinese Women's Eyes*. 52-minute documentary video. Distributed by Women Make Movies, New York City.

Yang, Mayfair. 1999a. "From Gender Erasure to Gender Difference." In *Spaces of Their Own: Women's Public Sphere in Transnational China*, edited by Mayfair Yang, 35–67. Minneapolis: University of Minnesota Press.

Yang, Mayfair. 1999b. "Introduction." In *Spaces of Their Own: Women's Public Sphere in Transnational China*, edited by Mayfair Yang, 1–34. Minneapolis: University of Minnesota Press.

Yang, Mayfair. 2004. "Spatial Struggles: State Disenchantment and Popular Reappropriation of Space in Rural Southeast China." *Journal of Asian Studies* 63, no. 3 (August): 719–755.

Yang, Mayfair. 2007a. "Ritual Economy and Rural Capitalism with Chinese Characteristics." In *Cultural Politics in a Global Age: Uncertainty, Solidarity and Innovation*, edited by David Held and Henrietta Moore, 226–233. Oxford: Oneworld.

Yang, Mayfair (Yang Meihui 楊美惠著). 2007b. 《傳統，旅行的人類學與中國的現代性話語》 [Tradition, traveling anthropology, and China's discourse of modernity] 葉南譯. 《農業大學社會科學》 第 24 期，2 號.

Yang, Mayfair. 2008a. "Goddess across the Taiwan Straits: Matrifocal Ritual Space, Nation-State, and Satellite Television Footprints." In *Chinese Religiosities: Afflictions of Modernity and State Formation*, edited by Mayfair Yang, 323–348. Berkeley: University of California Press.

Yang, Mayfair. 2008b. "Introduction." In *Chinese Religiosities: Afflictions of Modernity and State Formation*, edited by Mayfair Yang, 1-42. Berkeley: University of California Press.

Yang, Mayfair (Yang Meihui 楊美惠著). 2009. "'溫州模式' 的禮儀經濟" [The "Wenzhou Model's" ritual economy]. In 《學海》, September 2009.

Yang, Mayfair. 2011. "Postcoloniality and Religiosity in Modern China: The Disenchantments of Sovereignty." *Theory, Culture, and Society* 28, no. 2: 3-45.

Yang, Mayfair. 2013. "Gazing into the Future of Religion and the State in China." *Immanent Frame* (blog), Social Science Research Council, November 14. http://blogs .ssrc.org/tif/2013/11/14/gazing-into-the-future/.

Yang, Mayfair. 2015. "Shamanism and Spirit Possession in Chinese Modernity: Some Preliminary Reflections on a Gendered Religiosity of the Body." *Review of Religion and Chinese Society* 1, no. 2: 51-86.

Yang, Mayfair. 2018. "Millenarianism in the Soviet Union and Maoist China." *The Immanent Frame* (blog), November 23. https://tif.ssrc.org/2018/11/23/millenarianism-in -the-soviet-union-and-maoist-china/.

Yang, Mayfair. 2019a. "Chinese Maritime Economy: Historical Globalizing Forces." In *China, India and Alternative Modernities*, edited by Sanjay Kumar, Satya P. Mohanty, Archana Kumar, and Raj Kumar, 103-120. New York: Routledge.

Yang, Mayfair (Yang Meihui 楊美惠著). 2019b. 《禮物與宴會的兩個邏輯: 中國和西北海岸譜係》 [Two logics of gifts and banquets: Genealogies in China and the northwest coast]. 《西北民族研究》 [Northwest Ethnological Studies], 劉明月, 黃子逸, 蘭婕譯. 總第 102 期: 54-69 頁.

Yang, Nianqun. 2011. "'Civil Society' in Modern China Studies: Methodology and Limitations." In *State and Civil Society: The Chinese Perspective*, edited by Deng Zhenglai, 47-62. Hackensack, NJ: World Scientific.

Ye Dabing 葉大兵著. 1997. "二十一世紀中國宗祠向何處去?" [Whither is the lineage headed in the twenty-first century?]. In 《民俗博物館學刊》, 第一期, vol. 1, 3-10.

Ye Dabing and Ye Liya 葉大兵, 葉麗婭著. 1992. 陳靖姑信仰及其傳說的研究 [A study of the Chen Jinggu cult and its legends]. In 《中國民俗學》, 1-9.

Ye Maoheng 葉茂恒著. 2009. "龍灣陳十四信仰" [Chen the Fourteenth worship in Longwan District]. In 《守望記憶: 龍灣區非物質文化遺產選粹》. 龍灣區文化局寫作班子編纂. 溫州: 龍灣區文化局.

Ye Tao 葉濤著. 2009. "浙江民間信仰現狀及其調研述略" [The present condition of popular religion in Zhejiang and its studies]. In 《中國宗教報告 2009》 金澤, 邱永輝主編. 《宗教藍皮書》. 北京: 社會科學文獻出版社.

Ye Zhongming 葉中鳴編著. 1985. 《陳十四奇傳》 [Marvelous tales of Chen the Fourteenth]. 杭州: 浙江文藝出版社.

Ying Weixian and Jiang Ruihu 應維賢, 薑瑞虎主編, eds. 2008. 《東甌神仙傳記》 [Hagiographies of gods and immortals of eastern Ou]. 香港出版社.

Ying Weixian and Qian Shunqing 應維賢, 錢順青主編, eds. 2008. 《浙南洞天福地: 游東甌山水, 探神秘溫州》 [Daoist caverns and blessed lands of southern Zhejiang]. 香港: 香港出版社.

Yongchang Bao Minsu Wenhua Yanjiuhui (Yong Chang Fortress Folk Custom and Culture Study Society 永昌堡民俗文化研究會). 2007. 《溫州市龍灣區永昌堡民俗文化研究會章程》 [Wenzhou City Longwan District Yong Chang Fortress Folk Custom and Culture Study Society charter].

Yongjia Xianzhi. (based on the Qing Dynasty ed., 1879) 1983. 《永嘉縣志》 (浙江省) [Yongjia Gazetteer: Zhejiang Province]. 張寶琳修 ; 王棻等纂. 台北市 : 成文出版社.

Yu Bingyuan 余炳炎著, 攝影. 2007. 《千年臨水》 [A thousand years by the waterside]. 福州 : 海潮攝影藝術出版社.

Yü Chun-fang. 2001. *Kuan-yin: The Chinese Transformation of Avaloketesvara*. New York: Columbia University Press.

Yü Chun-fang. 2013. *Passing the Light: The Incense Light Community and Buddhist Nuns in Contemporary Taiwan*. Honolulu: University of Hawaiʻi Press.

Yu Keping. 2011a. "Civil Society in China: Concepts, Classification and Institutional Environment." In *State and Civil Society: The Chinese Perspective*, edited by Deng Zhenglai, 63–96. Hackensack, NJ: World Scientific.

Yu Keping 俞可平著. 2011b. 《走向官民共治的社會治理》 [Toward the co-governance of society by officialdom and the people]. 中國社會管理研究所. http://www.cssm.org.cn/view.php?id=31917.

Yueqingshi Renmin Zhengfu 樂清市政府. 2013. 《樂清市人民政府辦公室關于印發樂清市'三改一拆'三年行動計劃 (2013-2015 年) 的通知》 [Notification of plans to implement the "Three Transformations and One Demolition Rule" by Yueqing People's Government]. http://xxgk.yueqing.gov.cn/YQ001/zcwj/0202/201311/t20131108_432270.html.

Yunji Qiqian 《雲籍七簽》. (1029 BCE) 1988. 《道藏》 [The Daoist canon]. 第 22 冊 [vol. 22], 581~582 頁 [pp. 581–582].

Zhang Chuanjun 張傳君主編. 2016. 《蒼南民俗》 [Cangnan folk customs]. 杭州 : 浙江攝影出版社.

Zhang Jianjun 張建君著. 2007. "企業家階級結構與政治發展" [The class structure of entrepreneurs and political development]. In 《二十一世紀》 *Twenty-First Century*, 二月號, 第九十九期, 21–29.

Zhang Jintao, ed. 張金濤, 主編. 2000. 《中國龍虎山天師道》 [Daoism of the Celestial Masters in China's Dragon Tiger Mountain]. 南昌 : 江西人民出版社 (Nanchang: Jiangxi People's Press).

Zhang, Li. 2000. "The Interplay of Gender, Space, and Work in China's Floating Population." In *Redrawing Boundaries: Work, Households, and Gender in China*, edited by Barbara Entwisle and Gail E. Henderson, 171–196. Berkeley: University of California Press.

Zhang, Li. 2001. *Strangers in the City: Reconfigurations of Space, Power, and Social Networks within China's Floating Population*. Stanford, CA: Stanford University Press.

Zhang Qin 張琴著. 2003. 《鄉土溫州》 [Folk Wenzhou]. 杭州 : 浙江古籍出版社.

Zhang Yining 張以寧著. 1778. 《古田縣臨水順懿廟記》 [Memorial on the Shunyi Temple in Linshui, Gutian County]. In 《翠屏記》, 張以寧, 卷四: 48–50. In 《四庫全書》. http://ucsdskqs.eastview.com/ (accessed June 16, 2016).

Zhang Zehong 張澤洪著. 2003. "論道教的步罡踏斗" [On Daoism's *Stepping and leaping through the Big Dipper*]. In 《中國道教》, 第四期, no. 4.

Zhang Zhenzhong 張鎮中著. 1993. 《溫州地方史稿》 [Sources of Wenzhou local history]. 溫州： 中國人民政治協商會議, 浙江省溫州市鹿城區委員會.

Zhang Zhichen 章志城主編, ed. 1998. 《溫州市志》 上冊 [Wenzhou City gazetteer]. 北京： 中華書局.

Zhao, Dingxin. 2015. *The Confucian-Legalist State: New Theory of Chinese History*. Oxford: Oxford University Press.

Zhejiang Rui'an Shi 浙江瑞安市. 2014. 《關於做好'三改一拆'涉及宗教和民間信仰違法建築調查統計工作的通知》 [Communiqué regarding properly implementing the "Three Reforms and One Dismantling" and illegal construction by religious organizations]. http://www.yuhuan.gov.cn/yggc/shamen/zcwj/201312/t20131218_70014.html.

Zhejiangsheng Renmin Zhengfu 浙江省人民政府. 2013. "浙江省人民政府關於在全省開展'三改一拆'三年行動的通知" [Communiqué of the Zhejiang People's Government regarding the initiation of the "Three Reforms and One Dismantling" action]. http://www.zj.gov.cn/art/2013/3/13/art_13012_77021.html.

Zheng Zhenman 鄭振滿著. 1992. 《明清福建家族組織與社會變遷》 [Lineage organization and social change in Fujian during the Ming and Qing dynasties]. 長沙： 湖南教育出版社.

Zheng Zhenman 鄭振滿著. 1998. "明清福建里社考" [A study of the *li* and *she* administrative units in Fujian Province during the Ming and Qing dynasties]. In 《家庭、社區、大眾心態變遷國際學術研討會論文集》, 255–267. 合肥市： 黃山書社.

Zheng Zhenman. 2010. "Part II: Lineage and Religion on the Putian Plains: An Analysis Based on Stone Inscriptions." In *Ritual Alliances of the Putian Plain*, vol. 1, translated by Kenneth Dean, 285–339. Leiden: Brill.

Zhengxie Wenzhou Shi Longwanqu Weiyuanhui 政協溫州市龍灣區委員會. 2011. 《龍灣民俗》 [The customs of Longwan District]. 北京： 中國炎黃文化出版社.

Zhengxie Wenzhou Shiwei Wenshi Ziliao Yanweihui, ed. 政協溫州市委文史資料研委會. 1984. 《溫州文史資料》 [Wenzhou historical documents archives]. 第九輯, vol. 9. 杭州： 浙江人民出版社.

Zhonggong Shamenzhen Weiyuanhui 中共沙門鎮委員會. 2013. "關於印發《沙門鎮宗教和民間信仰活動場所違法建築專項整治工作實施方案》的通知" [Notification concerning the "Shamen Township Plan to Clean Up Illegal Constructions of Religious Sites"]. 53 號文件. http://www.pacilution.com/ShowArticle.asp?ArticleID=4877.

Zhonggong Zhongyang Weiyuanhui 中共中央委員會 [Chinese Communist Party Central Committee]. 2018. 《深化黨和國家機構改革方案》 [Method for deepening the reform of the Party and government organizations]. http://www.gov.cn/zhengce/2018-03/21/content_5276191.htm#1.

Zhonggong Zhongyang Wenxian Yanjiushi Zonghe Yanjiuzu 中共中央文獻研究室綜合研究組. (1980) 1995a. 《關於落實宗教團體房產政策等問題的報告》 [Report on implementing the policy regarding the buildings and properties of religious associations]. In 《新時期宗教工作文獻選編》. 北京： 宗教文化出版社, 23–26.

Zhonggong Zhongyang Wenxian Yanjiushi Zonghe Yanjiuzu 中共中央文獻研究室綜合研究組. (1982) 1995b. 《關於我國社會主義時期宗教問題的基本觀點和基本政策》 [Basic policies regarding religious issues] (中央 *19* 號文件; *Document 19*) in 《新時期宗教工作文獻選編》. 北京: 宗教文化出版社, 53–73.

Zhou Benshun 周本順著. 2011. "社會管理不能落入公民社會陷阱" [Management of society cannot fall into the civil society trap]. 《求是》, May.

Zhou, Kate Xiao. 1996. *How the Farmers Changed China: Power of the People.* Boulder, CO: Westview.

Zhou Konghua and Ruan Zhensheng 周孔華, 阮珍生, 主編, eds. 1999. 《溫州道教通覽》 [Survey of Daoism in Wenzhou]. 溫州: 溫州市道教協會編印.

Zhu Haibin 朱海濱著. 2008. 《祭祀政策與民間信仰變遷: 近世浙江民間信仰研究》 [The state ritual system and transformations of popular religion: Late Imperial Zhejiang]. 上海: 復旦大學出版社.

Zhu Kangdui 朱康對著. 1997. "宗族文化與鄉村社會秩序建構: 溫州農村宗族問題思考" [The construction of social order by rural lineage culture: Reflections on the problem of Wenzhou lineages]. In 《中共浙江省委黨校學報》 第一期.

Zhuang Zi 莊子著. 1977. 《新譯莊子讀本》 [A new translation of the Zhuangzi]. 黃錦鋐, 註譯. 台北: 三民書局.

Zito, Angela. 1987. "City Gods, Filiality, Hegemony." *Modern China* 13, no. 3: 333–371.

maritime culture, 35

Maritime Prohibitions (*haijin*), 42

market economy, 14, 25, 36, 163, 195, 240, 262, 266, 305, 307–311, 314

Marvelous Tales of Chen the Fourteenth (Ye Zhongming), 70

matrilineal descent, 69–70, 41

Mauss, Marcel, 283, 284, 313

May Fourth Movement, 7, 20

Mazu, 100, 184, 241, 252

meditation classes, 130, 149, 151, 176, 178

memorial halls (*jinian tang*), 195

merit (*gongde*): accumulating activities, 76, 79–80, 118, 121, 149–150, 180, 289, 293; as investment in the afterlife, 78, 118, 132–138, 164, 290, 305, 310, 313; in the Lotus Sutra, 125–126; in popular Buddhism, 132–136; sin, debt and, 77–80

merit foundations (*gongde hui*), 174

mianzi (face), 172, 204, 290

Mid-Primordial Universal Salvation Festival (*Zhongyuan pudu*), 88, 118, 286, 307

migrants, 8, 16, 13, 26, 24, 34–35, 43–46, 52, 175, 219, 221, 265, 314

migration, 16, 43, 98, 200, 268, 207

millenarianism, 30, 53

Ming dynasty, 16, 19, 45, 73, 89, 107–108, 115, 153, 167, 267; and history of Wang lineage, 198, 201, 205–207, 215

Ministry of Security (Guojia Anquan Bu), 28

minjian (nonstate "realm of the people"), 33, 37, 162, 182, 184, 287, 317

Minnan Buddhist Academy, 128, 176

Minnanese, 16, 128, 179–180

missionaries, 6–7, 11, 20, 23

modernity: in non-Western and post-colonial contexts, 162, 195, 259–277; as process of "purification," 4–7, 60, 69; the re-enchantment of, 8–9, 232, 254, 259, 317; and secular nationalism, 10–13, 278; in Wenzhou, 17, 47, 315, 319

modesty, 228–229, 233, 248, 250

money shops (*qian zhuang*), 40

Monkey King, 73–75, 242, 252

mono-organizational society, 261–263

morality books (*shanshu*), 115

Mother Chen the Fourteenth, 24, 57, 61, 65–71, 73, 77, 100, 179–180, 184, 238–257, 278, 293

Mother Lu, 63

Mulian, 88, 138

Nalanda Buddhist Academy, 129, 147, 175–176, 178

Nalanda Charitable Foundation, 129, 173, 174, 178

National Learning, 21

nationalism, 4, 10, 11, 12, 22, 231, 259, 260, 271, 315

nation-state, 8, 10–13, 19, 29, 241, 260–261, 274–275, 278, 315, 319

native-place associations, 25, 43, 258, 264, 266

nature, 5–9, 58, 73, 122, 275, 281, 283, 315

Neo-Confucianism, 55, 191, 222–225, 228, 231, 258, 262, 267, 282, 312, 314

neoliberalism, 41

New Youth (periodical), 7

nongovernmental organizations (NGOs), 35, 162, 182, 252–253, 256, 266

nonproductive expenditure, 281

nunnery (*an*), 133

oath-making, 76, 118, 240

"Ode to Incense Urns," 153

officialdom, 33, 35, 54, 108, 125, 136, 143, 162, 183, 214, 246, 250, 255. *See also guanfang*

old people, 83–84, 86, 87, 172, 205, 207

Old People's Associations (*laoren xiehui*), 84, 130, 172, 178, 288, 299

Old People's Pavilions (*laorenting*), 84, 178, 288, 289

opening the light (*kaiguang*), 58, 268

orientalism, 260

orphan souls (*guhun*), 88, 89, 118, 286

Song dynasty, 17, 30, 55, 67, 126, 195, 267, 290; Buddhism during, 126, 146, 153, 191; Daoism during, 30, 92, 99, 107–109; Wang lineage during, 200, 205

Southern Lineage, 98

spirit mediums, 51, 81–82, 100, 165, 167, 227, 231, 270, 286, 302, 304

spirit money (*mingbi*, *mingqian*), 65, 85, 117, 138–139, 155, 284, 290, 304, 307–309

State Administration for Religious Affairs (SARA), 22, 144, 187, 278

State Council, 22, 144, 181, 291

state feminism, 13, 196, 228–229, 332

Steps of Yü, 122–123

subnational commitments, 278

substantivists (in economic anthropology), 36

Sunan Model, 34–35

superstition, 53–54, 58, 110, 116, 167, 205; in Maoist-era discourse, 9–10, 301–302; in official Daoist and Buddhist discourse, 96, 154, 157, 167; as presumed obstacle to economic development, 303; in Protestant discourse, 20–21. *See also* feudal superstition

surname associations, 219–221, 223, 268

state capitalism, 33–34, 184, 311

syncretism, 56

Szonyi, Michael, 191

taiji quan, 96

Taiping Buddhist Temple, 140–144, 225, 291

talismanic writing, 61, 93, 98, 123

Tang dynasty, 16, 51, 64, 66, 92, 126, 144, 147, 167

Tao Hongjing, 97

Taylor, Charles, 6, 276

teleology, 12, 20, 314

television, 26, 39, 84, 132, 142–143, 148, 158, 175, 215, 218, 247, 285, 299, 302–304

temple management, 84, 108, 178–181, 245, 301

temple renovation, 13, 76, 90, 129–130, 141–145, 161, 165, 172–173, 177, 179, 244–245, 250, 309

Ten Judges of the Yin World (*Yinjie shidadianwang*), 78

Third Plenary Session of the Eleventh Party Congress, 20–21

Three Corpse Worms, 79

Three Officials and Great Emperors (*Sanguan Dadi*), 88, 104–105

Three Pure Ones (*San Qing*), 73, 100, 103–104, 120–121, 122

Three Reforms and One Demolition (*sangai yichai*), 21

Three Teachings (*Sanjiao*), 55–56

Three Teachings Combining in One (*Sanjiao heyi*), 56

Three Treasures (*San Bao*), 149

Tiantai Sect (*Tiantaizong*), 126, 236

tombs, 85–86, 89, 90, 202–203, 205–206, 209, 221, 291, 295–296, 305, 312

Tongbai Palace, 99

trade, 19, 25, 42, 60, 253, 255, 258, 306–307, 319

transmigration, 7, 78, 85, 134, 153

transnationalism, 12, 222–223, 268, 278, 316

Treaty of Westphalia, 11

tributary trade, 41

trigrams (*gua*), 75, 89, 123, 302

Ullambana Festival (*Yulanpeng jie*), 88–89, 138, 286

United Front Office, 115, 183, 187, 189, 278

Universal Salvation Festival. *See* Mid-Primordial Universal Salvation Festival (*Zhongyuan pudu*)

urbanization, 15, 16, 45

utilitarianism, 281, 282, 313

van der Veer, Peter, 11, 12

vegetarianism, 94, 144, 152–154

videos: of Buddhist sermons, 132, 143; ethnographic, 25, 27, 168, 208–209, 286 volunteer work, 76, 121, 136, 149, 151, 179–180, 213, 250, 318; of older and retired people, 270, 288

von Glahn, Richard, 59, 290

Wang Chongyang, 98

Wang Lineage. *See* Yingqiao Wang Lineage

Wang Mingming, 193

Wang Qinsheng, 264

Watson, James, 54, 268

Weber, Max, 4, 280, 310, 311

WeChat, 25, 132, 151

weddings, 83, 238, 267, 296, 297, 298, 312

Weller, Robert, 253, 268

Wenzhou: economy of, 19, 32–48, 318–319; geography of, 14–17, 315; languages of, 16

Wenzhou City, 14–15, 24, 26, 28, 180; ban on earth burials in, 86; "boss" Protestants, 311; Buddhist activities, 140, 174, 291; government administration of religion, 21–23, 140, 183–185

Wenzhou credit crisis, 40–41

Wenzhou drum chant (*guci*), 70–72

Wenzhou model, 14, 32–42, 278–319

Wenzhounese language, 16, 26, 80, 148

Western Paradise (*Xifang jile shijie*), 76, 78, 85, 127, 139

White Cloud Daoist Temple, 99, 111, 118, 170, 183, 293

wild monks (*ye heshang*), 133

women's religious agency, 13, 225–238, 241–245, 248, 253, 255, 318

Worshipping with Ten Sisters (*bai shijie-mei*), 238, 240

Wu language, 16

wu-wei, 9

Xianyan Buddhist Temple, 128–129, 144–146, 148, 151–152, 173–178

Xianyan Township, 15, 24

Yandang Mountains, 24, 111

Yang Chongye, 167

Yellow Turbans Rebellion, 30

Ye Shi, 195

Ye Shi Memorial Hall, 195

Yingqiao Wang Lineage, 23, 67, 198–223, 301, 317

Yong Chang Fortress, 198, 213, 218, 269, 317

Yong Quan Chan Buddhist Temple on Mei Peak, 126, 291

Yu Keping, 262

Yulanpen Festival (Ullambana Festival), 88–89, 138, 286

Zeng Jinglian (Golden Lotus), 248–255

Zhang Boduan, 92

Zhang Cong, 108

Zhang Daoling, 30, 92, 109, 114

Zhang Jianjun, 35

Zhao Dingxin, 258

Zhejiang Province, 4, 14, 16–17, 21, 60–66, 119, 157, 167, 174, 183, 213, 242

Zhejiang Village, 42

Zheng Zhenman, 267

Zhenzong, 107

Zhi Yi, 126

Zhongyuan pudu (Mid-Primordial Universal Salvation Festival), 88–89, 118, 138, 286, 307

Zhou Benshun, 264

Zhu River Triangle Area Model, 34